$5

D1068054

Significant Others

HISTORY OF ANTHROPOLOGY

Significant Others

INTERPERSONAL AND PROFESSIONAL COMMITMENTS IN ANTHROPOLOGY

Edited by

Richard Handler

HISTORY OF ANTHROPOLOGY
Volume 10

THE UNIVERSITY OF WISCONSIN PRESS

The University of Wisconsin Press
1930 Monroe Street
Madison, Wisconsin 53711

www.wisc.edu/wisconsinpress/

3 Henrietta Street
London WC2E 8LU, England

Copyright © 2004
The Board of Regents of the University of Wisconsin System
All rights reserved

1   3   5   4   2

Printed in the United States of America

Library of Congress Cataloging-in-Publication Data
Significant others interpersonal and professional commitments
in anthropology / edited by Richard Handler.
p. cm.—(History of anthropology: v. 10)
Includes bibliographical references and index.
ISBN 0-299-19470-1 (cloth alk. paper)
1. Ethnology—Field work. 2. Anthropologists' spouses. 3. Anthropologists—
Family relationships. 4. Women anthropologists—Family relationships.
5. Interpersonal relations. 6. Teacher-student relationships. 7. Ethnology—
Authorship. 8. Communication in ethnology. I. Handler, Richard, 1950– .
II. Series.
GN346 .S54 2004
306—dc21
2003014538

Information for Contributors

Normally, every volume of *History of Anthropology* will be organized around a particular theme of historical and contemporary anthropological significance, although each volume may also contain one or more "miscellaneous studies," and there may be occasional volumes devoted entirely to such studies. Since volume themes will be chosen and developed in the light of information available to the Editorial Board regarding research in progress, potential contributors from all areas in the history of anthropology are encouraged to communicate with the editor concerning their ongoing work.

Manuscripts submitted for consideration to HOA should be typed twenty-six lines to a page with 1¼-inch margins, with *all* material double-spaced, and documentation in the anthropological style. For exemplification of stylistic details, consult the published volumes; for guidance on any problematic issues, write to the editor. Unsolicited manuscripts will not be returned unless accompanied by adequate postage. All communications on editorial matters should be sent to the editor:

Richard Handler
Department of Anthropology
University of Virginia
P.O. Box 400120
Charlottesville, Virginia 22904-4120 U.S.A.

HISTORY OF ANTHROPOLOGY

EDITOR
Richard Handler
Department of Anthropology, University of Virginia

EDITORIAL BOARD
Talal Asad
Department of Anthropology, City University of New York
Lee D. Baker
Department of Anthropology, Duke University
James A. Boon
Department of Anthropology, Princeton University
Matti Bunzl
Department of Anthropology, University of Illinois
James Clifford
Board of Studies in the History of Consciousness,
University of California, Santa Cruz
Donna J. Haraway
Board of Studies in the History of Consciousness,
University of California, Santa Cruz
Curtis M. Hinsley
Department of History, Northern Arizona University
Dell Hymes
Department of Anthropology, University of Virginia
Henrika Kuklick
Department of History and Sociology of Science,
University of Pennsylvania
Daniel A. Segal
Department of Anthropology, Pitzer College
George W. Stocking, Jr. (Editor emeritus)
Department of Anthropology, University of Chicago

Bruce G. Trigger
Department of Anthropology, McGill University
Pauline Turner Strong
Department of Anthropology, University of Texas–Austin
Patrick Wolfe
Europe-Australia Institute, Victoria University of Technology

Contents

Significant Others

ANTHROPOLOGY'S
OTHER OTHERS

Anthropology is by definition about "significant others," with the word "others" (often, "Others") standing for cultural alterity, as anthropologists understand it. In the title of the present volume, however, "significant others" refers otherwise, drawing on the meaning of the phrase in recent middlebrow American English: "spouses and lovers." When we look at institutionalized anthropology from the end of the nineteenth to the middle of the twentieth centuries, spouses (that is, wives) can certainly appear as paradigmatic significant others, not just in their domestic roles, but more particularly in the work that many anthropologists' wives did when they accompanied their professional husbands to the field. Although the contributions of these wifely significant others is only now beginning to be recognized in scholarship (see Tedlock 1995 for references; also Kennedy 1995), it has long been understood that many women contributed both scholarly and domestic labor to their husbands' careers.[1] The present volume opens with two essays documenting the works and lives of anthropological couples: Matthew Engelke's on Edith and Victor Turner, and Harry West's on Jorge and Margot Dias. It closes with the "marriage," at the turn of the last century, of the [male] Anthropological Society of Washington to the Women's Anthropological Society of America, in the paper by Joy Rohde.

Beyond spouses, *Significant Others* looks at several kinds of personal relationships that have been important to anthropologists as they practice their craft; hence, the subtitle, which indicates the intertwining of personal and professional relationships in the history of anthropology, or, more particularly, a focus on relationships that were simultaneously deeply personal and professionally important for particular anthropologists' careers. The relationship between anthropologists and their informants or consultants is obviously an important

---

1. In his preface to the republication of Edward Sapir's long out-of-print essay on "Time Perspective in Aboriginal Culture" (1916), David Mandelbaum tells "the story of a winsome and intelligent young lady who used to do typing for [an anthropologist] . . . when he was a graduate student. On his birthday she brought him a sheaf of typescript in gift wrappings. It was the whole of 'Time Perspective,' which she had meticulously copied. He married her" (1949:387).

one, and has received much scholarly attention. West's paper on the Diases focuses also on the anthropologist-informant relationship—indeed, on a particularly complicated instance of it, as West, in the field in Mozambique, worked with Rafael Mwakala, who had worked a generation earlier with Jorge and Margot Dias, authors of the "classic" ethnographies in the area.

The teacher-student (or patron- or mentor-student) relationship is also one in which personal and professional commitments can become intertwined. The papers by Brightman, Rohde, Schumaker, and Silverstein are concerned, at least in part, with established or senior professionals directing, mentoring, or even obstructing junior colleagues and students. We should note that in all the cases they examine, more or less enterprising junior partners often try to wrest control of the relationship for their own ends. These stories about senior and junior interlocutors are often also stories in which the juniors become a cohort of significant others to one another, as in the case of Gluckman's students in the field (in Schumaker's essay) or various generations of Boas' students (in Silverstein's and Brightman's essays).

Teacher-student relationships are often discussed in a language of kinship, with mentors figured as ancestors—[fore]fathers and [fore]mothers of the "ego" in question. There has also been much discussion of "sibling," or same-generation, relationships—that of cohorts—and, now, increasing attention to the history of anthropological husbands and wives (including "conjugal" relationships between same-sex partners [see Grinker 2000]). But, looking down the genealogical tree, historians of anthropology have had less to say about anthropologists' relationships to their children (but see Cassell, 1987, Sutton and Fernandez 1998). One such relationship, that of A. I. Hallowell to his son, is at the heart of Stocking's paper, which compares influences of a "real" kinship relationship (Hallowell and his adopted son) to those exerted on the anthropologist by various "fictive" ancestors, his teachers and the traditions they fostered. The paper concludes with an extended meditation on the question of influence in anthropology and in scholarship more generally, and the relationship of "influence" to one's place in history—or in disciplinary genealogies, the anthropological family tree.

Given Stocking's discussion of influence, and more generally, the volume theme—"significant others"—I cannot help but treat the following editorial moment as paradigmatic: Stocking had sent an early draft of his paper on Hallowell (one of his teachers) to his dissertation advisor, Murray Murphey. Murphey offered a critique of the paper (as discussed in the version published here), which prompted Stocking (one of my mentors in graduate school) to telephone me to discuss ways to incorporate his responses to Murphey into the paper itself. Meanwhile, I was discussing the emerging volume regularly with Engelke, who was at the time my doctoral student, and who as an undergraduate had studied with Stocking. There are many other, crosscutting teacher-student and collegial relationships that link the authors collected in *Significant Others*. Although such links can be interpreted as a sign of the incestuousness of a small sub-discipline, I prefer to think that they demonstrate a common endeavor and a shared, albeit quirky, passion for the history of anthropology.

Acknowledgments

Several years ago, Matthew Engelke proposed "significant others" as a theme for an *HOA* volume. He has been instrumental both in shaping the project conceptually and in making connections to scholars working on the history of anthropology in Africa. As the volume took shape, I consulted freely and regularly with *HOA*'s founding editor, George Stocking; as always, he provided intellectual insight and editorial advice of the highest quality. All contributors to the present volume have been through several drafts of their papers, and have with great good will responded to my editorial initiatives; I thank them all, particularly, for their willingness to shape their work to speak to the volume theme. Ira Bashkow, Matti Bunzl, Adria LaViolette, Suzanne Menair, Daniel Segal, Michael Silverstein, and Pauline Turner Strong provided support and advice whenever I asked for their help. At the University of Wisconsin Press, Steve Salemson has been readily available to guide the volume through the editorial and production processes. Finally, Suzanne Menair has served ably as an editorial assistant.

References Cited

Cassell, J., ed. 1987. *Children in the field: Anthropological experiences*. Philadelphia.

Grinker, R. R. 2000. *In the arms of Africa: The life of Colin M. Turnbull*. New York.

Kennedy, E. L. 1995. In pursuit of connection: Reflections on collaborative fieldwork. *Am. Anth.* 97:26–33.

Mandelbaum, D. G., ed. 1949. *Selected writings of Edward Sapir in language, culture, and personality*. Berkeley.

Sutton, D. & R. L. Fernandez, eds. 1998. *In the field and at home: Families and anthropology. Anth. & Humanism* 23(2).

Tedlock, B. 1995. Works and wives: On the sexual division of textual labor. In *Women writing culture*, ed. R. Behar & D. Gordon, 267–86. Berkeley.

"THE ENDLESS CONVERSATION"

Fieldwork, Writing, and the Marriage of Victor and Edith Turner

MATTHEW ENGELKE

In 1975, Edith Turner described herself in a biographical note to the feminist literary magazine *Primavera* as "an (unofficial) anthropological fieldworker" who had done "quite a lot of research in Africa" (1975c:91). She had been working with her husband, the well-known anthropologist Victor Turner, for over thirty years. Together, they translated the French symbolist poets, conducted fieldwork among the Ndembu of Zambia, and on pilgrimage in Europe and Latin America, wrote, taught, and raised a family. And so Turner's self-description might seem an understatement. She is today a well-known proponent of humanistic anthropology and has been an influential contributor to the anthropology of religion. But Turner described herself with hesitation because she was not an anthropologist in the strict sense of the term. Edith Turner was an anthropologist's spouse—a significant other. This is something else altogether.

There is one moment in particular that captures the complexity of Edie's role as Victor Turner's significant other. Soon after that issue of *Primavera* came out in the winter of 1975, the Turners moved with their two youngest children to an apartment in Princeton, New Jersey at the Institute for Advanced Study, where Victor Turner took up a year-long fellowship. It was a "busy time" (ETI). The Turners had many visitors, and according to those around, Victor Turner was the center of attention for the fellows (DSI). James Fernandez, who was teaching nearby at Princeton University and saw the Turners on a regular ba-

---

Matthew Engelke is a lecturer in the Department of Anthropology at the London School of Economics. In addition to his work on the Turners, he has conducted field research in Zimbabwe on apostolic churches and on human rights.

sis, said, "Vic was the *bon vivant*" (JFI) of the cohort that year. David Sapir, also in residence at the Institute in 1975–76, said Vic provided "the conviviality" (DSI). As always, Vic and Edie tried to fold this conviviality into the work of intellectual production. Normally this strategy worked; the Turners never preferred Apollonian sobriety to Dionysian abandon. But something that year was different for Edie.

For Edie, Princeton was too social; the work she had done in *Primavera* just prior to the move had rekindled a fire to write on her own, in what she would later call a "woman-centered" approach to anthropology (1987). At the Institute she pulled out an old manuscript called "Kajima" she had first drafted in 1954, after she and Vic had returned to England from their fieldwork with the Ndembu. Edie now worked on the manuscript in their Institute apartment. There was no office for her, so she set up space in the closet of the master bedroom. It was a walk-in closet with a window (neither she nor Vic had large wardrobes and there was room to fit a small desk). It was "a room of my own," she said, with purposeful allusion to Virginia Woolf. It was in the closet that she reworked "Kajima" along the lines of the piece from *Primavera* as "the anthropologist's wife," and as someone interested in "the richness of the women's culture" (ETI).

In addition to the "Kajima" project, Edie worked with Vic. The purpose of his tenure in Princeton was to finish the manuscript for *Image and Pilgrimage in Christian Culture*, the research for which they had carried out in the late 1960s and early 1970s during Vic's sabbaticals and summer vacations at the University of Chicago. Edie would sometimes work on *Image* in her closet-office, but usually they worked on it together, as they always had. It was a process she loved—indeed thrived on. As Sapir described it, "they would sit in [Vic's] office; Edie was at the typewriter and they would face each other and do all this consultation" (DSI). They finished the manuscript, and Edie published "Kajima" on her own, as *The Spirit and the Drum* (see Engelke 2001). But Vic and Edie's consultation, as Sapir calls it, became more complicated from that point on. She felt the pull of "Kajima," of her own work.

As an historical figure, "the spouse" sheds interesting light on the history of anthropology with regard to at least two issues: fieldwork and writing. Both are central to understanding the Turners' relationship in the context of professional anthropology. Probably nothing generates more ambivalence in anthropology than fieldwork. Since Franz Boas and Bronislaw Malinowski helped establish anthropology within the academy (Stocking 1968, 1992; Kuklick 1991; Grimshaw and Hart 1993), the practice of fieldwork is what anthropologists have used to distinguish themselves from other academics. And yet, despite Malinowski's famous call in *Argonauts of the Western Pacific* for establishing the "law and order" (1922:9) of method, training for fieldwork "has most often been informal and unsystematic, and frequently lacking almost entirely" (Stocking

1992:14). In fact, anthropologists often pride themselves on their intellectual and methodological eclecticism. Since Malinowski's seminars at the London School of Economics, where many of the students were refugees from other departments and professions (Stocking 1995:293–95; Kuper 1983:69), anthropology has served as an intellectual haven for those who find themselves at odds in other disciplines. In short, anthropology has fostered an air of professional flexibility, and it has often cast the experience of fieldwork as something ineffable in order to reinforce this point. Nevertheless, anthropology has never relinquished the prerequisite of proper training or the professional certification to which Malinowski alludes. The implicit claim is a catch-22 in the profession: anthropologists must be trained to do fieldwork, but real fieldwork cannot be taught.

If fieldwork generates ambivalence among professional anthropologists, surely writing generates anxiety. The Turners' collaboration highlights this from an interesting angle. The literary critic Françoise Meltzer argues that academia is obsessed with "the cult of the individual" (1994:4; cf. Rose 1983). The figure of the writer, alone at a desk, is a central image in the Western literary imagination. Anthropology is not an exception to this rule. And yet it is implicitly understood that no one produces ideas in isolation, and even anthropologists—whose subject matter, after all, is groups of people—have been slow to acknowledge collaboration in "writing up" as anything less than putting pen to paper (see Schumaker 2001).

When significant others conduct fieldwork with their anthropologist partners, and when they write ethnography collaboratively or on their own, they highlight the problems of anthropology's catch-22 (see, for example, Fernea & Fernea 1989:43–44). Indeed, the paradoxes and tensions described in this essay obscure important moments in the history of anthropology in which collaboration between couples has been central to the development of anthropological scholarship. The work of significant others in these situations (usually wives, although by no means only so [see Kennedy 1995; Grinker 2000]) is often minimized or ignored altogether. Consultation and collaboration are usually erased. And yet significant others often shape both the careers of their partners (Papanek 1973) and the contours and concerns of anthropology (Ariëns & Strijp 1989; Behar & Gordon 1995).

This essay focuses on Edith Turner as the significant other of the well-known anthropologist Victor Turner. Edith Turner contributed significantly to ideas anthropologists often associate with her husband, such as the social drama, liminality and communitas, and the anthropology of performance. The Turners' collaboration in fieldwork and writing was more intimate than that of most couples who do not share similar professional training. But in general, anthropology is not, and never has been, the product of individuals. It is always collaborative, and in terms of understanding the more intimate of these relationships, there is still a good deal of work to be done (see Gottlieb 1995). Through a focus on collaborative fieldwork and writing with her husband—what she sees as part of an "endless conversation" (ETI)—I show how Edie Turner has taken advantage of anthropology's professional catch-22.

Childhood, War, Love, Poetry

Edith Lucy Brocklesby Davis was born on June 21, 1921 in the small town of Ely, England (just outside of Cambridge). The seventh child of two Anglican missionaries, Edie spent her childhood in a "very evangelical" home (ADI). Edie's father, George Brocklesby Davis, was a Cambridge-trained clergyman and doctor who spent thirteen years in Amritsa, India with the Church Missionary Society. Her mother, Lucy Howard, was a vice principal at the Alexandria Teacher's Training College, also in Amritsa, for eight years. Her parents married in India and there had their first five (of eight) children. When they returned to England her father established a medical practice in Cambridgeshire. Edie's mother continued to work for the CMS. During World War II the Davis family housed evacuees from London in their spacious home.

As a child Edie enjoyed stories of India. Dr. and Mrs. Davis brought a cosmopolitan air to the household. They were fluent in Hindi, and would often speak in that language around the children if they wanted to speak privately. Edie inherited a lifelong interest in traveling and different cultures from her parents. Missionary work, however, was not her calling. Indeed, she actively disliked the profession. By the time she was in her late teens, Edie had had "quite enough" of the Anglican Church (ETI), and it was only later in life, after time in Africa, that she came to terms with her own strong spirituality.

Edie left Perse High School in Cambridge in 1936 with a certificate in domestic sciences. She had no idea what she wanted to do. She told me she had a "bad attitude" toward authority figures, starting with her parents. Lucy Davis called her daughter a "rebel" (HBI) and would not support Edie's desire to attend university. Her older sister, Helen, became a mentor and role model during this time. Helen was studying at Cambridge and had become interested in a wide range of work, from Shakespeare to Stalin. Edie credits any enjoyment in reading and the life of the mind she had as a teenager to her exchanges with Helen. The two of them used to sit in Helen's room in Cambridge, which she had painted red and decorated with an oversized picture of Stalin, and talk the night away (ETI; HBI). When World War II broke out Edie joined the British Land Army and worked on a farm near Oxford milking cows.

Edie's husband, Victor Witter Turner, was born in Glasgow, Scotland on May 28, 1920. He was the only child of two "strong-willed" Scots (TTI). His mother, Violet Witter, was a well-known actress in the Scottish National

Edith Turner, 1923 (two years old), in Ely, England. (Courtesy of Edith Turner.)

Theater (Turner 1982:7; see also ETI; Babcock & MacAloon 1987; Manning 1991; TTI; JBI). His father, Norman Turner, was an electronics engineer and well-respected radio operator during World War I (TTI). Both of Victor's parents enjoyed success in their early days, but their careers never fully blossomed. Norman ended up in Blackpool, England in a number of dead-end electronics jobs (TTI). Violet's career as an actress declined after her work with the Scottish National Theater in the 1920s (ETI).

Victor Turner's parents divorced when he was eleven years old. He was sent to live with his maternal grandmother, Annie Witter (known affectionately as "Ga"), in Bournemouth, England. Violet moved to Bournemouth as well but was often away teaching drama at free schools (Turner 1982:7–8). Victor never saw his father after he moved to England and lost all contact with the Turner side of his family until the 1970s, when he sought them out through an ad in the Glasgow *Herald*. The "deep south" (8) of England, as Victor called it, could not have been further away in the British Isles both literally and figuratively from the working-class Scottish city of Glasgow Vic thought of as home. The years in Bournemouth with his mother and grandmother were difficult (Turner 1982; ETI; TTI). Victor was never attracted to the upper-class "culture" of the south of England, and remained "a fervent Scots nationalist" throughout his childhood (Turner 1982:8).

Violet and Ga raised Victor on their own, with help only from classic literature and a little football (Turner 1985a:5; Turner 1982:8; ETI). At school Victor excelled in both intellectual and athletic pursuits. His poetic sensibility and the inheritance of his mother's dramatic talents stood out. His schoolmates called him a sissy-boy (Turner 1982:7–8; Babcock & MacAloon 1987; ETI). On the football field he tempered his "feminine" side by playing an aggressive game, eventually earning him the nickname "tank" (Turner 1982:7–8; Babcock & MacAloon, 1987:3).

As a teenager Victor was a precocious thinker. This excerpt from a letter to his mother is typical (and provides an early glimpse of his lifelong interest in literature):

Dostoievsky and Tchekov although using a Russian background delve into that part of the human soul which is universal and whose problems remain unchanged in the vast mutability of time, creed and nationality. That is how I would like to write, and if I cannot I shall quit prose and turn entirely to the non-controversial realms of poetry where instinct takes pride of place over experience and sagacity.

Genius is stifled, nowadays, by the absurd, affected medium that every young writer feels constrained to use and which corrupts style as nothing else in history has done. When I write I take no notice of the idiosyncrasies of others and try to express in words my feelings about life and people. (VETA: VT/Violet Turner 6/12/38)

Victor Turner (standing, center) with some classmates, Bournemouth, circa 1937. (Courtesy of Edith Turner.)

Victor's genius must have escaped the stifling mood of the day, because he won a scholarship to University College, London in 1938 to study English literature. In his first year at UCL *Beowolf* and other medieval sagas caught his attention. World War II interrupted Victor's studies, however, and he was called up for armed service. Despite his reputation on the football field as a violent player, Turner declared himself a pacifist. Although not a religious youth, he wanted no part in the fighting; he held a lifelong abhorrence of violence (ETI). Nevertheless, he was required to serve in the army as a noncombatant—a class of men looked upon with derision, particularly as the war dragged on and the moral imperative to defeat Hitler grew (see E. S. Turner 1961:169). In his first detail Victor was stationed with a bomb disposal unit under the direction of the Royal Engineers in Oxfordshire.

Vic and Edie met in Oxford through Edie's brother, Charlie Davis. Charlie was also a conscientious objector and a member of the bomb disposal unit. As it happens, this army group was full of budding intellectuals. The men soon fell in with one another and started a literary magazine called *Oasis,* run by the company clerk, John Bate (who became a lifelong friend of the Turners). Charlie told Edie that Vic was "the most interesting guy in the group" (ETI), and he arranged a meeting in June 1942 between Vic and his intellectually isolated sister. They were married six months later on January 30, 1943, in an Oxford registry office. John Bate and Edie's sister, Anna, were the only witnesses. Dr. and Mrs. Davis were appalled that their daughter had been married in a civil service. Violet Turner was appalled that her son married the daughter of two "fanatical missionaries" (HBI; ADI; JBI). The newlyweds took a certain pleasure in their parents' discomfort (HBI).

It was love at first sight for Edie. "It's as if you've never read any poetry in your life and you suddenly come across it," she told me, "and you see the rhythms and the beauty and the depths of its meaning all of a sudden. That's what I felt when I met Vic" (ETI). She has also said Vic was "very handsome" (ETI) and that his good looks "stirred something in her insides" (SJ:ch. 1). On that first rendezvous they went to an army cafeteria and talked about movies and books. Vic was reading Kierkegaard at the time; she was reading from the Penguin "New Writing" book series edited by John Lehman. They met many times again at a small pub before the romance started, always to talk about their ideas, their poetry, and their books.

Vic was a lady's man. As a youth (and indeed throughout his life) Victor Turner was interested in generating what he later came to call "communitas": "a transformative experience that goes to the root of each person's being and finds in that root something profoundly communal and shared" (1969:138). This often involved intense personal relationships with colleagues and friends. Throughout the early days of his relationship with Edie, when they would meet to discuss the heady topics of the day, Vic dated other women. One in particular, a Creole (in Vic's parlance) from the West Indies named Gloria Delgado, was a serious girlfriend. But as Vic later told Edie's sister, Helen, he had a sudden realization one day that he was in love with Edie. At the time, he was on a bus with Gloria, coming back from a weekend rendezvous. At the next stop, he got off the bus and went to tell Edie his feelings (HBI).

Vic and Edie's relationship was defined by the passions of their youth. The most obvious of these was their love of the arts, which we can see in the way Edie describes falling in love with Vic as the "discovery of poetry." But there were other passions as well, some of which undercut their love of "high culture." They had a notable distaste for "the establishment," whether that meant the Church of England and the Bournemouth elite of their childhoods, or, much later in life, colonial administrators and the ivory tower of the academy. It was always difficult for the Turners to reconcile these two sides of their outlooks—their love for "the life of the mind" and their distaste for the places and attitudes with which it was so closely associated. They called themselves "anti-Wastelanders," not only because they saw the message of T. S. Eliot's poetry as so despondent, but also because they disliked the elite world of academics that Eliot personified. The patterns of collaboration and love that characterized their marriage, and the ways in which they handled their passions in life, were first played out in those early days in Oxford. These passions came to characterize their collaborations in anthropology as well. Their work for John Bate's literary magazine *Oasis* was the first step in this long process. Endless conversations about the value of the arts—with each other, with Bate—were central to their lives. Collaborating through *Oasis* was the medium through which they fit themselves into a war-torn society as pacifists and thinkers, and into two families that at the time were difficult for them to accept.

The mission statement in the first number of *Oasis*, published in January 1942, gleefully warned "at times the imagination must burst the bounds of mere assimilation and try a little endeavor on its own account." Contributions came in from Michael Tippett, the British composer, and there were endorsements from George Orwell and E. M. Forster. The latter wrote personally to John Bate, saying he read *Oasis* "with pleasure" (JBL: EMF/JB).

Vic and Edie contributed a number of pieces to *Oasis*, both separately and together. Vic wrote poems and essays on Beethoven and Rilke. Edie wrote some stories and did a number of translations of Baudelaire, who was an influential poet for them both. Together, Vic and Edie wrote a poem called "Poppy," which tells us something about their interest in Baudelaire and the French symbolists, as well as something about their nonconformist attitude at that time:

> Poppy, your greed of light has bared
> The spider's grinning fangs,
> Scarlet devotion to your God
> Has splayed your selfish wings.
>
> Your flag has drugged a continent
> With ensigns of decay,
> The sultry pressure of your love
> Aborts the genesis of joy.
>
> Caskets of pellets, bounteous
> As Onan, multiply the need
> For negatives throughout the sum
> Of time; the gravity of weed.
>
> Remain a sullen catalyst
> Of tragic choice; a musty torch,
> Transmit the blush of centuries
> To cauterise the last debauch.
> (1943:20)

At turns romantic and moralizing, this poem is characteristic of the ways in which the Turners embraced what was considered abject, immoral, and out of the ordinary. The symbolist poets of France were their intellectual role models. Baudelaire's drug addiction, Verlaine and Rimbaud's torrid love affair—these were part of a heroic snubbing of conventions that Vic and Edie admired. "Rimbaud called what he was doing *the reasoned deregulation of all the senses*. We didn't go this far," says Edie, "but what Rimbaud saw in this was immense beauty if you weren't hedged in by conventions. This is more or less what it was like for us. My mother-in-law called me a bohemian" (ETI).

That wasn't everything Violet Turner called her daughter-in-law. Edie and Violet were often at odds. In a July 1943 letter to John Bate (Violet had a way of keeping herself involved in Vic's life, and had befriended Bate), Violet expressed serious concern for the arrogance of the newlyweds, which was "gaining the upper hand" in her son's temperament. Edie—that "wench," Violet called her— was partly to blame. But it is also clear from the letter that Violet recognized "Edie fills a great need in Victor's nature" (JBL: Violet Turner/JB 7/20/44). Edie was taking Violet's place as the most important woman in Vic's life. Victor Turner once described his mother as "something of a feminist" (Turner 1982:7), and John Bate remembered her as a "strong minded" woman (JBI). These are characterizations many would use to describe Edie today (BBI; RAI).

In 1943, the bomb disposal unit was disbanded (Hitler had stopped dropping bombs in England and was concentrating efforts on the Eastern Front in Russia). The *Oasis* group scattered. Vic decided to join the Pioneer Corps, and he was sent to the midlands around Rugby to load supply trains. It was around this time that Vic and Edie's first son, Frederick, was born. But by late 1943 Vic had entered a period of "life crisis" (JBI). According to Bate, Vic "didn't know what he wanted to do" (JBI). While the horrors of World War II only reinforced their commitment to pacifism, Vic and Edie became disenchanted with literature and poetry during this time. Edie explains how it all started to look like "rubbish" in the face of what was happening in Europe (ETI). They began reading the natural sciences and thought seriously about the possibility of becoming sheep farmers in Scotland after the war. By 1944, while *Oasis* was still being published, it was clear that they had been slowly moving away from their interests in poetry. The only sign of their commitment to literature from the few years in Rugby was the fact that they named their second son, Robert, after the Scottish poet Robert Burns (ETI). Perhaps it had as much to do with Vic's nationalist sentiments. But the idea of going to Scotland was not only a way for Vic to connect with his ancestral roots, it was a way to stay "close to the earth," to what was happening in the "real world." It was during this more "scientific" and "naturalistic" period that they first came across anthropology. They read Margaret Mead's *Coming of Age in Samoa* and A. R. Radcliffe-Brown's *The Andaman Islanders*, which they checked out of the local library in Rugby (ETI; Turner 1985a).

From Manchester to Mwinilunga and Back Again

Vic and Edie did not become sheep farmers. Vic had a bad accident in the Pioneer Corps loading the trains and broke his leg (later in life he suffered from an arthritic hip as a result). Edie tore her stomach muscles giving birth to Bobbie in a gypsy caravan they had bought for £22 and a stolen bottle of army rum. They were in no condition at the end of the war to handle the rugged job of farming. And so, Vic enrolled back in UCL, this time in the new anthropology program under Darryl Forde, who had just been appointed professor there from Aberystwyth in Wales (Stocking 1995:429). Poetry and literature still looked meaningless, but anthropology had enough of a scientific air and humanistic bent to satisfy the Turners' inner conflicts. They lived in Hastings with Violet, some sixty miles from London. Vic spent most of the day away, but when he got home he used to talk with Edie about his seminars: "he used to read out all of his assignments to me while I was doing the chores around the house, and so I was getting quite an education under quite an interesting person who was a budding professor himself. Though now I feel I'd have given anything to have gone in and written the papers myself" (ETI). Those chores, of course, included taking care of the two young boys and soon a girl—their first daughter, Irene. The patterns of intellectual exchange Vic and Edie had developed in the *Oasis* circle were taking on new forms as the young couple was getting used to both parenthood and university life. The "endless conversation" they started in Oxford continued.

Vic was studying Radcliffe-Brown at UCL. Radcliffe-Brown's claim that social anthropology was "a branch of natural science" devoted to "a consideration of the continuity of social structure through time" (1952:188, 192) was, at the time, the dominant paradigm (see Stocking 1995:425–26; Kuper 1983:48–49), and both Turners found it compelling, even comforting. It fit nicely also with their growing interest in Communism—a seed that had been planted by Edie's sister, Helen, before the war, but grew as the Turners saw the working class suffering as "war profiteers" flourished (ETI).

The Turners' interests in anthropology and Marxism crossed in the person of Max Gluckman. Vic and Edie had read Gluckman's work prior to a chance meeting Vic had with him at a talk in London in 1949. They were taken by many of the essays now collected as *Analysis of a Social Situation in Modern Zululand* (ETI; see Gluckman 1958). Vic and Max got along well; according to Edie, Max "picked Vic out" (ETI). Gluckman convinced Vic to apply for a Rhodes-Livingstone Institute grant to conduct fieldwork in Northern Rhodesia, and then to come back and write up a Ph.D. in Manchester. Gluckman had just been made the first Professor of Social Anthropology there, and it was where he launched the "Manchester School" of anthropology.

Vic got the grant. Since the RLI also paid for dependents, Edie and the children were able to join him in the field (VETA: RLI/VT 8/17/50). Victor Turner first arrived in Africa in December 1950. Edie and their three children joined him in mid-February 1951 (they had to come separately because Vic could not find fives passages on the same ship). The Turner family stayed in Northern Rhodesia working with the Ndembu until March 1952, then spent six months in Cape Town, and seven months back in Manchester. They returned to work with the Ndembu in the Mwinilunga District from April 1953 to June 1954. In all, they spent twenty-eight months in the field. Edie Turner also returned to Mwinilunga after her husband died in 1985 for four more months of study of the Ihamba ritual (see Turner 1992).

Gluckman was hesitant about Vic having his wife and children with him, but ultimately he consented with the stipulation that Edie not get pregnant in the field (ETI). Gluckman may have understood the couple as separate individuals, but there is little indication Vic and Edie thought of themselves likewise: "As had always been the case with Vic and myself, he had ideas about what he had been studying and we were talking about them day and night. His getting a grant to go to Africa, and my getting travel money to go, too, was just like taking it for granted that we would go on doing this collaboration" (ETI). They assumed they would both work as much as possible on whatever they could in the field. Often this meant dividing the work by gender: Vic working with the men, Edie with the women. Edie also took all of the photographs in Mwinilunga and collected most of the genealogies that were such an important part of Vic's dissertation and first book, *Schism and Continuity* (Turner 1957, 1967; E. Turner 1987; ETI; VETA; Engelke 1996).

While it is true that the Manchester School possessed a good deal of "methodological self-consciousness" (Stocking 1992:14)—revolving principally around "the exciting possibilities opened up by the study of extended cases" (Epstein 1967:xvi)—Vic had little of such training before leaving for the field. He was scheduled to receive some at the RLI's Luanshya base under the acting director, Clyde Mitchell, with whom he corresponded before leaving for Africa. Vic wrote with enthusiasm: "At the moment it seems as if I shall be preceding my family. . . . I'm looking forward to my first field-trip with great gusto. . . . I'd very much like to do an initial spell under your guidance, if possible. Teamwork is always more rewarding than lone wolfing" (PJCM:7-2-1 10/7/50). Mitchell had to be "indefinite" in terms of how much hands-on guidance he could offer. In the end, it was a week with his "old friends" the Lamba (PJCM:7-2-2 10/14/50). On their second field trip in 1953–54, the Turners took the 1951 edition of *Notes and Queries*, but did not use it. Like most anthropologists, they learned to do fieldwork in the field through trial and error, working with each other and with the Ndembu to get at the "magic" of ritual (ETI).

In reading Turner's letter to Mitchell, it is important to consider the dual sense in which we can interpret his interest in "teamwork." For one, teamwork was a concern of the budding Manchester School (Epstein 1967; see also Werbner 1984; Schumaker 1996; 2001; Gottlieb 1995:22). It was something he had discussed with Gluckman before leaving on the RLI grant. This meant taking trips to the RLI headquarters in Luanshya to meet with the other researchers for occasional conferences, and, later, drawing on common experiences in

Northern Rhodesia with his colleagues in Manchester seminars to work out ethnographic problems and questions (AEI; ICI; RFI; see also DSL: Hilda Kuper/DS 6/26/84). In another sense, teamwork among the Ndembu meant working with Edie (and even the children) in the day-to-day exigencies of life and research in the field.

We can trace something of the Turners' relationship and ideas through their field notes. There are 1,983 numbered pages of typed notes, constituting the bulk of field materials (PVWT). Vic and Edie divided the labor of typing (ETI). They also each added handwritten annotations after the fact to mark important points or clarify translations from chiLunda text. The notes are not arranged chronologically, but by topic: "Chronology of Lunda chiefs," "witch doctors," "Chihamba ceremony," "brideprice," and so on. There are also two journal notebooks of handwritten notes (90 pages each), covering topics including Lunda genealogies and the various rituals they observed. There are four notebooks (70 pages each) of Lunda language notes (the Turners both learned chiLunda well, and many of the original notes are written entirely in that language). There is one notebook (100 pages) on village census material, and three shorthand notebooks (322 pages in all) entitled the "V. W. Turner Diary," actually written in Edie's hand (PVWT; VETA). In all, then, there are 2,800 pages of notes from the four-year period.

Nkang'a, the girl's puberty ritual, is a much-discussed topic in both their field-notes and published writing, and their work on it is representative of the more general ways in which they collaborated in ethnographic research. This work is also the clearest example of how issues of gender and sexuality influenced the patterns of their research (see Tedlock 1995). Because many Ndembu women's day-to-day activities and ritual roles were off-limits to men, Edie played a crucial role in getting "the women's point of view." But more generally, it seems, the idea was that having two ethnographers was better than one, because twice as much information could be collected. In many instances, whether it was a man's or a woman's point of view mattered little to the Turners (ETI), at least in these early years.

The Nkang'a ritual is central to a number of Victor Turner essays collected in *The Forest of Symbols: Aspects of Ndembu Ritual* (1967:19–58). Edie Turner has written about the ritual on her own in literary (1975b) and anthropological (1985b; 1987) styles. The Turners and others performed Nkang'a reenactments in the early 1980s, and it became an important point of departure for their writings on the anthropology of performance (see Turner & Turner 1987; PFI).

Edie Turner's earliest piece on Nkang'a is called "Girl into Woman" (1975b), which is an apt summary of the transformation involved. Nkang'a is performed as "a girl's breasts begin to ripen," and stands for "the tie of nurturing between mother and child" (Turner 1967:20–21). The dominant ritual symbol of Nkang'a is the "milk tree," or *mudyi*. This tree exudes a white, milky substance

Ikubi in the final stages of Nkang'a, 1951, Mwinilunga, Northern Rhodesia. (Courtesy of Edith Turner.)

when cut, which, for the Ndembu, who are matrilineal, "is supposed to produce a good supply of milk in the girl when she bears children" (PVWT:281). It also "symbolizes the total system of interrelations between groups and persons that makes up Ndembu society" (Turner 1967:21). Since the Ndembu are virilocal, with married couples settling in or near the husband's home, such interrelations are often strained, and indeed "the observer can hardly doubt that emotions are really aroused in the actors as well as formally represented by custom" (39) in this ritual.

The Turners' analysis of Nkang'a highlights their interest in thinking of rituals as moments of both social continuity and change. Rituals in the abstract sense help to define the social order, but no one enactment of a ritual is like another. "In other words, each ritual has its own teleology" (32). The Turners have argued that it is crucial to view each ritual in context, and to take account of the affective relationships between the various participants, above and beyond the structural roles they perform. This is put clearly in a related discussion of Mukanda (the boy's circumcision rite): "when we analyze the structure of a social field, we must regard as crucial properties of the field not only spatial relations and the framework of persisting relationships which anthropologists call 'structural,' but also the 'directed entities' at any given time operative in that field, the purposive activities of individuals and groups, in pursuit of their contemporary and long-term interests and aims" (264).

In addition to helping define their approach to the "ritual process," the discussions of Nkang'a are important because they contributed to the Turners' understanding of Ndembu systems of color classification (59–92) and, more importantly for our interests here, the discrepancies between idealized symbolic models and the politics of lived experience (48–58). Behind the white milk of the *mudyi* "lie the notions of harmony, continuity, purity, the manifest, the public, the appropriate, and the legitimate" (77). This is all part of the way in which matrilineal ties are celebrated and defined. But against these values lie the social tensions of separating a girl from her matrilineal kin by making her a woman, and thus eligible for marriage to a man from another village. Coming to terms with the "contradictions between principle and practice" (25) in ritual was a major concern of the Turners in much of their collaborative work.

Nkang'a was the first African ritual both Vic and Edie witnessed. Arriving in Mwinilunga District in December 1950, Vic saw the first phase of the ritual for a girl named Ikubi from Kajima village who was married out to the second headman of Shika village (see PVWT:285). Edie saw the final phase of Ikubi's ritual, in which the novice emerged from the seclusion hut after three months, in March 1951. Observing this Nkang'a was a moment of conversion. Less than a year later Vic wrote to Gluckman saying that he and Edie had struck into "the rich rift of ritual" (PVWT:1566; see also Engelke 1996:3) and were finding it hard to turn their attention away from that side of Ndembu life.

The organization of the Turners' fieldnotes provides clues to their collaboration. The five pages of typed notes Victor Turner wrote after witnessing this first phase of the ritual—before the kankang'a (novice) went into the seclusion hut—are attributed not primarily to his own observations, but to his informant, Windson (see PVWT:281–85). It was typical of Victor Turner in his publications to include large sections of "native exegesis," usually from his most well known informant, Muchona the Hornet (see Turner 1961; 1962; on Muchona see Turner 1959; cf. Tedlock 1983; Metcalf 1998). When, in late March of 1951, both Vic and Edie attended the *ritual d'aggregation* for Ikubi, "Mrs. Turner" is listed by Mr. Turner as the chief informant in the fieldnotes (PVWT:286).

Two years later, in April 1953, Edie Turner conducted a series of interviews about Nkang'a with her friend, Manyosa (who was the most influential female informant the Turners consulted). In that interview, which is included in the archived fieldnotes of Victor Turner (1458–95), Edie made a crucial breakthrough in understanding the "contradictions between principle and practice" in Nkang'a. Asking Manyosa about the importance of something called the chipwampwilu spoon, Edie learned that the spoon represents the kankang'a, and the chipwampwilu, which is a mixture of beans and cassava mush, represents her fertility. The novice's mother cooks the mush at the end of the first day of the ritual and a dollop is placed in the spoon. The mother then presents the spoonful of mush to the women, some of whom are from the novice's village, and some of whom are from other villages, often including the novice's bridegroom's or potential bridegroom's village. The women all rush to be the first to eat from the spoon. When Edie asked Manyosa why, she replied: "The person to snatch the spoon of chipwampwilu must be a person from Kankanga's own village, otherwise the mother believes that her child will go far away and die. The mother wants the child to stay near" (1464). In "Symbols in Ndembu Ritual," Victor Turner relies on this data for the crux of his argument. He explains the "symbolic struggle between the novice's matrilineal kin and those of her bridegroom, which makes explicit the conflict between virilocality and matriliny" (Turner 1967:25), and credits his wife in the essay for the research that went into the conclusion (24).

Work on Nkang'a is just one example of how the Turners collaborated in the field. But even this is just the tip of the iceberg. There are other ways to gauge their collaboration and trace how the Turners came to define themselves as an anthropological couple during the early 1950s. Victor Turner's letters are suggestive. An early example is from a letter he wrote to Gluckman in November 1951 from the Luinga River Camp in Mwinilunga (see PVWT:1565–70). The letter is typed, but like most of what the Turners typed, it has corrections and annotations in pencil. At the start of the letter, Turner explained to Gluckman what he had been doing since his arrival in the Luinga area. After a short summation of genealogical work, he writes: "Next, I (Edie did the bulk of work in this) took annual budgets for over 600 individuals, grouped into 37 families and a few odds and ends." But after the fact, he corrected his typing in pencil so the pronoun followed the logic of the sentence: "Next, we (Edie did the bulk of work in this) took annual budgets" (1566 [emphasis added]; see also Engelke 1996:3).

Victor Turner pointed out the importance of this collaboration in other letters, including one he wrote to Clyde Mitchell regarding the interim period in the RLI fellowship. The RLI Board of Trustees suggested Victor and the family spend several months together in Cape Town, and that Victor then head to Manchester for several more months on his own. Vic pushed hard for a vote (allowance) covering family passage to England. He explained his reasoning in a personal letter to Mitchell:

The family should not be separated. Edie and I have collaborated on almost every aspect of my work and have discussed its theory together. In addition, Edie has collected a lot of material on women's rituals and matters such as sex and child-birth which I could not have obtained myself and on which she hopes to write a paper or two. Moreover, I could not keep two homes going on a Research Officer's salary and the absence of a father is no good for kids, as I know from experience. (PJCM: 7-2-43 12/23/51)

Ultimately, the family was given the vote to make the trip to Manchester, but had to spend seven months in Cape Town because of an administrative gaffe. For Edie, Cape Town turned out to be a rewarding place. She was able to sit in on a seminar with Monica Wilson at the University of Cape Town, which to this day is her only "official" training in anthropology. "It was a great, enormous benefit," Edie said, "as she was giving classes on *rites de passage* starting with van Gennep" (ETI). Later, van Gennep's work figured prominently in many of Victor Turner's publications. *The Forest of Symbols* is dedicated to Monica Wilson, one of the few Victor Turner books not dedicated to Edie or the children.

In Cape Town the Turners wrote their first anthropology article together in the *Rhodes-Livingstone Journal*. The article, "Money Economy among the Mwinilunga Ndembu," is the "bare-bones numerical work" (ETI) that went into Vic's dissertation. Although it offers nothing more than "the most tentative conclusions" (Turner & Turner 1955:36) on cash budgets in Mwinilunga, and although it is a dry and uncharacteristic piece of writing, it is worth mentioning here because of its acknowledged coauthorship. As a couple, they used it to mark Edie's role in the work. With her name in print Edie acquired a measure of legitimacy. It boosted her confidence when they returned to the field.

We also have a sense of how Vic and Edie interacted in the field from fellow RLI research officers and from the Turners' children. A. L. Epstein, who was in Northern Rhodesia during much the same period as the Turners, remembers them as "unimaginably close." "I don't think there was anything they didn't discuss. She was so much involved. I think it is genuinely the case that they worked as a team among the Ndembu in which her part as fieldworker was no less important than Vic's" (AEI). Ian Cunnison also recalls the Turners' relationship, and remembers stories Vic used to tell him about working with Edie:

> They were very well matched, and it was teamwork that made the family operate so well together. There was a story which Vic used to relate from their period in the field, about how living in that way, tensions could not help but spring up between them. So once a week they'd go out into the bush, stand so many yards apart, and yell at one another for about an hour. And he reckoned this eased the tensions, so they could start life again. (ICI)

There were other patterns as well. For example, in addition to doing field-work and taking the photographs, Edie spent each morning teaching the children with materials from a Salisbury-based correspondence course (ETI; RTI; FTI). During these lessons Edie would often be interrupted by Ndembu villagers coming to her for medical supplies such as bandages and aspirin (ETI; RTI; E. Turner 1987). At night, Vic would often read out loud to the children from the classics of English literature to round out their education. Bob Turner remembers this as "the major part of the day" (RTI). But the children also saw their parents as anthropologists at work. Bob Turner cannot remember "a point at which Edie saw herself as being in any way more an amateur than Vic." For both of his parents, it was "dead serious stuff." His father, he says, "was very lucky to have a wife that could be that much of a partner" (RTI).

Fieldwork, that "which makes one a 'real anthropologist'" (Gupta and Ferguson 1997:1), changed Vic and Edie as individuals and as a couple. It became their "delight" in Africa, and was to remain so throughout their lives (Turner 1985a:4). They never felt at home in an institutional setting, no matter how prominent or well-received Victor became. When they went back to Manchester in 1955, writing up the results of their work only highlighted this fact. It also highlighted the discrepancy in their professional identities; Edie had none. She was not enrolled in the anthropology program and her marginality in Manchester was a stark contrast to her importance in the field.

The Spirit and the Dissertation

By the time the Turners returned to England in 1955, the Manchester School was in full swing. The seminars led by Gluckman often spilled over from Social Anthropology's Dover Street conference room to other venues, like the Transport Café and local pubs, where the members would drink pints of beer and continue their conversations (ICI; Richard Werbner personal communication, 6/11/97). It was, in many ways, Victor Turner's métier. Throughout the 1950s, Gluckman worked at establishing a new framework of political anthropology in these settings and through his students. Gluckman, of course, has become legendary as a personality above and beyond his anthropological work. He had a reputation as quick tempered, brilliant, somewhat paranoid, and zealous in his efforts to foster a sense of community amongst the researchers in his "school" (RFI; AEI; RVI; ETI; ICI; FTI; Schumaker 2001).

The "distinguishing mark" of Gluckman's anthropological message was "its emphasis on the significance of conflicts in values, interests, and beliefs for the maintenance of social cohesion within societies" (Gluckman, Mitchell, and Southwold 1970:78). While it would be an oversimplification to reduce the work of the Manchester School to this one line, it was a very influential one (Werbner 1984:157–58). In Gluckman's view, politics and social organization were fundamental. Everything else was "epiphenominal" (RFI).

Gluckman insisted that Vic write on social organization and Ndembu politics before turning his attention to ritual and symbolism. The process of coming to terms with this for Vic and Edie was not an easy one. Both pushed against Gluckman in their own ways. Vic was asked, like all department members returning from the field, to give a series of six "debriefing" papers in the seminar. Ronnie Frankenberg recalls Vic's presentations:

> We couldn't understand what he was talking about, because most of the words were in Ndembu. And when he was attacked for this, he said it was inevitable because they were untranslatable. And Max said, "Well they may be untranslatable, but you've got to bloody translate them!". . . And Gluckman said he wanted politics, and I don't know how long afterwards, but [Vic] eventually came up with six more papers which were about politics, and which formed the basis of his later work. (RFI)

Gluckman once criticized Fortes for using too many Tale terms in *The Dynamics of Clanship among the Tallensi* (Gluckman 1963:83). Turner was subject to the same objection. For Turner, using Ndembu terms must be seen in part as a rejection of what he had been asked to do: distill the essence of Ndembu life into the structural-functionalist framework of social organization. It was partly a sign of Vic's disagreement with Gluckman over the value of ritual and ritual language. For the Turners, using chiLunda (Ndembu) was a way of remaining true to something of what they had experienced. It was indicative of their growing concern with the ways in which anthropology could represent anthropological subjects, a kind of unwillingness to reduce their fieldwork experience in Mwinilunga to academic language.

Soon after Vic presented the seminar papers, the Turners got "down to business" on the dissertation (ETI), which became *Schism and Continuity in an African Society*, the "outstanding classic within the mainstream of [Manchester School] studies" (Werbner 1984:157): an ethnography "in a class of its own" (Kuper 1983:153). In their flats in Blakeley and Cheadle Hume, the Turners would spend every morning while the children were at school working "solidly" (ETI). Then Edie would prepare lunch. Edie says Vic did the "main writing" and she was editing it "all the time," as well as writing up the tables, genealogies, and maps that accompanied the dissertation and book (ETI). Vic would sit at the typewriter and compose, often out loud. Edie listened. Edie would then fire back an idea, challenge a point, or rework a sentence. *Schism and Continuity* is, in many ways, the result of a dialogue transformed into a monograph. Its production, in other words, was not so different from anything they had written previously, or much of what they wrote afterwards. In the afternoons and the evenings, even when the children were around, the Turners "were talking about the subject matter all the time" (ETI). Bob Turner recalls something of this from his childhood: "One of the things I remember very vividly was the sound of my father's study when I was going to sleep at night of him and Edie talking, talking, talking. Such long conversations, mostly Vic's voice. Things were getting thrashed out and decided. It was a very satisfying sound; like a large engine purring away, manufacturing great thoughts" (RTI).

Edie did not approve of everything that was "thrashed out and decided" in Vic's study late at night. Most importantly she felt *Schism and Continuity* had no "spirit" (ETI). Neither she nor Vic was happy with the account of the Chihamba near the end of the monograph (1957:303–17). It was "too sociological" (ETI). This was part of the concession they had to make for Vic to satisfy Gluckman. In a sense, however, the unsatisfying treatment of Chihamba in chapter ten of *Schism and Continuity* is the perfect ending to a book in which the tensions in Ndembu life seem insurmountable. Ndembu life is characterized as "a community of suffering" (xxix). Village fissions, the high divorce rates, and Sandombu's violent outbursts threaten to tear Ndembu life apart, but they don't because "in the course of a ritual, symbols and verbal behaviour are manipulated so as to discharge tensions in the social system" (300). The importance of ritual action to the creation of an overarching moral unity, then, is made even clearer after so many discussions tracing disunity. Unwittingly or not, the detailed, unresolved ethnography set out in *Schism and Continuity* served as the perfect point of departure for the Turners' later work on ritual and symbolism.

This idea of a "spirit" lacking in *Schism and Continuity* points to an important issue the Turners were grappling without throughout the 1950s. For Edie, any connection to religion she had as a child came back to her in Africa through the vibrant life of Ndembu ritual. Victor Turner had not been raised in a religious household, but it is clear from his interests as a young man that literature and poetry had religious dimensions. William Blake, after all, was one of his favorite authors. In Africa, immersed in the "real world" they had longed for during the war, the Turners' poetic sensibilities crept back in through their fascination with what Edie has repeatedly called the "magic" of Ndembu ritual. When Edie expressed her frustration with academia by criticizing the lack of "spirit" in *Schism and Continuity* she meant that many of the ineffable or "poetic" moments of day-to-day life in Mwinilunga did not come through in the text. Simply put, it was too "scientific" and not "humanistic" enough. In this instance, perhaps, it was a privilege for Edie to be working on the dissertation outside the official boundaries of academia. It is doubtful Victor Turner could have taken such a frank stance at the time, given his institutional position. He was subject to the whims of his advisor. But Edie's concern was something they shared at a deeper level. The epigraph in *Schism and Continuity*, which is taken from Blake's *Jerusalem*, signals something of a return to the concerns and passions of their youth: "General Forms have their vitality in Particulars, and every Particular is a Man." Sandombu and the other Ndembu characters were meant to invoke this vitality, but neither Vic nor Edie felt the task could be completed under Gluckman's supervision.

While they were working on Vic's dissertation, Edie wrote a book of her own, "Kajima," named after the Ndembu village in which they spent most of their time ("Mukanza" was the pseudonym in all the published work). "Kajima" was something of a therapeutic break from the sociological dissertation. In a note she wrote to herself in 1954 shortly after returning from the field, Edie confesses to being in a "hell of [a] state," depressed and somewhat anxious about writing, as many anthropologists have been after leaving the field. In the same note she says she wanted to write a "personal, passionate" account of the work she and Vic had done, "a series of stories or episodes" that might capture the more humanistic side of Ndembu village life (see "Kajima" manuscript, 1955, VETA). As she recalled, "[Africa] had such an effect on me, and I missed [the Ndembu] so much. I had this dream about them, and I just simply had to get it down the way I personally saw it and experienced it" (ETI).

The first draft of "Kajima" is a one-hundred-page handwritten manuscript "on extra long sheets of paper" (SJ:ch. 4); it is a piece filled with the "spirit" that was supposed to accompany Schism and Continuity. It focuses on day-to-day life in the village. It has the feel of a novel, with a good deal of dialogue and reflection on how personal relationships with the Ndembu affected the course of research. It is, at moments, full of sexually risque material. There is little attempt to make the text a systematic ethnography, and yet it conveys an ethnographic understanding. At the beginning of the text, Edie offers an explanation (deleted from the final version) for what they were doing in Mwinilunga, and describes her version of anthropology as studying "the panorama of a people's culture and religion set intimately within the events of each day's work: knitted together like the human body with its nerves and bones" (VETA:Kajima, 2).

Vic was supportive of Edie's project and saw it as a necessary perspective on the work they had done (ETI). "Kajima" can perhaps best be compared to something like Elenore Smith Bowen's (Laura Bohannon's) Return to Laughter (1954), the anthropological novel of life in Nigeria among the Tiv. While "Kajima" is not a fictional account, it is, like Return to Laughter, both a "work of ethnography" and an "autobiography of affective experience" (Riesman 1964:xvi). It was not published until 1987 as The Sprit and the Drum, but was hailed at that time by one critic as an exemplary postmodern text (Marcus 1987).

In 1957 the Turners started attending the Roman Catholic Church. This was another calling of "the spirit." In October 1959 the entire family was received into the Church in Stockport in Manchester (JBL; ETI; FTI). Vic wrote to his friend, John Bate, that they all came to "realize how rich and satisfying is a collective devotional life" (JBL: VT/JB 3/7/59). The family-centered nature of their conversion was quintessentially Turnerian, and so too was the way in which they came to an interest in the Catholic Church in the first place—through anthropology. Blending family life with anthropological pursuits was de rigueur by this time. According to Fred, Vic and Edie were "shopping" for a church into which they could fit their experiences in Africa. They wanted something "deeply ritualized, deeply incarnational, with tradition and a sense of community behind it" (FTI). The lines between their religious faith and anthropological work were blurred from then on. In the late 1960s, for example, the Turners began a long-term project on Catholic pilgrimage in Mexico and Ireland (see Turner & Turner 1978). Victor Turner also published later in life a number of essays on Church history, including his popular pieces on Thomas Beckett and Miguel Hidalgo (see 1974). Edie Turner is currently involved in research on Catholic pilgrimages in Ireland, building on the work she conducted with her husband in the early 1970s, as well as upon over forty years as a committed, if questioning, Roman Catholic.

The most notable sign of a connection between work and faith from the Manchester days is the short monograph *Chihamba, the White Spirit* (1962). Two points of personal biography mark this text. First, it was written in 1960, shortly after the Catholic conversion. Second, it was written following the tragic death of Vic and Edie's fourth child, a girl named Lucy who suffered from birth defects and died at less than three months old, in the winter of 1959. It has been suggested by others that *Chihamba* represents Victor Turner's "breach with the anthropological tradition in which he had been trained" (Babcock & MacAloon 1988:7), and that it "gives full flight to his own creative spirit" (Kapferer 1996:xi). The text develops some of the sentiments and ideas Victor Turner expressed in 1955 when he presented his six post-field seminar papers almost entirely in Ndembu. The point is that religion (or culture) cannot always be translated into academic prose. "Religion is not determined by anything other than itself" (Turner 1962:62). Turner moves away from Gluckman's models toward the ideas he and Edie spent the first fifteen years of their marriage working through. "Poetry" was back. Jung's psychoanalytic theories, Herman Melville's *Moby Dick,* and the Gospel of St. Matthew are all central points of departure in the piece. Religion is bigger than anything a scholar could fully grasp:

> In studying religious symbols, the product of humble vision, we must ourselves be humble if we are to glimpse, if not fully to comprehend, the spiritual truths represented by them. In this realm of data only innocence can hope to attain understanding. That is the reason why the attempts of such scholars and philosophers as Fraser and Durkheim to explain away religious phenomena in naturalistic terms have been so obviously unsuccessful. Like Captain Ahab, such scholars seek to destroy that which centrally menaces and wounds their self-sufficiency, that is, the belief in a Deity, and like Ahab they suffer shipwreck without transfixing the quick of their intended victim. (1962:92)

The parallels here with what the Turners were thinking about in terms of their newfound Catholic faith are striking. According to their friend and colleague

Bill Epstein, "Vic felt he had to rework all his thinking about anthropology" (AEI). Vic said as much himself in a letter to his longtime friend John Bate:

> [St. Thomas Aquinas] has shown all of us idiots who make our dough by thinking, writing and teaching how to be an "intellectual" without the faintest trace of intellectual pride; his whole writing has an aroma of innocence, what Charlie Davis used to call a "fathomless lucidity."
>
> All intellectual work, in our fallen state, is exceptionally vulnerable to the assaults of Lucifer that "bearer of (*intellectual*) light," for his primordial fall was precisely through *intellectual* arrogance. (JBL:VT/JB 3/7/59 [emphasis in original])

As a rejoinder to the "sociological" treatment of the same issues in *Schism and Continuity*, *Chihamba* should indeed be seen as a radical move. It brings together the Turners' concerns with literature, religion, and "real world" anthropology in a new way by consciously fusing the world of their daily lives with the world of their anthropological ideas. In fact, *Chihamba* was the most radical piece Victor Turner published in his lifetime. Later books, such as *The Drums of Affliction* (1968), pull back from the repudiation of Durkheim, the "anti-sociological" method, and the kind of "Dostoievskian mysticism" that characterizes *Chihamba*. For those familiar with Edie Turner's later work (1992; 1996) it will come as no surprise that *Chihamba* is her favorite "Victor Turner book" (ETI).

In this context it is worth taking a moment to break the historical frame to consider Edie Turner's critique of her husband's occasional sociological reductionism. In *Experiencing Ritual* (1992), published nearly a decade after her husband's death, Edie Turner levels her strongest critique of this tendency in Victor Turner's books, particularly *The Drums of Affliction*. Unlike *The Spirit and the Drum*, which was meant to be a "companion piece" to *Schism and Continuity*, the arguments in *Experiencing Ritual* are meant to eclipse the influence of *The Drums of Affliction* (see Ray 2000). Each book takes as its focus the Ihamba rituals of the Mwinilunga Ndembu—curing rites in which a diviner extracts the misfortunes and illnesses of a patient through the removal of a tooth, also called ihamba, from the patient's back. Victor Turner understood these rites to be symbolic of the "hidden animosities of the village" (1968:172). The tooth "epitomizes the aggressive drives in human nature," but it is only a symbol, and the diviner employs sleight of hand to "extract" the tooth from the back of a patient (182). As Benjamin Ray argues: "For Victor Turner the tooth was an effective 'symbol' of the back-biting envy of the villagers, nothing more" (2000:107).

On the other hand, Edie Turner argues in *Experiencing Ritual* that the tooth is an "outward and visible sign of an inward and spiritual being" (1992:82). The narrative in the book is organized around her attempt to make sense of having witnessed a spirit-form emerge from the back of a patient during a ritual session in 1985. In doing so, she remains faithful to an idea discussed above: that religious ritual cannot be reduced to the language of western academics, and that the attempt to explain away spiritual phenomena in terms of "social facts" will always fail to grasp the deeper realities of religious experience. "The result," as Ray argues, "is that the Ndembu ritual experience has become cross-culturally intelligible—without its being reduced to something different by the concepts of a more 'scientific' language—the alternative that Turner refused to accept" (2000:110). Edie describes the spirit as a "gray blob" and, drawing in part on the work of her colleague Roy Wagner, says that as a physical entity, the ihamba is a "symbol that stands for itself" (see Wagner 1986). In Ihamba, Turner concludes, "symbols and their meanings and the effect of them were one, not one *standing* for the other" (1992:73, emphasis in original). This argument is strikingly similar to what we find in the Victor Turner of Chihamba.

But as one might expect, neither Chihamba nor the Turner family's Catholic conversion were well received by colleagues in Manchester. Edie wrote that Gluckman and the others were "nervous about it" because it was "too daring" (1985a:7). For many, the conversion came as a surprise, even a discomfort. Ian Cunnison noted:

> When this one member—this charismatic member—of the Department changed his behavior, and the behavior of his family, by taking religion seriously (by going to church and talking about the effect of religious practice), we couldn't help thinking that something pretty big had happened. And I suppose it did some damage to the idea of consensus we had in the Department about society. This was one of the difficulties of the Manchester setup, perhaps. Max Gluckman was so intent on the idea of Manchester as a unified school with one general mood of thought, and one general way of analyzing society, that this change in Vic's position really brought that to an end. And this is why we all viewed it with such consternation at the time. (ICI)

The feeling was exacerbated by the fact that it was Roman Catholicism in particular to which Vic and Edie turned. With World War II still fresh in the minds of many leftist Mancunians, there was a "particularly anti-RC" (RVI) sentiment. Pope Pious XII was not well regarded; it was felt he had been complicit with the fascist regimes in Germany and Italy (see Lewy 1964; Cornwell 1999).

But within a year of publishing Chihamba, the Turners were gone. Vic was invited first to the Center for Advanced Study in the Behavioral Sciences in Palo Alto, California for a year-long fellowship. The Turners went back to England the following academic year, 1962–63, and while Vic was on staff at Manchester, the family spent most of their time in Hastings with Vic's mother. The Manchester days were over. At the Center for Advanced Study, Vic had caught the attention of a number of American departments. While at the Center, Cornell University offered him a full professorship, a position he took up in February 1964. The Turners never lived in England again.

Rebel Thinkers and Pious Pilgrims in the Promised Land

By the time the Turners left England, Vic was a senior lecturer at the University of Manchester. He was rising quickly through the ranks of the department, but it was still Gluckman's "school." Vic wanted his own ground. Moreover, by the late 1950s Manchester's vice chancellor began to require the Department of Social Anthropology to take first degree students—a responsibility the department as a whole had happily avoided in the first years of crafting the school when only postgraduate students were admitted. Vic, in particular, was miffed by the added responsibilities this change entailed (ICI; RFI). Perhaps swept up by the appreciation shown by the Cornell department—Robert Smith recalls that everyone was enthralled by his arrival (RSI)—and the image of American life shaped by their encounters with the Beats in California—their fellow misfits and contrarians—Vic and Edie assumed America would be a promised land.

The Turners were in Ithaca from 1964–68. They were fostering new ideas on the heels of *Chihamba*, and raising two new boys, Alexander and Rory. In the summer of 1966, the Turners went to Uganda to do some exploratory work with the Gisu on boys' circumcision rites. Vic also lectured at Makerere University in Kampala. But the Gisu fieldwork yielded few results, and it was a project to which they did not return. The 1960s turned out to be more a decade of "writing up." It was also when the Turners developed their "Thursday Night Seminar," a kind of alternative classroom experience run out of their living rooms in Ithaca, Chicago, and Charlottesville that involved late nights, heated discussions, alcohol, ritual reenactments, and as much communitas as they could muster (see Turner & Turner 1987).

The most important work from this period were the Lewis Henry Morgan Lectures, presented in the spring of 1966 at the University of Rochester and published three years later as *The Ritual Process*. The lectures were a chance to present the new ideas building up in their lives. Chief of these was an interest in van Gennep's work on liminality, first encountered by Edie in Monica Wilson's seminar, and then explored in "Betwixt and Between," a paper presented by Vic at the American Ethnological Society meetings in 1964 that still stands as the classic articulation of liminality. Their time in California also proved influential. In Palo Alto they came across some beatniks—fellow admirers of Rimbaud and detractors of "the establishment." These new friends had them read Jack Kerouac's *On the Road* and the poetry of Alan Ginsberg and Gary Snyder. Ithaca was also fertile intellectual ground. It was full of budding hippies and the site for Edie of her first "love-in" on the Arts and Sciences Quadrangle at Cornell.

The first two Morgan lectures are key documents in the Turners' criticism of Gluckman's emphasis on politics and social structure. "Planes of Classification in a Ritual of Life and Death," the first lecture, is a clear articulation of the

Turners' position written in a personal style. Vic portrays experience in the field as a conversion narrative, admitting "the reluctance [he] felt at first to collect ritual data" (1969:7). But soon it became obvious, from the constant pounding of drums, that ritual occupied a central place in Ndembu life. So, he says, "with eyes just opened to the importance of ritual in the lives of the Ndembu, my wife and I began to perceive many aspects of Ndembu culture that had previously been invisible to us because of our theoretical blinkers" (8). Those blinkers were off well before the spring of 1966, but this was the time to proclaim it, now that they were out from under the "servitude" of Gluckman and at a safe remove from their British roots (VETA:VT/ET 7/16/64).

The last three Morgan Lectures are more theoretical in scope. Like *Chihamba*, they move away from the ethnography of the Ndembu into new territory. In the third lecture, "Liminality and Communitas," Martin Buber and David Hume share space with the classic ethnographic literature on the Tallensi and Nuer in Turner's effort to describe and define the phenomenon of communitas—that which "emerges where social structure is not," an "existential quality [that] invokes the whole man in relation to other whole men" (126, 127). The lectures consider the characters of American subculture—their new friends—to reinforce the idea. "In modern Western Society," Turner writes, "the values of communitas are strikingly present in the literature and behavior of what came to be known as the 'beat generation,' who were succeeded by the 'hippies,' who, in turn, have a junior division known as the 'teeny boppers'" (112).

In the fourth lecture, when Turner is explaining how the idea of communitas differs from Durkheim's idea of solidarity (the latter depends on "an ingroup/out-group contrast" [132]), hippies are further put to use in describing a subtype of communitas, existential communitas—"[w]hat the hippies would today call 'a happening,' and William Blake might have called 'the winged moment as time flies'" (132). That Turner should juxtapose the hippies with William Blake is important to note, too. What hippies were doing was nothing new; it was simply another historical manifestation of a universal form not much different, in essence, from what Blake describes, or what the Beats call "crazy," or Rimbaud's *deréglement ordonné de tous les sens*.

One of the important points made in *The Ritual Process* is that in order for there to be communitas, or anti-structure, there has to be structure. Although I would argue that the Turners produced most of their best work while in Ithaca, Cornell University had too much "structure" for their taste (see ETI). Edie was not fond of Ivy League attitudes. Vic, whose stature was growing both inside and outside of anthropology, had a growing dislike of the bureaucratic responsibilities that came with a professorship. Hardly surprising, the Cornell department expected him to pull his weight on administrative duties, which Vic found increasingly difficult to bear (RSI). He wanted intellectual comrades, not colleagues or students, and he thought ideas were best explored in an environment that was as open as possible. Universities, he was slowly coming to realize, could not provide that. They demanded "structure" and bureaucratic responsibility.

An alternative came with an offer (one among many) from the Committee on Social Thought at the University of Chicago. Vic took up a professorship in the Committee in 1968, with a joint appointment in the anthropology department. While Chicago did not release Vic from all of a professor's duties, the Committee was more amenable to his diverse approaches to scholarship. It was something they fostered. Social Thought was once described to Vic by one of his colleagues there as a place for "solid scholars who are something else as well" (VETA: James Redfield/VT 10/14/69). The Committee was meant to be interdisciplinary; it provided Vic with more intellectual freedom within a university setting. He taught courses not only in anthropology but also on the writers and philosophers that had occupied his youth: Blake, Kierkegaard, Baudelaire. This, in turn, gave Vic and Edie more leeway to pursue new ideas—even if they led, as their work came more and more to suggest, away from the classic sites of anthropology.

Within a year of their arrival at Chicago the Turners wanted to start another major project. The 1968–69 academic calendar year had been a difficult one, full, in the minds of the Turners, of the anti-structure they had been writing about. The Chicago school year began with the infamous riots at the Democratic National Convention in August 1968, and was punctuated that February with a bitter and divisive student protest over the sociology department's refusal to renew the contract of a popular, if controversial, professor and feminist activist, Marlene Dixon (University of Chicago 1991:145–51; Stocking 1979: 47; JMI). Edie found it all overwhelming; the place was about to "explode" (ETI). Fieldwork, which had been their "lifeblood," became a way out (ETI). With the publication of *The Ritual Process* that year, and Vic's recent appointment to the Committee, it was the perfect opportunity to seize upon their interests that fell beyond the scope of traditional anthropological studies. "Vic and I talked seriously with each other about doing 'non-traditional' fieldwork," Edie told me. "Vic had written on anti-structure in *The Ritual Process* and its relation to modern life. And we were thinking about the idea of journeys, which was linked to Dante. It gradually became clear that we were going to take up this pilgrimage work. This was the anti-structural thing" (ETI).

The study of pilgrimage was thus an articulation of their expanding intellectual visions, as it drew on the ideas of liminality and communitas presented in *The Ritual Process* (BRI). They also saw the new work as a way to reconnect on more neutral grounds with Max Gluckman, a figure to whom they still felt attached, however ambivalently. Gluckman had in the early 1960s suggested Israel as a future fieldsite for Vic. Now, the Turners were reading and writing about Marian shrines (that is, shrines devoted to the Virgin Mary) in Palestine (see Turner & Turner 1978:163–66). For Vic and Edie it was an added bonus (a position not all anthropologists might take) that they were Catholics and could participate as "natives." Studying pilgrimages was yet another way in which they collapsed the boundaries between personal and professional life, a boundary they had little interest in maintaining. "It all seemed to fall into place for us on academic and personal levels" (ETI).

So within a year of arriving at Chicago Vic and Edie were off to Mexico, where they spent the summer and fall of 1969 conducting research for what became their next major project on Catholic pilgrimages. It culminated in the publication, in 1978, of *Image and Pilgrimage in Christian Culture*. This book is notable in their *oeuvre* because it is the only one they officially coauthored. This was due in large part, Edie says, to the rise of feminist sentiments within the university, sentiments for which they had a good deal of sympathy (ETI). Dixson's case in sociology at Chicago was a harbinger for Edie of the importance of the women's movement. But before the question of authorship ever came up, Vic and Edie worked through a number of practical and theoretical issues to get the pilgrimage fieldwork done.

Between 1969 and 1972 the Turners made four major field trips, two to Mexico (1969 and 1970) and two to Ireland (1971 and 1972). The first and longest trip to Mexico was during the summer and fall term of 1969. The other trips involved research done on summer holiday, a schedule Edie begrudgingly chalks up to Vic's teaching "constraints" at the university (ETI). In addition to this fieldwork, the Turners included observations and analyses of other pilgrimage sites from textual sources, most notably in England and Israel. They took their youngest sons, Rory and Alex, with them on the trips. Rory took the picture of the crucifix that appears on the cover of *Dramas, Fields, and Metaphors*. Edie studied Spanish so she and Vic could work through the Mexican materials (ACI). Vic used contacts from his colleagues and students to get established in Mexico. And in Ireland they had a Volkswagen bus that doubled as their holiday camper for the family.

Fieldwork for the pilgrimage study differed from their work in Northern Rhodesia, as already suggested, both in conception and scale. Not only was the Mancunian extended case method "temporarily set aside," "the social drama [was] abandoned, in order to expound the interrelations of symbols and meanings framing and motivating pilgrim behavior in a major world religion" (Turner & Turner 1978:xxiv). Moving away from the small-scale study of "micropolitics" and ritual in an African village meant moving away also from the kind of in-depth understanding of social relations behind daily life. The Turners would meet pilgrims only once or twice before having to move on, or before the pilgrims returned home. Outlining social dramas would have been difficult given the often superficial nature of their contacts. There are no Muchonas or Sandombus in this published work, no figures who stand out as complex characters negotiating the paradoxes of Mexican-Catholic or Irish-Catholic life in the way that Sandombu must negotiate Ndembu kinship and marriage alliances in *Schism and Continuity*. For Vic and Edie, such compromised fieldwork was a serious issue. Edie missed "integration with what the people were actually doing" (ETI). The irony of the setup did not escape them: in work that was devoted to the further exploration of communitas, that moment of social life that captures what David Hume called "the sentiment for humanity" (quoted in Turner 1969:111), there were no vivid actors through which to appreciate this sentiment. But the Turners tried to approach the emotions from other directions. Textual material was one source that filled the gap created by a lack of prolonged social interaction. *Image and Pilgrimage* is based on extracting feeling and the sense of religious faith from devotional materials and pamphlets, or such texts as John Bunyan's *Pilgrim's Progress*. Writing "from the devotees," then, was an integral part of the analysis. One of the best examples of this is their treatment of St. Patrick's Purgatory in Lough Derg, County Donegal. The discussion here is based primarily on textual material, although the Turners went on the pilgrimage themselves. The pilgrimage site in the middle of Lough Derg ("Red Lake") has been, they write, "the focus of acrimonious polemic between Irishman and Englishman, Protestant and Catholic" (Turner & Turner 1978:107). Through an examination of the polemics, pamphlets, and amateur histories of this site—ranging from the Irish nationalist poet Thomas D'Arcy McGee's verse to the Protestant landholder Shane Leslie's histories—the Turners trace how "[t]his pilgrimage shrine combines religion and nationalism in a unique way" (107). In the concluding analysis, they stress the vitality and importance of religious symbols in politics: "Far from being an opiate for the people, Lough Derg and other pilgrimage shrines in Ireland—as in Mexico, Poland, and elsewhere—may have kept alive the cultural basis for national struggle, providing it with its root paradigm: that martyrdom should be embraced, if necessary, for the good of the people. In such wise we may partially account for the tenacity and obstinacy of Irish resistance over the centuries of foreign occupation" (136–37).

Vic and Edie's fieldnotes and experiences can also be considered writing "from the devotees" since they participated in this work not only as anthropologists but as Catholics. "I did not put my hand on the holy images for fun," Edie writes (SJ:ch. 6). "We were worshipping at the shrines" (ETI).

By 1969 Edie had no interest in separating her fieldnotes into "scientific" and "personal" accounts the way she had in Northern Rhodesia, where what was full of affect was filtered after the fact through her personal diaries. "In Mwinilunga," Edie says, "I did not give any emotional reactions of my own at all." But in Mexico, she started to "give more to the 'feeling' side of things, and I knew after that that if I did write anthropology on my own it would have to be full of feelings" (ETI). Edie also told me: "It was on the pilgrimage research when I first began to write notes that were my own, that is, in my own right; the way *I* wanted to do them" (ETI; emphasis in original). This change was due in part to Edie's greater sense of confidence, not only in herself as a perceptive anthropological observer, but also because of the privileged position Vic enjoyed within the academy. Just as they could take more liberty in the scope of their anthropological inquiries, so too Edie took more in the style of her writing.

But the work with Vic was collaborative, and that demanded compromise. Despite a common reverence for Blake's motto, "All things have their vitality in particulars, and every particular is a man," Vic did not want to include everything Edie did on the pilgrims they encountered. "And so," Edie says, "I had a kind of ambivalent feeling about the presentation of this material on pilgrimage" (ETI). Where she did win out, in part, was in "The Center Out There" (1974:166–230), a wide-ranging essay on the centrality of liminality and communitas in pilgrimages of the world religions. The inclusion in that piece of the poem "Arrival at Compostella," about the shrine of Saint James the Great, was at Edie's insistence. (She was also the translator.) Edie argues that it "captures what the core of pilgrimage is to people" (ETI), something that cannot be captured in social scientific accounts. Victor Turner wrote in the essay that the poem suggests the "ideal model of communitas" (1974:181).

In the mid-1990s Edie conducted further research on pilgrimage in Ireland. This more recent research was, like the trip to Mwinilunga in 1985, a kind of follow-up study. Through it Edie hopes to address the experiences and people "left out" of the early work on pilgrimage with Vic. It is, like *Experiencing Ritual*, a reinterpretation or revision of their collaboration. In an unpublished book manuscript, "Strange Journey," Edie rounds out her approach to pilgrimage. She also writes at length about her and Vic's religious faith. "What Vic and I were chasing after [in the pilgrimage research] was the material world of people's religion. . . . We were getting used to coming across places and circumstances where the presence of a spirit was self-evident, was actually experienced" (SJ:ch. 6). They found this in the people they met, like a woman called "Bidgy," whom they accompanied on a pilgrimage to Knock Shrine. The description of Bidgy in "Strange Journey" brings to mind a much earlier piece on Muchona the Hornet (Turner 1959), their brilliant, if quirky, informant in Mwinilunga who provided them with a key analysis of Ndembu ritual symbols (see Metcalf, 1998; 2002). Muchona was an oddball and social misfit. Bidgy, writes Edie, was an old "spinster, slightly 'tongue-tied' . . . [who] seemed to have no address" (SJ:ch. 7). Through Bidgy the Turners helped confirm their own feelings about the experience of communitas on pilgrimage; "it is a true path," Edie has recently written, expressed largely through "the experience and devotion of hundreds of millions of women" (SJ:ch. 7; cf. Engelke 2000).

The Influence of Feminism

It would be difficult to position the Turners' work on pilgrimage in the mid-1970s without taking into consideration the rise of second-wave feminism. Lisa

Hogeland writes, "the 1970s was a crucial period for feminism in the United States, a period in which feminist issues and ideas . . . moved quickly into the mainstream" (1998:1). Membership in the National Organization for Women, for example, grew from three thousand to over fifty thousand between 1970 and 1974 (1–3). Anthologies of feminist writings like Robin Morgan's *Sisterhood is Powerful* (which includes a statement by Chicago Women's Liberation [1970:531] condemning the University of Chicago's handling of Dixson's case) enjoyed popular success. The novels of Erica Jong, Margaret Atwood, and Rita Mae Brown were popular, while those of writers like Doris Lessing were receiving scholarly attention. These "consciousness-raising novels" (Hogeland 1998) were of great interest to the Turners.

Unlike their interests in "hippie culture" or Communism or Catholicism, however, it is hard to trace the influence of feminism in Vic and Edie's collaborative work. The pilgrimage work does not focus on women per se; they are not a "group," like the hippies, explicitly put to use in the elaboration of a theory of communitas. This is ironic because many of the sites Vic and Edie discuss in the pilgrimage work are Marian shrines, something Edie writes about only later, in her preface to the 1995 edition of *Image and Pilgrimage*, where she argues that women pilgrims possess "their own kind of unshakable feminism" (1995:xx).

Where the influence of a feminist perspective does surface, at least for *Image and Pilgrimage*, is in the by-line. "I saw the justice in that," said Edie (ETI). This was a powerful means of legitimizing Edie's role in the Turners' collaborative anthropological project; it was a way of bringing her out of the field (and out of the Thursday evening seminar in their living room) and into the larger academic arena as a voice in anthropology. But we have also seen that for Edie such recognitions were not always enough. She wanted the women's side of things in the work because she saw women's roles in pilgrimage as central to its understanding.

Although Vic and Edie were influenced by the writings of feminists (Adrienne Rich, Doris Lessing), Edie has not always considered herself one, although she admits to having "feminist friends" (ETI). She also says that as a child she was "something of a feminist," but more the way a good socialist should be for the equality of the sexes than like Gloria Steinem, much less the Redstockings. Edie even claims that it was Vic who first took up an interest in reading second-wave feminist literature. He would have done so, according to Edie, with the same open-minded respect he gave to everything he read. "Vic never stood above an argument; he always tried out the other side's ideas on his own pulses, and got interested and upset if they made sense, and incorporated them into his own position next time" (Turner & Turner n. d.:6; see also BBI). But if Vic did indeed (re)introduce feminism to his wife, there is little doubt, despite her own hedging, that Edie created through the women's movement a valuable space in which to develop her own sense of self as a writer.

Edie's fieldnotes had become a testing ground. She also started to write po-

Edith Turner in Chicago, 1973, at home in the study. (Courtesy of Edith Turner.)

etry again on a regular basis, something she hadn't done since the Second World War. When Vic pointed out an ad in *The Maroon*, Chicago's student-run newspaper, calling for people to help start a women's literary magazine, Edie jumped at the opportunity. "I would have loved to do it anyway," Edie says, but "it was his suggestion that legitimized it for me" (ETI).

The magazine was called *Primavera*. Although it was published under the auspices of the University Feminist Organization, not all of its staff members and contributors were students or faculty at Chicago. There was Edie. There were also freelance journalists, part-time secretaries, and students from other universities in Chicago and other parts of northern Illinois. According to Edie's introductory statement in the inaugural issue: "The purpose of *Primavera* is to be the voice of women here in Chicago, the voice of woman's own intrinsic art"

(1975a:1). Another contributor, Paula Brown, writes. "the voices speak with the special inflection of feminine sensibilities" (1975a:1). Edie believed strongly in such inflection; she thought of women's writing as distinct from men's, as something "physical, bodily" (ETI; see also Tedlock 1995). Her contributions to *Primavera* relay something of that.

Edie's piece in *Primavera* on the Nkang'a ritual, "Girl into Woman," is a good example of this "physical, bodily" side to her writing. It is a style she went on to develop in her own books, particularly *The Spirit and the Drum* and *Experiencing Ritual.* "I once witnessed the initiation ceremony for a girl in Central Africa," Edie wrote (1975b:83). "I was then mainly the anthropologist's wife," she continued. "Nevertheless I was interested on my own account in the positive outlook and richness of women's culture." As captured here that richness has to do with Ndembu women's sexuality and desire (see Richman 2001). Ikubi, the kankang'a Vic and Edie first got to know in early 1951, and one who features prominently in many Victor Turner essays, is portrayed in the *Primavera* article as a curious and excited young woman whom Edie imagines with her new husband "dancing on the bed, circulating, making delicious the first attack, forgetting that she ever doubted her body" (86). Beyond a slight blush the reader is left with another understanding of the Nkang'a ritual, an important one in light of the motivation behind its enactment (to make a woman out of a girl), but one that nevertheless was not explored for over twenty years. Nkang'a is infused with sexual desire. Writing in *Primavera* was a way for Edie both to explore her own interests and push the limits of the anthropological project she and her husband had developed.

But for all the ways in which Edie saw *Primavera* as her own territory, a space in which she could develop self-esteem and skills as a writer, she places it within the larger context of what she and Vic were trying to do together within anthropology. *Primavera* was not "a great light breaking on the horizon; it was a chance to write and get among writers" (ETI). "I was doing work with Vic all along," Edie says, and "there was a great satisfaction to know that the ideas Vic and I were discussing from the Chicago seminars were being put to use in the new writing" (ETI). Inasmuch as *Primavera* could be folded into the Turners' overall work, it was a valuable outlet for Edie as an individual and as a member of "the team." And she does insist it was only an outlet, although descriptions of the closet-office in Princeton do give her pause.

Greener Pastures

Almost as soon as Edie got wrapped up in editing and writing for *Primavera*, she found herself pulled away. Vic accepted the fellowship at the Institute for Advanced Study for the 1975–76 academic year. He returned to Chicago the following fall, only to be lured away by the University of Virginia the next. Edie told me Vic left Chicago because of a disagreement he had with the anthropology department over the hire of a prominent (female) anthropologist. A number of people I spoke with, however, suggested that as with Cornell, Vic left because Chicago would not give him the freedom from university service he felt he deserved. By this point Victor Turner was world-renowned. While no one I spoke with ever accused him of being arrogant, he could get upset, even hurt, when colleagues did not follow his suggestions. With lovable aplomb, he saw himself as the center of anything with which he was involved. Vic had hopes of crafting a world that was one-half intellectual discussion and one-half party. The University of Chicago did not accommodate this view. And so, in the fall of 1977, Victor Turner took up the Kenan Professorship in Anthropology and Religious Studies at Virginia, which included a two-year appointment in the University's Center for Advanced Study. While in residence at the Center, Vic had no teaching responsibilities. The Committee on Social Thought had given Vic a good deal of intellectual room, but it could not (or did not) match Virginia's offer of freedom from bureaucratic responsibilities. Even after his tenure at the Center ended, it is clear from the recollections of his colleagues at Virginia that Vic was afforded a good deal of leeway in meeting his university duties (CCI; DSI; RWI; HSI). He had the uncanny ability, for example, to teach two courses at the same time—always on Thursday night (RLI)—and thus to meet the requirements of his teaching load. When he did bother to attend anthropology faculty meetings, "normally he fell asleep" (PFI). He was, however, "at every party" (KRI), and almost always with Edie.

The six years that Victor Turner taught at the University of Virginia, before his death in 1983, are remembered by Edie as a time of movement and freedom. Alex and Rory were in high school and could take care of themselves if their parents had to travel. Since Virginia was interested above all in supporting Vic's eminence (RWI)—and therefore contributing to its own—Vic and Edie did indeed take advantage of numerous offers to travel. They took extensive trips to India, Sri Lanka, Brazil, Japan, and Israel (twice). Many of these offers came from former students and colleagues with whom the Turners had developed close relationships. The Turners also attended conferences in Tucson, Houston, Minneapolis, Chicago, New York, Los Angeles, and London, sometimes under the auspices of the Wenner-Gren Foundation through which the Turners could gather their friends for rounds of discussion and communitas. In 1982, Vic delivered the Nielson Lectures at Smith College. Together, Vic and Edie participated in a number of workshops at New York University with their friend and colleague Richard Schechner, whose work on performance studies became central to the Turners' articulation of the anthropology of performance (V. Turner 1987) and the anthropology of experience (Turner & Bruner 1986). When they were not away from Charlottesville, Vic and Edie were running

At the Turners' house in Chicago, 1977; *from left*: Victor Turner, Mary Douglas, Edith Turner, Rory Turner, James Douglas. (Courtesy of Edith Turner.)

seminars out of their home that often included staged rituals, sometimes for up to forty students and faculty (Turner & Turner 1987:141–53).

While not fieldwork in a strict sense, the ritual reenactments Vic and Edie staged with their students at Virginia and with Schechner at NYU became central to their understanding of what it means to do anthropology. In this sense, it is important to consider the role of performances in the development of the Turners' intellectual collaborations. They were interested in performance as "teachers of anthropology," but also because it contributed to a "kinetic understanding" of how people "experience the richness of their social existence" (Turner & Turner 1987:140).

One key enactment took place at the Performance Garage, Schechner's theater space in New York, over the course of a two-week workshop at NYU. A group of anthropology and theater students played out the social dramas of Sandombu in Mukanza village. These performances are notable, then, because they drew on material from *Schism and Continuity*. By 1982, when they were staged, the Turners were worlds away, ethnographically and theoretically, from their Ndembu work. Yet this is precisely why they chose to enact Sandombu's plight. Not only did Sandombu's case highlight the Turners' continued interest in the social drama, it helped suggest the universality of performance as a human condition. If an Ndembu social drama can be performed to learn about the nature of Ndembu social life, then indeed, with Shakespeare's "All the world's a stage" in mind, Vic and Edie were deeply invested in making this point by the early 1980s.

To stage Sandombu's case, Vic and Edie selected relevant passages from *Schism and Continuity* for the workshop participants to read (see Turner 1957:82–130). Edie and he "had to try to create the illusion of what it is to live Ndembu village life" (Turner 1982:92). They decided to focus on the "name inheritance" ritual which was part of the redressive phase of the second social drama described in *Schism and Continuity* (1957:116–30), in which Sandombu is invited back to the village after a year's exile to plant a *muyombu* tree to mark the inheritance by Manyosa of Nyamuwaha's name (Manyosa, Edie's best friend in the village, was Nyamuwaha's daughter), the very person Sandombu had once been accused of killing by sorcery. For the tree, they used a broom handle stuck in a crack of the Performance Garage floor. For the libation beer, unfortunately, "a cup of water would have to do" (Turner 1982:95). A kitchen knife was procured to pare the top of the "tree," and wet salt was used in place of white clay to anoint the ritual's participants. After the texts had been read and the ritual performed, the participants "agreed that the enactment of the Ndembu ritual was the turning point which brought to them . . . the affectual structure of the social drama" (96).

For Vic, the experiences in that two-week workshop held a number of lessons prefigured in Edie's interest in feminism and women's writing. It was in the context of this seminar, and after such experiences with his wife (as well as challenges from a number of the women in the workshop regarding the gendered assumptions of his work), that Vic posed the following reflexive question: "Does a male ethnographer, like myself, really understand or take into full analytical account the nature of matrilineal structure and its embodiment, not only in women but also in men, as a powerful factor in all their actions—political, legal, kinship, ritual, economic?" (98). Recognizing the centrality of this question to the anthropological project was, I argue, yet another way in which Victor Turner marked the collaborative nature of his work with Edie. It is also one of the few places in which a feminist argument is given his explicit attention. But "Dramatic Ritual/Ritual Drama" is not a feminist piece; he ultimately treats this question, and the feminist perspective, with tempered ambivalence, arguing, in last-word fashion, that "the feminist mode of staging ethnography assumed and enacted modern ideological notions in a situation in which those ideas are simply irrelevant" (97). It is not clear if the irony of this conclusion was lost on Vic. Twenty-five years before, Turner had been criticized by Gluckman in the same fashion for introducing the idea of the "social drama" into his analysis of Ndembu village life. Gluckman thought the drama metaphor was a "modern ideological notion" as well (see Gluckman 1972:xviii).

In the midst of all this travel and performance, Edie found time to enroll in the University of Virginia's continuing education program. It was the first time in her life she sat in a university classroom as a registered student. Despite the fact that she had never earned a bachelor's degree, the University granted her a master's degree in English in 1980. She wrote her thesis on William Shakespeare's *Measure for Measure*. Enrolling in classes for a master's degree at the age of fifty-seven was both a privilege she enjoyed as the wife of a famous professor and a stark reminder that she needed the academic credentials to carry on in her work with a public identity (ETI). It was a decision sparked in part from her experience with *Primavera* and the growing sense within herself that she wanted her own intellectual space (see ETI; AGI). Publishing *Image and Pilgrimage* with her name on the cover was liberating, but it also induced professional anxieties. She enrolled for a degree in English because she thought there would be something "invidious" about going for anthropology (ETI). She had spent the better part of her life a *de facto* anthropologist and felt too settled in her ways to take a structured course. It would also have changed her position in relation to the discipline by defining her in a more exact way. As the significant other of Victor Turner, Edie could always try to play on her liminality. To earn a master's in anthropology would have positioned her within a concrete professional hierarchy. English was, in any case, a natural choice. She had always seen literature as an avenue through which to explore the potential of anthropological writing. "I wanted to see how narrative would work in the marvelous field of anthropological material," she says (ETI). The courses she took in the English Department, including some with the novelist, John Casey, and the poet, Gregory Orr, helped hone her skills as a writer and bolster her professional confidence.

Edie did not apply for a Ph.D. after completing her master's degree. It was a difficult decision, but she and Vic were due to leave for a lengthy trip to Japan. Her attention was on the performance work. It is now a decision she regrets. As a lecturer today at the University of Virginia, she knows there are "downsides" to not having a Ph.D. in anthropology (ETI). For example, she is limited by university policy in her ability to work with graduate students in an official capacity. She is also ineligible for tenure, or for advancing to even the rank of assistant professor. Writing a doctoral thesis, then, is a *rite de passage* Edie has never completed for herself. Her work on Victor Turner's dissertation had to suffice as the experience.

In 1983, the good life in Virginia caught up with Vic. He was drinking, eating, and traveling too much. He was exercising too little because of his arthritic hip (stemming from his rail-car injury during the war). In October 1983, at the age of 63, Vic had a heart attack just before leaving for a board meeting at the University of Virginia's Bayly Art Museum. He was hospitalized for over a week, placed on a strict diet, given a plan of light exercise and physical therapy, and told not to do too much heavy work. Edie spent that fall trying to help him recover. But on December 18, 1983, Victor Turner had a second heart attack and died. He had been having breakfast with Edie and their son, Bob, in town for Christmas, when pains gripped his chest. He was reading the newspaper. He got up quickly from the breakfast table, stumbled down the hall to the bedroom and died, his body falling back against the door and slamming it shut. "I've always had the idea that his going to all those meetings is what killed him," says Edie (ETI). Like so much else in their lives, this fits into a Turnerian narrative: the free spirit of communitas killed by too much structure. But communitas alone might have been enough, particularly at the rate with which it was devoured by Victor Turner.

Victor Turner had two funerals. The first was Roman Catholic, and was held at the Holy Comforter Church in downtown Charlottesville. Selections were read from Rilke's *Duino Elegies* and Psalms. The second was African, and was held later that same day in the basement of the Turners' house. It was an "Ndembu funerary rite," scripted from the pages of Vic's own *Lunda Rites and Ceremonies* (1953). Roy Wagner played the role of Vic's Ikishi and danced his death (RWI; ETI; PFI). Edie was sitting atop a pile of carpets, a makeshift ash heap symbolizing the usual spot for the Ndembu widow.

Edie was "broken in half" when her husband died (SJ:ch. 9). But she was resolved to carry on with their work—what would become her work. She surprised her family and friends by turning "into a complete ball of fire" (FTI). Soon after Vic's death, Wagner secured for Edie a part-time lectureship. This gave her institutional support. Since January 1984, Edie has been on the faculty at the University of Virginia. This is the first and only academic position she has held. Wagner's efforts must be seen as a gracious gesture on the part of Edie's supporters within the university; it certainly made her life as a widow that much easier by providing her with a salary (however meager). But it must also be seen, in the larger context, as a commentary on the influence the academy exerts on our notions of professionalism: it is doubtful Edie would have been able to carry on with her anthropology projects to the extent she has outside of any institutional framework. She would have become, for those who didn't know better, the widow of a famous anthropologist. She is still Victor Turner's widow, but she has become something else as well.

Edie was sixty-one years old when she was hired for the job of anthropologist. In addition to continuing the Thursday night seminar, Edie was soon busy with other work and invitations from colleagues around the country. For the 1984 AAA meetings, held that year in Denver, Edie organized a memorial session for her husband. She was reluctant to do it because the anthropology meetings had always seemed so intimidating. "I felt that I would be doing something all the high-and-mighty anthropology professors were doing. I felt I was butting into worlds in which I was not fully a part before" (ETI). But the session was an awakening for Edie, in her eyes and the eyes of many others. Edie realized for the first time she had been a "professional" all along, not simply within the context of a world she had created with her husband, but the discipline at large. Those meetings, Alma Gottlieb concurs, "marked Edie's own coming out; I think they liberated her in the way a good ritual should" (AGI).

Edie's colleagues at Virginia were pleasantly surprised by her flowering. Ben Ray recalls Edie's appointment to the lectureship: "we thought that the whole point of it would be to kind of tidy up, and bring to completion anything that was almost ready. . . . But we didn't know, I didn't know, there was a whole new anthropological career germinating" (BRI). Wagner felt likewise. But now, he says, he can see that at "the time when most anthropologists are contemplating retirement, Edie started her career" (RWI; see also Wagner 2001).

These beginnings and endings are not so clear. Edie was starting a career, yes, but she was also finishing one up, as many of her friends initially suspected would be the case, and, on top of it all, refusing to do either. It was still in some respects the same as it ever was, except worse, because Vic was gone, and better, because now she could take time to clear up the parts she and Vic had got wrong, or never properly finished.

Epilogue

In 1985, Edie published a collection of Victor Turner's essays called *On the Edge of the Bush: Anthropology as Experience*. One of the most interesting pieces in this collection is Edie's prologue. Edward Bruner, in his review of the book (1991), rightly puzzles over it. For the first time in print, Edie explains to the anthropology community at large what colleagues and friends (including Bruner) had known all along: she called herself the "principal collaborator in every field that Vic explored" (1985a:1). This is something Vic never denied, although as we have seen the ways in which it was recognized shifted over time and in relation to his position within the institutional landscape. The farther along he got, the more visible Edie became. But as Bruner notes, Edie's presentation of herself is complex and contradictory. He tells us, for example, that he saw Vic and Edie present a paper together at the 1980 AAA meetings that is included in *On the Edge of the Bush* under Vic's name alone (Bruner 1991:197). Bruner asks why, after staking out her claim in the prologue, and with ample witnesses to corroborate her story, did Edie not include her name in the by-line of this essay?

Phyllis Rose (1983:125–37) has written about the hostility the public can have toward a significant other when this person is seen to be infringing on the genius of his or her partner. Rose and others (Meltzer 1994; Bayley 1998) also remind us that ideas are never born in isolation without some form of relationship with other ideas and other people. The kind of intimate relationship Victor and Edith Turner shared is a particularly vivid example of this fact. It is hardly unique and it is only one of many patterns. But Rose is correct to say that we are often hostile to the recognition of such connections. Edie was, I think, anxious about such hostility when she was compiling *On the Edge of the Bush*.

Her husband had just died, and her own position within anthropology was frag-ile. She was an anthropologist's widow, and risked a certain amount of scorn for trying to rewrite that role.

Edie will always be a significant other. She could never outgrow her identity as "the wife of Victor Turner." Then again, she would not feel comfortable do-ing so. But she is also, now, significant herself within anthropology. In the years since her husband has died, Turner has, in addition to tidying up her husband's oeuvre, published three books of her own (1987; 1992; 1996) and numerous ar-ticles. She received an honorary Ph.D. for her contributions to anthropology from the College of Wooster and has been integral to the development of what she calls, after the work with Vic she copresented at the 1980 AAA meetings, the anthropology of experience. Her best work, *Experiencing Ritual*, is, as I dis-cussed briefly, both a rejoinder to her husband's unreformed sociological side and the fullest articulation of their common interest in "the spirit."

Edie is not nervous about the consequences of becoming what Wagner calls a "prodigy-after-the-fact" (2001:190). She has never had a sustained, articu-lated dissatisfaction with how her intellectual ambitions were folded into the career of her husband. She has never fully cared. Edie is, like an anthropologist, ambivalent about the idea of a career, not only because she is a "rebel," but also because she perceives a career in academia to have killed her husband. Victor Turner was a man bothered, and sometimes torn apart, by the academy. It sus-tained him and shot him to the lofty heights of intellectual celebrity but he could never come to terms with its demands.

For Edie, legitimacy is only partly troubling, because she rarely slows down long enough to consider the consequences. Edie is a woman of ideas; ultimately, she is beholden to her intellectual curiosity. She has never allowed herself to get fully caught up in the machinations of the academy or the anxieties of profes-sionalism. Her marginal position in the academy has not been without its dif-ficulties, and in talking to her one can, on rare occasions, detect hints of anger and regret. But, with a generous spirit, she always expresses gratitude to Vic, whom she sees as having made sacrifices for them both. Malinowski might have called Edie an amateur anthropologist, and perhaps not even that—perhaps "just a wife." But if so, Edie Turner is a person who can teach us an important lesson about the shaping of a professional career in anthropology. Careers are not crafted in isolation, and perhaps it is time for the academy to reconsider the emphasis on individual genius in the construction of its intellectual histories.

Acknowledgments

Funding for this project was provided by the Wenner-Gren Foundation for Anthropo-logical Research Historical Archives Program and a Raven Society Fellowship at the

University of Virginia. Liam Buckley commented on the first sections of the manuscript and gave important advice. I would like to thank Barbara Babcock, Alma Gottlieb, Harry West and, especially, Richard Handler and Rebecca Nash for reading the whole draft and offering valuable suggestions and critiques. I would also like to thank Sandra Bamford, Keith Hart, John MacAloon, Mary McConnell, Susan McKinnon, Peter Metcalf, Richard Schechner, Lyn Schumaker, John Tresch, Richard Werbner, Margery Wolf and the Turners' children for discussing this project with me at various points along the way. Above all, my gratitude goes out to the people I interviewed. A few of these individuals are not directly cited in this essay, but their reflections were nevertheless invaluable. They are: Bernhard Kendal, Bernd Lambert, Gary Witherspoon, Mihayli Csikszentmihayli, and Ray Fogelson. The others are listed in the "Manuscript Sources" below. Edie Turner, of course, takes pride of place on the list. My apologies to all those mentioned here for the shortcomings in my writing, which I am afraid could never capture the richness of their insights.

References Cited

Ariëns I. & R. Strijp, eds. 1989. Anthropological couples. Special issue of *Focaal*, vol. 10.

Babcock, B. & J. MacAloon. 1987. Victor W. Turner (1920–83). *Semiotica* 65(1/2):1–27.

Bayley, J. 1998. *Elegy for Iris*. New York.

Behar, R. & D. Gordon, eds. 1995. *Women writing culture*. Berkeley.

Bowen, E. S. (Laura Bohannon). 1964. *Return to laughter: An anthropological novel*. New York.

Brown, P. 1975. Introductory statement. *Primavera* 1:1.

Bruner, E. 1991. Man alive, woman alive. *Revs. in Anth.* 16:195–201.

Chicago Women's Liberation. 1971. Statement on Marlene Dixson. In *Sisterhood is powerful: An anthology of writings from the women's liberation movement*, ed. R. Morgan, 111. New York.

Cornwell, J. 1999. *Hitler's Pope: The secret history of Pious XII*. New York.

Engelke, M. 1996. "Dear Max:" Victor Turner from the field in 1951. *Hist. Anth. Newsl.* 23(2):3–6.

———. 2000. An interview with Edith Turner. *Curr. Anth.* 41(5):843–52.

———. 2001. Books can be deceiving: Edith Turner and the problem of categories. *Anth. & Humanism* 26(2):124–33.

Epstein, A. L., ed. 1967. *The craft of social anthropology*. London.

Fernea, R. & E. Fernea. 1989. The practicing of our marriage. In Ariëns & Strijp 1989:36–44.

Gluckman, M. 1958. *Analysis of a social situation in modern Zululand*. Manchester.

———. 1963. *Order and rebellion in tribal Africa*. London.

———. 1972. Preface. In Turner 1957[1996]:xv–xix.

Gluckman, M., J. C. Mitchell & A. Southwold. 1970. Social anthropology and sociology. In *University perspectives*, eds. J. Knapp, M. Swanton, & F. R. Jevons, 75–89. Manchester.

Gottlieb, A. 1995. Beyond the lonely anthropologist: Collaboration in research and writing. *Am. Anth.* 97(1):21–26.

Grimshaw, A. & K. Hart. 1993. *Anthropology and the crisis of the intellectuals.* Prickly Pear Pamphlet 1.

Grinker, R. R. 2000. *In the arms of Africa: The life of Colin M. Turnbull.* New York.

Gupta, A. & J. Ferguson. 1997. Discipline and practice: "The field" as site, method, and location in anthropology. In *Anthropological locations: Boundaries and grounds of a field science,* 1–46. Berkeley.

Hogeland, L. 1998. *Feminism and its fictions: The consciousness-raising novel and the women's liberation movement.* Philadelphia.

Kapferer, B. 1996. Preface. In Turner 1957[1996]:vii–xiii.

Kennedy, E. L. 1995. In pursuit of connection: Reflections on collaborative fieldwork. *Am. Anth.* 97(1):26–33.

Kuper, A. 1983. *Anthropology and anthropologists: The modern British school.* 2nd ed. London.

Kuklick, H. 1991. *The savage within: The social history of British anthropology, 1885–1945.* Cambridge, UK.

Lewy, G. 1964. *The Catholic Church and Nazi Germany.* New York.

Malinowski, B. 1922. *Argonauts of the western Pacific.* Prospect Heights, IL (1984).

Manning, F. 1991. Victor Turner's career and publications. In *Victor Turner and the construction of cultural criticism: Between literature and anthropology,* ed. K. Ashley, 170–77. Bloomington.

Marcus, G. 1987. Review of Turner 1987. *Parabola* 12(3):116–19.

Meltzer, F. 1994. *Hot property: The stakes and claims of literary originality.* Chicago.

Metcalf, P. 1998. The book in the coffin: On the ambiguities of "informants." *Cult. Anth.* 13:326–43.

———. 2002. *They lie, we lie: Getting on with anthropology.* New York.

Papanek, H. 1973. Men, women, and work: Reflections on the two-person career. *AJS* 78(4):90–110.

Radcliffe-Brown, A. R. 1952. On social structure. In *Structure and function in primitive society,* 188–204. New York (1965).

Ray, B. C. 2000. Discourse about difference: Understanding African ritual language. In *A magic still dwells: Comparative religion in the postmodern age,* eds. K. Patton & B. C. Ray, 101–16. Berkeley.

Richman, K. 2001. Discussion comments for the session "Anthropology, undisciplined: Essays in honor of Edie Turner." Am. Anth. Assn. Meetings, 12/1, Washington, DC.

Riesman, D. 1964. Foreword. In Bowen 1964:ix–xviii.

Rose, P. 1983. *Parallel lives: Five Victorian marriages.* New York.

Schumaker, L. 1996. A tent with a view: Colonial officers, anthropologists, and the making of the field in Northern Rhodesia, 1937–60. *Osiris* 11:237–58.

———. 2001. *Africanizing anthropology: Fieldwork, networks, and the making of cultural knowledge in central Africa.* Durham, NC.

Stocking, G. W. 1968. *Race, culture, and evolution: Essays in the history of anthropology.* New York.

———. 1979. *Anthropology at Chicago: Tradition, discipline, department.* Chicago.

———. 1992. The ethnographer's magic: Fieldwork in British anthropology from Tylor to Malinowski. In *The ethnographer's magic and other essays in the history of anthropology*, 12–59. Madison, WI.

———. 1995. *After Tylor: British social anthropology, 1888–1951*. Madison, WI.

Tedlock, B. 1995. Works and wives: On the sexual division of textual labor. In Behar & Gordon 1995:267–86.

Tedlock, D. 1983. *The spoken word and the work of interpretation*. Philadelphia.

Turner, E. 1975a. Introductory statement. *Primavera* 1:1.

———. 1975b. Girl into woman. *Primavera* 1:83–86.

———. 1975c. Notes on contributors. *Primavera* 1:91.

———. 1985a. Prologue: From the Ndembu to Broadway. In V. Turner 1985:1–15.

———. 1985b. The milk tree. *Anth. & Humanism* 10(2):27–32.

———. 1987. *The Spirit and the drum: A memoir of Africa*. Tucson, AZ.

———. 1992. *Experiencing ritual: A new interpretation of African healing*. Philadelphia.

———. 1995. Preface. In Turner & Turner 1978:xiii–xxi (1995).

———. 1996. *The hands feel it: Healing and spirit presence among a Northern Alaskan people*. DeKalb, IL.

Turner, E. S. 1961. *The phoney war*. New York.

Turner, E. & F. Turner. n. d. (1984). Victor Turner as we remember him. Ms.

Turner, E. & V. Turner. 1955. Money economy among the Mwinilunga Ndembu: A study of some individual cash budgets. *Rhodes-Livingstone J.* 18:19–37.

Turner, V. 1953. *Lunda rites and ceremonies*. Occasional papers of the Rhodes-Livingstone Institute, no. 10. Manchester.

———. 1957. *Schism and continuity in an African society: A study of Ndembu village life*. Oxford (1996).

———. 1959. Muchona the Hornet, interpreter of religion. In *In the company of man: Twenty portraits by anthropologists*, ed. J. Cassagrande, 333–55. New York.

———. 1961. *Ndembu divination: Its symbolism and techniques*. Occasional papers of the Rhodes-Livingstone Institute, no. 31. Manchester.

———. 1962. *Chihamba, the white spirit: A ritual drama of the Ndembu*. Occasional papers of the Rhodes-Livingstone Institute, no. 33. Manchester.

———. 1967. *The forest of symbols: Aspects of Ndembu ritual*. Ithaca, NY.

———. 1968. *The drums of affliction: A study of religious process among the Ndembu of Zambia*. Oxford.

———. 1969. *The ritual process: Structure and anti-structure*. Ithaca, NY (1977).

———. 1974. *Dramas, fields, and metaphors: Symbolic action in human society*. Ithaca, NY.

———. 1982. *From ritual to theatre: The human seriousness of play*. New York.

———. 1985. *On the edge of the bush: The anthropology of experience*. Tucson, AZ.

———. 1987. *The anthropology of performance*. New York.

Turner, V. & E. Bruner, eds. 1986. *The anthropology of experience*. Urbana-Champaign, IL.

Turner, V. & E. Turner. 1943. Poppy. *Oasis* 1:20.

———. 1978. *Image and pilgrimage in Christian culture*. New York (1995).

———. 1987. Performing ethnography. In V. Turner 1987:139–55.

University of Chicago. 1991. *One in spirit: A retrospective of the University of Chicago on the occasion of its centennial*. Chicago.

Wagner, R. 1986. *Symbols that stand for themselves*. Chicago.
————. 2001. Edith Turner: The gender of giftedness. *Anth. & Humanism* 26(2):190–94.
Werbner, R. 1984. The Manchester School in south-central Africa. *Ann. Revs. Anth.* 13:157–85.

Manuscript Sources

Interviews (all interviews conducted by the author and recorded on tape):

ACI   Ann Chambers interview, July 1, 1997, Skibbereen, Ireland.
ADI   Anna Davis interview, June 24, 1997, Hastings, England.
AEI   A. L. Epstein interview, July 4, 1997, Hove, England.
AGI   Alma Gottlieb interview, March 7, 1997, Seattle, WA.
BBI   Barbara Babcock interview, April 11, 1997, Evanston, IL.
BRI   Benjamin Ray interview, April 18, 1997, Charlottesville.
CCI   J. Christopher Crocker interview, October 7, 1998, Charlottesville.
DSI   J. David Sapir interview, March 27, 1997, Charlottesville.
ETI   Edith Turner interviews. 17 interviews conducted between January and October 1997 in Charlottesville and Skibbereen, Ireland.
FTI   Frederick Turner interview, September 18, 1998, Charlottesville.
HBI   Helen Barnard interview, July 7, 1997, Hastings, England.
HSI   H. L. Seneviratne interview, September 28, 1998, Charlottesville.
ICI   Ian Cunnison interview, June 14, 1997, Heddon, England.
JBI   John Bate interviews, June 6, 1997, April 23, 1998, and June 2, 2000, Oxford.
JFI   James Fernandez interview, April 10, 1997, Chicago.
JMI   John MacAloon interview, April 11, 1997, Evanston, IL.
KRI   Karen Richman interview, April 10, 1997, Chicago.
PFI   Pam Frese interview, October 19, 1998, Charlottesville.
RAI   Roger Abrahams interview, March 6, 1997, Seattle, WA.
RFI   Ronald Frakenberg interview, June 10, 1997, Newcastle-under-Lyme, England.
RLI   Robert Langbaum interview, May 15, 1997, Charlottesville.
RSI   Robert Smith interview, July 21, 1998, Ithaca, NY.
RTI   Robert Turner interview, July 3, 1997, London, England.
RVI   Ruth Van Velsen interview, June 20, 1997, Cambridge, England.
RWI   Roy Wagner interview, March 20, 1997, Charlottesville.
TTI   Toni Thomas interview, June 17, 1997, Edinburgh, Scotland.

Other sources:

DSL   David Sapir letters. Personal correspondence held by J. David Sapir, Charlottesville.
JBL   John Bate letters. Personal correspondence held by John Bate, Oxford.
PJCM   Papers of James Clyde Mitchell. Rhodes House Archives, Oxford. Box 7.
PVWT   Papers of Victor Witter Turner. Fieldnotes made by V. and E. Turner,

Mwinilunga District, Northern Rhodesia, 1950–52 and 1953–54. University of Virginia Library, Special Collections Department.

SJ   "Strange Journey: The Spiritual Path of an Anthropologist." Jan. 2000 ms., E. Turner.

VETA   Victor and Edith Turner Archives. Fieldnotes, correspondence, photographs, diaries, and manuscripts of V. and E. Turner, held by E. Turner, Charlottesville.

INVERTING THE CAMEL'S HUMP

Jorge Dias, His Wife, Their Interpreter, and I

HARRY G. WEST

I had been in the northern Mozambican province of Cabo Delgado only a day when my initial research contact, the director of the provincial nucleus of the cultural archives, told me that he had arranged for me to meet Rafael Mwakala. When I asked who Mwakala was and why I should meet him, I was told, "Rafael has experience with people like you; he worked with Jorge Dias." Over the next year and a half, as I conducted research among the Makonde-speaking people of the Mueda plateau, my presence repeatedly conjured up the ghost of Dias, the Portuguese anthropologist who worked in the same region nearly forty years before me. Today, anthropologists seeking others of various sorts among whom to study frequently find beneath them the well-preserved footprints of those who were in many regards like themselves—other anthropologists. The significance of these others to our work can vary, but it is increasingly difficult to ignore them. Indeed, my experience with "the Makonde of Mozambique" (*Os Macondes de Moçambique*) was, and continues to be, mediated in substantial ways by Dias and the work of his research team.

For most of us, the encounter with anthropological precursors is laden with anxieties (Limón 1991:118). The readers of our grant applications and ethnographic manuscripts require that we demonstrate familiarity with "the literature," while those among whom we work do not easily permit us to forget the visitors who came before us. Often, we are expected both to live up to standards

Harry G. West is Lecturer in Anthropology at the School of Oriental and African Studies (University of London). He is the author of numerous articles based on research he has conducted in Mozambique since 1991 on governance and political discourse. He is editor, with Todd Sanders, of *Transparency and Conspiracy: Ethnographies of Suspicion in the New World Order* (2003).

of conduct and/or scholarship laid down by our predecessors and to "correct their errors" and "go beyond" them. Our precursors can often be of greatest significance to us, however, when we transcend critique of the texts they have produced and focus on the motives behind their work and the forces that gave shape to their perspectives (Limón 1994:12). Such study can afford new insights not only into the texts they produced and the ethnographic contexts from which those texts derived, but also into epistemological and political issues that we, as they before us, inevitably face.

In the case of António Jorge Dias this is no small task. Dias wrote more than 150 published works (see Oliveira 1968; Instituto de Alta Cultura 1974; Lupi 1984), and is widely considered the most influential anthropologist to have written in the Portuguese language (Lupi 1984:11). When he was invited in 1947 to head the ethnography section of the newly created *Centro de Estudos de Etnologia Peninsular* (CEEP), Dias was the only individual in Portugal with a doctorate in ethnology (Oliveira 1968:7–11, 19).[1] He remained so for more than two decades, but during that time he laid the foundation for a generation to follow him, teaching ethnology at the University of Porto, the University of Coimbra, and the University of Lisbon, and establishing a degree-granting program in ethnology at the *Instituto Superior de Estudos Ultramarinos* (ISEU), Portugal's colonial training institute, established in 1906 (Gallo 1988:26). Ernesto Veiga de Oliveira, a colleague and contemporary of Dias, has written:

> To Jorge Dias alone . . . is due the renascence of ethnological study in Portugal, its scientific, methodological and systematic attainment . . . , the expansion of such studies and the founding of institutions in which they could be pursued . . . [and the] university professorships forming its basis, as well as the training of those first researchers and their assistants who were to give this study the necessary consistency and continuity. (Oliveira 1974:17)

Dias, however, is not an uncontroversial figure in the history of Portuguese anthropology, particularly for those interested in his work in Africa. While his research team's publications on the Makonde continue to be regarded as Portuguese-language anthropology classics, these were not the only texts the team produced on the Makonde. After each of the five research trips that Dias

---

1. There is some disagreement in the literature about the title of the degree Dias earned in Germany: Branco (1986:82) states that the degree was in "*Volkskunde,*" which would translate more accurately as "folklore" than as "ethnology"; James Dow (personal communication, 1/22/99) told me that the degree was in Romance languages with a specialization in modern history and German literature; R. Pereira writes in one place that the degree was in philosophy (1998:xxvii)—perhaps merely reflecting that the degree was a Ph.D.—and elsewhere that it was in ethnology (1998:xxxii).

António Jorge Dias conversing informally with a woman in the field. (Courtesy Arquivo do Museu Nacional de Etnologia [Lisboa].)

and his colleagues made to the overseas territories between 1956 and 1960, they submitted a confidential report to the Portuguese Overseas Ministry, which had funded their research. In their published works, the Dias team celebrated "traditional" Makonde culture, scarcely commenting on the impact of colonialism. In justifying this stance, they defined their work among the Makonde as "scientific" and "apolitical." Nonetheless, in the confidential reports, the team described continuing political processes, such as the emergence of a nationalist movement among the Makonde, and provided the colonial regime with information that could be used to consolidate the colonial agenda. One might easily conclude that Dias and his colleagues acted with duplicity, betraying the trust of their *research* subjects to a regime that saw these people only as *colonial* subjects. Simplistic judgments of Dias and his colleagues, however, ignore the politically complex institutional and intellectual environments in which they worked—environments shaped by the authoritarian Salazar regime that ruled Portugal throughout Dias's career. Closer study of Dias and his work reveals valuable lessons about the complexity of relations between power and academic inquiry in the colonial context and, as I will argue at the end of this essay, in post-colonial contexts as well.

My attempt to treat Dias as an ethnographic subject in his own right has been complicated by the fact that he passed away in 1973 (for obituaries, see Oliveira 1972–74; Redinha 1973), long before I took an interest in the Makonde and his work among them. My relationship with Jorge Dias has, therefore, been mediated through *his* surviving significant others—principal among them his wife and research colleague, Margot Dias, and Mwakala, one of his "native informants." Such significant others are often substantial contributors to the ethnographic productions of anthropologists. Such was certainly the case with Mwakala, who served as interpreter to a Dias team that was never able to conduct research in the local *Shimakonde* language. Such was also the case with Margot Dias, who not only accompanied her husband to the field and did research among the Makonde (and elsewhere in Mozambique) on her own, but was also the coauthor of substantial portions of the works on the Makonde published by the Dias team, and eventually published several works of her own.

In this essay, I approach Jorge Dias and the work of his team as I did during the course of my research. The chronology of my account thus moves against the grain of history, following instead the flow of my investigations as I conducted an archaeology of the Dias team's work that involved digging through layers of events and narratives, seeking revelations of each strata in the one underlying it. I begin with a reading of the published works of the Dias team on the Makonde of Mozambique, focusing on the construction of the Makonde as a "traditional" people. I then present my encounter with Mwakala, whose life history, including his involvement with the Dias research team, calls into question the timelessness of the Makonde that the team encountered in Mozambique in the late 1950s. I next turn my attention to the confidential reports (now publicly available) that were written by the team during their years of field research. These reports not only reveal the historical and political understandings of the team—notwithstanding their public professions of disinterest in such matters—but also raise questions about the ethical stance of Dias and his colleagues regarding their research subjects and the state. Such questions, I suggest, can be adequately addressed only within the context of an examination of the life and career histories of Dias and his colleagues. I do this in the following section, where I seek to understand them as "native" to their own time and place through an examination of the institutional and intellectual milieus in which they came of age and worked as anthropologists. I conclude with reflections on how my own experiences in the field influenced by complex political issues lead me to judge my ethnographic precursors with rigor, but also with humility.

"It Was Like This, You See": Jorge Dias and the Makonde Without History

In transit to my dissertation field research site in Mozambique in the summer of 1993, I stopped off for a month in Portugal to take the Advanced Intensive Portuguese Language Course at the University of Lisbon. After class during hot July afternoons, I sat reading on the shaded veranda outside the second-story room that I had rented from a family in Campo de Ourique. Having previously read only selected sections, I now read straight through the 1168 pages of the four-volume ethnography, *Os Macondes de Moçambique*, written by Jorge Dias and his research team comprising his wife, Margot Schmidt Dias, and Manuel Viegas Guerreiro (Dias 1964; Dias & Dias 1964; Dias & Dias 1970; Guerreiro 1966).

This study of the Makonde ethnic group, located in the north of Portugal's Mozambican colony, constituted the first Portuguese-language ethnography of significant interest to an international audience. Some have suggested that *Os Macondes de Moçambique* remains the most comprehensive ethnographic study of an African society ever produced (see Pereira 1986a:3; Pereira 1986b:220). The work conforms to the conceptual and organizational logic of a "classic ethnography" (Rosaldo 1989), surveying and systematizing Makonde society. The table of contents, summarized in Figure 1, is revealing. Tucked among the pages of text are 577 photographic plates, 45 diagrams, and 7 maps. Where Dias and his team were unable to gain the perspective they desired on their subject with the camera, they relied upon Fernando Galhano, a childhood friend of Dias who joined him at the CEEP in 1948, to recreate the Makonde world in 62 sketches distributed throughout the work.

Volume 1: Historical and Economic Aspects (Dias 1964)
    Natural Environment
    Anthropomorphology
    History and Origins
    Economy
Volume 2: Material Culture (Dias & Dias 1964)
    The Village
    Diet
    Bodily Practices
    Artisanry
Volume 3: Social and Ritual Life (Dias & Dias 1970)
    Social Structure
    The Social Life of the Individual

Political and Juridical Structure
Magical and Religious Beliefs and Rituals
Volume 4: Knowledge, Language, Literature and Games (Guerreiro 1966)
Knowledge
Language
Oral Literature
Games, Toys and Other Diversions
Stories and Riddles

Turning the pages of Os Macondes de Moçambique, I was at once enchanted and disturbed, for Dias and his colleagues succeeded all too well in their attempts to "capture" the Makonde on paper, making of them "monuments" to their own "tradition." It came as a surprise to me that the Dias team, conducting field research in the late 1950s and publishing their works in the following decade, would produce ethnography of this genre. Anthropologists of other nationalities had long since begun to focus on the impact of colonialism on the peoples they studied, and to produce ethnographic works that portrayed social change through process-oriented analysis. Foremost among anthropologists contributing to this shift within the discipline were those working just across Mozambique's borders in conjunction with the Rhodes-Livingstone Institute (see Kuper 1983:99–120; Moore 1994:29–73). The titles of their works, which highlight such phrases as "social change," "economic development" and "migrant labor," are telling of emergent interests within the discipline at that time (Gluckman 1940, 1942, 1943; Wilson & Wilson 1945; Schapera 1947; Richards 1955; Epstein 1958; Southall 1961).

Dias and his colleagues did not ignore contemporary events and processes in their ethnographic works on the Makonde so much as they circumvented them. In an essay Dias first published in 1949, before he had done fieldwork outside of Portugal, he echoed Boas when he argued for ethnographic research focused not on historical processes but on the "authentic" research subjects those very processes were destroying:

> And it is necessary that we hurry, because we are arriving in a period of history in which the loss of traditional values is more rapid and relentless. From day to day, precious elements of culture are lost that we can never again recover and that we are obliged to conserve because they are the legacy of our grandparents and constitute the base of our national characteristics in addition to being the patrimony of all humanity. (Dias 1961b:95)

Dias might have written similar words a decade later with reference to the Makonde. Where the Dias team saw the forces of historical change, they portrayed them not as legitimate subjects of scientific analysis but as pollutants that adulterated Makonde "tradition" and disrupted their study of it. Whenever possible, the Dias team sought to filter out the impurities brought to Makonde society from an apolitically conceived modern world and to "salvage" a record of Makonde "custom."

Notwithstanding this critique, the record of Makonde culture that the Dias team produced was a richly detailed one. As I sat reading in Lisbon, on the threshold of fieldwork, I came to think of the team's work both as a resource and as a point of departure for my own research. I could "move beyond" the work of the Dias team merely by focusing on differences between the Makonde the Dias team had portrayed and the Makonde I would encounter. I was soon to discover, however, that my task would not be so simple. *Os Macondes de Moçambique* had taken on an historical life of its own as a cultural artifact both about and within Makonde society. Upon arrival in Mozambique, I was told in conversation with a prominent sociologist in Maputo that Makonde elite in government and in the military might treat my research with suspicion in the tense environment produced by the Mozambican civil war (that began in 1977, just two years after Mozambican independence) and the recent (1992) peace accord. To my advantage, it was explained to me, most high-ranking Makonde officials took great pride in *Os Macondes de Moçambique*, and many even had copies of the volumes in their homes. Should my motives be questioned, I was instructed, it would be best to explain that I was conducting research "as Jorge Dias had done." In many of my subsequent encounters with political and military leaders of Makonde origin, I did, in fact, find *Os Macondes de Moçambique* to be a valuable conversation piece over which to establish rapport through mutual admiration (attesting to the wealth of Makonde culture) and "corrective" critique (challenging the "authority," even if only ethnographic, of the Portuguese who once ruled Mozambique while at the same time establishing my own ethnographic authority among people who were at once my ethnographic subjects and my most "interested" readers).

The coup de grâce, however, occurred in the field, where I kept a photocopy of *Os Macondes de Moçambique* to which I sometimes referred before or after conducting interviews. On my first research excursion to the plateau, I asked Mwakala to accompany me. Several times in the first days of this trip, he disputed the information given me by my informants. To clinch his case against them, he turned to the ethnography he had assisted in producing. Eventually, for a variety of reasons I will later discuss, I stopped working with Mwakala. To my surprise and frustration, I was still unable to keep the Dias team out of sight and out of the minds of my interviewees. On several occasions, in response to my questions, they arose and retreated into their mud and bamboo houses only to return with their own copy of *Os Macondes de Moçambique*. Paging through it, they would point to a photo or a passage and tell me, "It was like this, you see."

Rafael Mwakala holding *Os Macondes de Moçambique* open to the page with a photo of his wife and child. (Courtesy Harry G. West.)

Over time, in the field, my appreciation deepened for the complex impact of the Dias team's work upon the historical consciousness of its subjects. *Os Macondes de Moçambique* portrayed a dignified African people with rich traditions and was, therefore, generally embraced with pride by Makonde. Where the life-ways of other Mozambican ethnic groups had been all but destroyed, Dias and his colleagues suggested, the Makonde had sustained a vibrant African identity. Forty years later, as those I worked among looked with ambivalence upon a recent post-colonial past of failed "socialist modernization" and a vague future of "development" promised by Western donors and a liberalizing state, the idea of a noble "tradition" remained attractive. At the same time, those Makonde whom I witnessed turning the pages of *Os Macondes de Moçambique* betrayed a deep ambivalence toward "tradition" deriving from their sense that, despite the books' words, they were now but a shadow of their former selves. Their references to a passage or a photo were generally accompanied by a lament to the effect that "it's no longer like this," or "people today don't know this anymore," or, simply, "the way we do it now is wrong." The Makonde of Mozambique with whom I conversed seemed always to be, in their words, suspended between a "modern" world that cast them as a "traditional" people, and a "tradition" they could no longer quite get right.

"Anti-Anthropology": Rafael Mwakala
and the Makonde With History

I began my research through the collection of life histories. The dynamic view of Makonde society afforded by the composite picture of the lives of my informants—many of which span the period between the research of the Dias team and my own—offers a substantial "corrective" to Os Macondes de Moçambique. These life histories provide "data" on the lived experiences of the very people among whom the Dias team worked, and demonstrate that Dias and his colleagues might have seen all around them the forces of colonialism at work, not to mention the dynamic and increasingly assertive responses of the Makonde they studied so intensively. In fact, these life histories show that few, if any, of the Makonde alive when the Dias team conducted its research had, in fact, lived the life of "Makonde tradition" portrayed in Os Macondes de Moçambique.

For students of African history, the Makonde lived–experience of Portuguese colonialism is all too familiar. Makonde settlement heads had been co-opted by the colonial administration and forced to collect taxes and recruit laborers for colonial public works and plantations (West 1998). This not only transformed local power relations, it gave rise to massive migrations of Makonde across the Rovuma River border into Tanganyika, where labor relations were more advantageous to them. By conservative estimates, more than one seventh of the total population of the Mueda plateau—the region most Mozambican Makonde call home—were temporarily living and working beyond its borders by 1957 (see Alpers 1984:377). As Makonde migrant laborers returned from Tanganyika, they caused dramatic changes within their communities, altering patterns of economic consumption and distribution, propagating new fashions in language, dress and architecture, questioning local cosmologies and challenging kin-based figures of authority. They also repatriated significant experiences gained in Tanganyika in plantation labor unions and in nationalist political movements. Returning migrants in combination with mission-educated youth back home laid the foundations for a nationalist movement and eventually for guerrilla war against the Portuguese colonial regime (West 1997a).

The story of Rafael Mwakala provides a poignantly illustrative counterpoint to the "typical Makonde" depicted by Dias and his colleagues. During that first arranged meeting with Mwakala, he and I sat together at a beachside restaurant—once a modest colonial resort—in Pemba, the capital of Cabo Delgado province. Mwakala's eyes moved about restlessly, rarely meeting mine. He told me that he worked with Jorge Dias and his wife, Margot Dias, as an interpreter during the time they had spent in the Makonde-speaking Mueda region in the late 1950s. His responses to my questions about the Diases, however, drifted time and again to scattered bits and pieces of his own life.

Over the next two years, I met with Mwakala in his home on nine separate occasions to record his story. These sessions lasted from two to five hours. To my frustration, Mwakala presented his life to me as shards of a broken pot, picking up one piece, considering it for a while and then casting it aside for another, in an order that made little sense to me. He seemed eager to please, but at the same time he often appeared agitated by his own memories. As we talked, we were constantly interrupted, not only by members of the large family who depended on Mwakala for support, but also by visitors, some of whom Mwakala nervously asked to return later, and others who acted with hostility toward Mwakala, toward me, or both. I eventually constructed the following narrative of Mwakala's life.

Rafael Pedro Mwakala was born on September 10, 1933 to Cecília Boniface and Pedro Mwakala. The exact date of his birth was recorded because Mwakala's parents lived with a small group of Catholic Makonde adjacent to the Nang'ololo mission staffed by Dutch padres and Italian sisters. Mwakala's father had been one of the first two converts won by the Catholic missionaries of the Montfort order who had come to the Mueda plateau in 1924. After his baptism in May 1928, Mwakala's father had continued studying with the padres, and in 1932, he and eleven other converts—Nang'ololo's first "twelve disciples"—began to teach the catechism in small settlements in the Nang'ololo region.

By the time Mwakala was old enough to learn to read and write, the padres had completed construction of an elementary school on the Nang'ololo mission grounds. Mwakala began his studies there in 1944. After he completed standards one- , two-, and three-rudimentary (the only standards offered at Nang'ololo), in 1948 Mwakala was included among the first group of Makonde boys to travel off the plateau to the Montfort mission school at Mariri in the Makua-speaking region of southern Cabo Delgado. Between 1948 and 1951, Mwakala completed standards three-elementary and four.

The 1940 Concordat between the Vatican and the Portuguese government had charged the Catholic church with the task of educating "native" Mozambicans, but it stipulated that education beyond the fourth grade be limited to clerical training. Only Africans who had achieved "*assimilado*" status by adopting "civilized" ways of speaking, dressing, eating, and the like, and who were, consequently, considered to be Portuguese, were allowed to send their children for further schooling (see Penvenne 1989). The padres, however, circumvented these limitations by placing "native" graduates of the fourth grade in a seminary school where broader academic training was given along with classes on church doctrine. Mwakala passed standards five, six and seven at the *Seminário Pio XII de Mariri* before abandoning his studies in 1956 when recurrent bouts with severe headaches forced him to return home. Mwakala's illness appears to have been related to the anxieties produced by his experience as one of the first Makonde to approach status as an *assimilado*. In unpublished writings, Dias suggested that Mwakala and the others who worked for the Dias team as field interpreters were "difficult people, who knew little of Makonde culture" due to their mission up-bringing. Of one of these interpreters in particular (perhaps Mwakala), Dias wrote that he was "full of complexes and inhibitions, which in part come from being considered indigenous [not 'civilized'] despite his literacy" (DG 1959:14).

Upon returning to the plateau, Mwakala sought treatment for his illness from a Makonde healer. Back at Nang'ololo, however, Mwakala was also given work by the mission as a catechist and later as a teacher. He earned 150 *escudos* (approximately $5.18) a month as a catechist, and 500 to 600 *escudos* a month as a teacher. When Dias inquired about the possibility of arranging a Makonde interpreter to work with him in the field, the district administrator of Mueda referred Dias to the Nang'ololo mission where Padre Jan Janssen identified Mwakala as the best-educated young man in the congregation. Mwakala worked with Dias in 1957 and 1958 as he conducted research during academic holidays. Mwakala was paid 500 *escudos* per week. Mwakala told me, "I used the money I made in the first year to pay bridewealth." The lucrative opportunity to work with the Dias research team was one Mwakala shared with only two other Makonde, fellow catechists Zacharias Vanomba and José Cosme. Still, the need to earn a cash income was one Mwakala shared with most Makonde, all of whom had to pay the annual hut tax of 120 *escudos* and to procure the basic consumer goods—such as salt, sugar, cooking oil, matches, clothing—on which they had come to depend.

Even as Mwakala worked for the Dias team, he also became involved in political activities. Having gained a "broader view of the world" (his words) through mission education, Mwakala was considered a potential supporter by Mozambican nationalists based in Tanganyika who sought to develop networks in the Mozambican interior. As early as 1958, Mwakala was approached by Clementino Nandang'a, a returning labor migrant, who suggested to him that a party modeled after Julius Nyerere's Tanganyika African National Union (TANU) would soon be built in Mozambique. Mwakala listened to Nandang'a's ideas and expressed sympathy, but at that moment there was nothing for Mozambicans living at home to do. As he traveled with the Diases, however, Mwakala shared his sentiments with young Makonde in villages throughout the plateau during conversations after the day's ethnographic work was done. In part because of this, and in part because he was a member of the educated church community, Mwakala eventually felt the suspicious eye of the Por-tuguese security police on him, and in late 1958, he fled across the border to Tanganyika. In Lindi, a Catholic priest convinced him to return to Mozam-bique, which he did in 1959.

Mwakala posing for his anthropologist employer in his finest "modern" apparel while holding a "traditional" Makonde spear.(Courtesy Arquivo do Museu Nacional de Etnologia [Lisboa].)

On June 16, 1960 the tense political atmosphere on the Mueda plateau erupted. Representatives of an organization called the Tanganyika-Mozambique Makonde Union (TMMU), who had returned to Mueda from their temporary homes in Tanganyika a few days earlier to approach the district administrator with a list of demands, were summoned to the administration building in the town of Mueda. Before the day was over, shots had been fired on the crowd that had gathered to see what would happen. News of the "Mueda Massacre" spread, with rumors suggesting that as many as 600 had been killed. After the massacre, Mwakala purchased a card making him a member of the Makonde African National Union (MANU), the proto-nationalist movement created after the Massacre through restructuring of the TMMU. He later assisted in selling membership cards to others.

The Diases were not in Mueda at the time of the Massacre.[2] According to Mwakala, Jorge Dias, Margot Dias and Manuel Viegas Guerreiro passed through Mueda a year later, and in conversation with him expressed grief over the tragic

2. Jorge and Margot Dias were attending to the visit of an American professor of anthropology, Charles Wagley, whose home institution, Columbia University, had expressed interest in supporting Dias's teaching activities in Lisbon under the auspices of a Ford Foundation grant (DGD 1961:2; Wagley n.d.). I thank Charles Wagley's daughter, Isabel Wagley Kottak, for providing me with a copy of Wagley's report and field diary.

events that had taken place.[3] Mwakala never saw the Diases or Guerreiro again. Due to concerns for their security in what was considered a dangerous environment, they were not permitted by the colonial government to return to Mueda. Although the Diases sent copies of preliminary research publications to Mwakala on the plateau, he never received them, for soon after the Massacre, he fled once more across the border to Tanganyika.

In 1962, the *Frente de Libertação de Moçambique* (FRELIMO) was formed in Dar es Salaam of three smaller Mozambican nationalist movements, including MANU. Mwakala was included among the first FRELIMO recruits sent to Algeria in 1963 for guerrilla training. After eighteen months, he returned to what had become Tanzania. In FRELIMO camps in Bagamoyo, Kongwa and, finally, Nachingwea, Mwakala trained new guerrilla recruits. In 1968, the fourth year of the FRELIMO insurgency, he was dispatched to the Mozambican interior where he served the guerrilla army first in Mocímboa de Praia as Secretary of Operations for the Inhambane Detachment and, from 1972 onwards, in FRELIMO's Central Base on the Mueda plateau as both Secretary of Operations and Secretary of the Political Commissariat for the Second Sector. He participated in several combat operations over the course of the decade-long war that culminated in Mozambican independence in 1975.

From the beginning, the Dias team considered Mwakala an exceptional case due to his mission upbringing and education. While unique in some regards, however, Mwakala's story interlaces with those of other Makonde, none of whom were immune to the forces of change in the late 1950s. Could the Dias team have failed to see these life stories, failed to recognize that the Makonde among whom they worked were all living lives of dramatic historical transformation?

Apparently so. In April of 1996, after completing my field research in northern Mozambique, I spent several weeks conducting research in Portugal. On several occasions, I met Dias's widow in her home in Oeiras, just outside of Lisbon. She asked me about people she had known on the plateau and I offered news of them as I was able. When she asked about Mwakala, I gave her a letter he had written to her and placed in my hands more than a year before. The delight in her eyes was genuine. I then informed her of the path Mwakala's life had taken after she last saw him. She displayed surprise that Mwakala, whom she had known so well, had been a FRELIMO guerrilla. The young man Jorge Dias saw as "full of complexes and inhibitions" had hidden

3. This visit is not documented in any of the reports made by the Dias team on their research activities in northern Mozambique. However, during one of my conversations with Mwakala, he showed me a photo of himself with his wife (Agata Tomé Akalenge) and two children (Celestina and Pedro Ernesto—the second of whom was born February 27, 1961); the photo was taken by Margot Dias and dated 1961 in her handwriting.

Margot Dias conducting an interview, surrounded by onlookers. (Courtesy Arquivo do Museu Nacional de Etnologia [Lisboa].)

from the Dias team political perspectives and aspirations that would define his life's trajectory.

I remembered a conversation with Mwakala about Margot and her husband; I had asked him to compare the Diases' research methods with mine. Mwakala responded:

> They worked in much the same way you do. People didn't resist answering their questions. But there was a difference. Now people have a certain liberty. At that time, there was fear of the white. People acquiesced in everything. For example, you always request permission before taping a conversation or a story someone tells you. They just showed up and started working. Who could refuse? Of course, people could never really be sure they didn't work for the government or the security police. Some thought that they were there to trick people into talking about things. So there were many things people didn't tell.

Mwakala then said, "I generally trusted them, though. They were truly different. I saw it in the way they worked." On another occasion, he told me, "They were not like other Portuguese. They shook our hands and they ate with us. They were extraordinary people. We had never seen whites like them."

When I had asked Mwakala, however, if the Diases knew at the time he worked with them of his sympathies with the nationalist movement, or when they visited with him in 1961, of his membership in MANU, he smiled and said: "They were, after all, Portuguese. It would have been very dangerous for me if they had known." And so, Mwakala, one of the three Makonde the Dias team came to know best of all, a man whose life told the story in microcosm of social transformation among the Makonde in the late colonial period, conducted a form of "anti-anthropology," to use Alfredo Margarido's term (1975), concealing from his ethnographers the very details I have criticized them for not presenting in their work.

"As an Ethnologist": Colonialism and the Dias Research Team

Margot Dias's response to my news of Mwakala's FRELIMO career may confirm that she shared ignorance with her husband and Guerreiro of the sentiments and extracurricular activities of their own interpreters.[4] Digging deeper, however, one finds that the Dias team was anything but oblivious to the political environment in which they conducted their research. Despite the near total omission of references to colonial processes in the Dias team's published works, the northernmost regions of Mozambique had been chosen as a site for their research in part because of its contemporary situation. Upon hearing that the team's confidential reports to the Portuguese Overseas Ministry had been made available to the public after the fall of the Salazar regime and the granting of independence to Mozambique's African colonies, I sought them out, finding them scattered in various libraries and archives in Mozambique, Portugal and the United States. To understand what they tell us about the late colonial period in Mueda and about the involvement of the Dias team in that historical moment, it is essential that we first look at the institutional context in which Dias and his colleagues worked both at home and in the field.

The Diases and Guerreiro conducted research in northern Mozambique between 1957 and 1959 under the auspices of the *Missão de Estudos das Minorias Étnicas do Ultramar Português* (MEMEUP). The MEMEUP was organized by the *Centro de Estudos Políticos e Sociais* (CEPS), a research institute housed within the ISEU, which was under the charge of the *Ministério do Ultramar* (the Portuguese Overseas Ministry). Although Jorge Dias had previously been teaching at the University of Coimbra, Portugal's most prestigious academic institution, he was attracted to the newly created CEPS in 1956 by its director, the soon-to-be Overseas Minister, Adriano Moreira. For Dias, coming to Lisbon was an attractive career move. Prior to that time, there were no degree-granting

---

4. The Dias team was most likely also unaware that Margot Dias's interpreter, Zacharias Vanomba, had a brother named Faustino who was a leading mobilizer for the Mozambican nationalist movement in Tanganyika. It was Faustino Vanomba and Kibiliti Diwani who led the demonstration that resulted in the Mueda Massacre in 1960.

programs in ethnology anywhere in Portugal; ethnology was taught as a *cadeira* (class) in other disciplinary programs. At the ISEU Dias was mandated to set up an ethnology degree program and thus was able to advance to the level of full professor (Branco 1986:94). Dias himself taught courses at the ISEU in cultural anthropology, "native" institutions, and regional ethnology.

The CEPS was also to provide Dias with the opportunity, and the institutional and financial support, to conduct ethnological fieldwork for the first time outside Portugal. Dias's proven skills as a field researcher were to be put to use in support of a CEPS mandate that Moreira had been instrumental in defining. As British and French colonies in Africa moved toward independence, and as the United Nations criticized Portugal's resistance to the independence movement, the Portuguese regime sought ways to rearticulate its colonial policy and to defend its continuing claims to empire. Moreira was a dynamic representative of a new generation on the Portuguese political scene who argued the need for "liberalization" and "modernization" of Portuguese colonial policy, but ultimately defended the colonial idea (see Moreira 1956, 1960; Instituto Superior de Ciências Sociais e Políticas 1995; Instituto Superior de Ciências Sociais e Políticas 1996). Under Moreira's directorship, CEPS was to cultivate the growth of a heretofore nonexistent applied social science (Pereira 1989a; 1998:xxiv), serving the regime as a research center and think tank in support of colonial policy reform (Gallo 1988; Pereira 1986b:219).

As its name indicated, MEMEUP was to provide the Ministry with data on ethnic minorities resident in its overseas territories. In 1956, Dias traveled alone to Guinea, Angola and Mozambique, surveying ethnic minorities including Indians, Chinese, and even Europeans (such as Boers) in each of these territories. Despite the defining agenda of the MEMEUP, Dias concentrated most of his time in subsequent years on the Makonde. Guerreiro—the MEMEUP "first assistant" and, later, "adjunct"—spent substantial time in Angola working among the Bochimanes and the Cabindas, and also among Boers. At the same time Margot Dias—"auxiliary" and, later, "first assistant" in MEMEUP—worked alone among the Chopi and Shangaan of southern Mozambique, and among the Maganja da Costa of central Mozambique. However, they too spent much of their time among the Makonde. Guerreiro accompanied Jorge Dias to Mueda in 1957 and worked alone among the Makonde in 1959. Margot Dias worked in Mueda with Jorge Dias in 1957 and 1958 and accompanied him during work done among the Makonde on the Tanganyikan side of the border in 1959.[5] By 1958 the MEMEUP team was in the midst of a full-blown ethnographic research project among the Makonde, as Jorge Dias recognized in his

5. Manuel Viegas Guerreiro published his own works based upon his research with the Makonde and elsewhere during this time, (1958, 1960, 1962, 1963, 1974), as did Margot Dias (1960, 1962a, 1962b, 1965, 1973, 1986).

report that year.[6] In reference to the work he intended to publish, he wrote, "this monograph will come to have 500 or 600 pages and must be the most complete work realized to date by the Portuguese in relation to an overseas population" (DG 1959:4).

In focusing so much attention on the Makonde, the historian of Portuguese anthropology Rui Pereira suggests, Jorge Dias "inverted a hierarchy of interests previously determined by those who sponsored his research in the north of Mozambique . . . raising eminently ethnological objectives to the top of the agenda" (Pereira 1986b:222; see also Margarido 1975, Gallo 1988:83).[7] At the same time, the interests of the MEMEUP's sponsoring institutions continued to be served by the team's "confidential reports." According to Moreira, the reports were no more than an exercise in internal institutional accounting necessary to justify the funds being spent by the CEPS on MEMEUP research activities (personal communication, 4/3/96). Others have taken a different view, suggesting that these reports were more integral to Overseas Ministry intelligence gathering initiatives (Gallo 1988:35). Dias himself repeatedly indicated in a summary report of MEMEUP activities in reference to individual years that one of his primary objectives was to analyze "politico-social problems in the north of Mozambique as they could be seen from the Makonde plateau," and that "given that the nature of [this information] prevents its publication, the Mission gives detailed description in a confidential report" (Dias 1961c:1). Such comments may reflect Dias's perceived need to pitch his work to sponsoring institutions (see Gallo 1988, Margarido 1975, and Pereira, 1987; 1998:xiv–xx), much like anthropologists working within other contexts, ranging from the British Empire (Kuper 1983) to the contemporary development industry (Ferguson 1990), regardless of his actual commitment to fulfilling this mandate. Before conclusions can be drawn, however, evaluation must move beyond "confessions" and justifications to an analysis of what the Dias team actually furnished the Salazar regime.

In the first report, written by Jorge Dias after his 1956 whirlwind tour of Portuguese African colonies, he warned of the growing importance of Indian traders, and specifically of the potentially deleterious effects of the spread of Islam in northern Mozambique: "These Indians . . . are nearly always propagating agents of the Mohamedian religion with political elements in the mix" (Dias 1957:5). Linking the Indian population and the Islamic faith to anti-colonial

6. Although the cover of each of these reports bears the names of all team members participating in field research in that year, Jorge Dias wrote them, as various first-person constructions make clear.

7. The first volume of the ethnography Dias succeeded in producing on the Makonde (Dias 1964) also earned him a doctorate from the University of Lisbon in 1965 (Oliveira 1968:22; Lupi 1984:42). These credentials were of great importance to Dias, as the doctorate he had earned in Munich was not fully recognized in Portugal (Lupi 1984:385).

nationalism on a regional scale, he further suggested that "Indian-Muslim missionary activity . . . indisputably constitutes a danger to national security" (8). The confidential report Dias and Guerreiro submitted the following year continued to comment on the Muslim threat, now carried by Swahili-speakers: "Swahili is the idiom of a group that is strongly Islamisized and in full expansion. Its system of teaching disseminates religious principles that involve political ideas dangerous to our sovereignty" (DG 1958:25). Speaking about "numerous clandestine schools spread along the coast," Dias and Guerreiro warned, "each padre (*mualimo*) is a teacher, and today's student will be tomorrow's teacher" (26).

The 1957 research campaign saw both Diases and Guerreiro spend most of their time in Mueda, and consequently nearly half the report on that year's activities was dedicated to the Makonde. So too were the reports on the 1958 research campaign—during which the Diases again worked primarily in Mueda, and on the 1959 campaign—during which they worked on the other side of the Rovuma and Guerreiro worked in Mueda. Whether or not the Overseas Ministry had encouraged Dias to concentrate on the Makonde, its personnel must have found the MEMEUP reports on them of interest. In their report on the 1960 research campaign, the team noted that "the people responsible for the Government of Mozambique showed interest in the information furnished in our reports, and look positively upon the continuation and intensification of our work in northern Mozambique" (DGD 1961:2). In the report on the 1958 campaign, Jorge Dias and Guerreiro wrote that the ex-Minister of the Overseas Ministry, Raul Ventura, requested that Dias travel across the borders of northern Mozambique into Rhodesia and Nyassaland to gather "information relative to the political and social situation," but explained that he was unable to accomplish this due to the difficulty he experienced in crossing borders (DG 1959:20). The following year, however, he traveled into Tanganyika with the same agenda (DGD 1960).

Passages from the reports speak for themselves:

> The diffusion of ideas coming from Tanganyika is gaining ground and many are those who return [from Tanganyika to Mozambique] infected and who will infect those who remain here. Today, there are many who say that there is a black, John [i.e., Julius] Nyerere, who has studied greatly and is head of the Government of Tanganyika, and who requires Portuguese natives who wish to work there to pay him a tax of ten *escudos*.[8] It can be seen that they are pleased to see a black rule, levy taxes, and edit pamphlets in Swahili, which give him a large profit and permit him to drive around in a car and live like a white. As the more active natives have spent time on the other side of our borders, and the more conservative and loyal to tradition have remained in our territory, such a rapid spread of subversive

---

8. This most likely refers to the union dues collected by Nyerere's TANU.

ideas is not seen among our natives as in Tanganyika. For this reason we must take care to avoid the return of dangerous elements. (DG 1958:57)

The fact that Swahili is the language of communication between various populations creates the great danger of opening a door to propaganda from Tanganyika and to association of the populations of the north of Mozambique with the Swahili bloc that extends into a vast area north of the Rovuma, separating them from the populations of the center and south of the Province. On the plateau radios are rare, but on the coast they are multiplying and propaganda from Cairo and Russia is being felt there. . . . For certain, the few [radios] that there are serve to disseminate news that is dangerous to our sovereignty. (DG 1959:12)

The Dias team's most substantial piece of intelligence gathering, however, related to the emergent TMMU. In the report on the 1959 MEMEUP campaign, they wrote with apparent concern of the activities of the organization whose members' requests of the Mueda administrator a year later would spark the Mueda Massacre. After explaining that Jorge Dias's inquiries among Catholic padres in Tanganyika revealed that the Union was not initially formed for political reasons, but rather to expand the community of Catholic Makonde in Tanganyika (whether of Mozambican or Tanganyikan origin), the team went on to share their doubts about its future:

It is clear that this association, even in its initial form and with better objectives, constitutes a danger to Portuguese sovereignty, as it intends to reinforce the links of solidarity and social cohabitation between two groups up to now differentiated and independent, intending to ignore the existence of a political boundary which separates them. At any rate, the true danger is not in the intentions of those who inspired the association, but in the purposes of those who take advantage of this magnificent instrument of political propaganda that, tomorrow, could be a powerful weapon in the hands of the so-called African nationalists. Even more so with the way politics are unfolding in Tanganyika, one must fear the victory of the more numerous Islamic elements, as we will see. If this happens, instead of Portuguese Makonde being an element of conversion among Tanganyikan Makonde through the Union, we will see precisely the opposite, and it will be Tanganyikan Makonde who exercise religious and political influence on ours. Some political leaders know perfectly well that on the day Tanganyika gains independence, "The Tanganyika-Mozambique Makonde Union" will be a wedge in place in Portuguese territory and a powerful motive of demands and conflicts with Portugal. (DGD 1960:6)

As an appendix to this report, the Dias team reproduced the constitution of the TMMU (53).

Critics refer to such passages to substantiate the argument that Dias and his colleagues betrayed the trust of their ethnographic informants and collaborated with Portuguese colonialism (for example, Moutinho 1982; Barradas 1997). Nonetheless, any fair assessment of the confidential MEMEUP reports must

conclude that the Dias team's intelligence gathering was uninspired and medi-
ocre at best. Moreover the team spent more ink in their reports castigating Portuguese colonials than informing on the Makonde. Time and again, they criticized Portuguese colonial policy and the effect it had on plateau Makonde. In
the report on the 1957 campaign, they drew attention to the fact that prices offered to agricultural producers were significantly higher in Tanganyika than in
Mozambique, and that salaries there were also much higher (DG 1958:56; also
DGD 1960:22). Employment opportunities for educated Africans were almost
nonexistent in Mozambique, they noted, resulting in a very small number of
"natives" who wished to acquire "assimilated" status and to become loyal citizens of Portugal (DG 1958:61; also DGD 1960:22). The trip the Diases took to
Tanganyika in 1959 led the team to make several unfavorable comparisons between Portuguese and British colonialism:

> We must think about the fact that the native observes a greater economic devel-
> opment on the other side of the Rovuma. Newala, which by its geographic posi-
> tion can be compared to Mueda, is an incomparably more active commercial cen-
> ter with dozens of stores and a lot of life. . . . Between Mueda and Newala there
> exists a chronological abyss that will be very difficult for us to cross, and which I
> remain unsure we have the will to cross. (DGD 1960:24, 26)

What is more, they pointed out, the British and their colonial administration
were held in greater respect than their Portuguese counterparts (8, 21).

For the Portuguese colonials, the Dias team also had sharp words. Whether
government functionaries, managers of private colonial enterprises, or settlers,
they were, according to the team, disgraceful representatives of the *pátria*. In
the academic record, Jorge Dias had subscribed to the ideology of Lusotropicalism—defined by the notion that the Portuguese, by nature, geographical
proximity, and historical experience had a greater affinity and empathy for colonial peoples than other European colonial powers (Freyre 1958)—and had
written that the Portuguese, unlike white South Africans, not only permitted
miscegenation in their colonies but also treated their *mestiço* children as off-
spring with an undiminished birthright (see Dias 1960:25; Dias 1965:64). Now,
he and his colleagues admitted in this confidential forum that Portuguese
abroad were less than the myth of Lusotropicalism assumed. Dias blamed colonials' defects on lower-class origins and "lack of culture":

> [U]nfortunately, many Portuguese in Mozambique, above all individuals without
> culture or of middle culture, because they drink whiskey, drive cars, know how to
> say a few things in English and have obtained a touch of culture which translates
> into having obtained a few prints of foreign paintings, or furniture and trinkets
> to which they were not accustomed, feel an inferiority complex in relation to
> their neighbors in the Union [of South Africa]. For many of these individuals,
> who come from any old place in our province, Johannesburg takes on proportions
> like Mecca for the Mohamedians. . . . Some of them, who in our land had the

lowest social *status*, avidly seize the opportunity to rise and they judge that in order to do so it is necessary to put down the negro, brutalizing him at times,
whether morally or physically. (Dias 1957:8–9, 10).

Dias concluded that "the Portuguese is turning much more racist than he was"
(15). Not surprisingly, Dias and his colleagues suggested, most Makonde felt
less than admiration for the Portuguese: "Contrary to what is generally
thought, and to what I also thought by the way, the blacks, today, in this region,
fear us, many detest us, and when they compare us with other whites it is always
in a manner unfavorable to us" (DG 1958:59). What is more, they asserted,
"the native is convinced that we bring him nothing of value" (72).

The Dias team's descriptive first-hand accounts of Portuguese colonials might
have provided Moreira with evidence supporting his argument that Portuguese
colonialism was in need of reform. Dias and his colleagues, however, shielded
themselves from accountability for their bolder assertions, tempering their
positions with self-effacing qualifications like "although we are not *politicos*
[politicians], and we are reluctant to make forays into domains alien to our professional interests, we are obliged to do so given the intimate relations between
the political and social" (DGD 1960:7). This considerably softened their critique at times. For example, on one occasion, Jorge Dias wrote of the practice
of flogging: "As an ethnologist, I don't know if these methods are indispensable
or not to dominate these populations. But from what certain administrative
authorities with great experience tell me, respect and discipline are easily
achieved without constant corporal punishment" (DG 1958:63).

Generally, the team remained timid and refused to follow observations
through to logical conclusions. They attributed the economic chaos witnessed
among Makonde to their exposure to the cash economy, but not to the brutal
colonial labor regime designed to extract wealth from the colonies to stimulate
the ossified metropolitan economy (DG 1958:8; cf. Dias 1970:265). Jorge Dias
alluded to "cultural conflict" on occasion, but preferred to talk about the conflict between the genders that he suggested lay at the foundations of Makonde
society (Dias 1961a:111) rather than about conflict between Portuguese and
Africans. Dias's muted "critique" of the abuses of Portuguese colonialism is
neatly summed up in the following statement: "It doesn't fall upon me, a simple
ethnologist, to say how [these problems] can be resolved, but I must not conceal heightened discontent, and that [this discontent] is not only a consequence of ideologies spread through subversive propaganda" (DG 1959:16).

Ultimately, the team left the Portuguese colonial mandate unchallenged.
None of the solutions they proposed questioned the right of colonial government or the European civilizing mission. For example, they wrote of the need
for more profound contact between Mozambican natives and various categories
of Portuguese colonials (DG 1958:84–85; DG 1959:11). To make this possible,
they suggested, the social environment in northern Mozambique would have to

be improved. To this end, they proposed development of a safari hunting and tourism industry in northern Mozambique that would draw other Europeans with whom resident Portuguese could fraternize (DG 1958:79; DG 1959:17). Portuguese colonials—many of them of peasant origins themselves—would have to be better educated regarding appropriate behavior in the colonial context, they also advised (DG 1958:74; DGD 1960:30); this would entail teaching them how to show greater respect for educated "natives," and even for elders held in esteem by virtue of their positions of authority within local kin-based social institutions (DGD 1960:31–32). Although not practicing Catholics, they advocated continuing conversion of the "natives" to Catholicism (DG 1958:83). Finally, they called for more effective propaganda to demonstrate to "native" Mozambicans the benefits they derived from the presence of the Portuguese (DG 1958:73; DG 1959:12). Clearly, the professed faith of the team in the colonial mission remained uncompromised. Jorge Dias put it this way:

> My attitude in relating so many negative facts and in making so many unsettling observations might appear rather pessimistic. Nevertheless, if I dare do this, it is precisely because I am animated by a grand ideal and enormous belief in our capacity as colonizers. If one such as I, who has dedicated the best years of my life to the study of the Portuguese people, criticizes some aspects of its performance in the north of Mozambique, it is not because I don't believe in its virtues, or in its potential, but because I believe that it is possible to remedy much of that which is wrong. (DG 1958:85)

"Cavorting with Rural Folk": Jorge Dias, with History

The stark contrast between *Os Macondes de Moçambique* and the MEMEUP confidential reports is disturbing, to say the least. In their published works, the Dias team romanticizes Makonde "tradition," and where they see them, bemoans the forces of change that threaten its integrity. In their unpublished communiqués, on the other hand, they provide justification for the very regime that was bringing devastating change to those among whom they studied, suggesting that observed problems could be corrected within the framework of colonial rule. One might be tempted to interpret such contradictions as evidence of intellectual pliancy or, even, duplicity. To do so, however, would be to oversimplify Jorge Dias and his colleagues, taking them out of historical context. To come to terms with the Dias team as anthropological precursors and significant others, I have turned to an examination of *their* life histories, with a particular focus on that of Jorge Dias. Only through understanding the intellectual, institutional and political environment in which he came of age, and came to define ethnology in Portugal, I suggest, can one gain a full appreciation of the meaning of the contradictions presented by his team's work on the Makonde, and ultimately learn from them.

António Jorge Dias was born to a bourgeois family in northern Portugal in 1907. He spent his youth between a family house in the city of Porto and a country estate in Guimarães (Oliveira 1968:16; Oliveira 1974:11; Lupi 1984:379). In his teen years, he enjoyed success in track and field, traveling the northern region of Portugal winning competitions and local notoriety. So fond was he of life in the rural areas he visited that he took to passing time there whenever he could. His longtime colleague, Ernesto Veiga de Oliveira, describes it:

> He would often join workers on their pilgrimages and visit fairs with them, strumming on a guitar, dancing and playing at quarterstaff. . . . [In the village of Gralheira, which he would often frequent,] he fraternized with peasants and shepherds. . . . [H]e hunted and tramped the mountain ranges . . . giving full range to his love of hiking; and all this contributed to mold his philosophy of life and his sense of values. . . . [He and his traveling companions] would visit village after village, tramping with knapsack from one to the other, spending the night in haylofts and country cottages, eating where and how they might, and harried by authorities who, failing to understand what was then virtually unknown in this country, looked upon them with suspicion as tramps and vagabonds. In this way did he gain a profound and real knowledge of the life and culture of the country-folk of Portugal to which he was later to give an ethnological dimension. (1974:11–12)

When António (as he was called by his family and friends) reached the age of twenty, his father tired of his lack of both discipline and interest in pursuing further studies and put him to work as a traveling salesman in one of his commercial firms. Within two years, António made the decision to return to school. After finishing the *liceu* in 1932, he continued studies at Coimbra University in German philology, traveling to Germany during holidays in 1935. Upon completing his *licenciatura* at Coimbra in 1937, António took the opportunity in 1938 to lecture in Portuguese at the University of Rostock, in Germany. A year later, he accepted an offer to set up a Portuguese course at the University of Munich. While in Munich, he met Margot Schmidt, who was then studying piano at the Munich Music Academy (Lupi 1984:411). In November 1941, they were married.

Margot Schmidt, born in 1908, had spent her adolescence in Nuremberg, the child of a middle-class German family.[9] Her father worked as a *braumeister* in a beer factory. Her mother came from a family of artisans, but worked only a short time as a salesgirl in a jewelry shop before marrying. Margot took an interest in piano as a girl, learning at first from her older sister. At the age of eighteen, she moved alone to Munich to continue her studies in music. She earned money to

---

9. Biographical information on Margot Schmidt Dias draws upon a letter written to me by her daughter, Karin (11/30/98).

support herself by offering piano lessons. While in Munich, she cultivated her interests in the arts and became an avid reader of the illustrated geographical review, *Atlantis,* for its articles on artisanship in places around the world.

When she met Dias, Margot told me, he was unaware that one could make a profession of "cavorting with rural folk" as he had loved to do in his youth. António was then continuing his studies in German philology while teaching Portuguese, but once Margot introduced him to *Atlantis,* he discovered the academic discipline of ethnology (Oliveira 1974:12). When offered the opportunity to lecture in Portuguese at the University of Berlin in 1942, António accepted with enthusiasm because of the more reputable ethnology program there. He attended lectures by Richard Thurnwald and continued work begun at Munich in 1940 on a doctoral thesis on the Portuguese village of Vilarinho da Furna (Oliveira 1968:12; Lupi 1984:48). Notwithstanding his move to Berlin, Dias submitted his doctoral thesis at Munich in 1944. In the same year, he returned to Portugal with Margot.

When I visited Margot Dias in 1996, she was vibrant despite her 87 years. Within the closed confines of Portuguese academic life, Margot had been treated throughout her career more as an anthropologist's spouse than as an anthropologist in her own right. She seemed pleased that I sought her out to speak with me as a colleague about a place so dear to both of us. Our shared professional orientation seemed often to transcend the forty years that separated our experiences in Mueda. Still, having been warned, as she told me, about my intent to "politicize" her and her husband's work, she remained guarded, even suspicious. She once opened a drawer and pointed to notebooks that she explained were field diaries kept by her and her husband, but she told me that she did not want to share them with anyone. When the name Manuel Viegas Guerreiro came up, she told me she had nothing to say about him. I learned around the same time that he had nothing to say to me—nor to anyone else, for that matter—about the Diases or about the Makonde of Mozambique.[10] Whenever I asked Margot to comment on the institutional and intellectual environment in which they worked, she cut off further questions by asserting that the work she and the Dias team had done was in no way "political," that they had not been interested in "politics" or "political issues"—that they had been "simple scientists."

10. I can only speculate about the causes of this tension between the Diases and Guerreiro, who passed away on May 1, 1997. Unlike Jorge Dias, Guerreiro was of rural origins (Fonseca & Ferreira 1997:12). He was, perhaps, closer akin to the rural class Portuguese colonials of whom Dias wrote so critically. People I spoke with in Mueda often told me that he was more gruff and authoritative in his demeanor with them. Nonetheless, Guerreiro appears to have accepted the Overseas Ministry mandate to provide confidential information on contemporary issues with deeper ambivalence than did Jorge Dias (Gallo 1988:70). In the late colonial period, he sought to leave Portugal, and he was pleased by the revolution that toppled Marcelo Caetano (heir to the Salazar regime) in 1974 and ultimately brought independence to Portugal's African colonies (Fonseca & Ferreira 1997:13).

Margot Dias and the author, discussing pronunciation of the name of a village on the map before them, in her home in Oeiras. (Courtesy Henry G. West.)

Manuel Viegas Guerreiro with his interpreter, José Cosme. (Courtesy Arquivo do Museu Nacional de Etnologia [Lisboa].)

Ultimately, it proved impossible to have her comment directly on the contradiction between the published and unpublished works of the Dias team.

Margot Dias's evasive responses reminded me of the "anti-anthropology" Rafael Mwakala had once deployed against her. Two years later, when I had the chance to visit her once more, I first sent a letter telling her when I planned to come and outlining my questions. I wrote her that I was particularly interested in the lessons her husband had learned as a student of folklore and ethnology in Germany during the Nazi period, and about the pressures placed upon scholars in Salazar's Portugal to support the state agenda—whether national consolidation or colonial rule. Days before my flight to Lisbon, I received an e-mail from Margot's daughter informing me that she had fallen and been hospitalized. She would not again be able to meet with me.[11] And so, I am left once more piecing together shards of a broken pot, trying to make sense of my ethnographic precursors qua ethnographic subjects.

We can at least imagine what Jorge Dias witnessed during his time in Germany—a period that coincided almost exactly with the Second World War[12]—

11. Margot Dias was uncommunicative after her fall, I was told; she passed away November 26, 2001.

12. Political ties between Germany and Portugal were complex in the inter-War period and during World War II; despite Portugal's alliance with England, it maintained strong links with Germany. Dias's experience of travel to and from Germany during World War II was by no means unusual for a Portuguese intellectual.

if we draw upon the recent literature constituting an emerging field of study of the history of German anthropology. Hitler's attempts to ground the Nazi regime in a mythic nation drew substantially upon the longstanding German philosophical tradition of romantic nationalism, including in particular Herder's idea that a nation polluted by external influences could rediscover its defining "national character" through the collection and celebration of its folklore (Wilson 1973). Although Herder's romantic nationalism was tempered by the assertion that each nation possessed a "national character" worth celebrating and folklore worth preserving, Nazi ideology fostered intolerance for the Aryan nation's inferior others (Bausinger 1994), and attempted to mask internal class divisions by making a scapegoat of cultural others, such as Jews, as "enemies within" the nation (Jell-Bahlsen 1985; Hauschild 1997). The prior division in German anthropological studies between *Volkskunde* (generally translated as "folklore," but implying the study of one's own people) and *Völkerkunde* (generally translated as "ethnology," but implying the comparative study of other peoples) rendered each of these fields vulnerable to the Nazi agenda (Jell-Bahlsen 1985; Jeggle 1988). *Volkskunde,* in particular, became what Helge Gerndt has called a "booming business" (1994:2).

Preliminary studies indicate that scholars of both *Volkskunde* and *Völkerkunde* adopted a variety of strategies regarding the Nazi regime. Many lost their academic posts and/or were forced into exile (Jell-Bahlsen 1985:319; Jeggle 1988:114). Others sought to accommodate the regime, either embracing Nazi politics or remaining politically aloof, or even avowedly "apolitical" (Jeggle 1988:114). According to Hans Fischer's account, many German academics considered themselves "above politics" (see Wolf 1992:474), although Fischer suggests that this "position" itself constituted a form of *political resistance* (Fischer 1990). No matter their predisposition, German scholars of both *Volkskunde* and *Völkerkunde* were drawn into complex relationships with the Nazi regime. Among them were Richard Thurnwald (whom Dias greatly admired) and Thurnwald's protégé, Wilhelm Emil Mühlmann. Functionalists in their general theoretical orientation, Thurnwald and Mühlmann are described in some contemporary accounts as "Nazi anthropologists" (for example, Jell-Bahlsen 1985). Thurnwald is criticized in particular for published works that constituted a blueprint for German colonial administration of "native" peoples (Fischer 1990; Thomas Hauschild, personal communication, 6/21/99)—works that were inspirational to a generation of South African *Volkekundiges* who studied in Germany and later made substantial contributions to the architecture of apartheid (Fischer 1990; Conte & Essner 1994:156; Hauschild 1995; Sharp 1981; Gordon 1988; Hammond-Tooke 1997). Other accounts suggest that Thurnwald and Mühlmann's work was largely irrelevant to, and ignored by, the Nazi regime (Jeggle 1988). It is clear, in any case, that Nazi ideology provided a language through which career opportunism and petty personal rivalries among scholars were expressed in this period. If debates between functionalists and diffusionists were of minimal interest to the regime, the protagonists did not hesitate to use the power of the regime to their ends, accusing one another of drawing on theoretical traditions defined by Jewish scholars, or of hiring them or publishing their work (Jell-Bahlsen 1985; Hauschild 1987; Fischer 1990).

As Jorge Dias studied first German language and folklore, and later ethnology, he witnessed at close range the high-stakes institutional and intellectual politicking produced by the Nazi regime in these fields. Perhaps he gravitated away from *Volkskunde* and toward *Völkerkunde* in part because the latter was less politicized than the former. We cannot know for certain. In any case, when they arrived in Portugal in 1944, the Diases witnessed affinities between Germany and Portugal that had particular salience for them given Jorge's new profession. Salazar's bureaucratic authoritarian regime survived a war in which it had not participated as a combatant. In spite of its bland and internationally inoffensive ideology,[13] the "New State," as it was called, sought to root itself like the Third Reich and other authoritarian regimes in a mythic nation. As in 1930s and 1940s Germany, folklore and ethnology were used by the regime to construct its myth of nation and to legitimate its rule (Branco 1986:93; Pais de Brito 1982). The historian of Portuguese anthropology, João Leal, argues that despite the absence of a "classical national problem" in Portugal in the first half of the twentieth century, and despite its relatively substantial colonial possessions, Portugal produced (in George Stocking's terms) an "anthropology of nation-building" rather than an "anthropology of empire-building" (Leal 1999b; 1999c; Stocking 1982). As a consequence, the anthropological sciences in Portugal were focused almost exclusively upon domestic communities.

This state of affairs is reflected in the early development of Dias's career upon his return from Germany. In 1947, as mentioned above, Dias was recruited to head up the ethnography section at the newly created CEEP at the University of Porto. The only Ph.D. in ethnology in the country, Dias focused his energies for the next decade on organizing the systematic study of Portuguese folk culture, giving definition, in romantic nationalist fashion, to the Portuguese "national character" (Oliveira 1968:12; Leal 1999b:5). His most salient expression of the romantic nationalist project was published in 1953 under the title "Os Elementos Fundamentais da Cultura Portuguesa" (1953).

In relation to the work of his contemporaries in America and elsewhere in Europe, Dias's work among rural Portuguese communities in the late 1940s

13. The historian of fascism, Stanley Payne, argues that the Salazar regime cannot accurately be labeled fascist, owing to the absence of genuine mass politics due to a variety of social factors, including the essentially agrarian nature of Portuguese society, the weakness of the worker left as a "threat," and the strength of the Catholic Church, as well as historical factors including the nation's "satisfied" and defensive imperial policy, and the fact that Portugal had not recently experienced traumatic loss at war (Payne 1995:317).

and early 1950s appears "theoretically anachronistic" (to borrow the term that the historian of Portuguese anthropology João Pina Cabral uses to describe Portuguese anthropologists in the Salazar period in general [1991:27]). One must appreciate, however, that Dias worked within an institutional and intellectual environment that was shaped by the "nation-building" enterprise of the "New State." At the same time, it was Dias and the work of his research team in Africa that initiated a gradual, if partial, shift in Portuguese anthropology away from "nation-building" and toward "empire-building." Ironically, Dias and his colleagues did so at an historical moment when other European nations were closing the book on empire building as a state mandate and as an anthropological project. Thus, it can be argued that Dias "lagged behind" his contemporaries who worked in places like the Rhodes-Livingstone Institute only if it is also argued that Portuguese Imperialism—the framing context for Dias's work—"lagged behind" as well (merely by persisting long into an era defined by decolonization).

In any case, Dias's work, both in Portugal and Africa, bore the marks of the discursive field in which it was embedded. In his work on rural Portuguese societies, Dias and his colleagues elaborated a "community studies" methodology (Branco 1986:89). In seeking to identify the defining characteristics of such communities, and in the larger project, of Portuguese society, they focused their research on such things as material culture and the techniques of its production, as well as, of course, folklore. They did not ignore history; Dias, who was instrumental in introducing Boas' ideas into Portuguese anthropology (Branco 1986:81; Leal 1999a:14–15), sought out and celebrated the deep historical roots of Portuguese society. However, they considered contemporary historical processes as polluting influences that produced methodological obstacles and threatened the integrity of their research subjects. Ultimately, Dias (1948; 1952) echoed his predecessor, Leite de Vasconcellos, romanticizing Portuguese customs—celebrating northern Portuguese communities, in particular, as loci of an egalitarian ethic—and expressing disdain for the corrupting forces of modernity (Branco 1986:85, 92; Leal 1999a:12–13). As can be seen from the descriptions above of *Os Macondes de Moçambique*, Dias carried with him from rural Portugal to rural Africa essential components of the methodological approach he would there employ; he presented the Makonde in much the same generic fashion as he had earlier presented the peasantry of northern Portugal. In both cases, Dias was paternalistic and overly romantic toward his subject. Among his proudest professional accomplishments was the founding in 1965 of the Portuguese *Museu de Etnologia*—a place where the societies he and his colleagues studied could be forever preserved. He even dreamed, at one point, of creating an open-air living museum of Portuguese rural life, although the project was never realized (Pereira 1996:76).

Even so, aspects of Dias's career project were quite radical. In coming to the CEEP, Dias substantially redefined anthropological studies in Portugal. Where interest had been focused on the physical and biological subfields of the discipline (Pereira 1998:vii), Dias's classic works on rural Portuguese communities (1948, 1952) brought rigorous ethnography to ethnological studies in Portugal in the post–World War II era (Pereira 1998:xxvii). Where skulls had been measured and cultural hierarchies charted, and where mythmaking had gone unchallenged, Dias asserted that the ethnological study of human culture was a "science" that lay beyond the grasp of politics; he celebrated the diversity of human culture and the integrity of its varied traditions. Another of Dias's proudest professional achievements was his success in 1955 in passing a motion at the International Congress of Regional Ethnography in Arnhem which called for Volkskunde to be considered a subfield of the broader discipline of Völkerkunde in which all societies, whether "civilized" or "primitive," would be studied on equal terms (Oliveira 1968:49; Dias 1961b:1–22, 23–38). With this motion, Dias echoed arguments made by the German Jewish anthropologist, Fritz Krause, before he was forced to flee Nazi Germany (Fischer 1990; Conte & Essner 1994:151).

While Dias looked upon Makonde society with the same romanticism and paternalism as he had Portuguese society, his treating Africans just like Portuguese constituted a dramatic shift in the typical perspective. In the same spirit, in Dias's Museu de Etnologia, artifacts of Portuguese society and artifacts of the societies of Portugal's colonial subjects were eventually exhibited side by side (Pereira 1996:78). Just as Dias argued against the scientific separation of human societies, he never supported the idea of administrative separation or isolation of peoples as did his German mentor Thurnwald and the South African Volkekundiges (Sharp 1981; Gordon 1988; Hammond-Tooke 1997).

It was, according to Rui Pereira at least, precisely because of Dias's "apolitical" reputation that he was selected to head up the MEMEUP research project in Africa:

> The Overseas Ministry intended, by way of its investigative organs, to know the opinion of someone who was not compromised with the colonial situation and who could gain a relatively impartial and scientific appreciation of the Portuguese colonial administration, comparing it with the British colonial administration on the other side of the Rovuma and with the politico-social problems that were being raised there by the increasing popularity of Julius Nyerere's [TANU] nationalist movement. (Pereira 1986b:220–21)

According to Pereira, "in naming Jorge Dias as head of the MEMEUP . . . the Overseas Ministry knew that it could count on a relatively impartial opinion from one who placed his ethic as a social scientist above ideological and political compromises" (Pereira 1986a:114). Time and again, those I interviewed in Lisbon—including Margot Dias, Benjamim Pereira (a colleague from the CEEP) and especially ex–Overseas Minister Adriano Moreira—asserted with almost disturbing conviction that Dias's work was "not politically oriented," and that Dias himself was a man "without interest in politics." Moreira, who was once keenly interested in making political hay of Dias's work, offered this powerful image: "Where most men carry their politics on their back like a camel's hump, Jorge Dias bore an indentation" (personal communication, 4/3/96).

Certainly, Jorge Dias was not the "apolitical man" he and his colleagues made him out to be, for no one working in such a charged political environment could survive without their own brand of "politics." At the same time, Moreira's statement is revealing of the nature of Dias's politics. Within the Byzantine political climate of the "New State," political positions that defined themselves as such drew attention. Those who espoused them either rose closer to power or suffered beneath its weight. A more tenable strategy, for most, was to carve out space around themselves to accommodate those "positions" they found either essential or inescapable, and when possible, redefining the spaces they occupied as "outside of politics." This Dias did when he celebrated the scientific foundations of ethnology.[14]

In sculpting one's environment, however, one also sculpted oneself. The indentation Moreira saw on Dias's back might be understood in this way, and its depth might be attributed to the unusually complicated circumstances in which Dias spent time sculpting his (a)political being. His experience began, of course, in the midst of Nazi Germany as he studied the deeply politicized subjects of folklore and ethnology. It is telling that Dias's biographers do not mention the war, or the impact it had on a man who made his life studying humanity. Lupi mentions only that the Diases left Munich on the last plane before allied bombers attacked the city, and that most of his books and notebooks burned at the airport (1984:381). Nowhere in the written record does Dias himself speak of the holocaust, or even of the war that he witnessed from its epicenter. The same is true of Margot Dias. What is more, in my interviews with her she quickly changed the subject whenever I approached the war years. Their daughter, Karin, told me in a letter that her mother "was always against Nazi politics but she was never actively against." Jorge, Karin told me, sometimes talked with his children about the war years. Margot, Karin remembered, "never liked very much to speak about those years," although Karin remembers when she and her mother traveled to America that they visited Jewish friends of her mother who had escaped Nazi Germany.

In any case, Jorge and Margot Dias must have been well practiced in "avoiding politics" when they arrived in Portugal, and undoubtedly they found their

14. Hans Fischer (1990:203) makes a similar argument for some of the ethnologists working in Germany during the Nazi period. It should be noted, however, that not all those anthropologists working in Portugal during the Salazar regime took this path. Leal (1999c) directs us to the work of Pais de Brito (1995) on Ernesto de Sousa and of Branco & Oliveira (1993) on Michel Giacometti as examples of alternate and oppositional anthropologies.

skills useful in a somewhat similar environment, even if the written record is as devoid of commentary on this issue as it is on the Diases' experiences of Nazi Germany. For the Diases, war did not end with the fall of Berlin. Like all subjects of Portugal, they continued to struggle with the dilemma of self-distorting compliance with authoritarian power or self-destructive resistance to it even past the day when the Salazar regime, weakened by wars waged against it by African nationalists like Rafael Mwakala, fell in 1974.

How do the complex life experiences of Jorge and Margot Dias illuminate the contradictions in their work on the Makonde of Mozambique? Taking the Diases as ethnographic subjects in their own right requires that we understand not only their academic productions and the impact of these on Makonde society, but also the power of the Salazar regime and the manner in which it flowed through the Dias research team, making them both *subjects* and *instruments* of the state. As Gramsci explains, the state exercises hegemony not only through coercive force but also, more importantly, through civil society, that is, through institutions staffed by "intellectuals." The loyalty of intellectuals to the state is by no means secure, for they remain on the margins of the dominant group on whose behalf the state rules (Gramsci 1971:3–23). Consequently, the state must focus disproportionate energy on policing them in order to insure that most of them serve it as deputies—loyal *subjects* through whom the power of the state flows and proliferates. As Salazar's New State reproduced its power, then, it placed enormous pressure on people like Jorge Dias and his colleagues, forcing them to contract their political vision. In George Orwell's novel *1984*, "intellectuals," much like Dias and his colleagues, are portrayed as living under the constant surveillance of "Thought Police." They must, therefore, practice a technique Orwell called "Crimestop," defined as "the faculty of stopping short, as though by instinct, at the threshold of any dangerous thought." Orwell says of this intellectual self-policing: "It includes the power of not grasping ideologies, of failing to perceive logical errors, of misunderstanding the simplest arguments . . . and of being bored or repelled by any train of thought which is capable of leading in a heretical direction" (Orwell 1949:174–75). Tellingly, Orwell summarizes the effects of Crimestop by stating that "orthodoxy in the full sense demands a control over one's own mental processes as complete as that of a *contortionist* over his body" (my emphasis). It is not unreasonable to imagine that "contortion" over an extended period of time might lead to "distortions" such as the inverted camel's hump Moreira saw on Jorge Dias's back.

We cannot know for certain what Dias and his colleagues thought about the New State and its policies in Mozambique; we can, however, assess the written record they produced. There, we might suggest, "logical errors" appear at the threshold of "dangerous thoughts." The images Dias and his colleagues produced of the Makonde in their ethnographic work celebrated the Makonde's humanity, but at the same time, rendered them defenseless before the forces of the modern world, justifying the protective oversight of colonial rule. This same rule, they failed to recognize, facilitated the catastrophic destruction of the Makonde "traditions" they celebrated. In producing images useful to the perpetuation of colonial domination, the Dias team not only extended the power of the Salazar regime over the Makonde as colonial subjects, but also deepened the regime's power over themselves as intellectual subjects.

Stepping Outside Jorge Dias's Footprints? Harry G. West and the Makonde with History

In the foreword to a volume on folklore in the Third Reich, Dan Ben-Amos quotes from "The Chapter of Our Fathers," a mishnaic tractate from the second century: "Judge not thy fellow-man until thou hast reached his place" (1994:ix). Perhaps now that I have conducted ethnographic field research among the Makonde, I have in some small measure reached a place once occupied by Dias and his colleagues. Not only am I now able to judge my ethnographic prede- cessors, I feel a certain obligation to do so given the friendship that I have with many of those about whom the Dias team wrote and upon whose lives they ex- ercised enormous—perhaps detrimental—power. I feel a certain obligation to tell the tale of others now significant to me, including Mwakala, whose stories give testimony of the "errors" of the Dias team. At the same time, I remain cau- tious, for in having shared conversation and food with Margot Dias, having talked with her about her husband, having corresponded with their daughter, Karin, and having spoken with their colleagues, I consider them significant others as well. Having "reached their place," I am more inclined to comprehend than to judge.

An ironic turn of events during my fieldwork leads me to look upon the short- comings of the Dias team with humility and to accept that it is from their "er- rors" that I have the most to *learn*. I began my field research in Mueda only one year after the October 1992 peace accord brought an end to armed hostilities between the FRELIMO government and the South African-backed RENAMO insurgents that had challenged FRELIMO since soon after independence. As I worked in Mueda, FRELIMO and RENAMO troops were being demobilized and disarmed under United Nations supervision, and both parties were prepar- ing for the national-level elections that were held in October 1994 (while I was still in the field). Because the FRELIMO war against Portuguese colonialism was initiated on the Mueda plateau, and because FRELIMO maintained its central base there amidst loyal Makonde supporters, Mueda had long since been con- sidered "FRELIMO's cradle." Even so, two decades after independence, many Muedans had become frustrated with the failures of the post-independence regime, and some accused FRELIMO of failure to fulfill promises made to them during the independence war (West 1997b). As elections approached, tensions mounted in Mueda. FRELIMO officials patrolled the region to insure that

RENAMO campaigners received no welcome. Villagers sometimes chaffed at FRELIMO attempts to line them up, but generally remained hostile to the few RENAMO party mobilizers and supporters with whom they came into contact.

Early in my research, I had chosen to focus on historical events that predated independence so as to establish rapport before working on more immediate and more sensitive topics. Suddenly, my strategy came under threat. One of my field assistants informed me of rumors that Mwakala—now traveling with me as a field assistant just as he had done nearly forty years earlier with the Dias team— was, after the day's ethnographic work, canvassing the villages to mobilize support for RENAMO in the upcoming elections. I thought immediately of Mwakala's evasive eyes, of the strange comings and goings of people as we met at his house to record his life history. Could it be true? Could it be that I was as naive as the Dias team—that Mwakala had worked his "anti-anthropology" on me just as he had done forty years before with the Dias team?

I knew from my interviews with him that Mwakala's situation was complicated. After the war, he lamented, he was "forgotten" by FRELIMO leaders who failed to offer him any substantial post in the new government. Still, he received a pension from FRELIMO as a registered member of the Association for Veterans of the War for National Liberation. With this pension, he supported a large extended family. Mwakala denied all accusations of RENAMO activism. Because allegations were never proven, he continued to receive his pension. His situation was compromised, however, by the fact that his younger brother, a Catholic priest in the Pemba diocese, openly encouraged his congregation to vote against FRELIMO, the socialist party that had persecuted the church in the years following independence.

Rather than taking a clear position—aligning myself with either political party, or with Mwakala and his freedom of political expression—I lay low. Even as I sought to maintain a distance from both political parties, I knew that if I alienated FRELIMO officials and adherents, I would no longer be able to work in Mueda. After completion of the research excursion during which the conflict between my field assistants had erupted, I decided not to work with Mwakala in the field again. My reasons were many, including a need to distance myself from the Dias team's work while establishing my own field methodology and network of informants. The political cloud that hung over Mwakala, however, figured in my decision as well. The irony of these events, and of my responses to them, did not escape me. The political environments in which the Dias team and I worked were different in myriad ways. Furthermore, I had never claimed to be disinterested in the complex politics of my day. Still, beneath my nose things were happening that I did not fully recognize, and when they were pointed out to me, I felt paralyzed and unable to deal with them.

My published works on contemporary Mueda, I hope, will demonstrate my engagement both with the people among whom I worked and with the political

Rafael Mwakala with the author at his home in Pemba. (Courtesy Harry G. West.)

issues that structured their world. To that extent, I have tried to step outside of the footprints left by Jorge Dias and his colleagues. Even so, I am reluctant to judge my anthropological precursors too harshly. Through looking at the works of Dias and his colleagues, I may have learned little about how the power of the New State worked upon the communities they studied, but I have learned a great deal about how that power worked upon and through the ethnographers. Appreciation of our precursors as subjects in their own right allows us to recognize that we, as researchers, are also complex *subjects*, susceptible to similar dilemmas.

Acknowledgements

I wish to acknowledge the late Margot Dias, who graciously shared with me remembrances of her husband, António Jorge Dias, and the time they spent conducting research in Mozambique; and Karin Dias, who provided me with biographical information about both her father, António Jorge Dias, and her mother, Margot Dias. I also wish to thank Rafael Pedro Mwakala, who recounted his life history to me and shared memories of his time working with the Dias research team. Adriano Moreira and Benjamim Pereira provided me with personal reminiscences, and Rui Pereira with historical insights, on Jorge Dias and his team's work. I wish to acknowledge the assistance of archivists and librarians in Lisbon at: the *Biblioteca Nacional;* the *Arquivos Nacionais/Torre de Tombo;* the *Museu Nacional de Etnologia;* the *Centro de Documentação e Informação do Instituto de Investigação Científica Tropical;* the *Biblioteca do Instituto Superior de Ciências Sociais e Políticas;* the *Biblioteca da Universidade Nova de Lisboa* and the *Centro de Documentação do Departemento de Antropologia* at the same institution. I also wish to thank the Paixão family (João, Anita, Paulo and Jorge) and Ana Barradas for facilitating my research in Lisbon. Funding for research conducted in Portugal was generously provided by the *Fundação Calouste Gulbenkian.* Research in Mozambique was made possible by grants from the Fulbright-Hays program, the United States Institute of Peace and the Wenner-Gren Foundation. A preliminary version of this paper was presented at the annual meetings of the American Ethnological Society in Seattle, Washington on March 7, 1997. Jorge Freitas Branco, James Dow, Matthew Engelke, Richard Flores, Eric Gable, Richard Handler, Thomas Hauschild, Conrad Kottak, João Leal, Jennifer Lewis, Luis Madureira, Brian O'Neill, Nuno Porto, and Lyn Schumaker all provided commentary on draft versions. Konstanze Frischen and Timm Lau assisted in bibliographic research on the history of anthropological studies in Germany. Translations of Portuguese language texts quoted in English in this essay are my own.

References

Alpers, E. 1984. "To seek a better life": The implications of migration from Mozambique to Tanganyika for class formation and political behavior. *Canadian J. Af. Studs.* 18(2):367–88.

Barradas, A. 1997. O pensamento colonial de Jorge Dias. *História* 19(30):36–47.

Bausinger, H. 1994. Nazi folk ideology and folk research. In Dow & Lixfeld 1994:11–33.

Ben-Amos, D. 1994. Forward. In Dow & Lixfeld 1994:ix–x.

Branco, J. 1986. Cultura como ciência? Da consolidação do discurso antropológico à institucionalização da disciplina. *Ler História* 8:75–101.

Branco, J. & L. T. de Oliveira. 1993. *Ao encontro do povo*. Oeiras.

Conte, É. & C. Essner. 1994. Völkerkunde et Nazisme, ou l'ethnologie sous l'empire des raciologues. *Homme* 34(129):147–73.

DG. See under Dias and Guerreiro.

DGD. See under Dias, Guerreiro, & Dias.

Dias, A. J. 1948. *Vilarinho da furna*. Porto.

———1952. *Rio de onor: Communitarismo Agro-Pastoril*. Lisbon.

———. 1953. Os elementos fundamentais da cultura Portuguesa. In *Proceedings of the International Coloquium on Luso-Brasilian Studies*, 51–65. Nashville.

———. 1957. *Relatório da campanha de 1956*. Lisbon.

———. 1960. Convivio entre Pretos e Brancos nas provincias ultramarinas Portuguesas. *Estudos Ultramarinos* 3:21–32.

———. 1961a. Conflitos de cultura. In *Colóquios sobre problemas humanos nas regiões tropicais*, ed. Centro de Estudos Políticos e Sociais da Junta de Investigações do Ultramar, 109–25. Lisbon.

———. 1961b. *Ensaios etnológicos*. Lisbon.

———. 1961c. *Relatório sucinto da actividade da MEMEUP desde a Sua Criação*. Lisbon.

———. 1964. *Os Macondes de Moçambique (v. I): Aspectos históricos e económicos*. Lisbon (1998).

———. 1965. Contrabuição para o estudo da ouestão racial e da miscegenação. *Boletim da Sociedade de Geografia de Lisboa* 83(1–3 & 4–6):63–72.

———. 1970. Mudança de cultura entre os Macondes de Moçambique. *Universitas* 6/7:261–66.

Dias, A. J. & M. S. Dias. 1964. *Os Macondes de Moçambique (v. II): Cultura material*. Lisbon.

———. 1970. *Os Macondes de Moçambique (v. III): Vida social e ritual*. Lisbon.

Dias, A. J. & M. V. Guerreiro. 1958. *Relatório da campanha de 1957*. Lisbon.

———. 1959. *Relatório da campanha de 1958*. Lisbon.

Dias, A. J., M. V. Guerreiro & M. S. Dias. 1960. *Relatório da campanha de 1959*. Lisbon.

———. 1961. *Relatório da campanha de 1960*. Lisbon.

Dias, M. S. 1960. Aspectos técnicos e sociais da Olaria dos Chopes. *Garcia de Orta* 8(4):779–85.

———. 1962a. Os iântaros de ir à agua dos Macondes. In *Estudos científicos oferecidos em homenagem ao Prof. Doutor Carrington da Costa*, ed. Junta de Investigações do Ultramar , 219–23. Lisbon.

———. 1962b. Preparação da farinha de mandioca torrada (farinha dos musseques). *Garcia de Orta* 10(1):59–76.

———. 1965. *Os Maganjas da Costa: Contribuição para o estudo dos sistemas de parentesco dos povos de Moçambique*. Lisbon.

———. 1973. *O fenómeno da escultura Maconde chamada "Moderna."* Lisbon.

————. 1986. *Instrumentos musicais de Moçambique*. Lisbon.

Dow, J. & H. Lixfeld, eds. 1994. *The Nazification of an academic discipline: Folklore in the Third Reich*. Bloomington, IN.

Epstein, A. L. 1958. *Politics in an urban African community*. Manchester.

Ferguson, J. 1990. *The anti-politics machine: "Development," depoliticization and bureaucratic power in Lesotho*. Cambridge, UK.

Fischer, H. 1990. *Völkerkunde im nationalsozialismus: Aspekte der anpassung, affinität und behauptung einer wissenschaftlichen disziplin*. Berlin.

Fonseca, M. L. & F. M. Ferreira. 1997. Mestre na ciência e na vida. *J. de Letras* 4 June: 12–17, 36.

Freyre, G. 1958. Integração Portuguesa nos trópicos. Lisbon.

Gallo, D. 1988. Antropologia e colonialismo: O saber Português. Lisbon.

Gerndt, H. 1994. Folklore and national socialism: Questions for further investigation. In Dow & Lixfeld 1994:1–10.

Gluckman, M. 1940. Analysis of a social situation in modern Zululand. *Bantu Studs.* 14:1–30, 147–74.

————. 1942. Some processes of social change, illustrated with Zululand data. *Af. Studs.* 1:243–60.

————. 1943. Administrative organization of the Barotse native authorities. Rhodes-Livingstone Communications, no. 10.

Gordon, R. 1988. Apartheid's anthropologists: The genealogy of Afrikaner anthropology. *Am. Eth.* 15(3):535–53.

Gramsci, A. 1971. *Selections from the prison notebooks of Antonio Gramsci*. New York.

Guerreiro, M. V. 1958. Boers de Angola. *Garcia de Orta* 6(1):11–31.

————. 1960. Ovakwankala (Bochimanes) e Ovakwannyama (Bantos): Aspectos do seu convívio. *Garcia de Orta* 8(3):529–34.

————. 1962. Jogos, brinquedos e outras diversões do povo Maconde. *Garcia de Orta* 10(2):283–303.

————. 1963. *Rudimentos da língua Maconde*. Lourenço Marques.

————. 1966. *Os Macondes de Moçambique (v. IV): Sabedoria, língua, literatura e jogos*. Lisbon.

————. 1974. *Novos contos Macondes*. Lisbon.

Hammond-Tooke, W. D. 1997. *Imperfect interpreters: South Africa's anthropologists (1920–1990)*. Johannesburg.

Hauschild, T. 1987. Völkerkunde im "Dritten Reich" In *Volkskunde und nationalsozialismus: Referate und diskussionen einert tagung*, ed. H. Gerndt, 245–59. Munich.

————. 1995. "Dem Lebendigen Geist": Warum die geschichte der völkerkunde in "Dritten Reich" auch für nichtethnologen von interesse sein kann. In *Lebenslust und fremdenfurcht: Ethnologie in Dritten Reich*, 13–61. Frankfurt am Main.

————. 1997. Christians, Jews, and the other in German anthropology. *Am. Anth.* 99(4):746–53.

Instituto de Alta Cultura. 1974. Bibliografia de António Jorge Dias. In *In memórium: António Jorge Dias*, ed. Instituto de Alta Cultura: Junta de Investigações Científicas do Ultramar, 21–28. Lisbon.

Instituto Superior de Ciências Sociais e Políticas, ed. 1995. *Estudos em homenagem ao Professor Adriano Moreira*. Lisbon.

————. 1996. *ISCSP—90 Anos: 1906–1996*. Lisbon.

Jeggle, U. 1988. L'ethnologie de l'Allemagne sous le régime Nazi: Un regard sur la volkskunde deux générations après. *Eth. Francaise* 18:114–19.

Jell-Bahlsen, S. 1985. Ethnology and fascism in Germany. *Dialectical Anth.* 9(1–4): 313–35.

Kuper, A. 1983. *Anthropology and anthropologists: The modern British school*. London.

Leal, J. 1999a. Mapping Mediterranean Portugal: Pastoral and counter-pastoral. In Proceedings of the conference "Where does the Mediterranean begin? Mediterranean anthropology from local perspectives." *Narodna Umjetnost* (Croatia) 36(1): 9–31.

————. 1999b. "Tylorean professors" and "Japanese corporals": Anthropological theory and national identity in Portuguese ethnography. In *L'anthropologie et la Méditerranée: Unité, diversité, perspectives*, eds. D. Albera and A. Blok. Paris.

————. 1999c. The history of Portuguese anthropology. *Hist. Anth. Newsl.* 26(2):10–18.

Limón, J. E. 1991. Representation, ethnicity, and the precursory ethnography: Notes of a native anthropologist. In *Recapturing anthropology: Working in the present*, ed. R. G. Fox, 115–35. Santa Fe, NM.

————. 1994. *Dancing with the devil: Society and cultural poetics in Mexican-American South Texas*. Madison, WI.

Lupi, J. E. P. B. 1984. *A concepção de etnologia em António Jorge Dias*. Braga.

Margarido, A. 1975. Le colonialisme Portugais et l'anthropologie. In *Anthropologie et impérialisme*, ed. J. Copans, 307–44. Paris.

Moore, S. F. 1994. *Anthropology and Africa: Changing perspectives on a changing scene*. Charlottesville, VA.

Moreira, A. 1956. *Política ultramarina*. Lisbon.

————. 1960. *Ensaios*. Lisbon.

Moutinho, M. C. 1982. A etnologia colonial Portuguesa e o Estado Novo. In Regra do Jogo 1982:415–42.

Oliveira, E. V. de. 1968. *Vinte anos de investigação etnológica do Centro de Estudos de Etnologia Peninsular*. Lisbon.

————. 1972–74. Professor Jorge Dias (1907–73). *Revista Portuguesa deFilologia* 16(1–2):797–802.

————. 1974. António Jorge Dias. In *In Memoriam: António Jorge Dias*, ed. Instituto de Alta Cultura: Junta de Investigações Científicas do Ultramar, 10–28. Lisbon.

Orwell, G. 1949. *Nineteen eighty-four*. New York (1984).

Pais de Brito, J. 1982. O Estado Novo e a Aldeia Mais Portuguesa de Portugal. In Regra do Jogo 1982:511–32.

————. 1995. Onde Mora o Franklin? Um escultor do acaso. Lisbon.

Payne, S. 1995. A history of fascism, 1914–45. Madison, WI.

Penvenne, J. 1989. "We are all Portuguese!" Challenging the political economy of assimilation: Lourenço Marques, 1870–1933. In *The creation of tribalism in southern Africa*, ed. L. Vail, 255–88. Berkeley.

Pereira, B. 1996. A luz da memória: Benjamim Enes Pereira e os caminhos da antropologia em Portugal, an interview by P. Godinho and C. Lavado. *Arquivos da Memória* 1:69–93.

Pereira, R. 1986a. *Antropologia aplicada na política colonial Portuguesa: A missão de estudos das minorias etnicas do ultramar Português (1956–1961)*. Masters thesis, Universidade Nova de Lisboa.

————. 1986b. Antropologia aplicada na política colonial Portuguesa do Estado Novo. *Revista Internacional de Estudos Af.* 4–5:191–235.

————. 1987. O desenvolvimento da ciência antropológica na empresa colonial do Estado Novo. In *O Estado Novo das origens ao fim da autarcia (1926–1959)*, ed. F. Rosas, 89–100. Lisbon.

————. 1989a. A ouestão colonial na etnologia ultramarina. *Antropologia Portuguesa* 7:61–78.

————. 1989b. Colonialismo e antropologia: A especulação simbólica. *Revista Internacional de Estudos Af.* 10–11:269–81.

————. 1998. Introdução à reedição de 1998. In Dias 1964[1998].

Pina Cabral, J. 1991. *Os contextos da antropologia.* Lisbon.

Redinha, J. 1973. Necrológia-António Jorge Dias. *Cadernos de Artes e Tradições Populares* 1(1):129–33.

Regra do Jogo, A., ed. 1982. *O fascismo em Portugal: Actas do colóquio realizado na faculdade de letras de Lisboa em março de 1980.* Lisbon.

Richards, A. 1955. *Economic development and tribal change.* Cambridge, UK.

Rosaldo, R. 1989. *Culture and truth: The remaking of social analysis.* Boston.

Schapera, I. 1947. *Migrant labor and tribal life.* London.

Sharp, J.S. 1981. The roots and development of volkekunde in South Africa. *J. of Southern Af. Studs.* 8:16–36.

Southall, A. 1961. *Social change in modern Africa.* Oxford.

Stocking, G.W. 1982. Afterword: A view from the center. *Ethnos* 72–86.

Wagley, C. n.d. Report on a visit to Portugal and Portuguese Africa. Ms.

West, H. G. 1997a. Sorcery of construction and sorcery of ruin: Power and ambivalence on the Mueda Plateau, Mozambique (1882–1994). Doctoral dissertation, University of Wisconsin–Madison.

————. 1997b. Creative destruction and sorcery of construction: Power, hope and suspicion in post-war Mozambique. *Cahier d'Études Af.* 147, 37 (3):675–98.

————. 1998. "This neighbor is not my uncle!" Changing relations of power and authority on the Mueda Plateau. *J. of Southern Af. Studs.* 24(1):141–60.

Wilson, G. & M. Wilson. 1945. *The analysis of social change.* Cambridge, UK.

Wilson, W. A. 1973. Herder, folklore and romantic nationalism. *J. Popular Cul.* 6(4):819–35.

Wolf, J. J. de. 1992. Ethnology in the Third Reich. *Cur. Anth.* 33(4):473–75.

THE DIRECTOR AS SIGNIFICANT OTHER

Max Gluckman and Team Fieldwork at the Rhodes-Livingstone Institute

LYN SCHUMAKER

Max Gluckman, the well-known South African social anthropologist, conducted extensive fieldwork in South Africa and Northern Rhodesia (Zambia) from the mid-1930s to 1947. In 1941, he became the second director of the Rhodes-Livingstone Institute (RLI) in Northern Rhodesia, and after World War II, led its first team of researchers. He left the RLI for Oxford in 1947, and in 1949 became the first chair of social anthropology at the University of Manchester. There he founded the "Manchester School" of social anthropology, based on the approaches he and his team pioneered in their RLI work.

The products of Gluckman's individual fieldwork, both in South Africa and Northern Rhodesia, included not only his publications but also a photographic collection preserved at the Royal Anthropological Institute (RAI) in London. A skilled amateur photographer, Gluckman recorded the everyday life of the Zulu and Lozi peoples he studied. He also frequently captured his own and other Europeans' presence in the field (Schumaker 2001:49–50). His interest in Europeans in the field developed out of his particular style of anthropological reflexivity, expressed in his famous work, "The Analysis of a Social Situation in Modern Zululand" (Gluckman 1958). There he analyzed his own movements and those of others—European and African—within and between the Zulu

Lyn Schumaker is a lecturer in the Wellcome Unit for the History of Medicine at the Centre for the History of Science, Technology and Medicine, University of Manchester. Her book on the Rhodes-Livingstone Institute, *Africanizing Anthropology: Fieldwork, Networks and the Making of Cultural Knowledge in Central Africa*, was published in 2001. She is currently researching the history of mining and medicine in Zambia.

and European groups that had gathered to celebrate the opening of a bridge. Then he used this reflexive analysis to paint a picture of South Africa as a racially diverse but single interconnected society, in what was a politically radical and anthropologically innovative move in the context of South Africa between the world wars.

Gluckman's reflexivity also extended to the profession of social anthropology itself. While in Barotseland in Northern Rhodesia (studying the Lozi people), he photographed his field camp and titled the picture "The Ethnographer's Tent." This image and its title made a conscious reference to Bronislaw Malinowski's photographs of *his* tent in *Argonauts of the Western Pacific*, and perhaps also to Audrey Richards's photograph of *her* tent in a village as the frontispiece to her book, *Land, Labour and Diet in Northern Rhodesia* (Malinowski 1922:16, 481; see also Stocking 1983:55; Richards 1939). For Gluckman and other social anthropologists in the 1930s, Malinowski stood as the founder of modern fieldwork methods, while Richards was his most famous protégé and pioneer of those methods in the Northern Rhodesian field. Like them, Gluckman intended to shape the future of the discipline's new fieldwork methods.

This fieldwork revolution, generally credited to Malinowski (but see Kuklick 1991), ushered in participant observation by a lone ethnographer as the model for functionalist anthropology. Prior to Malinowski, the fieldworker usually did not work alone, but as part of a team of two or more members, as in the 1898 Cambridge Torres Straits Expedition, an exemplar of fieldwork in late-nineteenth-century anthropology (Kuklick 1991). By the 1930s, however, Malinowski had transformed the image of anthropological fieldwork into that of an enterprise that not only allowed, but also demanded that the ethnographer work alone in order to produce valid results. Professional anthropologists came to believe that true understanding of another culture could be achieved only through total immersion in that culture and the continuous observation of the self undergoing the process of adaptation to an alien form of life—the main constituents of the participant observation method. But this ideal could not be achieved in the presence of significant numbers of anthropological (or other European) others. This led to the image of the anthropologist as a "lone ranger with a notebook," which has dominated twentieth century conceptions of fieldwork (Grimshaw and Hart 1993:15).

The legitimation of this new form of singular observing—participant observation—took place not through the corroborating testimony of one's anthropological team mates, as it would on an expedition, but through textual innovations like those found in Malinowski's published work. These included passages that invited readers to imagine themselves in the field as witnesses to the events described by the author, both creating the "ethnographic present" in the text and convincing anthropologists that participant observation

Max Gluckman's tent at Nanjeko, Barotseland. (Courtesy RAI.)

worked. Stocking has argued that this provided the new method with its "mythic charter" (1983:56–57). The texts also included visual images that testified to the ethnographer's presence in the field—most famously, the photos of Malinowski's tent.

Missing, however, from the literature on these textual strategies, and on the much-remarked divergence of Malinowski's published accounts of his fieldwork from his daily field diary, is the question of how anthropologists establish their credibility during fieldwork (Stocking 1983:17; Clifford 1983). Not only do anthropologists engage in legitimating strategies in their texts, they also must establish their legitimacy in the field itself. And they must do it not for an audience of readers from their profession but for a wide array of significant others who can help or hinder their work. Legitimating strategies are essential to successful fieldwork whether the anthropologist works alone or in a team: All researchers must engage in demonstrations of competence to observers who may act as gatekeepers to the field site or witnesses to the quality of their fieldwork.

Although anthropologists find legitimating strategies necessary in all fieldwork, cases of team fieldwork exhibit them more clearly because teamwork in the field elicits a wide range of explicit communications and public reactions. The team of anthropologists who worked under Gluckman at the RLI left a rich archive that reveals their strategies for legitimating their fieldwork in the eyes of others who included colonial administrators, African nationalists, missionaries, and white settlers, and most importantly, in the observing anthropological eyes of the director himself. This context holds the key to the "more widespread methodological self-consciousness" that Stocking has noted in the work of the Manchester School in the 1950s (1983:14; see also Epstein 1967).

The central problem confronting the RLI team in devising its field strategies was to find ways to observe and participate in African societies while not too flagrantly violating the strictures of the colonial society of central Africa, the society from which most of these observing others came. Thus, in this essay I pay close attention to the spoken and unspoken "rules" for field behavior that the RLI team negotiated with their director and other observers. I will focus on colonial rituals and etiquette, the distinct styles of fieldwork practiced by different communities of anthropologists, and the everyday sociality out of which all researchers develop their practices and methods. Indeed, anthropological fieldwork—colonial, postcolonial, at home or abroad—always involves negotiating the differential power of conflicting social groups, the anthropologist's professional group among them. And these struggles are always voiced through appeals to character, credibility, and ultimately to what is seen as proper or improper in human relations (and in the case of southern Africa, race relations).

Thus, principles of civility and etiquette will be key to my argument, for these are terms that draw attention to the standards of everyday behavior upon which scientists, like any others, are judged in a social context. Moreover, these standards interact with and help to shape the standards researchers establish for their *scientific* behavior and credibility. This is especially the case in that most social of the sciences, social anthropology.

The Wicker Toilet Seat, or Civility in the Field

Some of the most prominent young British social anthropologists of the 1930s helped to establish and direct the RLI. Two of Malinowski's best students inaugurated the Institute's work: Richards played a key role in founding the Institute in 1937, and Godfrey Wilson became its first director (1938–41) (Richards

1977; Wilson 1977). Richards did her fieldwork among the Bemba in Northern Rhodesia in the 1930s. While director, Wilson carried out fieldwork in one of Northern Rhodesia's mining towns, Broken Hill (now Kabwe). Gluckman was a young South African anthropologist and former Rhodes Scholar who became the Institute's second director in 1941. Already seen as one of the most promising anthropologists in the discipline, he had trained both at Oxford and in Malinowski's famous London School of Economics (LSE) seminar. It was he who developed the Institute's first seven-year research plan and fielded its first team of researchers shortly after World War II, using funds provided by the British Colonial Development and Welfare Fund (CDWF).

Initially Gluckman joined the Institute in 1939 as senior sociologist. He had earned his doctorate at Oxford and had done fieldwork in Zululand from 1936 to 1938. While senior sociologist at the RLI, he did fieldwork with the Lozi people of Northern Rhodesia's Barotseland Protectorate, work that led to numerous publications over the next three decades (Gluckman 1942, 1944, 1955, 1965). At first, he spent most of his time in Barotseland where he lived near the administrative capital, Mongu, at a site called Katongo Camp. After Wilson resigned from the Institute in 1941, Gluckman became director and worked mainly at the RLI headquarters in Livingstone. During World War II, he ran the Institute alone after the only other staff member left for war service—the archaeologist, J. Desmond Clark, who directed the Rhodes-Livingstone Museum.

Gluckman took over the RLI directorship in the anxious early days of the war, when the colonial government was considerably ambivalent about anthropology, and the mining companies that dominated Northern Rhodesia's economy expressed sometimes-overt hostility to the idea of anthropological work in the mining towns. Both saw anthropologists as potentially subversive of African loyalty at a time when African military service and labor on the mines and railways were crucial to the war effort. This general atmosphere and his own and Wilson's field experiences gave Gluckman reason for being sensitive to issues of researchers' behavior in the field. He concerned himself particularly about the observation of anthropologists by crucial others in the field—by administrators, technical officers, and white settlers—for negative as well as positive reasons: such people could block fieldwork, yet some aspects of their behavior could provide models that anthropologists might use to make their work more acceptable. Administrators and settlers had the power to affirm or deny the truth of anthropological claims, a power that anthropologists took seriously because many of them in the interwar and immediate post–World War II periods hoped their work would be used for practical purposes of planning and development in the colonies. This did not make them mere "handmaidens" of the colonial government, however. At least in the case of the RLI, anthropologists' research often became a springboard for criticism of administrators' preferred policies, and administrators often responded by dismissing anthropologists' work as irrelevant or impractical. Whatever the frustrations in this relationship, RLI anthropologists had to seek approval for their research from government authorities. And they often turned the tables by claiming a greater legitimacy for their fieldwork than that of the administration's own political officers, whose role as experts on Africans they were attempting to usurp (Kuklick 1991; Schumaker 2001).

The politics that vexed colonial fieldwork more than once threatened Gluckman's research. He had a difficult entry to fieldwork in Northern Rhodesia in 1939, nearly losing his permission to stay in Barotseland due to two incidents that took place shortly after his arrival. The first was his accidental shooting of a Lozi man (of which he was cleared of any criminal charges), and the second involved the colonial government's suspicion of his loyalty based on remarks he made at the beginning of the war (Brown 1979:529). Similarly, his prior fieldwork in Zululand in South Africa had not been without incident, and there he had been required to leave because he took the part of a man being punished by the Zulu regent. He had also been criticized for wearing Zulu traditional dress (Macmillan 1995:41–43, 51).

Equally distressing, Gluckman observed some of the consequences of Wilson's banning from his field site, which led to the first director's resignation (and may have contributed to his later suicide). His banning came at the instigation of mining company managers concerned that chance remarks by a pacifist anthropologist like Wilson might inspire African disloyalty (Brown 1973:192). But rumors about Wilson's behavior during fieldwork also contributed to his banning: he was "too familiar," smoking cigarettes with African miners, and he and his wife became the subject of European gossip because he gave lifts to African women, and with his wife, visited a retired colonial administrator who had two African wives. Privately, the mine owners also thought him guilty of professional arrogance for assuming that his social research at the RLI counted as an important justification for exemption from war service (Schumaker 2001:62–64).

Most of these concerns can be interpreted as a criticism of the participant observation method and anthropologists' claims for its importance. This was at a time when a new emphasis in colonial society on sexual and racial boundaries had curtailed an older administrative style that involved total immersion in African life (in Northern Rhodesia symbolized by the retired colonial administrator and his two African wives). Rumors about sexual impropriety or smoking with Africans pointed either to violations of newly established boundaries or to a greater policing of old rules about status-related behavior in interracial situations. Anthropologists' use of participant observation, and sometimes their liberal views on race, violated these increasingly rigid colonial standards. Intensive fieldwork also offended government administrators' sense of their own professionalism. Many felt that research by these relative latecomers, professional anthropologists, could not replace the work of administrator-ethnographers who, ideally at least, based their observations on lengthy colonial service, local language learning, and sensitivity to the political ramifications of their behavior in the field.

Because of his history of difficulties during fieldwork, Gluckman acquired an acute understanding of the etiquette of fieldwork in a colonial situation. Thus, he paid particular attention to dress, to colonial rituals of power, and to the ways that administrators defended their legitimacy through references to their own fieldwork—administrative touring for the collection of taxes and enforcement of colonial authority and development campaigns. His guidance of the RLI team on these matters extended from the heights of colonial civility—paying respect to governors and chiefs—to the most mundane details, such as pitching tents and organizing clothing and equipment. When interviewed about his experiences in central Africa, J. Clyde Mitchell, a member of the first RLI team, often referred to the director's rules for fieldwork as "Gluckman's dictums" (JCMI 1). Although this term expressed Mitchell's resentment of the director's rigidity about these rules, many of Gluckman's "dictums" pointed to areas of likely conflict that the RLI team members would encounter in the course of their fieldwork.

The most mundane of Gluckman's rules was the toilet-seat dictum: "Max believed a latrine with a proper European-style toilet seat was an absolute necessity in the field," recalled J. A. (John) Barnes, another RLI team member (JABI). Institute records contain references to toilet seats being issued as standard equipment to RLI researchers, and Gluckman's photographic collection at the RAI contains a picture of an African version of a toilet seat, constructed out of wicker and offered for sale to Europeans. The photographer's intent may have been more humorous than sociological in this case, but the photo is nevertheless significant. Both Gluckman and the African who made the wicker toilet seat had noticed a key site of difference between European and African behavior, and Gluckman had noticed the African noticing.

Touring administrators and other Europeans who ventured into the African countryside took pride in overcoming the difficulties of everyday life in the field. An insistence upon hygiene and high standards, with the occasional touch of luxury, proved that one had not gone native—thus, the power of the image, repeated in travel literature and film, of Europeans dining on tables set with china and wine glasses in the bush. The missionaries' "knife and fork doctrine," which they saw as central to their work of christianizing "cannibal" Africans, is another part of this discourse on the cultivation of civilized character through instruction in etiquette (Hunt 1999:118–33). In the colonial setting, one's table manners became a demonstration of civilized status, and an opportunity to enhance the education of observing Africans. Although not so comfortably discussed as dinner table etiquette, the toilet-seat dictum represented the opposite side of the same colonial coin, and the government pursued it with vigor through a multitude of latrine-building campaigns.

Barotse-made latrine seat for whites. (Courtesy RAI.)

No studies have been made of administrators' toilet habits, but it is likely that in the late colonial period touring officers built latrines wherever they remained for a length of time and that they expected to find latrines already built in villages touched by previous latrine-building campaigns. Colonial civil servants in remote administrative centers would have had permanent latrines, as would settler farmers and the residents of many towns, for running water and modern toilet facilities only spread slowly across the country in the period after the Second World War.

The RLI researchers followed local European behavior in this area, though in some cases with a sense of irony about European hygienic obsessions. During their more settled periods of fieldwork, RLI researchers built latrines. Some of them lived with their families in houses in the field; others lived in large "cottage tents" in semi-permanent campsites, arrangements settled enough to justify the effort. Latrine-building in semi-permanent European camps may have also been required by law at a certain point in the late colonial period, just as other aspects of European camp life were regulated. For example, because of fire danger, Europeans were not allowed to live in "grass camps"—grass and pole huts used as temporary accommodation by Africans living seasonally in fishing camps or near their gardens in the bush (Turner 1987:54, cf. Schumaker 2001:143).

In short, the judgments of researchers' living arrangements in the field made by outsiders could affect the credibility of their research. The accusation that one was going native or becoming too familiar with Africans spoke not only to one's character or propriety, but also to the credibility of one's scientific observations. This has been true of European science since its beginning, when scientific observations achieved legitimacy based on the character of the person making them and the appropriateness of the site in which they were made (Shapin 1994). In early modern Europe, for example, the only legitimate observer was a gentleman, and the first experimental science was carried out in the homes of gentlemen (Shapin 1988). Even in nineteenth-century anthropology, the armchair anthropologist was seen as the most appropriate arbiter of travelers' and fieldworkers' observations; seated at home, he could achieve the objectivity and breadth of theoretical vision necessary to make statements of scientific truth.

With the advent of the participant observation method, the key site of scientific judgment shifted decisively from the armchair to the field. But this did not mean a cessation of concern about the character of the observer or the appropriateness (and propriety) of the site in which scientific observations and analysis took place. Instead, attention shifted to the anthropologists' behavior in the field and the appropriateness of their field camps as sites for the making of science in alien racial and cultural settings.

The toilet-seat dictum and Gluckman's other rules represented the director's attempt to develop a style of anthropological fieldwork (and of everyday behavior in the field) that would legitimate the RLI team's research. He directed his efforts simultaneously at two audiences: at professional anthropologists in the academic context and at the administrators and other people working or living in the field who would be the RLI researchers' most immediate observers and rivals. This dual concern motivated the two most important training experiences that the director arranged for the team before its members began their fieldwork: a field training session in Northern Rhodesia and a stay in South Africa that inducted them into a community of anthropologists already cognizant of the politics of southern African fieldwork. The training session also introduced them to a group of professionals—the colonial technical officers—whose field behavior represented a successful model for gaining credibility in the field.

"Hobnobbing with the Agriculturists"

In addition to the photos of the wicker toilet seat and Gluckman's tent, the collection at the RAI contains a photo of a wicker tent. This photo appeared in a popular magazine article, "Human Laboratory Across the Zambezi," that Gluckman wrote to publicize the RLI and the aims and methods of "sociological research" in Africa (Gluckman 1946). The aim, according to Gluckman,

The DC's tent in wicker. (Courtesy RAI.)

was to produce knowledge of the social changes taking place in African societies, knowledge that would prove useful both to governments and to the larger public, black and white. As he explained in the caption, the tent in the photo was a Lozi version of a touring administrator's tent, and the fact that a Lozi had considered it a suitable object for artistic reproduction demonstrated that administrators were an integral part of African society. From this he concluded that anthropologists must study the administrators, too. In the colonial context of Gluckman's work, this was a controversial statement, advocating research on the colonial system itself and not simply on the African subjects of that system. Although controversial, this approach had deep roots in the director's professional training and South African background.

These South African roots are revealed in Gluckman's claims for the *scientific* status of "sociological studies," a term he used more frequently than "social anthropology" to describe his discipline. Previously A. R. Radcliffe-Brown had promoted the use of the term "sociology" to emphasize social anthropology's break with the supposedly antiquarian evolutionary or diffusionist interests of earlier types of anthropology. He also used the term to emphasize the potential of the discipline for the study of specifically modern aspects of society and the potential of quantitative methods for enhancing the scientific status of the discipline. (Although they admired statistics, neither Radcliffe-Brown nor Gluckman used them to any extent in their work.) Gluckman followed this usage because of the strong influence Radcliffe-Brown had exerted on the South African academic and political scene in the 1920s, as well as on his education when he was a Rhodes Scholar at Oxford.

Another motivation came more directly from Gluckman's South African liberal background—his exposure to the ideas of William Macmillan, a prominent historian of South Africa. Macmillan portrayed South Africa as a single multiracial society, a view very different from that of most South African scholars of the time, who saw the country's history as that of a white frontier of civilization advancing across a landscape of culturally distinct and uncivilized African tribes. This predominant view obscured any social, economic, or political connections between Europeans and Africans, and it could be used to justify segregationist policies and schemes for separate development, which Macmillan also attacked. Another scholar, Isaac Schapera, influenced Gluckman in a similar direction. Like Macmillan, Schapera advocated studying African societies in their colonial situations. He felt anthropologists must include white missionaries and administrators in their ethnography, rather than attempting to recover a pristine precolonial society. Africans and whites must be studied in the same way, using sociological methods, because they were part of the same colonial society (Macmillan 1989).

To study social change, Gluckman laid the template of the South African situation upon central Africa, and especially upon Northern Rhodesia, using the region as a field "laboratory" in which research into these questions could be carried out far more easily than would have been the case in South Africa itself. He also saw such a research program as relevant to Northern Rhodesia's own situation, where as in South Africa, African urbanization and European immigration both were on the rise. He expressed concern about segregationist pressures moving northwards from the "white South," as white South Africans migrated to work in the mining towns of Northern Rhodesia's Copperbelt. This, and the later immigration of British war veterans after 1945, would rapidly increase the size and political influence of the small settler community who opposed the paternalistic but more pro-African colonial administration of Northern Rhodesia. The settlers hoped for a white-dominated state like that of

Southern Rhodesia. In contrast, Northern Rhodesia's administrators sought the eventual creation of an African independent state at some, admittedly very distant, future date—the ultimate goal of the indirect rule system in which they had been trained.

Gluckman also had a political stance in the midst of this conflict-ridden situation. A Marxist at the time, he supported African aspirations for political equality in South Africa, as well as the later African nationalist efforts for independence in Northern Rhodesia. Moreover, he hoped that his anthropology itself could prove useful to Africans in their debates with the colonial government about their political development and social well-being, fulfilling an Africanized version of the "science for the people" movement that inspired many social critics in Britain and elsewhere after World War One. Gluckman was not alone in his ambitions for social anthropology to be a critique of colonial government. Malinowski (1930), among others, had written on the importance of anthropology for the improvement of colonial administration and had also advocated studying the colonial situation, though from a somewhat different perspective. In addition, Lord Hailey's influential *African Survey* had endorsed the need for anthropological research as a foundation for successful African development; the *Survey* as a whole reflected the realization of many colonial scientists in the period between the world wars that scientific research, as well as colonial administration and development planning, needed to be more sensitive to African knowledge and practices (Tilley 2001; Hailey 1938).

It was this politically and sociologically motivated approach that can be seen at work in Gluckman's photo of the wicker tent, which symbolized the African view of the touring administrator and signaled the photographer's interest in studying the administration. Unlike Malinowski's tent, which pointed to the ethnographer's solitary existence among the natives, the wicker tent pointed to the existence of other Europeans within the field and within the territory for observation claimed by Gluckman's (and Schapera's) version of social anthropology.

The RLI itself had originated in an earlier confluence of local interest that included Northern Rhodesia's white settlers, who wanted a museum, and a proactive governor, who wanted a scientific research institute in his territory (Schumaker 2001:32). But it was the larger British strategy for the development of its African colonies that made funding available for the RLI's first team of researchers. Gluckman submitted his seven-year plan for the RLI to the Colonial Social Science Research Council (CSSRC) in 1943, which subsequently awarded the Institute a generous CDWF grant. Subsequently in 1945, Gluckman played a major role in selecting the researchers who would take up the CDWF posts, and became field supervisor for those chosen for the non-CDWF fellowships in central Africa, who would also be affiliated with the Institute.

Mitchell, a South African; Elizabeth Colson, an American; and Barnes, a Briton were hired under the CDWF grant. They were to study the Yao of Nyasaland and the Tonga and Ngoni of Northern Rhodesia, respectively. Max Marwick, a South African social psychologist, obtained a Colonial Research Fellowship, and his fieldwork on the Cewa of Nyasaland and Northern Rhodesia was to be supervised by Gluckman. In addition, a Dutch South African, J. F. (Hans) Holleman, filled a Beit Trust post to do research on the Southern Rhodesian Shona.

Of this first team, Holleman and Colson had had previous fieldwork experience—Colson's quite extensive—and only Colson had a Ph. D. (Colson 1953). Gluckman acted in some respects as a thesis supervisor for some members of the team, though each had an official university-based supervisor as well. He also acted as a *field* supervisor for the entire team. It was in this capacity that he arranged early training experiences—the fieldwork session in Northern Rhodesia and the lengthy stay in South Africa that involved training in African linguistics, sociology, and anthropology, meetings with prominent South African scholars, and visits to significant sites. Both of these experiences introduced the team to the director's view of the key questions guiding the research, as well as to the methods—and, just as important, the etiquette—of fieldwork in a colonial situation.

When Barnes, Mitchell, and Max and Joan Marwick arrived in Northern Rhodesia in 1946, Gluckman took them immediately to the field. They focused on a resettlement area that was of interest to the colonial administration, an area occupied by members of the Lamba people, a group who had lost their best land to the white mining towns of Northern Rhodesia's Copperbelt. Gluckman chose the site in accordance with his design for the overall research project of the RLI: the Lamba area allowed for study of colonial resettlement practices and issues of land tenure, agricultural improvement, local government, and the consequences for kinship structure that resulted from changes in settlement patterns brought about by colonialism. The Lamba people also represented a type of adaptation to industrial society different from that studied by Richards, who previously had examined the consequences of labor migration to the mines by a more distant group, the Bemba. Despite living near the mines, Lamba people rarely worked in the mines themselves, but rather developed local agricultural production and trade in foodstuffs to take advantage of the urban market created by the mining industry (Siegel 1989).

Gluckman and the newly arrived researchers worked together as a group for a few days, joined by the government technical officers, D. U. Peters, Colin Trapnell, and William Allan (all specialists in agriculture), as well as David Sianga, a research assistant who had worked with Gluckman on previous studies. Sianga and Gluckman demonstrated the central fieldwork relationship of anthropologist and research assistant to the new researchers. The agricultural officers, on the other hand, showed them how to deal scientifically with their material environment and how to understand the ways it had been shaped by human action. For example, Trapnell, an ecologist by training, taught Mitchell and Marwick how to interpret signs of previous cultivation in fallow land and other practices of reading the landscape that would be helpful in the anthropologists' future land tenure inquiries and mapping of village gardens. (Barnes missed the first day or two of the Lamba fieldwork and did not meet Trapnell until later.) Trapnell had worked extensively in Northern Rhodesia prior to Gluckman's arrival, and one of his studies (Trapnell and Clothier 1957) had influenced Gluckman's view of Barotseland.[1]

"Hobnobbing with the agriculturists was a very valuable experience," Mitchell observed of the field training session (JCMI 1). By including agricultural officers in the group, Gluckman may have intended to train his new researchers in the kind of interdisciplinary teamwork he himself had experienced in an earlier government survey, which had given him the hope that the colonial government would request future team studies by anthropologists and government technical officers (Allan et al. 1948). Anthropology, as conceived by Gluckman in this period, shared the technical services' professional interest in the problems associated with development. Sharing the field with technical officers as part of a survey team had given him enormous optimism for future work, which was later eroded by the government's failure to act on his recommendations (Brown 1979). By giving them this opportunity to develop working relationships with technical officers, Gluckman also enabled his team to become participant observers in the culture of colonial administrative fieldwork, an activity consistent with his view that anthropologists must study the administration.

Working with the agriculturists also familiarized the new researchers with a terminology and a way of seeing the field that would give their descriptions of fieldwork and their research results greater credence with the colonial administration. Colonial administrators possessed their own tradition of ethnographic enquiry for administrative purposes, which most of them considered perfectly adequate for answering questions about African behavior. In response to this attitude, Gluckman deployed a strategy of identification with government technical officers when dealing with the problem of rivalry between social anthropologists and all the other "amateurs"—missionaries and administrators who laid claim to greater familiarity with African societies. Like anthropologists, technical officers had found themselves in a position of rivalry with administrators when they first arrived, but nevertheless had made a place

---

1. John Barnes, however, recalls that Gluckman wrote "Economy of the Central Barotse Plain" (1942) because Trapnell hadn't yet worked in the area at that time (personal communication).

for their expertise. Anthropologists perhaps could do likewise (see Schumaker 1996:246–47). Thus, in his seven-year research plan for the RLI, Gluckman emphasized the special professional expertise that sociologists brought to the study of African societies. He repeatedly stated that sociologists' terms of employment should be equal to those for government technical officers because they were "in equal demand" in the wider world and that colonial governments would need to provide for their work just as they did "for the work of their chemists, botanists, and other scientists" (Gluckman 1945:2–4).

The technical officers also provided a model for daily fieldwork behavior that Gluckman believed anthropologists should emulate if they were to succeed. Of all the people working in central Africa, these technical experts worked in the field in a way most like the role Gluckman hoped to carve out for anthropologists—as members of scientific professions (and increasingly university-based disciplines) with distinctive standards and expertise. As professionals they commanded respect from administrators but also derived their knowledge from close observation of African life. Like anthropologists, they relied on extended periods of fieldwork that involved greater contact with Africans than the district administrator's traditional tour of villages. This characterization was especially true of the agricultural service in Northern Rhodesia in Gluckman's time, when men like Trapnell and Allan promoted the idea that African knowledge of soils and plants had to be understood in great detail before the government could successfully introduce new practices (Tilley 2001:110–21).

Subsequent personal relationships between agricultural officers and RLI researchers followed the pattern established by Gluckman in the field training session, even though formal collaboration in research never took off as he had hoped. In the field, agricultural stations often represented the closest European outpost and provided basic support for the anthropologists, including a place to collect their mail and get transport or guidance on tenting sites. And nearly all the former RLI anthropologists mentioned that technical officers often provided the nearest friendly ears for discussion of research problems and theoretical issues in those areas where agricultural and anthropological expertise overlapped.

The field training session, and the close relationships later established by many of the RLI team members with technical officers in their field sites, thus provided the anthropologists with training in proper field behavior—in field etiquette—and in a style of self-presentation that would help them to establish their legitimacy to the colonial government. The subsequent period of academic training in South Africa would also comprise a learning exercise in the etiquette of anthropological work, but this time outside of the field, in an academic world centered in Africa rather than Britain. It would, as well, provide the new researchers with a set of local intellectual elders, ancestors, and fictive kin in a South African anthropological community that boasted a matrilineal structure as unique and interesting as that of many of the societies in central Africa that the RLI team would study.

The Mother of Social Anthropology

When the RLI team visited South Africa in 1946, most liberals in South Africa did not foresee the adoption of apartheid policies that would take place in 1948 with the election of the Afrikaner Nationalist Party. A few, indeed, hoped that postwar economic growth would lead to the moderation of segregationist policies. They thought that recognition of the importance of African labor to the development of South African industry and the need for its availability in the urban industrial areas might lead white elites to allow Africans a place in the towns and increased political and economic rights. It was this academic and socially activist community of liberal and left-wing thinkers who became the intellectual network for the RLI researchers during their fieldwork in Africa. It seems likely that Gluckman intended this South African intellectual network to help them to acquire not only a basic knowledge of the scholarship on southern Africa, but also the social skills necessary to work in the segregated society of central Africa. Most important, through meetings with scholars, training in previous scholarship, and visits to important economic, social, and political sites, the South African tour enabled the RLI team to learn to recognize the kinds of social situation Gluckman wanted them to study in central Africa.

Gluckman had developed the concept of a "social situation" out of earlier anthropological models and used it (rather than "tribe") as his primary unit of sociological analysis. This approach had informed his Zululand work prior to his appointment at the RLI. In the article based on this research, "The Analysis of a Social Situation in Modern Zululand," Gluckman took the events of a single day and built a picture of the history and contemporary state of relations between Europeans and Zulus in South Africa. He further analyzed differences within the Zulu and European groups and discussed the interests that divided them into factions despite their overt racial or ethnic unity. He also pinpointed the ways that whites and blacks were bound by ties that transcended race and ethnicity, such as in church organizations and in African participation in native government under European indirect rule.

While the training arranged for the RLI team was a training *toward* how to "see" social situations like the ones used in Gluckman's work, it was also a training *away* from another approach to African societies—the dominant approach of Malinowski and his students, called the culture contact method (Mair 1938, 1946; Malinowski 1938). This approach emphasized the importance of cultural differences between African and European societies and focused on the difficulties Africans faced in the wake of the changes colonialism had brought to the continent. Many of its adherents put great effort into recovering an ideal state of African society before the advent of change (though the generally recognized importance of studying social change in the 1930s meant that no one completely neglected the colonial context). The work of British anthropologists like Margaret Read, Lucy Mair, and Richards, and to some extent that of Godfrey and Monica (Hunter) Wilson, provided the best examples of this approach.

Gluckman, however, wanted to stress political and economic factors above the cultural in looking at African societies, and he wanted to train his team of researchers to look for positive as well as negative African adaptations to changes brought by colonialism, especially urbanization and industrialization.[2] The team's training at Cape Town and the later visits to various South African people and places seemed designed to introduce them to this approach.

Meeting South African scholars and paying respect to their work was as important to the new team as learning proper fieldwork behavior from the administrators and technical officers in Northern Rhodesia. Although South African academics did not have the power to ban an erring young anthropologist from the field, they represented an influential and supportive alternative anthropological community for those RLI researchers who were far away from the American and British anthropological communities where they had been trained. And although Mitchell, Holleman, and Marwick had studied in South Africa, their training had taken place in disciplines other than anthropology or in universities other than the Universities of Cape Town (UCT) and Witwatersrand (Wits), where Gluckman's mentors and contemporaries had trained and worked. So they too were outsiders to that particular community of scholars.[3]

This community was a well established and dynamic group with its own concerns (see Dubow 1995; Gordon 1990; Hammond-Tooke 1997), many of which were relevant to the social situations in central Africa where the RLI researchers would work. Moreover, some of these scholars (or other South African scholars who had been part of this community before taking academic posts in Britain) had participated in choosing the RLI team or would play important

---

2. For Gluckman's critique of Malinowski's approach, see Gluckman 1949. While pointing out some important weaknesses in the culture contact approach, his critique was heavily motivated by intradisciplinary rivalry and did not give credit for the nuanced (and not entirely negative) accounts of African adaptations to social change of those who had produced the best examples of this work.

3. Mitchell and Marwick had trained as undergraduates at Natal University College (later the University of Durban)–Mitchell in social work and Marwick in social psychology. Holleman had gone to the Afrikaner-dominated University of Stellenbosch. Gluckman also had encouraged RLI researchers to meet important British scholars, before coming out to Africa or during subsequent visits to Britain.

roles advising the RLI's Board of Trustees in Northern Rhodesia or its primary funders, the CSSRC in Britain or the Beit Trust of South Africa. In this capacity they could influence the young researchers' future careers.

After the Lamba field training session, Barnes, Mitchell, and Max and Joan Marwick traveled to Cape Town, where Colson joined them on her arrival from the U.S. Gluckman had arranged their academic work to take place at UCT, where they could familiarize themselves with African linguistics and sociology, taught through intensive courses given by Schapera and the linguist, G. P. Lestrade. They were also introduced to African urban research by H. J. Simons, who had done extensive (unpublished) work on Langa, an African housing area in Cape Town. Because he was on leave in Britain at the time, Gluckman asked Colson, the most senior member of the team, to arrange the meetings with scholars at Wits. There the team visited the department of Bantu Studies, which reflected the context that had shaped Gluckman's views during his time as an undergraduate. In 1946 this was a community of scholars in the process of being displaced. In that year the social anthropologist, Hilda Kuper, left for the University of Natal, being replaced by the former British colonial administrator, M. D. W. Jeffreys, a diffusionist, who turned the department away from contemporary sociological concerns. Gluckman later played a role in restoring social anthropology to Wits through his support for Max Marwick to become that university's first professor of social anthropology in 1957 (Murray 1997:255).

Gluckman often pointed to his former teacher at Wits, Winifred Hoernlé, as the strongest influence on his choice of social anthropology for a career. Her combination of academic work with strongly principled social activism may have been as important to Gluckman as her support for Radcliffe-Brown's introduction of structural-functionalism to South African anthropology in the 1920s. It was in the latter role, however, that she became known as "the mother of social anthropology in South Africa" (Hammond-Tooke 1997:38, citing Krige & Krige 1943). She had learned a large number of important diffusionist and sociological approaches during her education and effectively transmitted them to numerous students while she was at Wits. She first studied philosophy at UCT and later anthropology and experimental psychology under Haddon and Rivers at Cambridge (where she had also been exposed to Radcliffe-Brown), Wundt and Kulpe at Leipzig and Bonn, and Durkheim at the Sorbonne (Carstens et al. 1987:3–4). In addition, she spent time in the U.S. and came to know the work of anthropologists at Harvard (Colson, personal communication).

After she became Lecturer in Ethnology at Wits in 1923, she began work there with Radcliffe-Brown on a comparative study of African social institutions in southern Africa. He, however, took up the chair of social anthropology at Sidney in 1926, leaving Hoernlé alone to develop the structural-functionalist approach (Carstens et al. 1987:9). She also promoted Malinowskian-style fieldwork, though her own fieldwork had employed the older expedition style. Students influenced by her interpretation of structural-functionalism focused their research on the contemporary problems of South Africa and became some of the first anthropologists to confront social change as an object of study. Ultimately, Hoernlé's belief that public service was as important for the anthropologist as academic research led her to resign from her senior lectureship at Wits in 1938 to pursue a more socially activist path at the South African Institute of Race Relations for the rest of her career (Carstens et al. 1987:11).

While in South Africa the members of the first RLI team (and most members of subsequent teams) met with Hoernlé and a number of those scholars who had been at Wits under her supervision when Gluckman studied there. These latter included Ellen Hellmann, Eileen Krige, and Hilda Kuper. Hellmann's research on an African slum yard in Johannesburg drew the team's special attention, for it pointed to Africans' increasingly permanent urbanization and its consequences, processes also at work in central Africa. Some also visited Monica Wilson at Ft. Hare College or toured her field site in Pondoland. Wilson's work got special attention because she had incorporated material on the urban life of Pondo migrants, as well as their work on European commercial farms into her largely rural study of Pondo society. The book on social change that she and Godfrey Wilson wrote before his death also drew on their Northern Rhodesian and Tanganyikan fieldwork, in addition to knowledge of conditions in South Africa, for its conclusions about African responses to global economic and local social change (Wilson 1936, Wilson & Wilson 1945).

Gluckman urged the RLI researchers to visit places where they could observe social processes similar to those they would examine in central Africa. Thus, they visited Sophiatown, a multi-ethnic, multiracial suburb of Johannesburg. Some of them had a tour of a gold mine, going underground to examine miners' working conditions. Although team members, such as Holleman, Mitchell, and Marwick, were familiar with social conditions in South Africa, they nevertheless would have benefited from seeing these things in new ways, influenced by the training they had at UCT and the concept of the social situation.

In general, the RLI researchers' introduction to the scholarly hierarchy in South Africa placed them within a political, intellectual, and social network that would give them the materials for building a local southern African identity useful for their fieldwork. This was an identity that could resist as well as adapt to the pressures of the segregationist society they would face in central Africa. The tour of sites in South Africa also gave them a consciousness of certain social processes—not merely in African societies, but also in the white communities with which they would have to interact in central Africa. These included the debates over liberalism and radicalism that went on within the small anti-segregationist camp, as well as skirmishes across the broader cleavage between segregationist and anti-segregationist thinkers. Although once in their Northern and Southern Rhodesian and Nyasaland field sites some of the researchers would experience their move to the rural field as an escape from the pressures of white society, the escape was never complete. Observation by administrators and local white farmers (or even pressure from Africans for certain types of behavior based on what they had experienced previously from whites) would continue to shape the researchers' choices regardless of the remoteness of their research sites.

The importance of sharing a style of behavior with a larger anthropological community in southern Africa should not be underestimated. It was an essential element for the success of the RLI team in making a place for itself in the field in central Africa. But this style of behavior was more than a mode of professional self-presentation, more than a social or professional form of etiquette. The developing RLI style of anthropology was also a "thought style," a way of seeing that shapes the way scientists approach their object of study (Harwood 1993). The Lamba field-training session and their training in Gluckman's South African academic community prepared them to look at colonial politics, regional processes, and the individual networks and strategies of Africans in rapidly changing rural and urban societies—all the hallmarks of what would later be called the Manchester School approach.

The Web of Anthropological Relations

The RLI researchers became a cohesive team through experiences of cleavage, as well as of cooperation. Throughout, the director played a dominant role, even in the most mundane aspects of the team's existence. His advice on the practical aspects of life in the field mainly dealt with African workers, transport and camping, and supplies and equipment, some of the latter provided by the Institute. Gluckman often recommended specific articles of clothing, tents, and camping furniture, as, for example, in the following list:

> [The RLI supplies] a good tent[,] and a bell tent for your servants and interpreter; camp chairs and tables; bath; one stretcher (not for your wife); and if we can get it, at least one power lamp . . . (but these latter are hard to come by in NR) . . . We also provide a typewriter—again, if we can get it. . . . Most comfortable wear is bush shirt and slacks, or shorts. I prefer slacks where there are lots of flies and find them cooler. I have just had a good bush shirt made by Indians. . . . If you can get a double terai hat I found it pleasanter than a topee. Good dark glasses are essential. . . . Get mosquito boots if you can. Gum boots are invaluable. Burberry rather than Macintosh. Umbrella useful. (JAB:MG/JAB 9/8/45)

Advice of this kind, and its specificity about styles and brand names, had a long history in the material culture of African exploration (see Fabian 2000:71–

72). Such lists and advice demonstrated one's experience of life in the bush, and in published memoirs lent credibility to the account. But Gluckman had also tailored his list (and perhaps the range of equipment provided by the Institute) to his view of appropriate practices for everyday life in the field, indicating the behavior he expected of his team. Thus, the reference to the lack of a "stretcher" for one's wife probably reflected his advice to male researchers not to bring their wives along.

Gluckman also gave specific instructions for "signing the governor's book," calling on the provincial and district commissioners, and paying respect to chiefs: "go and see the Chief and then keep away from him." To some of the first team, the director also sent a numbered list of instructions for behavior in the field, which included such advice as "Don't set up as herdsmen, kill a beast when it is given to you. You are entitled to give your carriers a beast once a month. . . . Salt is useful for informants . . . , [and] Never strike an African" (JAB:Instructions from Director to Officers [undated]).

This practical advice, like the toilet-seat dictum, pointed to important aspects of field etiquette. Some of this advice was based on Gluckman's knowledge of colonial administrators' touring regulations and his attempt to get similar conditions for anthropologists in the field. This is likely to be the source of the entitlement to give one's carriers a beast once a month, which the researchers might be expected to pay for out of their fieldwork allowances. Giving salt as a gift had been a standard practice of travelers in Africa since the beginning of exploration. The admonition never to strike an African derived from the need to distance anthropologists' field behavior from that of many white settlers and administrators (and perhaps some colonial anthropologists), who used beatings and outbursts of temper to maintain their authority.

The director also gave instructions about the researchers' personal lives, such as the advice to male researchers not to bring their families. He wrote to Barnes (whose wife, Frances, would soon qualify as a medical doctor) that there would be plenty of scope for a doctor to work alongside an anthropologist, but that a wife could not go into the field with a child. She should preferably remain in England or get a house in the nearby provincial administrative center (JAB:MG/JAB 11/10/45). Gluckman's wife, Mary, echoed this advice in a letter to Frances Barnes, in which she gave tips on family health and raising children in Northern Rhodesia while assuming that Frances would live in the nearest administrative center rather than in the field (JAB:MG/FB undated). In the end, Frances joined her husband in the field for the initial period of research when their first child was small and remained in England during the second period of fieldwork, after the child learned to walk and was harder to look after. Mitchell's wife and child also lived with him in the field, as did the wives and children of most of the male researchers throughout the RLI's history (JCMI 1).

Although Mary Gluckman and their children lived most of the time in Livingstone, she sometimes stayed in Mongu, the local administrative center in Barotseland, and occasionally joined Gluckman in nearby Katongo where he based himself during fieldwork before he became director and before the children were born (Colson, personal communication). Mary also participated in some of the fieldwork according to stories remembered by her children (T. J. Gluckman, personal communication).

As with his advice about chiefs, the director's concern about families in the field had to do with their potential effect on the research, his fear being that the anthropologist might interact more with family than with informants. Most of the researchers, however, disagreed and pointed out the benefits of having families in the field, particularly the effect of humanizing the male anthropologist in the eyes of local people (JCMI 1). With regard to the director's advice about chiefs, as well, there was considerable divergence from the ideal, both by Gluckman himself (some of whose assistants belonged to the Lozi royal family) and by the others. Entanglements with royalty had the potential to enhance some aspects of the research, and regardless of their effect, often could neither be avoided nor foreseen. One of the researchers complained, "The Director instructed us to avoid getting too entangled with Chiefs. 1. The site of my house, selected by D[istrict] C[ommissioner] . . . is only 7 miles from the Paramount [Chief]. 2. My interpreter is a. the schoolboy chum of the Paramount. b. the sister's husband [of the Paramount]. c. the wife's brother [of the Paramount]. And I have just found out that 3. The brother's wife's sister of the boy who does the washing up is a mistress of the aforesaid Paramount" (JAB:JAB/JCM 10/16/46).

Nevertheless, members of the team strove to follow the director's advice when they could. And some of Gluckman's advice became embedded in RLI practice through the standard issue equipment provided by the Institute—the tents, stretchers, camping boxes, camp chairs, baths, and toilet seats they picked up at the Institute before going into the field. As Barnes noted in his final inventory of RLI-provided equipment before leaving his field site, Chenjela Camp: "1 lavatory seat (permanent fixture at Chenjela)" (JAB:JAB/EC 5/9/49).

Such standard equipment and advice helped in a material and unacknowledged way to unite the team in its daily experience of the African field. Teamwork, however, also developed out of a cluster of more conscious experiences of observing each other's field practices and sharing communication networks. Gluckman actively arranged many of these experiences, including the initial field training session and the visit to South Africa. The director also visited some of the researchers in their field sites, and he usually encouraged them to visit each other in the field or travel to administrative centers to gather information from government records and local administrators. The latter was the purpose of a visit Barnes made to Nyasaland, which Gluckman, despite his general en-

Relaxing during the 1947 RLI conference, Livingstone, Northern Rhodesia. From left to right: John Barnes, Phyllis Deane, Elizabeth Colson, Hans Holleman. (Courtesy Jean Mitchell.)

couragement of such trips, had attempted to forestall: "Max sent telegrams to Fort Jameson, but we ignored the one that said 'Don't go to Nyasaland.' [In the field] you got a feeling of being way far away from where the spider was sitting in its web" (JABI). Most important of all, the director required the team members' attendance at a field conference, held in Livingstone in 1947, where they gave preliminary accounts of their research and critiqued each other's methods. Such field conferences became a standard feature of the RLI experience.

Outside influences also contributed to the researchers' emerging cohesiveness. Phyllis Deane, a colonial research fellow engaged in a study of colonial national incomes, did fieldwork in rural areas to gauge the contribution of villages to the British central African economy. In addition to gathering statistics from government sources, she visited each RLI researcher's field site and used their already established contacts to collect the data she needed. Strange as it may seem today that an economist could share the field with anthropologists, such was the case with Deane, who enjoyed fieldwork and thought it essential to the practice of her discipline. (This was at a time when economics had not yet exclusively embraced the practice of modeling economic systems on the basis of statistics gathered by others—its standard disciplinary practice today.) Her visits to the RLI field sites led her to recommend the practice enthusiastically to

At a later conference in Salisbury, Southern Rhodesia, 1948; standing, from left to right: Max Marwick, Ian Cunnison, John Barnes, Clyde Mitchell; seated, from left to right: Joan Marwick, Elizabeth Colson, Marjorie Elliot, Hans Holleman. (Courtesy Jean Mitchell.)

the team, and this encouraged more visiting and more comparative observation of the variations in the societies being studied. As Gluckman reported to Barnes, during Deane's visit to the director's Lozi field site, "[she says] it would be of great benefit to your political study to visit Barotseland—she is very impressed with the different attitude of the people [here compared to the Ngoni] both to Government and the N[ative] A[uthority]" (JAB:MG/JAB 5/15/47).

Supervisors' visits to students in the field had happened occasionally before the founding of the RLI (most significantly in Malinowski's visits to his students in Africa engaged in the International African Institute–supported culture contact studies), but it also became more important as a means of developing a coherent group field practice when Gluckman made it part of the RLI experience (see Richards 1963:16–17). And both of these practices—the director's visits and the team members' visits—helped forge a set of "integrated research procedures" that Mitchell later felt was the key to the RLI's capacity to produce a body of work with regional relevance, one of the hallmarks of the RLI approach (JCMI 1).

One of the most crucial of the group experiences that made the RLI into a team took place at the first conference in 1947, was repeated at subsequent conferences, and became an integral part of the later Manchester social anthropology seminars that functioned as the testing ground for subsequent RLI researchers recruited there. At that first conference Gluckman required each researcher to present his or her initial results. Each presentation was then critiqued by the director and other members of the group, who pointed out gaps in the material that would have to be addressed in further fieldwork, as well as comparisons that could be made between conditions in the different societies being studied by members of the team. This undoubtedly helped to mold the RLI approach. It may also have functioned as a not altogether pleasant initiation rite, which, if successfully endured, led to stronger group identification.

The solidification of an RLI group identity also may have contributed to the researchers' professional solidarity with respect to those other "others" with whom they interacted in the field—in particular, the colonial administrators who were discussed to some extent in most of the RLI monographs and at length in a later study by Holleman (1969). But anthropological solidarity also figured in the kind of sociality that developed *within* the group, which involved joking about the colonial administration and other people with whom they had ambivalent or competitive relationships in the field, including at times the director himself.

This social solidarity can be seen in a humorous yet pointed account of a visit by the Marwicks and Barnes to see the government files at the provincial administrative center that catered to their field sites. Their purpose was to get a picture of the history of the area through examining records made by past and present district-level administrators. In a letter to Mitchell, Barnes gave his impressions of the administrators whose records he had been reading:

> As far as I can make out, no one has the time or inclination to read anything written by their predecessors in office, and each new jack-in-office gaily writes down his personal impression of what he thinks he has seen with all the self confidence that makes a good D[istrict] C[ommissioner]. E. g., this year, the cadet, a man of less seniority north of the Zambezi than I, which is saying a lot, reports of the people where Max lives that they regard the latrine as one of the more menacing aspects of European acculturation, and that in these circumstances he has

advised the people (did they ask him for advice, one wonders?) to use a hole in the bush. Little does he know that in the very same area, as recently as December 1938, a wave of latrine digging swept through this part, and under the leadership of two Jeanes [Training School] supervisors, as many as 2000 were dug, a performance said at the time to reflect great credit on the local chief. What does the patient seeker after truth do in a case like this? Assume that the present cadet is more perspicacious than his forerunner; that the opinion of the people has changed radically in the last 9 years; or that the Jeanes supervisors, perhaps unconsciously, imagined latrines where there were none in their effort to win approval from their latrine-using superiors? . . . I must confess myself very much in the dark. Perhaps the naivety of the Administration is exceeded only by my own naivety in attempting to understand them. (JAB:JAB/JCM 7/31/47)[4]

Barnes's description of the colonial administration uses particular rhetorical devices to convince the reader of the credentials of the author. In this case, the legitimating rhetoric works to solidify the mutual identity of the researchers at a time when they needed encouragement to withstand the pressures of fieldwork. As the letter suggests, they faced competition with administrators who considered themselves the best experts on African societies. Thus, Barnes mentions his seniority with respect to the cadet because administrators commonly claimed greater knowledge of Africans due to their lengthier field experience. History is also an underlying issue, for the RLI researchers paid attention to history as few social anthropologists had done before, stimulated by Gluckman's reverence for Macmillan's historical analysis of South African society. Barnes and the Marwicks, in examining the government files, saw themselves as taking more care about the history of the societies they studied than the administrators who had produced the files but did not read them and thus, unknowingly, promoted contradictory policies.

"Don't Tell Max"

Gluckman's guidance of his team extended well beyond matters of integrated research procedures or daily comforts in the field. His most essential contribution to the success of the RLI research grew from his understanding of the politics of fieldwork, as he devised strategies for researchers to maintain their right to work in the central African field despite the sometimes controversial nature of their research agendas and personal politics. So-called academic politics also

4. The Jeanes Schools trained Africans for teaching and extension work in the rural areas, based on the model of schools founded for African Americans in the American South by Anna Jeanes in the early twentieth century. The Carnegie Corporation helped to fund the transfer of this model to Africa (Snelson 1974:157).

motivated the director's surveillance of the team's work, especially his strong and constant attention to the translation of the influential disciplinary approaches of the day into the team's field practices and writing.

No one had more reason to be concerned about the politics of fieldwork than Gluckman. As a Marxist in a context in which liberalism (and even colonial government paternalism) were viewed as radical by white settlers, the director had had more than one narrow escape from disaster during his own fieldwork. He had benefited from Wilson's staunch defense when the government considered throwing him out of his Lozi field site for making politically suspect statements at the beginning of World War II. In Wilson's estimation, anti-Semitism had played a role in shaping certain aspects of Gluckman's personality, including at times a retreat into intellectualism in response to prejudice (Brown 1979:529). Anti–Semitism, doubtless, had an effect on Gluckman's expectations of his treatment by others, but many other factors in the history and structural position of the Institute and its director also influenced his behavior in ways that his colleagues at times saw as difficult.

Within Northern Rhodesia, the RLI found itself in an insecure position because of events at the beginning of World War II. All three of its staff (Gluckman, Wilson, and Clark) had claimed conscientious objector status, leading many in the colonial administration to view the Institute as a haven for pacifists, despite Gluckman's later attempt to join the armed forces. The arrival after the war of new administrators who had done war service, as well as men in the new RLI team who had been in the military, may have made Gluckman feel isolated. In addition, the Institute had a difficult relationship with the CSSRC, the arm of the Colonial Office that determined the standards for its funding after the war. The RLI occupied an anomalous position in the view of the CSSRC because it was a product of local initiatives and predated the planning and siting of other CSSRC-funded colonial research institutes. The RLI's location in Northern Rhodesia and its continued funding often became the subject of debates within the CSSRC, requiring considerable effort on the part of its directors to preserve its access to funding (Schumaker 2001:61–65, 146–47).

Gluckman's history and position, too, gave him cause for worry. The directorship of the RLI, though highly prestigious, did not guarantee secure employment or a pension, and he would leave eventually for a lectureship in Britain. Perhaps he was also concerned about attitudes toward his membership in the small South African community of liberals and radicals. This may have been one reason for his fear that his articles might not be published. In addition, his "colonial" origin as a South African student at Oxford may have made him insecure about his acceptance in British anthropology in general, though he quickly gained the support of many central figures in the discipline. Later, as the chair of the Manchester social anthropology department, he responded to Manchester's marginality vis-à-vis Oxford, Cambridge, and London by developing ambitious plans for the department's expansion using his RLI network, rather than relying entirely on his British connections.

Political concerns continued to haunt him during his British career. Like Hoernlé, his first teacher, Gluckman pursued a socially activist role in addition to his academic work. During the 1950s and early 1960s, he became an outspoken supporter of the British-based Movement for Colonial Freedom, and he was told not to return to Northern Rhodesia for a visit in 1957 because of his public statements critical of the British Central African Federation (which Northern Rhodesia had joined in 1953). He later felt that the attitude of the academic establishment to his anticolonial political work might have prevented his further advancement in Britain (though there were few higher posts aside from Oxford after Evans-Pritchard's death) and his attempt to move to an American university (T. J. Gluckman, personal communication).

The director's relations with the RLI team reflected these stresses. Gluckman's tendency to retreat into intellectualism and express feelings of persecution were captured in a letter from Max Marwick to Mitchell, in which Marwick referred to the director as "His Paranoid Obscureness." (The mocking titles given the director by members of the team paralleled colonial honorific titles—such as the title of the governor of the colony, His Excellency, abbreviated as H. E.) Marwick complained about the number of articles the director had written for journals and had been sending to team members, apparently fearing that "his persecutors will prevent [them] from being published" (JCM:MM/JCM 11/19/46). Marwick's relationship with Gluckman was strained at the time because the director had been given authority over the administration of Marwick's Colonial Development Fellowship, which was separate from and less generously funded than the posts funded by the RLI's CDWF grant. Thus, both Marwick and Gluckman came under pressure to keep spending within limits (limits which were often exceeded even by the more generously funded RLI officers). Their conflict was compounded by their political difference at the time, and by the fact that neither enjoyed bureaucratic paperwork.

Marwick had also come to the RLI from social psychology and resisted some (though not all) of the pressure exerted upon him to convert to social anthropology. In a subsequent letter to Mitchell, Marwick admitted he was not good at "cooperative bullshit" and was glad that the director had handed back responsibility for his grant to the Colonial Office. He also referred to Gluckman as "'The Directator' (alias H.D. in chibarnes—to distinguish him from Sir John, H. E.)" (JCM:MM/JCM 2/11/47). Sir John Maybin was governor of the colony, and "chibarnes" was a reference to words perhaps invented by John Barnes. (The names of many of the central African languages which team members were learning begin with "chi," as in chicheŵa, chitonga, and so on.)

Despite these problems Marwick enriched the team's joint project with his social psychology approach. Later he and Gluckman resolved their differences, and Gluckman played a supportive role in Marwick's subsequent career. And Marwick was not the only researcher to have trouble with Gluckman's plans for RLI teamwork. Mitchell chafed against certain aspects of teamwork, complaining to Barnes that he did not like to do research on political structure but must do it because Barnes and Colson were doing it (JAB:JCM/JAB 5/18/47). Colson too had concerns about the advisability of some of their joint research ventures—in particular, the "snap censuses" they used to gather basic demographic information, which she found unreliable on subsequent investigation in her own area (JAB:EC/JAB 11/7/48). Holleman, like Marwick funded by different sources but initially placed under Gluckman's field supervision, had rebelled against Gluckman's advice immediately during his first discussions with the director and had gone his own way in his Shona studies, both in intellectual terms and fieldwork style. His work took a much more traditional approach to African societies than the other RLI studies, for he focused on reconstructing precolonial religious and political structures. Nonetheless, he later produced the finest example of the RLI approach to the study of colonial administration (Holleman 1969).

Some researchers also felt hemmed in by the director's favorite theories and what seemed like a rigid adherence to ideas he shared with his mentors and teachers. Mitchell put it this way in a series of letters to Barnes, reacting to his correspondence with Gluckman: "Incidentally I got myself into hot water by making some derogatory witticisms about Fortes' book. In his lashing he [Gluckman] said that it was only 'an aspect of the social structure' [with which Fortes dealt]. I wrote back saying that it is impossible owing to the dynamic nature of social structure (i.e. social relations) to have an aspect of it. As soon as you isolate any aspect for study the whole social structure changes" (JAB:JCM/JAB, ?/?/46). Here Mitchell probably referred to criticism he made of Fortes' *Dynamics of Clanship among the Tallensi*; as he later put it, "the Tallensi have been tortured on the rack of clanship" (JCMI 2; see also Fortes 1945, 1949).

Mitchell's daring even stretched to criticism of the preeminent British anthropologist, E. E. Evans-Pritchard, who had been one of Gluckman's mentors at Oxford. Objecting to the interpretive focus of both Fortes' and Evans-Pritchard's work, he wrote to Barnes: "Boy do I feel guilty at the apostasy that I commit . . . their writings are interpretive. I feel (so far) that our writings ought to be descriptive. I think it was you who was telling me that Firth was made to write his book in two parts. The first part is descriptive and the second interpretive. I see now that it is a good idea" (JAB:JCM/JAB 12/12/46). Firth's two-part practice had a long history in anthropological writing, but in any case, the use of detailed descriptions that preceded or accompanied theoretical interpretation would become a hallmark of the RLI approach, partly due to Mitchell's "apostasy."

Nevertheless, this approach also derived from Gluckman's own work. Despite his admiration of Fortes' and Evans-Pritchard's studies, Gluckman previously had organized his "Analysis of a Social Situation in Modern Zululand" into separate descriptive and analytical sections, which provided a template for later RLI work. Moreover, from the beginning of his training of the team, the director had stressed the importance of gathering and writing up more than enough descriptive material to support theoretical inferences in the researchers' work, a practice that allowed for subsequent reanalysis, either by the researchers themselves or by others. This practice of reanalysis became characteristic of the Manchester School approach. For example, Gluckman had insisted that the team gather extensive descriptive material during the Lamba field-training session, beyond what at the time they may have foreseen they would need. Barnes and Mitchell later found this material extremely useful when writing a paper based on that research. This perhaps explains why Mitchell objected so strenuously to Fortes's and Evans-Pritchard's failure to put "the dope" first and then draw the inferences (JAB:JCM/JAB 12/12/46).

In a subsequent letter about his fieldwork Mitchell noted with some irony that "just because I consider it rather dangerous to touch I have been finding nothing else but witchcraft these days." The dangers of witchcraft stemmed not, however, from his subjects, the Yao, but from other anthropologists:

> With Gluckman and Evans-Pritchard as holders of the field [of witchcraft studies] do you think they would be very pleased if I tried to come into the arena against them [?] As far as I can see the Yao idea of witchcraft can only work *within* the kinship system (with certain exceptions) which seems to go slap bang against what Gluckman wrote in one of the journals—something to the effect that witchcraft worked across the kinship system and [the] ancestor cult inside it hence the increase of witchcraft. When I pointed this out to him he carefully explained that the Yao don't have witches. Certainly not witches by the Azande definition apparently. I saw Max Marwick at the Lake [Lake Nyasa] for a weekend and his account of the Chewa situation is identical with the Yao in nearly all aspects and it is certainly so of witchcraft. (JAB:JCM/JAB 5/18/47)

Differences over witchcraft aside, Mitchell's concerns here have to do with disciplinary territoriality—and the politics of going against a director who, along with his illustrious mentor, Evans-Pritchard, could be essential to a young researcher's subsequent career.[5]

Private correspondence can function as a way of blowing off steam and must be interpreted within its context (see Stocking 1983:49). When Mitchell and

5. Many subsequent scholars have complained that Evans-Pritchard's definition does not fit their material, especially in southern and central Africa. See Evans-Pritchard (1937:387), Turner (1964), and Geschiere (1997:225).

others used "derogatory witticisms" against Gluckman and other powerful fig-ures, they responded to the tensions involved in the formation of the RLI team. Male team members may have also felt a comradery based on military service, which Gluckman did not share, and which may have contributed to the ten-sions between him and them. These comments also reflect the more general pressures inherent in the early stages of fieldwork—pressures they all were ex-periencing at the time. The frustrations of language-learning and their inform-ants' resistance to some aspects of the research led Mitchell and the others, on occasion, to use strong language about their informants, and it was primarily at this difficult stage and often in the same letters that they used strong language about the director.[6] The impression this language gives is not a good indicator of the quality of their long-term relationships with either the director or their informants. During later interviews, many of the former RLI researchers men-tioned difficulties, but stressed that Gluckman's fine intelligence, perceptive comments on their work, and unfailing support for their careers compensated for any abrasiveness or overbearing qualities in his style of direction.

Gluckman's move to Oxford in 1947 and then to Manchester in 1949 meant the end of his directorship of the RLI. This change transformed rather than ended his leading role, however, because he developed Manchester's new social anthropology department as a colony of the RLI, transplanting most of the members of the first team into lectureships or fellowships there and making the RLI approach and its theoretical products into the core of what would become the Manchester School. The RLI continued to develop in close association with the Manchester department, with Gluckman offering advice about its di-rection and preparing Manchester students for research posts there. He gener-ally warned his students to avoid political activities in Africa and advised them instead to join the anticolonial movement in Britain.[7]

6. Mitchell sometimes used racist language when he expressed his frustrations about the "neg-atively hostile" Yao. This was at a time when the Yao's impressions of him were being manipulated by an African court messenger sent with him by the colonial administration (JCM:JCM/JAB 12/12/46). The Yao quite sensibly treated him as they would a colonial administrator and kept him at a distance until his wife and new baby arrived and broke the ice. Another problem with inter-preting Mitchell's strong language is that it was often laden with irony, and he frequently parodied colonial attitudes in his choice of words. Both can be missed in written language, which does not contain the signals in tone of voice or facial expression that give clues to the speaker's attitude. An African's view of him at the time perhaps gives a truer idea of Mitchell's relations with colleagues and informants. In a letter to Mitchell, Colson commented that her research assistant, Benjamin Shipopa, compensated for all the difficulties of fieldwork she was experiencing at the time, but that he adored Clyde more than herself or any of the other researchers he had met because Clyde was always laughing (JCM:EC/JCM 4/26/47).

7. This advice was mentioned in several interviews with researchers who studied at Manches-ter prior to going to central Africa.

Like Gluckman himself, however, subsequent researchers often ran into trouble in the field, and subsequent directors had to deal with their problems. In 1952, the RLI's fourth director, Mitchell, recounted in a letter to the third director, Colson (then in a Manchester lectureship): "Watson and v[an] Velsen have made entries to their societies . . . Watson typically enough by talking himself into it. Watson has also talked himself into hot water twice with the Administration and eventually I had to fly up to Abercorn to sort it all out. Not very successful. . . . Don't tell Max" (JCM:JCM/EC 11/26/52).[8]

The RLI Rapids

Work in the history of science has shown that various socially and culturally prescribed forms of witnessing must occur during scientific experiments in or-der for a scientist to claim to have discovered scientific truths. Witnessing re-quires the presence of certain types of others—observers with particular cre-dentials or social statuses—as, for example, the gentleman scientists of the early modern period. These gentleman scientists observed not only the key scenes of scientific practice, but also in their daily conduct the key rules of ci-vility commensurate with their status in society. And their status in society was considered by other gentleman scientists to ensure their objectivity and the va-lidity of their observations. The latter process is evidence of the importation of standards from a prestigious arena of *social* relations—gentlemanly manners—to the emerging arena of *scientific* relations, which was in need of a language and a set of practices that would ensure its credibility. Thus, the construction of scientific truth became linked to particular standards of civility, while scien-tific methods themselves grew out of historically and culturally specific forms of etiquette. In this way the language of science came to reflect the ways that gentlemen spoke and wrote about their activities (Shapin 1994:xxviii).

Scholars such as Steven Shapin have suggested that many of the social val-ues and relationships that shaped early modern science continue to have rele-vance for understanding twentieth-century science (Shapin 1994:409–17). Early modern scientists constructed and legitimated their findings in the con-text of small face-to-face groups, reflective of premodern social relations that were being displaced in the early modern period by the less personal, more in-stitutionalized relations associated with urbanization and industrialization. Nevertheless, "core-sets"—the small groups of specialists who make up most

8. The two research officers were Jaap van Velsen and William Watson, both of whom later published monographs (Watson 1958; van Velsen 1964). Abercorn (present-day Mbala) was one of the colonial administrative centers in the country's Northern Province.

scientific subdisciplines today—still practice face-to-face relationships and engage in legitimating practices not unlike gentlemanly witnessing and practices of civility. Trust is established among members of these core-sets, linked as they are by networks created during education and apprenticeship, and reinforced by personal communication at conferences and written communication in specialist journals.

This model of scientific legitimation, however, has been largely based on research on laboratory sciences from the early modern period to the present. Anthropology, as a field science with social and cultural behavior as its subject matter, both conforms to and diverges from it. For the discipline as a whole, observation (both as witnessing and as adherence to etiquette) is essential to legitimating not just the finished work of the anthropologist, but also the anthropologist's right to a place in the field, the crucial site for the researcher's construction of knowledge. In the case of the RLI, evidence for this can be found at several key points in the development of the first team's fieldwork practices.

"Dictums" involving tents and latrines point to the importance Gluckman placed on rules of etiquette and standards of civility in the field. The "laboratory in the field" was also the home of the anthropologist, just as the laboratory of the early modern scientist was part of the gentleman scientist's home. A gentleman's home and his behavior there, as elsewhere, demonstrated his moral status in society, and thus, his credibility as a producer of (or witness to) scientific truth. Similarly, the moral and scientific status of professional anthropologists had to be demonstrated while in the field, through both their research practices and their private (at home or in camp) behavior. Marking the behavioral boundaries between European researchers and their African subjects, latrines, in particular, symbolized conflicts about appropriate field behavior, both in research and daily life. Moreover, they were one item among many distinctions in living and research practices that separated anthropological participant observation from administrator-ethnographers' more socially distant style of fieldwork. Both styles required making one's home in the field, but participant observation also demanded being "at home" with one's African subjects in a more intimate way than that required by administrative touring in the late colonial period.

Barnes's letter about the naive cadet continued with witty speculation about his Freudian anxieties regarding excrement, anxieties that Barnes thought the cadet projected as a fear of latrines on the part of his African subjects. An important point can be found in this humor. Whether or not people—African or European—used latrines, and what kind of latrine they preferred, made a difference in how they would be perceived by others. Thus, Gluckman and the RLI researchers had to tread a fine line between acceptable and unacceptable behavior in a segregated society, living under the eyes of a tiny European community that policed itself through gossip, social ostracism, and the occasional deportation of undesirables. Where to draw the line in participant observation became doubly important for the RLI group because of the left-wing and/or antisegregationist politics of some team members.

In addition, the notion of a core-set can be useful for understanding the purpose of the RLI team's training in South Africa, especially the introductions to eminent scholars suggested by Gluckman. These introductions, along with meetings with Gluckman's associates and mentors in Britain, helped to establish the kind of face-to-face relationships on which scientific trust is built. But the usefulness of the idea of a core-set breaks down when one considers the behavior of the RLI anthropologists in the field. Unlike laboratory scientists, whose relationships this concept was intended to elucidate, field scientists work in a "laboratory" quite different from those of today's physicists and chemists, or from those at-home laboratories of earlier gentlemen scientists.

The "human laboratory across the Zambezi," as Gluckman called it, could not be closed off for the purposes of observation, experiment, or witnessing. The field was and is a laboratory with permeable boundaries. This is true not just in the geographic sense, in that human societies have blurred edges and exist in territories that may not be clearly demarcated or bounded at all. Nor is it true only in the theoretical sense, in that entities such as "tribes" and other anthropological units of analysis cannot be taken as bounded or isolated in the real world. (Indeed, RLI anthropologists developed the concept of the "network" precisely to deal with the difficulty of finding clear boundaries for human societies.) It is also true in the sense that observation and witnessing by anthropologists could not be closed off from the judgments of others whom the anthropologists considered outside the profession. This was particularly true in the early days of social anthropology, when administrator-ethnographers' and missionary-ethnographers' claims to professional status and priority in the field were taken seriously, both by colonial governments and metropolitan universities. And it still is true in fieldwork, where debate continues over the role of nonprofessionals in the field (anthropologists' spouses, assistants, friends, subjects, and rivals) and over the status of their contributions to the finished work of anthropology and the power of their witnessing to affirm, limit, or deny anthropologists' access to the field.

Thus, for anthropology, the process of becoming a modern science has not been simply one of transforming gentlemanly civility into scientific credibility. More importantly the task has been to incorporate into the methods of fieldwork some way to deal with the standards of gatekeepers in the field and to acknowledge or deny the utility of their contributions to anthropological knowledge. The significance of the RLI experience for this disciplinary goal is exceptional. Gluckman and the team developed their methods during a key period in the development of participant observation as anthropology's central method, and this process took place in relation to the discipline's struggle for professional status and separation from administrative and missionary ethnography. That this consciousness of method and the processes involved in its innovation became one of the hallmarks of the Manchester School should not be surprising.

Finally, as is the case with Malinowski's photographs, the images discussed throughout this essay also make the argument. The photo of Gluckman's tent, with its allusion to other photos of ethnographers' tents, illustrates the legitimating strategy of the professionalizing social anthropologists of his time. They claimed credibility on the basis of the participant observation method and the experience of intensive fieldwork by a lone ethnographer, to whose presence in the village the photograph of the tent attests. On the other hand, the image of the wicker toilet seat represents the anthropologist's unavoidable confrontation with the etiquette of a colonial society that had to be mastered or sidestepped by the anthropologist if he or she was to remain in the field. And the image of the wicker tent indicates the most powerful of the gatekeepers of the African field encountered by social anthropologists in the period between the world wars— the colonial administrators who, as administrator-ethnographers, were also anthropologists' chief rivals in the production of knowledge about Africans.

For the RLI researchers, however, the most significant of these observing others was the director himself, and one verbal image that recurs in the interviews I conducted during my research on the RLI's history can be interpreted as a metaphor for the creativity and tensions that forged RLI teamwork into a major research school. This was an image of the "RLI Rapids" where the researchers went swimming during that first and formative conference in Livingstone (JCM:JCM/RLI secretary 3/17/47). Gluckman had initiated these conferences in 1947 in Livingstone, Northern Rhodesia, not far from Victoria Falls on the Zambezi River. My informants' stories of their relationship with Gluckman often focused on the events of that first conference. More than one informant recalled Gluckman being shaved by a barber in the middle of a seminar (Barnes, Colson, personal communications). Such recollections suggest both an aspect of the director's personality and the need of some team members to poke fun at such a dominant character.

Mitchell captured one such moment in a photograph he took of Gluckman at the first conference. Gluckman, who had used photography to capture the presence of the European in the African field, now became the subject of Mitchell's ironic gaze. The photo shows the director sitting in the rapids, smoking a pipe with all the confidence of an Oxford don seated in the proverbial armchair. But perhaps the director's expression contains a hint of ambivalence regarding the photographer's motives, as he looks self-consciously into the camera's eye?

Clyde Mitchell, throwing stones in the rapids above Victoria Falls, during the 1947 conference at Livingstone. (Courtesy Jean Mitchell.)

Max Gluckman in the rapids above Victoria Falls, during the 1947 RLI Conference in Livingstone. (Courtesy Jean Mitchell.)

Acknowledgments

Some of the topics dealt with here I discuss at further length in Schumaker 2001. I am grateful to Henrika Kuklick, Elizabeth Colson, John Barnes, and Richard Handler for their insightful comments on draft versions of this essay.

References Cited

Allan, W., M. Gluckman, D. U. Peters, & C. G. Trapnell. 1948. Land holding and land usage among the Plateau Tonga of Mazabuka District: A reconnaissance survey, 1945. *Rhodes-Livingstone Paper* 14.

Brown, R. 1973. Anthropology and colonial rule: Godfrey Wilson and the Rhodes-Livingstone Institute, Northern Rhodesia. In *Anthropology and the colonial encounter*, ed. T. Asad, 173–98. New York.

———. 1979. Passages in the life of a White anthropologist: Max Gluckman in Northern Rhodesia. *J. Af. Hist.* 20:525–41.

Carstens, P., G. Klinghardt, & M. West, eds. 1987. *Trails in the Thirstland: The anthropological field diaries of Winifred Hoernlé*. Centre Af. Studs. Communications No. 14.

Clifford, J. 1983. On ethnographic authority. *Representations* 1:118–46.

Colson, E. 1953. *The Makah Indians: A study of an Indian tribe in modern American society*. Minneapolis, MN.

Dubow, S. 1995. *Scientific racism in modern South Africa*. Cambridge, UK.

Epstein, A. L., ed. 1967. *The craft of social anthropology*. London.

Evans-Pritchard, E. E. 1937. *Witchcraft, oracles and magic among the Azande*. Oxford.

Fabian, J. 2000. *Out of our minds: Reason and madness in the exploration of central Africa*. Berkeley.

Fortes, M. 1945. *The dynamics of clanship among the Tallensi*. London.

———. 1949. *The web of kinship among the Tallensi*. London.

Geschiere, P. 1997. *The modernity of witchcraft: Politics and the occult in postcolonial Africa*. Charlottesville, VA.

Gluckman, M. 1942. Economy of the central Barotse plain. *Rhodes-Livingstone Paper* 7.

———. 1944. Essays on Lozi land and royal property. *Rhodes-Livingstone Paper* 10.

———. 1945. Seven-year research plan of the Rhodes-Livingstone Institute of Social Studies in central Africa. *Rhodes-Livingstone J.* 4:1–33.

———. 1946. Human laboratory across the Zambesi. *Libertas* 6 (4):38–49.

———. 1949. Malinowski's sociological theories. *Rhodes-Livingstone Paper* 16.

———. 1955. *The judicial process among the Barotse of Northern Rhodesia*. Manchester.

———. 1958. Analysis of a social situation in modern Zululand. *Rhodes-Livingstone Paper* 28 (previously published in *Bantu Studs*. [*Af. Studs.*] 1940 and 1942).

———. 1965. *The ideas in Barotse jurisprudence*. New Haven, CT.

Gordon, R. 1990. Early social anthropology in South Africa. *Af. Studs.* 49(1):15–48.

Grimshaw, A. & K. Hart. 1993. *Anthropology and the crisis of the intellectuals*. Prickly Pear Pamphlet No. 1. Cambridge, UK.

Hailey, M. (Lord). 1938. *African survey*. London.

Hammond-Tooke, W. D. 1997. *Imperfect interpreters: South Africa's anthropologists, 1920–1990.* Johannesburg.

Harwood, J. 1993. *Styles of scientific thought: The German genetics community, 1900–33.* London.

Holleman, J. F. 1969. *Chief, council and commissioner.* Assen, The Netherlands.

Hunt, N. 1999. *A colonial lexicon of birth ritual, medicalization, and mobility in the Congo.* Durham, NC.

Krige, E. J. & Krige J. D. 1943. *The realm of the Rain Queen.* London.

Kuklick, H. 1991. *The savage within: The social history of British anthropology, 1885–1945.* Cambridge, UK.

Macmillan, H. 1989. 'Paralyzed conservatives': W. M. Macmillan, the social scientists and 'the common society.' In *Africa and empire,* eds. H. Macmillan & S. Marks, 72–90. London.

———. 1995. Return to the Malungwana drift—Max Gluckman, the Zulu nation and the common society. *Af. Affairs* 94 (374):39–65.

Mair, L., ed. 1938. *Materials for the study of culture contact.* London.

———, ed. 1946. *Methods of study of culture contact in Africa. Memorandum 15 of the International Af. Inst.*

Malinowski, B. 1922. *Argonauts of the western Pacific: An account of native enterprise and adventure in the archipelagoes of Melanesian New Guinea.* London.

———. 1930. Rationalization of anthropology and administration. *Africa* 3:405–29.

———. 1938. *The Dynamics of culture contact.* New Haven, CT.

Murray, B. K. 1997. *Wits: The 'open' years.* Johannesburg.

Richards, A. 1939. *Land, labour and diet: An economic study of the Bemba tribe.* London.

———. 1963. Malinowski. *New Society* 41:16–17.

———. 1977. The Rhodes-Livingstone Institute: An experiment in research, 1933–38. *Af. Social Research* 24:275–78.

Schumaker, L. 1996. A tent with a view: Colonial officers, anthropologists, and the making of the field in northern Rhodesia, 1937–1960. *Osiris* 11:237–58.

———. 2001. *Africanizing anthropology: Fieldwork, networks, and the making of cultural knowledge in central Africa.* Durham, NC.

Shapin, S. 1988. The house of experiment in seventeenth-century England. *Isis* 79: 373–404.

———. 1994. *A social history of truth: Civility and science in seventeenth-century England.* Chicago.

Siegel, B. 1989. The 'wild' and 'lazy' Lamba: Ethnic stereotypes on the central African copperbelt. In *The creation of tribalism in southern Africa,* ed. L. Vail, 372–94. London.

Snelson, P. D. 1974. *Educational development in Northern Rhodesia.* Lusaka.

Stocking, G. W. 1983. The ethnographer's magic: Fieldwork in British anthropology from Tylor to Malinowski. In *The ethnographer's magic and other essays in the history of anthropology,* 12–59. Madison, WI (1992).

Tilley, H. 2001. Africa as a 'living laboratory': The African research survey and the British colonial empire: Consolidating environmental, medical, and anthropological debates, 1920–1940. Doctoral dissertation, Oxford U.

Trapnell, C. & J. N. Clothier. 1957. *The soils, vegetation and agricultural systems of north-western Rhodesia*. Lusaka.

Turner, E. 1987. *The spirit and the drum: A memoir of Africa*. Tucson, AZ.

Turner, V. 1964. Witchcraft and sorcery: Taxonomy versus dynamics. *Africa* 34:314–25.

Van Velsen, J. 1964. *The politics of kinship: A study in social manipulation among the lakeside Tonga of Nyasaland*. Manchester.

Watson, W. 1958. *Tribal cohesion in a money economy: A study of the Mambwe people of Northern Rhodesia*. Manchester.

Wilson, G. & M. Wilson. 1945. *The analysis of social change: Based on observations in central Africa*. Cambridge, UK.

Wilson, M. 1936. *Reaction to conquest: Effects of contact with Europeans on the Pondo of South Africa*. London.

———. 1977. The first three years, 1938–41. *Af. Social Research* 24:279–84.

Interviews

All of the following interviews were conducted by the author:

JCMI 1   J. Clyde Mitchell interview, October 31, 1990, Oxford, UK.
JCMI 2   J. Clyde Mitchell interview, November 27, 1990, Oxford, UK.
JABI   J. A. Barnes interview, August 12, 1993, Cambridge, UK.

Manuscript Sources

The following abbreviations are used for manuscript sources:
JAB   J. A. Barnes Papers, University of Cambridge
JCM   J. Clyde Mitchell Papers, Rhodes House Library, University of Oxford

BOASIAN COSMOGRAPHIC ANTHROPOLOGY AND THE SOCIOCENTRIC COMPONENT OF MIND

MICHAEL SILVERSTEIN

Six years after his Kiel dissertation on psychophysics, Franz Boas, at the age of 29, and inspired by Alexander von Humboldt, announced in his famous 1887 paper, "The study of geography," the epistemological program of Boasian "cosmographic" anthropology.[1] This "anthropo-geography" took as its discursive object the individual-in-society's unique consciousness of phenomena in the world—"the native's point of view," as Malinowski would later (1922:25) call it. It situated that outlook on experience at the intersection of two kinds of frameworks. One is the macro-social framework of societies, namely their

---

1. Boas himself (1940) reprinted the paper as one of three "miscellaneous" early writings "because they indicate the general attitude underlying [his] later work" (1940:vi). It is the very last paper in the volume, perhaps a last-minute decision (Boas's preface actually referred to "two" such miscellaneous papers). Presuming its fundamental nature (see Stocking 1996:5), Stocking, too, reprints it (1996:7–16) as the very first item of Volksgeist *as Method and Ethic: Essays on Boasian Ethnography and the German Anthropological Tradition*. Many of the paper's somewhat slogan-like formulations were realized only gradually, as Boas could transform the personnel and central intellectual issues of American anthropology. For some of its institutional aspects as Americanist anthropology, see now Darnell 1998.

Michael Silverstein is currently Charles F. Grey Distinguished Service Professor in the Departments of Anthropology, Linguistics, and Psychology, and in the Committee on General Studies in the Humanities at The University of Chicago. He has long been interested in the historical sociology of knowledge of anthropology and of linguistics, on which he has published a continuing series of articles and chapters in such places as *International Journal of American Linguistics*, *Language*, *Historiographia Linguistica*, and *American Anthropologist*

history—not their functionally or universally determined evolution. The other is the micro-social framework, in which individual "psychic processes"—revealed in perception, conceptualization, and affect—provide the basis for the individual human organism to be goal-directed in its context of being. The realm of Boasian "psychology" lies at the intersection of these two frameworks, where native subjectivity lies and gives intensional, categorial coherence to phenomena at least in part *as* "culture."[2]

For some decades, as is well known, the predominant Boasian discourse developed in the first mode, the historical.[3] In certain areas, for example, the sound systems of languages, such Boas students as Edward Sapir began to develop innovatively its intersection with the second realm as well, founding phonology, the "psychology" of speech sounds on this basis (Silverstein 1986, 1992). For the most part, however, there was a 30-year period of predominantly North American collecting, classifying, and comparing in every anthropological realm from material culture to human phenotypic physical form to kinship to mythology to linguistic grammar and lexis. The material was used to constitute negative theoretical arguments against universal, unilinear social evolutionism in both its pre-Darwinian and Darwin-inspired forms.

By demonstrating the relative independence of race, culture, and language as they varied across North American time and space, such phenomena were used to show the out-of-synch localizations, the contingencies, of their historical development. In this way, Boas and his students showed again and again that processes of culture-history are counterarguments to any would-be evolutionary scheme. Thus, a (mere) typology in any one of these areas could not be interpreted as a transparent picture of its diachrony, and even less so of the overall history of peoples in all these respects. In extending the critique to ever more fundamental levels, Boas and his students repeatedly attacked the very constitutive notions of received typologies in all of these areas.

In this mode of work, one studies the coming-into-being in time and space of "complexes" of racial, linguistic, or cultural "traits," defining and locating

2. Hence we can understand Boas's critique (1889) of the "alternating sounds" phenomenon, discussed so (ap)perceptively by Stocking (1968:157–60), and the relationship of Boasian "anthropo-psychophysics," as we might term it, to Helmholtz, Wundt et al. (see Mackert 1993, 1994; Silverstein 1986, 1992).

3. We differentiate here history—causally connected specificities, no matter on which scale they must be described—from "evolution." Boas's fierce critiques of the older social evolutionism were sometimes directed against his own students. Boas's Columbia first-"born," Kroeber, strayed to what for Boas was the evolutionary camp with his notions of "superorganic" (1917) cultural forms moving in historical trajectories to configurational climaxes of a clearly quasi-functionalist, macro-institutional nature (1931, 1935). Responding to Kroeber's 1935 piece, Boas called him sharply to task (1936).

something culminatively configurational about a group's phenotype, language, or culture.[4] One looked to the way these dynamisms showed no impediment at the accepted boundaries, even of received racial groupings (these, too, are complexes of biological traits that move a population through time in only statistical relative synch). Of course, diffusion shows that there is no impediment at the boundaries of social groups as well. At the end of this first Boasian period, when A. L. Kroeber published his synthesizing textbook, *Anthropology* (1923), Edward Sapir wrote to the author,

> [The book] stands out because it tacitly eliminates a great deal of that fruitless and cumbersome discussion about social origins and developments that used to be considered peculiarly the province of anthropology and because it not only makes the gesture of anthropology's being a historical discipline but actually ties up the data of anthropology with those of history. So much so that some people will ask, "What after all *is* anthropology as distinct from culture history?" and your implicit answer is, of course, that there is really no difference between the two disciplines except that anthropology asks a few more fundamental questions about the relation of culture to heredity. (ES/AK 6/15/24; see Golla 1984:412)

Such questions, of course, allude to what Boasians termed the "psychology" of cultural beings, and these questions develop the other framework, the second one, already implicit in Boasianism. The tilt to investigation of this second framework takes place, I wish to show, in 1924, the very year of Sapir's appreciative letter to Kroeber. And it takes place at first probably much outside of the awareness of the leading players—Boas and the biographically intertwined Benedict, Mead, and Sapir.

Why and how? I would like to sketch here the various events and forces that came together that year, subsequently evolved, and ultimately produced Boasian "culture and personality" studies.[5] This constitutes part of the distinctive

---

4. We might note that the problem of "when" a "complex"—see Tylor's (1888) 'adhesions'—properly or stably configures, presents the riddle of 'culture'; compare Boas's trenchant critique (1896:270–80). One can list attempts to solve this riddle in the various theories of autonomous culturological principles of structure, pattern, configuration, etc. as a time-independent metric—from configurationalism, to structural-functionalism, to structuralism, to biosocial reductionism. In one way, some of the later—second-phase, as I shall call it—Boasians can be seen as attempting to provide a kind of reductive end-run around the riddle of culture, declining to see it as a level of organization immanent in, but distinct from, the individual's psychobiological makeup.

5. I call attention to four interesting takes on "culture and personality." First, Alexander Goldenweiser's (1941) posthumously published "Recent trends in American anthropology," the close-up and savvy perspective of a "native" of the psychoanalytically informed New York cultural as well as anthropological scenes of the 1920s and 1930s. Second, Melville Herskovits' postwar pedagogical account in his chapter on "Culture and the Individual" of the textbook, *Man and His Works* (1948:43–60). Third, David Aberle's (1960) rejectionist explication of culture-and-personality in

history of psychologically oriented anthropological investigations that see
"mind"—in its categorially structured knowledge and cognitive characteristics, its affective modes and the dynamics of their operation,—as at least partly
sociohistorically located and sociohistorically emergent.[6]

It is clear that psychology, not anthropology, was the educated discourse of
reflective selfhood throughout avant garde, Euro-left-of-center culture maven-
dom, where so many Boasians placed themselves. (The early Boasian brethren's
personal epistolary currency—acts of paying mutual attention—was self- and
reciprocal analyses, with critiques and denunciations straight out of Freud, Jung,
and the like.) Yet I would emphasize that whatever the "etiology" or "epidemi-
ology" of these approaches in the central characters' fascination with various
psychologies, a second-phase Boasian anthropology grew out of it. Here was anthropology being turned to urgent societal "relevance" long before its self-styled
applied "reinventions," first as post-Boasian wartime[7] or Murdockian Cold War[8]

---

the Leslie White Festschrift, seeing it as a kind of culture-as-grammar aberration on the road to
materialist-friendly sociocultural anthropology. Fourth, the psychoanalysis-centered account in
William C. Manson's essay on Abram Kardiner (1986:72–94). See also Caffrey (1989) and Howard
(1984), focusing on Benedict and Mead, respectively.

6. Its other aspect, "worldview" (weltanschauung), emerges in the Boasian idiom as the problem
of culture-specific "secondary rationalizations" disturbing to a scientific culture history, as clearly articulated in the "Introduction" to the Handbook of American Indian Languages (see Boas 1911a:64–
73). Until World War II it was especially identified with Boasian anthropological linguistics and
Benjamin Lee Whorf (1956). (For discussion see especially Joseph 1996; Lee 1997:180–201; Lucy
1992:11–68; Silverstein 1979; 2000:86–109; n.d.) After World War II, the "cultural-consciousness-
as-false-consciousness" aspect of the problem was suppressed in America (did this have a Marxist
aroma during the Cold War?). Bloomfieldian structural linguistics (and its then-ascendant behav-
iorist epistemological penumbra) provided the nonpolitical, analogically formalist key to the problem of conceptual variability. What eventually became "cognitive anthropology" (see D'Andrade
1995; Tyler 1969; Tyler 1978 [discussed by Silverstein 1981]) sought to continue at least the "cultural relativity" theme in the sense of specific cognitive conceptual schemata shared and transmitted by members of a social group.

7. Benedict, Mead, Rhoda Métraux, Geoffrey Gorer, and others associated with the Columbia
University and Barnard College Departments of Anthropology all contributed their professional
efforts to various wartime projects, for example, "culture [and personality] at a distance"—see Yans-
McLaughlin (1986)—as did anthropologists and linguists all over the United States. Together
with language pedagogy projects during those years either at the various university sites or out of
"165 Broadway," under the ACLS and then the War Department (see Hall 1991; Joos 1986), these
established the template of "language and area" studies in crash courses for personnel shipping out
overseas.

8. The "Coordinated Investigation of Micronesian Anthropology" trained postwar graduate
students at Harvard and Yale, under the general direction, respectively, of Clyde Kluckhohn and
especially George Peter Murdock (1948). Ward Goodenough, John L. Fischer, Paul Garvin,
William Davenport, David Schneider, Robert Ritzenthaler, John Useem, Arthur Vidich, Homer
Barnett, and many others, were supported by the National Research Council, Pacific Science Board
for fieldwork conceptualized as strategic exploration for successful anticommunist trusteeship of
these U.N. territories (see Bashkow 1991:178–90 on Schneider, for example).

policy science, and second as Vietnam-era empowering cultural science of, by, and for "the people."[9]

It is perhaps best to sketch 1924 Boasianism by using the activities of Franz Boas himself as a vantage point.[10] At the age of 66 Boas was, as usual, operating in all four subfields of anthropology as some combination of researcher, author, editor, impresario, and organizer; he maintained substantive connections, then, to all the relevant related disciplinary fields.[11] Second, he was a public figure in New York civic life, especially in affiliating with good causes of one or another sort, for example, post–World War I reconstruction of Europe, child welfare, et cetera. This made him an intimate of a range of wealthy, philanthropically inclined people of the group that included left-liberal, humanist, German-Jewish and related networks during their most active interwar period. Third, and perhaps most important for our story, he was a scientist-citizen, whose learning, technique, knowledge, and, importantly, dispassionately mounted authority in his realms of science—recall his wonderful phrase, "icy enthusiasm"—were available on demand in relatively public forums beyond the confines of academic anthropology at Columbia and other similar places.

In his guise as scientist-citizen, in 1924 Boas was driven by a single overriding

9. Dell Hymes, ed., *Reinventing Anthropology* of 1972 was published as one of the "Pantheon [Publishers] Antitextbooks" for the newly empowered, even radicalized youth professoriate and student bodies of the era. "Other Pantheon Antitextbooks" listed on the half-title page, *verso*, include *The Dissenting Academy; Towards a New Past; Power and Community; America's Asia;* and *The Politics of Literature*—the titles or subtitles of which, couched in terms of "dissent," summon college and university youth to ramparts of minority political truth and [therefore?] empowerment—heady stuff indeed! The authors and editors position themselves as breaking that *assenting* or *consenting* political silence of which they are, in essence, accusing their fields and their scholarly elders. See now Hymes's (1999) reminiscences of the circumstances.

10. This work follows upon the fundamental works on Boas by my colleague George Stocking (1968, 1974), as well as those his work has stimulated (e.g., Stocking, ed. 1996). Among other investigative techniques, I have used a careful rereading (for this specific project, items from mid-1923 to mid-1925) of the Boas Professional Papers available on microfilm (originals in the Library of the American Philosophical Society, Philadelphia) as the starting point. Following out where possible from my knowledge of various other Boasians' writings and letter collections, some of the latter even partially published, for example, Benedict, Kroeber, Lowie, Mead, Sapir, I worked to collateral sources indicated by those tiers of reading. I have also followed public events in similar reading of *The New York Times* and collateral political and social history.

11. And, where subdisciplinary relations were threatened, Boas was concerned to protect the disciplinary field, anthropology. In early 1924, he lends his name to the "call" for an organizational meeting of what was to be the Linguistic Society of America (Leonard Bloomfield/FB 1/18/24). In late 1924, he tries to convince Ales Hrdlicka not to establish a separate American Association of Physical Anthropology. Worrying about the distance between physical anthropologists' and ethnologists' views on race, in particular, Boas preferred that the *American Journal of Physical Anthropology* remain a publication of the American Anthropological Association (AH/FB 12/16/24; FB/AH 12/18/24; FB/AH 12/24/24).

theme: race[12] and "mentality," the latter in its nineteenth-century sense. This nexus was then culminating in a general postwar hysteria in the United States—particularly in Congress—about the mental, moral, and especially political fitness of aliens, immigrants, and minorities.[13] Early in 1924, a lawyer named M. Vartan Malcom wrote to notify Boas of a "suit [that] has been commenced by the Attorney-General of the United States, with a view of taking it to the United States Supreme Court, to test the right of an Armenian born in Asia Minor to American citizenship" (MVM/FB 1/24/24). This was based on racially restrictive naturalization legislation already in existence that excluded all people of "Asiatic race" from citizenship. If Asia Minor was a part of Asia, the reasoning presumably went, then people from Asia Minor should probably be considered a special subcategory of "Asiatics"! At the time, the rhetoric of exclusion was couched in terms of mentality and fitness of various "races," and the issue in consideration was which "race" Armenians belonged to, so as to determine the legal applicability of the already mandated exclusion. Boas's opinion, and eventually his legal deposition of scientific fact, was thus solicited for U.S. v. Cartozian on whether or not Armenians of "Asia Minor" were Caucasian. (Since the exclusionary statute already existed, Boas's charge in the case by Mr. Cartozian's lawyer was to put Armenians into a favorable classificatory position with respect to that statute.) Boas recruited Roland B. Dixon, then at Harvard's Peabody Museum, to work on the case as well. The letter archives show them occupied with it far into the year; Boas did not hear from the defendant's chief counsel, William D. Guthrie, until October 30 that a decision was expected in federal trial court in early November.

12. Somewhat anachronistically, many authors now forget that the term had not yet been clearly differentiated in popular usage from ethnicity, nationality, etc. It seems to have more clearly become so today as a result of generations of dialectic interaction with more learned and scientific usage, as consciousness of the conceptual terminologies of both biological and social sciences has been more informative of contemporary folk usage. (Consider words like sibling, subculture, and many others, lexical chestnuts of scholarly prose that have moved into pop-cultural usage.) In the period we are considering, the French, thus, could be a "race," no different from "Asiatics" being a "race." The post-Darwinian identification of race with what in the biological realm would be variety (taxonomically—and in evolutionary process—below the level of species) exists in an unstable (dis)equilibrium in the larger discursive cauldron of racial and cultural politics in the 1920s. See Barkan 1992, where the discussion seems to founder anachronistically at the border of the scientific and lay conceptualizations in many respects; and see Glazer 1997 for some ramifications of these changing terminological and conceptual relationships in such a practical institution as public education.

13. The United States' isolationist retreat from the experience of World War I should not be forgotten here, as well as the imaginative hallucinations that the Bolshevik Revolution was threatening its shores in the form of unionism (not just the IWW Wobblies!), etc. We must not forget such indicators of the temper of the times as then U.S. Attorney General A. Mitchell Palmer's Red Squads, and the U.S. Senate's rejection of the League of Nations that President Wilson had negotiated at the Versailles peace conference of 1919.

Boas, who was long famous for his empirical measurements of immigrants' "bodily form" begun during his Clark University days (Barkan 1992:83ff), did not perform his own new empirical study for this case. But he was ingenious in soliciting from every repository of medical records he could find data with which to compare Armenians—those from Europe as well as those from "Asia Minor"—to other labeled groups of people. One of his most important lines of attack was to seek to show developmental data on the maturational course of children into adults, to show that Armenian children matured physically more like Caucasians than others (FB/MVM 2/25/24, 9/26/24; FB/RD 3/2/24; FB/WG 3/21/24). Observe the irony in Boas's quasi-reductive biologism, using the data of morphological—and, thence, physiological—development (ontogenesis) as a classificatory metric; Boas always sought to beat his antagonists on their own ground!

This shift in framing classification-relevant data from culture history—what one might metaphorically call the phylogenesis of the whole social group—to the ontogenetic course of maturation in a contemporary population, was the decisive link between the two conceptual realms spanned by cosmographic anthropology. Indeed, one sees it in many parallel formulations revealed in Boas's correspondence of 1925 and years following concerning Mead's doctoral field-work, where it is focused upon the psychic maturation of pubescent and adolescent young women in Samoa as they "come of age."[14] The development of the individual, as available to measurement or other determination in various "psychic" realms, might be at least in part an *enculturation* based upon social-ization patterns. This constitutes the logical equivalent of what Boas had al-ready demonstrated in bodily form, myth, language, etc. as "instability of type" under the pressure of the sociohistorical context. Here, however, it is of an in-dividual's ontogenetic development, that is, the second cosmographic sphere of Boasian anthropology. (From the 1890s to the 1910s Boas used his time cross-sectional studies to argue against transparent and fixed morphological conti-nuities of racial types in the first, "phylogenetic" sphere.) As we can see, a great number of Boas's activities as scientist-citizen involved just this transition in cosmographic focus.

14. There is an interesting passage in a letter of late 1924, in fact, to one Joseph Ralph, of Long Beach, California (12/29/24), in which Boas asserts that the anthropological "we" "find very com-monly among young unmarried people sexual license, along with restrictions in married life." Boas was preparing at that time to travel to Chicago (January 3–5, 1925) at the invitation of Herman M. Adler of the Institute for Juvenile Research of the Illinois Department of Public Welfare, to ad-dress a celebratory meeting of January 4 on the twenty-fifth anniversary of the Cook County Juve-nile Court. His address was billed as "The growth and development of children as determined by heredity and environment" (HMA/FB 12/3/24; 12/10/24; 12/19/24). Such matters must have been very much on his mind in the immediately practical legal work, as well as in more conceptual and scholarly senses.

Interestingly—and as we might surmise—racial talk pervaded American politics. There was, for example, the continuing question of the Ku Klux Klan's opposition to Alfred E. Smith's candidacy for the Democratic nomination for President because he was an Irish Catholic. Most importantly, there was legislation that was widely followed that was introduced in the first session of the 68th Congress in early February, debated, amended, sent to conference, passed by both houses (May 26), and signed into law by President Coolidge: the Immigration Act of 1924 (Hutchinson 1981:159–96). The act sets up an interim period until July 1, 1927, during which time two per cent of any particular nationality's population in the United States, according to the 1890 census [!] would be allowed in as new immigrants with the potential to become naturalized citizens. After that interim period, each nationality's quota was to be computed on the basis of a total annual immigration of 150,000 people, its fractional share based on a ratio determined by its total presence among foreign born according to the most recent census, that of 1920.

Boas had been involved in studies for the 1911 Commission, and in 1924 became centrally involved in immigration matters once again through the solicitation of his son's Columbia classmate ('10), Congressman Emanuel Celler of Brooklyn's Tenth District. The Congressman wrote on February 11 saying that he, Celler, wanted to play a role—and wanted Boas to play a role—in the Johnson immigration bill debate (the House version, H.R. 6540, had just been favorably reported out of committee on February 9). The beginning of a long correspondence and set of roles for Boas to play as expert witness, et cetera, Celler's letter notes that Boas was mentioned in the racist best-seller by Madison Grant, *The Passing of the Great Race*,[15] the intellectual underpinnings of arguments of the important members of the committee considering the legislation. He appeals to Boas for "some statement from you concerning the alleged Nordic superiority." By March 11, Celler is writing to ask Boas to supply three skulls that will allow him to dramatize House debate, a Nordic, an Alpine or Mediterranean, and a "[N]egro" one. In this way, he thought, "we could forcefully im-

---

15. Its subtitle: *The racial basis of European history*. The first edition (245 pp.) had come out from Charles Scribner in New York in 1916 (as America was being dragged by President Wilson from its isolationist neutrality into World War I), followed by an English printing in 1917 (London: G. Bell). A second, revised edition of 296 pp. appeared in 1918 (the third edition apparently just a reprinting in 1920 and following years). In 1923, a fourth edition, "revised and amplified" to some 476 pp. appeared in time for the immigration bill debates in Congress, complete with prefatory essay by Henry Fairfield Osborn, head of the American Museum of Natural History. One imagines that this edition is the reference in Congressman Celler's letter to Boas. Scribner was reprinting this fourth edition as late as 1936, in time for the next racialist calamity going on in Europe. (A German translation, *Der Untergang der grossen Rasse; die Rassen als Grundlage der Geschichte Europas* [München: J. F. Lehmann] had been available, we should note, since 1925; a French translation, *Le déclin de la grande race* [Paris: Payot] since 1926.)

press upon the Congressmen the fallacy of Madison Grant's theory. . . . [S]ome of the Congressmen who are afflicted with the Nordic mania might become worried when they realize that the Nordic skull is no better and no worse than the Negro's. . . . [A]rgument could be made in a humorous vein. We could ask Congressmen to come up and have their [own] skulls measured."

One imagines the young Representative Celler had that same ironic faith in rationality in the face of political experience that still animated Boas at his advanced stage of life (and would characterize even his legendary final utterance at the very moment of his last breath in 1942). Against a backdrop of skillfully cloaked racism, these ideas circulated popularly as "scientifically" authorized commonplaces of red-white-and-blue Americanism. Congress rushing to legislate against certain immigrants on its basis, Boas accepted invitation after invitation to write, to speak, and, importantly, to debate the relationship between race and mentality, assumptions about which underlay what materialized politically in 1924 as immigration and naturalization anxieties and legislation.

For example, on the same day, January 24, that the Armenian exclusionary case came his way, Boas received an invitation from G. B. Gordon at the Museum of the University of Pennsylvania, who had been asked to organize an April 26 symposium by the American Philosophical Society's General Committee for the Annual Meeting. The topic was to be "Are the Races of Mankind Potentially Equal," and Gordon proposed Kroeber, Ales Hrdlicka, and Clark Wissler, in addition to Boas. Note the characteristically Boasian rephrasing of the acceptance he fired back the next day (FB/GBG 1/25/24): "I shall be glad to take part in the symposium, although . . . I should rather be inclined to formulate it: What proof can be given for the potential inequality of races? My standpoint is a critical one, and my conclusion is that no proof can be given that races are potentially unequal, but on the other hand I should not commit myself to the statement that all races have absolutely the same mental make-up."

The session took place on April 25 with only a slightly re-entitled topic: "Are the various races of man potentially equal?" but without the others mentioned (APS 1924:viii–ix). Boas did speak, as well as that inimitable Boasian character, Alexander A. Goldenweiser (then at the New School). The anti-Boasian adversary was Henry Usher Hall, listed as "Curator of General Ethnology, University Museum, University of Pennsylvania."[16] Hall presented a frankly racist

16. Hall (1876–1944) had taken part in an expedition to Siberia in 1914–15 as the University Museum's representative. He was appointed Assistant Curator in 1916, Curator from 1924 of the "Section of General Ethnology" at the Museum, a title he seems to have held until 1935, though as late as 1936–37 we find him undertaking a Museum expedition to Sierra Leone. (See *American Journal of Archaeology* 49(1) [January–March 1945]: 82.) He seems to have published only in the Museum's *Journal* and *Bulletin*, not in regular professional outlets, and one gathers was an example of a nondegreed practitioner of the type common to the non-Boasian museological and related worlds of collecting in Cambridge, Washington, and Philadelphia. The peak incident mobilizing

position on the alien, superstition-driven and autocracy-seeking "slave" mentality of African Americans worthy of an Imperial Kleagle of the KKK: "The history of the negro [sic] in the New World shows that even where he has been removed from the surroundings in which his own institutions were developed the mental disposition out of which those institutions grew has persisted unchanged in essentials" (APS 1924:214).

Saturday's *New York Times* (April 26:17) devoted nearly two columns to the symposium with the headline, "Scientists at Odds on Superior Race / Majority at Philadelphia Philosophical Convention Sees No Inherent Difference / Nordic Claims Dismissed / Controversy Narrows to the Question of White Superiority Over the Blacks / H. U. Hall Analyzes Negro / Points to African Superstitions and Their History in America to Prove Fundamental Inferiority." The newspaper characterizes Hall's argument this way:

> The weak-willed natives, afraid of all responsibility, insisted on having autocracies, according to Mr. Hall, in order to shift all responsibility away from themselves, and this, he said, was a hereditary perpetual defect of negro [sic] character. . . . [In the America of today] white philanthropists and leaders of mixed race [constitute the] external superior force.

It is important to see that concepts of racial heredity of an individual's sociopolitical orientations are at the basis of Hall's claims, and hence only "lightening" or "whitening" of Black peoples will transform their fitness for participating in democracy.

If the newspaper account is to be believed, Boas countered by example, noting that "a few thousand years ago . . . the Egyptians might have said the same thing [as Hall did] of the [coeval Nordic] whites [of Europe]. Looking at the backwardness of the white races, they might have said, 'They are shiftless, superstitious, mentally inferior, and nothing can ever be made of them.'" Taking another example of coeval developments, the vaunted "Nordic race" in comparison to the Maya of the Classic Period, the *Times* reports that Boas pointed out, "The Nordic was then an uncouth barbarian without arts and without knowledge to be compared to those of the Maya. Would not the Maya be justified like our modern race enthusiasts in calling the [coeval] Nordic an inferior race that could never achieve eminence?" He sought to drive home the very epistemological and methodological argument he had reformulated in replying to Gordon in January, that, as the *Times* paraphrases him, "no scientific method has been found of measuring the fundamental capacity of different races as dis-

---

this side of a demographic as well as professional chasm to its last hurrah was the December 30, 1919 censure of Boas at the American Anthropological Association meeting in Cambridge (see Stocking 1968:270–307, 356–63).

tinct from the mental and moral development due to custom, history, economic and social environment," and that, therefore, such projections by coeval others were judgments from within some other, historically locatable cultural framework. (Hence, his examples of plausible Egyptian and Maya judgments—inevitably "cultural" or ideological ones—with respect to the coeval "Nordic race"—they are identical to contemporary racialist arguments!)[17]

Clearly this was no mere scholarly or scientific debate. Goldenweiser's blood was boiling in recollecting their reception, as shown by an angry six-page, handwritten letter he dashed off to Boas—choleric disfluencies and all—at 1:00 A.M., probably written immediately after returning to New York: "I suppose you and I must have appeared to [William B. Scott, APS President, in the chair] as two colored men disguised as Jews dishing out our black magic before that 'symposium' (vide The Century) of blue-blooded(or red blooded—which is it?) gathering of sapientes" (AG/FB n.d. [4/26/24?]).

Ironically, just as "Goldie" wrote this in his sleepless rage, the New York Times of April 27 was going to press. Here (sec. 9, p. 3) Senator David A. Reed, recently elected Republican of Pennsylvania, took a whole page to explain, in terms much like Hall's, why the Immigration Act of 1924, which he championed, would be good for American democracy. "America of the melting pot comes to end," announced the headline, and introduces Senator Reed as "sponsor of the idea which it embodies." This idea, the Times summarizes, is "to preserve racial type as it exists here today" by "chang[ing] the flow of immigration from Europe to the United States."[18]

But what, according to Senator Reed, is the importance of "preserving racial type?" He is convinced that the future of our American democracy as a way of

17. The Times has caught Boas's negative rhetoric about how racists confound relevant variables brought forth as allegedly independent ones. Here, the variables are "fundamental [sc., biological] capacity" vs. perceived capacities due to "custom/history/economic & social environment," "nature" vs. "nurture" viewed in the cosmographic macro-framework of historical stability or instability of racial and mental classificatory schemes and categories over time and space. Note, moreover, the parallel to the "Alternating Sounds" article (Boas 1889) on 'apperceptive' norms of speakers of particular languages and their perception, transcription, and allegedly scientific classification of sounds that are apperceptively noncanonical, i.e., those for which the linguistically enculturated hearing has not been trained. What we now know as phonological categories are thus "psychologically" real in the cosmographic sense of this term—and only "psychologically" real!

18. Europe can indeed be the focus of the bill, because, as Senator Reed noted, existing immigration law already barred from admission to the United States as "aliens ineligible for citizenship" "all Chinese, East Indians, Afghans, Burmese, Siamese, Japanese, and other Asiatic and Malay peoples." (Note the relevance to U.S. v. Cartozian then pending in U.S. District Court, on which Boas was consulting.) Senator Reed approvingly observes that the new immigration bill of 1924 has this exclusion taxonomically "expanded impartially to all Asiatic and Malay nations" as a blanket provision.

life depends on "recognition of the excluded peoples' fundamental dissimilarity from ourselves," justifying exclusion of such racially "unassimilable . . . aliens." In this way the "America of our grandchildren will be a vastly better place to live in. It will mean a more homogeneous nation, more self-reliant, more independent, and more closely knit by common purpose and common ideas." Homogeneous, with common purpose and ideas that celebrate being self-reliant and independent: a kind of nostalgic racialist vision of a vigorous "Anglo-Saxon" body politic out of Emerson, Teddy Roosevelt, and many others in the preacherly tradition of American virtue, including the *Boy Scout Handbook*!

The critical point is that for the senator and similarly-thinking folks, there is a conceptual story that makes sense of the connection between democratic government and Anglo-Saxon (or "Nordic") nativism; it is indeed the cluster of folk concepts that racialize these virtues. Madison Grant had indeed already made such sense to Senator Reed and others. Here is the senator's account, under the subheading "Fate of Roman Empire Recalled," which I quote at length:

> There has come about a general realization of the fact that the races of men who have been coming to us in the recent [post-1885] years are wholly dissimilar to the native-born Americans, that they are untrained in self-government—a faculty that it has taken the Northwestern Europeans many centuries to acquire. Thoughtful Americans have been despondent for the future of our country when the suffrage should be exercised by men whose inexperience in popular forms of government would lead them to demand too much of their Government, and to rely too heavily upon it, and too little upon their own initiative.
>
> America was beginning also to smart under the irritation of her "foreign colonies"—those groups of aliens, either in city slums or in country districts, who speak a foreign language and live a foreign life, and who want neither to learn our common speech nor to share our common life. From all this has grown the conviction that it was best for America that our incoming immigrants should hereafter be of the same races as those of us who are already here, so that each year's immigration should so far as possible be a miniature America, resembling in national origins the persons who are already settled in our country.

Here's the "juuuuust right" Goldilocks Principle for ethnic acceptability: it ceases to be a principle in any politically relevant way.

Consider the terms of Senator Reed's argument. On the one hand, "self-government" has become a kind of psychological "faculty" through which true Americans, of the Northwestern European "races," express their self-reliance and autonomy from government. "We," then, are unlike those to be excluded, who seem rather to ask of their governments—especially, perhaps, socialist and communist ones?—what they can do for their dependent citizens. So we surely do not want them among us, they of the craven, dependent, autocracy-seeking mentality, as Hall termed it. On the other hand, curiously, there are those self-reliant enclaves of immigrants—"foreign colonies"—already present but without "our common speech" and "our common life."[19] They must be *too* visibly "self-reliant," since they seem not to want to "melt" into the erstwhile melting pot as mere individuals under the Northern European banner of leadership. They retain group identity, which allows a certain autonomy of functioning; they are obviously suspicious to the senator and like-minded citizens. While we cannot deport them now (though consider Mr. Cartozian's fate under the "Asiatic" exclusionary provisions), we can certainly fix it so that they cannot add to their unassimilated and perhaps Democratic-leaning numbers through continued immigration and naturalization.

It is not my purpose to emphasize the political interests here, but rather to point out that the racializing discourse about immigration policy reconceptualizes certain foreign born residents of America as mental, political, and moral deviants. Relentless discourses of promoting exclusion and idealizing homogeneity led to the passage of the Immigration Act of 1924; that is the simple political reality. We can trace in this discourse, however, the clustering of certain issues in its ideological apologetics. Here, cultural difference reinterpreted as racially based mentality and psychological disposition once more is considered as the *cause* of social problems at what are perceived as the fringes of American society, that is in urban ethnic slums, or in isolated rural enclaves like Native American reservations, where deviance lurks. Senator Reed addresses not merely the lack of assimilation of "American" norms by these marginal people, as it can be empirically measured, but far worse, the enduring, and even biological impossibility that they will ever be effectively assimilated. The group's difference from the norms is an *immutable* one; it is a "racial" one. (It is interesting to note the parallel to the premises in the argument of special creationism underlying the Scopes Trial, just then taking shape in Tennessee.)

If Americans of the senator's kind were increasingly worried about persisting statistical prevalence of crime in such populations, here was the justification for their anxiety. Social deviance is explained by the fundamental deviance of mentality—in any of its measurable indices—of the kinds of foreigners the Immigration Act of 1924 intended to bar or to restrict from entering the country. The phenomenon of statistical "deviance" is quietly joined with the issue of absolute and immutable "racial deviance"—which seemed to many in power to go a long way toward explaining those very statistics!

But the restricted or excluded foreign-born are, in fact, the foreign tout court,

---

19. American English, thought of as "monoglot Standard" (Silverstein 1996), periodically surfaces as a symbol of unity in the form of waves of enacted and proposed amendments to both state and federal constitutions making English the "official language" of the polity. For an historical overview, see Baron (1990); for a documentary sourcebook, see Crawford (1992); for essays on particular communities, see Adams & Brink (1990). See Woolard (1989) for a case study of recent California politics of monoglottism.

just happening to reside within these borders. They are, however, the folk who constitute anthropology's subject matter (and, like Boas himself and many of his earlier students, they are anthropology's own personnel in 1924). They are people characterized by "cultural" difference, not racial "deviance," in Boas's default cosmographic conceptualization. But the conjunction of these issues seemed to present itself everywhere that Boasian anthropology would be called upon to discuss phenomena of "cultural" difference, as it was at the American Philosophical Society. Hence, there was an extraordinary number of similar occasions for Boas and others throughout this year and the beginning of 1925, each focused on a variant of the APS theme. These included a joint meeting of sections H [Anthropology] and I [Psychology] of the American Association for the Advancement of Science at its Christmas meeting in Washington, D.C., on "the value of [intelligence as well as anthropometric] tests upon immigrants" (E. Hooten/FB 9/21/24; FB/EH 9/26/24; R. Terry/FB 11/30/24); and numerous other professional and popular speaking engagements and publications.[20]

20. Here is a list of the major ones, in addition to those already discussed in my text, documented in the microfilmed files of Boas' professional papers:

speaking to the Inter-Racial Conference, New York City, early 1924;

convened a joint meeting of the American Ethnological Society and the New York Academy of Sciences at Schermerhorn Hall, Columbia University, March 26, on "American racial problems" (FB/John Elliott 3/8/[?24]);

speaking to The Get–Together Club of the Community Church of New York (Blanche Watson et al./FB 4/6/24);

letter to the editor, *New York Times*, 4/9/24, re: H. F. Osborn, President of AMNH, on "race." Note that Osborn had written a laudatory preface to Madison Grant's book;

letter in *The Nation* on anti–immigration bill work of Congressman E. Celler (FB/Lewis Gannett 9/26/24);

speaking to the International Club of the City of New York, November 2, on "What is a race?" (Leah Levinson/FB, 10/9/24; FB/LL 10/10/24);

article on "The question of racial purity" in *American Mercury*, October 1924;

address as guest of honor of a conference on immigration, 11/25/24, of the League of Foreign Born Citizens, "The anthropological basis that should underlie a constructive immigration measure" (Harold Fields/FB 11/7/24; Nathaniel Phillips/FB 11/11/24; HF/FB 11/26/24);

speaking to twenty-fifth anniversary commemoration, January 4, 1925, of Juvenile Court of Cook County (see n. 14, this chapter);

book proposal for revision of *The Mind of Primitive Man* (Boas 1911b), to be entitled *Race and Progress* (FB/Macmillan Co. 12/4/24; R. R. Smith/FB 12/8/24). This came out as *Anthropology and Modern Life* (Boas 1928);

commission to write first article of a proposed 1925 series of articles on "race," *The Nation* (Freda Kirchwey/FB 12/22/24).

Note that all these activities were in addition to a continuing role in numerous civic and international organizations, as well as his full load of professional, scientific, and pedagogical activities at Columbia University and nationally. Boas sailed for Europe in late June, 1924, and did not return until the middle of the summer.

But the most fateful of all of these gatherings for our story was the joint meeting, on August 11, 1924, of Sections H (Anthropology) and J (Psychology) of the *British* Association for the Advancement of Science, during its 92nd meeting held August 6–13 in Toronto. This meeting might well have been the model for the one Hooten later proposed to Boas for the American AAAS. The topic for the BAAS joint meeting was "Racial Mental Differences" (BAAS 1925:417–24). Sapir, then at the Victoria Memorial Museum in Ottawa, was Secretary of the Local Committee of Section H. In this capacity, he tried to get Boas and others to attend (ES/FB 3/3/24[?]; 6/11/24; FB/ES 3/5/24). But Boas and numerous others had been intending to leave for Europe to attend the 21st International Congress of Americanists in Göteborg and The Hague that August (Boas sailed the last week of June). Benedict was off on fieldwork in Zuni, as was Ruth Bunzel.

Various of the anthropologists in the general Boasian orbit were, ultimately, able to go up to Toronto, among them Wissler, Goldenweiser, Erna Gunther [Spier], Frank Speck, and a remarkable, energetic newcomer to Columbia anthropology, "Miss Margaret Mead," or Mrs. Luther Cressman since September 3, 1923 (Howard 1984:61). On August 11 she read her paper, "Rank in Polynesia," having three days earlier read "Mrs. Benedict's" paper, "Religious complexes of the North American Indians" (Mead 1972:124; 1959:207).

Of course, what was important about Toronto was more than this intellectual tussle between McDougallian[21] psychology's "nature" and Boasian anthropology's "nurture." A set of personal and intellectual relationships of the next Boasian generations seems to have crystallized there so as to shift decisively the intellectual center of gravity of Boasianism. Sapir and Mead began what would culminate in an intimate relationship, the recently widowed Sapir desirous of marrying the seemingly unencumbered Mead some seventeen years his junior. Mead, just finished with her psychology M.A. under R. S. Woodworth during

21. William McDougall had been a student of W. H. R. Rivers at Cambridge University, and became a member of the famous Cambridge Anthropological Expedition to Torres Straits of 1898 organized by A. C. Haddon. Stocking describes his career in these terms: "McDougall [was] in the long run to remain in psychology. . . . [He] wrote influential textbooks on physiological psychology and social psychology, before turning to racially oriented speculations about the 'group mind'; he subsequently emigrated to the United States, where he instituted parapsychological research at Duke University and published a critique of American democracy" (1995:117). Indeed, by the time of the Toronto meetings, McDougall's textbook, *Social Psychology*, had appeared in its sixteenth edition! It should also be noted that a book he himself termed a "sequel" to this had already appeared and been revised all in 1920, the title of which is significant: *The group mind; a sketch of the principles of collective psychology, with some attempt to apply them to the interpretation of national life and character.* Could Mead's presence at Toronto be significant in this respect, given the studies of "national character" later undertaken at Columbia during wartime? The conceptual precedents for this kind of work clearly are wider than Benedict's and Mead's use of notions of "culture" as "personality writ large" and inversely in the 1930s.

1923–24, was definitively moving into the orbit of Boas, especially as mediated by Benedict, the already established confidante and soulmate of Sapir. She was falling into a relationship with Sapir that was exactly parallel to and in a sense competitive with the one the older woman, Benedict, already had—a relationship filled with intense intellectual exchange, Culture, and a reflexivity strangely sublimated and figured on a number of levels, including the aesthetic as expressed in poetry and its criticism (see Caffrey 1989; Darnell 1990; Handler 1983, 1986a, 1986b, 1989; Howard 1984; Mead 1959; and Modell 1983, 1989).

By the next summer of 1925, as Mead was preparing to leave husband Luther Cressman, sail off to American Samoa and thence to her destiny of celebrity, she apparently consummated the intimacy both with Sapir in New York (Howard 1984:66–67) and then—on a side visit to the Grand Canyon on her way to San Francisco for the steamer—with Benedict as well (Caffrey 1989:188)! Only the Benedict-Sapir relationship of this intense triangle had not been and was apparently not to be sexually consummated.

Sapir introduced Mead to Carl Jung's *Psychological Types* (1921).[22] It was a book whose ideas had become an undercurrent in the serious fraternal banter about each other's psychodynamics of the second-generation Boasian men— Sapir, Kroeber, Radin, Lowie, "Goldie" et al. (Sapir had reviewed the English translation of Jung in *The Freeman* in 1923.)[23] It was still highly influential in Sapir's "Psychology of Culture" classes down to the 1930s (see Sapir 1994, Irvine's collated edition of these; cf. Preston 1986). And observe that Benedict's *Patterns of Culture* (1934b) was originally to have been titled *Primitive Peoples*, and subtitled, by analogy, *An Introduction to Cultural Types* (Caffrey 1989:206; cf. the title of Benedict 1930, delivered in 1928). Mead (1959:207; 1972:125) claims to have returned the favor of the loan in 1925—Koffka's *Growth of the Mind* (1921).[24]

22. Howard (1984:43) quotes Mead from late-in-life interviews with Jean Houston (on whom see Howard 1984:370–71, 409–10) about the period of ca. 1925, when the "Ash Can Cats" group of friends lived at 606 West 116th Street on Morningside Heights, to the effect that she "began thinking in Jungian terms. I was at that point supposed to be an 'intuitive introvert,' which everybody wanted to be because that was what Jung admired most. And we decided that Luther [Cressman] was a 'sensation extrovert.'" The more general orientation of psychoanalysis as such had already made an impression on the group even while Mead (class of 1923) was an undergraduate (Howard 1984:49–50).

23. Homans (1979:93ff) makes a nice case that the psychological types of Jung's book are really projective mechanisms by which Jung was able psychologically to differentiate himself from Freud and Adler. Jung assigned Freud and his approach to extraversion, Adler and his to introversion, and hoped to "create a psychological system that would include and thereby surpass the other two" (Homans 1979:94). Note the book's subtitle.

24. ES/RB, 4/15/25 (Mead 1959:177): "I've been reading Koffka's 'Growth of the Mind' (Margaret's copy) and it's like some echo telling me what my intuition never quite had the courage to say out loud" (see Caffrey 1989:154).

Mead was apparently infatuated with Sapir's intellect, learning, aesthetics, and psychologizing, as was Benedict, Mead's older, symbolic rival. The Samoan trip came just in time for Mead to extricate herself from Sapir's stifling expectations and his somewhat less-than-candid machinations. He tried to prevent her from going (Mead 1959:288, 290–91; Howard 1984:74; Caffrey 1989:198–99), and tried to relocate himself from Ottawa to New York instead of to Chicago (ES/FB 10/2/24; 4/13/25; 4/22/25) to enable her to render second-wifely service to the marriage-with-children already in progress.

Psychoanalysis, with its conceptualization of the meaning of symbols for the ego's functioning in personality, was a universalizing, and easily medicalized developmental story of mind.[25] It provided an idiom in which to conceptualize such things as normality ("normalcy," as President Harding had made immortal in his campaign slogan in 1920) versus deviance over a population. It looked like a psychiatric science in which the case history, in the medical sense—the record of the developmental course of a personality no less than that of a personality "disorder"—could be joined to large-scale testing and description of whole populations no less than in anthropometrics. This had already been done in the much-touted area of intelligence testing, in which Mead had done her M.A. (on second-generation immigrant Italian Americans; see Howard [1984:64], who observes, "what an instinct she had for issues of enduring interest!"). There is an intersection of analogies. First, the developmental case histories of many individuals could be related to a summary, whether statistical or typological. One could compare the genealogical charts of individuals as they are related in social anthropology to a diagram of "the" group's kinship system and to statistical rates of realization of the normative rules of genealogical and affinal relationship. In a second analogy, one can see the evaluative logic of the psychiatric profile of growth and development from infancy to adulthood—the very stuff of psychoanalytic and related diagnosis and therapy. Its logic might be compared to the anthropometric profiles of longitudinal growth and development of bodily characteristics in which Boas was such a world-famous

25. The course of psychological degeneration of Sapir's first wife, Florence, no less than her lung abscess (from treatment of which she died in April, 1924; see Darnell 1990:133–37), was a personal tragedy that drew in Kroeber, Boas and his physician son, Ernst; Lowie, Radin, Benedict, and Mead (and others) to try to render one or another sort of help as friends of the medically afflicted family. Indeed, Sapir clearly cried out in anguish to each of them in a particular way, and the continuing discourse about personality and psychiatric matters has a poignantly personal quality no less than an intellectual one for this reason until Mrs. Sapir's death in 1924. Note that Kroeber had even briefly "hung out a shingle" as a psychoanalyst on Sutter Street in San Francisco in mid-1920, though he gave up the idea of a practice in addition to, or in place of, his academic appointment in 1922 (Golla 1984:342–43). That this discourse became a major professional counterfoil to the older, historicist idiom of Boasian anthropology for Sapir, Benedict, Mead, and others *after* 1925 is the critical fact here, however.

expert, arguing on the side of a complex relation between genetic and environmental factors.

Although Boas was never an admirer of psychoanalysis as such, he clearly saw the relationship of these former students' emerging interests to his own concerns for looking for new scientific tools with which to investigate problems of "heredity and environment"—whether in America or elsewhere.[26] As we have seen, in 1924 he had started to reconceptualize these as requiring or at least supporting the kind of ontogenetic or developmental evidence that he had long established in the study of children's phenotypic patterns of skeletal growth and bodily maturation. Insofar as "psychological" evidence could be gathered and deployed to the same ends, it was so much the better for heading off approaches he considered beyond "science" in his sense.

It was also almost as though at the same time he were settling an ancient score with G. Stanley Hall, author of *Adolescence* (1904), an extremely influential account of psychological as well as phenotypic development (he was something of a Haeckelian recapitulationist; see Stocking 1968:125–26; 254–55). As President of Clark University, Hall had once been Boas's employer in the "psychological department" (employment that ended badly; see Ross 1972:222–26). So, once he was resigned to Mead's making a field trip outside North America, Boas set her to work on the problem of female adolescence in American Samoa

---

26. Caffrey (1989:158) notes this, too. Boas refers to Freud in a footnote in *The Mind of Primitive Man*, as background for a passage remarking on "the influence of habits of thought, feeling, and action acquired in early childhood, and of which no recollection is retained . . . [though they] remain a living force throughout life—the more potent, the more thoroughly they are forgotten" (1911b:288, 121). But such positive reference, translated into Boas's rather psychophysicalist view of unconscious reaction mechanisms as sociohistorically learned or acquired, despite being "unconscious," gave way later to a certain antipathy to the second- and third-generation psychoanalytically inspired psychologizing—especially in anthropology. See his pungent remarks against W.H.R. Rivers and others (1920:281–89). Still recognizing that "the social behavior of man depends to a great extent upon the earliest habits which are established before the time when connected memory begins, and that many so-called racial or hereditary traits are to be considered rather as a result of early exposure to certain forms of social conditions" (288; cf. 1911b:121), Boas compares psychoanalytic interpretation to philosophy and then theology (!), and concludes with a fairly blanket condemnation that must indeed have left his 1920s circle of students somewhat bashful about bringing up the subject: "While, therefore, we may welcome the application of every advance in the method of psychological investigation, we cannot accept as an advance in ethnological method the crude transfer of a novel, one-sided method of psychological investigation of the individual to social phenomena the origin of which can be shown to be historically determined and to be subject to influences that are not at all comparable to those that control the psychology of the individual" (1920:289). Here is Boas, reiterating that the "psychology" of an anthropologically relevant subjectivity lies at the intersection of the two frames of cosmographical epistemology. It should also be noted that in passing, Boas locates theological and psychoanalytic thought precisely as equivalents within a cosmographic analysis of them as cultural phenomena: "depend[ing] primarily upon the subjective attitude of the investigator who arranges phenomena according to his leading concept" (289; cf. 1887:645).

(she settled on Ta'u as the locale), and couched it in terms that placed it precisely at the cosmographic "psychological" intersection of culture-in-time and the development of individual attitudes in a cultural milieu. He used, however, innovative developmentalist terms for investigating "(in)stability of 'type'."

Mead's actual doctoral dissertation (1928b) seems to have been for her a triviality; something to be gotten out of the way (Howard 1984:64). No less than Benedict's comparison of Amerindian guardian spirit quests (1923), it was to be a Boasian product of the old mold. What was central, rather, to Mead's first field trip was the research that became *Coming of Age in Samoa* (Mead 1928a), and more technical works on social organization (for example, Mead 1930).

Mead's fieldwork thus brought together, at Boas's behest (Mead 1972:126–32), two of the themes he had been mulling over and developing in his work against the racialists. In his recommendation letter about her to the NRC (FB/R. S. Woodworth 2/24/25), Boas describes "[t]he fundamental question to be solved" as "in how far the removal of traditional restrictions upon the young and the substitution of other types of restrictions may influence behavior"—in the classic pattern of observation of change (here, behavioral) in sociohistorical circumstance (compare to "bodily form"). To Mead herself (FB/MM 7/14/25), however, Boas suggests studying adolescent girls' rebelliousness, bashfulness, and "crushes"—a selection out of American folk wisdom, as well as evident in Hall (see Mead 1972:138–39). The status of all these as aspects of a necessary, biological developmental stage of psychic life Boas doubted, just as he came to formulate doubts about the pre- or acultural universality of development in children's physique. He notes (in a passage *not* reproduced by Mead in *Blackberry Winter* [1972]) that "whatever you decide to do . . . the most important contribution that we hope you will make will be the psychological attitude of the individual to [sic] under the pressure of the general pattern of culture. . . . [A]nything that pertains to this subject will be of greatest importance for the methodological development of ethnological research"—indeed setting into motion a move into the second Boasian cosmographic moment, which, in all probability, neither Mead nor Benedict realized until much later, if at all (Mead 1972:126–27). For the terms in which they were explicitly conceptualizing this second Boasian moment seem to have been quite different in the period from 1926–27, as Mead was organizing her material from Samoa, and to the Second World War and beyond.

Boas was taking on psychoanalysis, medicalized or not, and any other purportedly universal ontogenetic accounts of the course of human mental life, as our culture's "psychologically real" though essentializing secondary rationalizations (see Stocking 1995:278–83 on Malinowski's contrasting Freudian revisionism). This was to reveal them as being neither better or worse than how the Classic Period Mayan would view coeval "Nordics," as he put it in Philadelphia. He was also seeking to test the strength of the "cultural" in development, at the intersection of two axes of cosmographically dictated variation. One was culture change (hence, "removal" and "substitution" of "restrictions" in psychic development), and the other "the general pattern of the culture," as it relates to constraint on developmental stages of each individual's psychological attitudes.

Licensed by this charge or brief, nevertheless Mead, Benedict—and in later years the large enterprises they either directed or participated in as "culture and personality" studies—went off in distinctly different directions. Even Sapir, an essential participant up to the time of Mead's sailing for Samoa, maintained his more cosmographical framing of the issues involved in his essays of the later 1920s and 1930s, as he became personally distant after relocating to Chicago in 1925 and remarrying in September 1926 (Darnell 1990:177–83). It is interesting that Mead, writing in the late 1950s, tells about what we can now recognize as Benedict's essentially cosmographic sensibility regarding "personality" and "culture" in their intense discussions during the winter of 1927–28, and the next several years: "We spent hours discussing how a given temperamental approach to living could come so to dominate a culture that all who were born in it would become the willing or unwilling heirs to that view of the world. From the first Ruth Benedict resisted any idea of schematization in terms of a given number of temperaments—Jung's fourfold scheme, for instance" (1959:206). In a long footnote of explanation (546–47), Mead describes her own use of psychoanalytic or other "temperament" typologies as universals. For her, cultures merely exaggerate or suppress these in molding a person's development. Benedict—still oriented to Boasian cosmography, as we now can easily recognize—rejected this approach in a universalizing comparative "science":

> In this preference she belonged more to the humanities than to the sciences and was more interested in the rich complexity of the real, historically unique situation than in the [sic] those types of scientific analysis which, by devising a formula which could be applied to all cultures, stripped the cultures of the very uniqueness which she valued. Some of our most lively theoretical battles were fought over this point—when I would argue for the usefulness of such an analytical method and she would smile and dispose of the carefully constructed analytical scheme as if it were little more than a bit of Zuñi cosmology, as of course from one point of view it was. (547)

Indeed, one should compare Boas's discussions of psychoanalysis in such a cosmographic scheme (see n. 26, this chapter) to understand the epistemological attitude that so irritated Mead as anti-scientific stubbornness even in retrospect decades later.

There is a profound irony in what the two cosmographers, Papa Franz and Edward Sapir had wrought, the one with his turn to the individual's psychic—even "psychological"—development as antiracialist data, the other with his enthusiasm for making cosmographic Boasians see their doubly-framed "psychology" in yet a third framework, the one sought by theorists of psychoanalytic and psychodynamic bent. The irony is that increasingly this led to the dissolution of cosmographic Boasianism in favor of a "science." In this approach, culture indeed became empirically investigable personalities (or ego-mechanisms) writ large, and personalities were causally influenced, in socialization and "enculturation," as well as in (mal)adjustment in later life, by such variables experienced by the individual as cultural pressures.[27] Certainly in the 1930s and beyond, this was the way "culture and personality" pursued these issues as an ongoing empirical research enterprise of Mead, her husbands, associates, and interlocutors.

It is clear that the cosmographic moment of 1924, the Boasian view of the mind, was increasingly frustrated in all the worldly modalities of support. Sapir and his psychiatric sidekick, Harry Stack Sullivan (Perry 1982:242–301), for example, could never make any serious headway with their perspective in places like SSRC, NRC, and so forth (though a few crumbs were forthcoming; see Darnell 1990:288–358, 383–414). Benedict was drawn along somewhat by Mead, and then in the milieu of Columbia in the 1930s was eclipsed as an organizer of interdisciplinary work there by Abram Kardiner (Manson 1986:78–79), and eventually by Ralph Linton, Boas's designated replacement (Caffrey 1989:276–78; Manson 1986:81). Mead herself increasingly became the major figure in a comparative "science" of culture and personality. In turn, she looked to people like Yale's John Dollard, a like-minded "go getter" and academic entrepreneur (on whom, see Darnell's coverage in relation to his scuttling of Sapir's plans, 1990:334–35, 394–97; see also Perry 1982:366 and 446, n. 3).

Normativity, normality and deviance, in a statistical as well as collective sense, and as political as well as intellectual ideas, were the key themes that were addressed by those trying to fit the next phase of anthropology into the larger social science scene. This had already been developing between foundations and universities in America from the mid-1920s on, frustrating much of the earlier sensitivity to, and sensibility about "culture" that Boasian anthropology sought to bring to social science and its publics (Stocking 1985; 1989; Darnell 1990:218–30). That it was also a highly personal and reflexive moment for all the key players, for which the discourse of neo-Freudianism was ready to hand as an analogic springboard, a "fashion of speaking" about "individual"and the "socio-cultural," should now be clear.

I have already made mention of the anxieties of "deviance" under which both Mead and Benedict operated (see Benedict 1934a; Caffrey 1989:196–98). These anxieties were compounded when Sapir published what to them must have been a shocking set of papers (1928; 1929a; 1930), two of them quite

---

27. A term invented by Herskovits: "The aspects of the learning experience which mark off man from other creatures, and by means of which, initially and in later life, he achieves competence in his culture, may be called *enculturation*. This is in essence a process of conscious or unconscious conditioning, exercised within the limits sanctioned by a given body of custom" (1948:39; cf. Hoebel 1949:473).

public, in the *American Mercury*. They had the effect of ending any further possibilities for intellectual collaboration with Sapir. He wrote from within the "safe" psychiatric confines of a new (heterosexual, legitimate, and monogamous) marriage. It is probable they took some of his passages on sexuality, marriage, and family relationships as directed with disappointment and a certain vindictiveness toward them. It was as though he had come to a realization that Mead had chosen Benedict and "freedom" from heterosexuality, legitimacy, and monogamy over him (Caffrey 1989:198–99; Darnell 1990:180–81; Mead 1959:195–96).[28]

As they sensed and hesitatingly articulated (or symbolically repressed or sup-

28. Sapir was particularly critical of Mead in print, going out of his way to mention her negatively. In his "Observations on the sex problem in America" (Sapir 1928), for example, he alludes to *Coming of Age in Samoa* (Mead 1928a) and Malinowski's (1927) *Sex and Repression in Savage Society* in the same deprecatory breath: "It does not seem to occur to the readers of excited books about pleasure-loving Samoans and Trobriand Islanders that perhaps these communities are not as primitive as they seem. . . . [W]hat should be denied is that sex conduct is truly unregulated even in these societies. A closer examination shows that the community has certain very definite ideas as to what is allowable and what is not allowable. . . . If we cannot sympathetically understand their sex taboos, why do we pretend to understand their freedom from our sex taboos?" (1928:523–24). Again, in reviewing—somewhat archly and churlishly—Boas's *Anthropology and Modern Life* (Boas 1928) in *New Republic* in 1929, Sapir (1929b) warns about "popular" anthropology "that its data and its varying interpretations will be chosen *ad libitum* to justify every whim and every form of spiritual sloth. 'Anthropology and Modern Life' is a brave warning against such misuse of the comparative study of culture, but the warning is in vain. Already a generation of 'applied anthropologists' has begun. What we have been waiting for is already on sale. It is brilliant now and then, like Malinowski's 'Sex and Repression in Savage Society'; more often it will be cheap and dull, like Margaret Mead's 'Coming of Age in Samoa.'"

Whatever the peevishness of these published reports, by the end of his life Sapir no doubt understood at last what was the situation with both Mead and Benedict. In a letter (10/25/38; reproduced in part in Stocking 1980) to the then young Philip Selznick (later Professor of Sociology at Berkeley), a Xerox of which came into my possession some years ago, Sapir condemns the "altogether too great readiness to translate psychological analogies into psychological realities," as he retrospectively reads Benedict's *Patterns of Culture* through its aftereffects in the culture-and-personality movement. He goes on at some length, in a somewhat shocking peroration, about the refusal of some—whom he actually names to the young student!—to recognize the possibility of culture-transcending "normality" in personality development. He refers to "an [often] unconscious or at least an unacknowledged motive for the denial of normalities which transcend the compulsions of culture. This motive," Sapir goes on, "comes out very sharply in the work of certain writers . . . who have heavy problems of personal morbidity to contend with and are, of course, interested consciously or unconsciously in transferring the scene of battle, as it were, from the psyche to the impersonal field of culture. One could write a very interesting paper on the usefulness of the concept of cultural relativity as a sophisticated form of what the psychiatrist somewhat brutally refers to as a flight from reality." Of course, by this time, Benedict had been living together with Natalie Raymond since 1931, though the relationship was about at its end (Caffrey 1989:202–3; 300–301); Mead, by contrast, labored mightily to keep at the surface of things only those of her various sexual relationships that looked "normal," though perhaps gossip had reached Sapir by then.

pressed) their own (and each other's) demographics and subjectivities relative to their own society and culture, they moved off into other lives and careers—and into others' lives and careers. In these circumstances various distinct, non-cosmographic versions emerged of what has come to be called the "culture and personality" approach in anthropology, certainly definitively so by the end of the Great Depression.

So the duplex—and if one includes ego dynamics, even triplex—particularity of the Boasian *sociocentric* in 'mind' or subjectivity constituted a scholarly, but outwardly directable set of issues in 1924. The writings about them announced a continuing brief for anthropology as a discipline relevant to our engagement in the fine art—and politics—of "modern life," as the success of Mead's Samoan book made clear. The cultural sociocentric also furthered anthropological theorizing and empirical work as one of the various disciplines recognized as "social science." During the 1930s and beyond, however, those interested in the problem of how an individual "mind" could be suffused with that which was a property of a group—namely, "culture"—increasingly accepted the terms of psychology and psychiatry to discuss the issues. Consequently, the issues became increasingly redefined as "inter-" disciplinary ones, which resulted in them being considered as either "psychological anthropology" or "cross-cultural psychiatry" or "psychology of culture" (Herskovits 1948:45). So the loss, during the 1930s, of the specifically Boasian, cosmographic "psychological" goes together with the loss of "mind" for anthropology. (Not coincidentally, self-captioned "social anthropology" with its horror of "mind"—though not without its own psychological presuppositions—emerged in America at just this time.)

Yet every era's anthropology has grappled with its own sense of what the "sociocentric" is in "mind"—this seems to remain a constant of our field; as well as how it can be demonstrated through empirical work that the sociocentric is one of mind's irreducible aspects. Here we have seen how the major figures in the moment of Boasian transition were poised between issues of policy and practicality on the one side, and matters of deep, reflexive concerns with selfhood on the other—their personal cosmographic nexus.

Acknowledgments

I thank Matti Bunzl and Richard Handler for the invitation to participate in a symposium held Saturday, 20 November 1999 at the 98th (Chicago) annual meeting of the American Anthropological Association, entitled "The Pasts, Presents, and Futures of Boasian Anthropology"; preserving its title, this paper expands on the first part of my symposium paper. I am grateful to my colleague Raymond D. Fogelson for extensive commentary on the earlier version, and likewise to Benjamin G. Zimmer. I acknowledge, with thanks, the following institutions for responding positively to my requests for permission to incorporate quotations from copyrighted material: Alfred A. Knopf, a division of Random House, Inc.; American Journal of Psychiatry; American Philosophical Society; The Bancroft Library (University of California, Berkeley); Institute for Intercultural Studies, Inc.; The Library of the American Philosophical Society; the *New York Times*; Simon & Schuster, Inc. (all such institutions and copyright holders having been contacted).

References Cited

AA   *American Anthropologist*
AQ   *Anthropological Quarterly*
HL   *Historiographica Linguistica*
HOA   *History of Anthropology*

Aberle, D. 1960. The influence of linguistics on early culture and personality theory. In *Essays in the Science of Culture; in honor of Leslie A. White, in celebration of his sixtieth birthday and his thirtieth year of teaching at the University of Michigan*, eds. G. E. Dole & R. L. Carneiro, 1–29. New York.

Adams, K. & D. Brink, eds. 1990. *Perspectives on official English: The campaign for English as the official language of the USA*. Berlin.

APS [American Philosophical Society]. 1924. *Proceedings*, vol. 63. Philadelphia.

Barkan, E. 1992. *The retreat of scientific racism: Changing concepts of race in Britain and the United States between the world wars*. Cambridge, UK.

Baron, D. 1990. *The English-only question: An official language for Americans?* New Haven, CT.

Bashkow, I. 1991. The dynamics of rapport in a colonial situation: David Schneider's fieldwork on the islands of Yap. HOA 7:170–242.

Benedict, R. 1923. *The concept of the guardian spirit in North America*. Menasha, WI.

———. 1930. Psychological types in the cultures of the Southwest. In *Proceedings of the Twenty-third International Congress of Americanists, Held at New York, September 17–22, 1928*, 527–81. New York.

———. 1934a. Anthropology and the abnormal. *J. Gen. Psych.* 10:59–82. [Reprinted in Mead 1959:268–83.]

———. 1934b. *Patterns of culture*. Boston.

Boas, F. 1887. The study of geography. In Boas 1940:639–47.

———. 1889. On alternating sounds. In Stocking 1974:72–77.

———. 1896. The limitations of the comparative method of anthropology. In Boas 1940:270–80.

———. 1911a. Introduction. *Handbook of American Indian Languages*, part 1, 1–83. *Bur. Am. Ethn. Bul.* 40. Washington, DC.

———. 1911b. *The mind of primitive man*. New York.

———. 1920. The methods of ethnology. In Boas 1940:281–89.

———. 1928. *Anthropology and modern life*. New York.

————. 1936. History and science in anthropology: A reply. In Boas 1940:305–11.

————. 1940. *Race, language, and culture*. New York.

BAAS [British Association for the Advancement of Science]. 1925. *Report of the 92nd meeting (94th Year) of the BAAS, Toronto—1924, August 6–13*. London.

Caffrey, M. 1989. *Ruth Benedict: Stranger in this land*. Austin, TX.

Cowan, W., M. K. Foster, & K. Koerner, eds. 1986. *New perspectives in language, culture, and personality*. Amsterdam.

Crawford, J. 1992. *Language loyalties: A source book on the official English controversy*. Chicago.

D'Andrade, R. 1995. *The development of cognitive anthropology*. Cambridge, UK.

Darnell, R. 1990. *Edward Sapir: Linguist, anthropologist, humanist*. Berkeley.

————. 1998. *And along came Boas: Continuity and revolution in Americanist anthropology*. Amsterdam.

Glazer, N. 1997. *We are all multiculturalists now*. Cambridge, MA.

Goldenweiser, A. 1941. Recent trends in American anthropology. AA 43:151–63.

Golla, V., ed. 1984. *The Sapir-Kroeber correspondence: Letters between Edward Sapir and A. L. Kroeber, 1905–1925*. Berkeley.

Grant, M. 1916. *The passing of the great race; or, The racial basis of European history*. New York (1923).

Hall, G. S. 1904. *Adolescence: Its psychology and its relations to physiology, anthropology, sociology, sex, crime, religion and education*. 2 vols. New York.

Hall, R. A., Jr. 1991. 165 Broadway—A crucial node in American structural linguistics. HL 8:153–66.

Handler, R. 1983. The dainty and the hungry man: Literature and anthropology in the work of Edward Sapir. HOA 1:208–31.

————. 1986a. The aesthetics of Sapir's *Language*. In Cowan et al. 1986:433–54.

————. 1986b. Vigorous male and aspiring female: Poetry, personality, and culture in Edward Sapir and Ruth Benedict. HOA 4:127–55.

————. 1989. Anti-romantic romanticism: Edward Sapir and the critique of American individualism. AQ 62:1–13.

Herskovits, M. 1948. *Man and his works: The science of cultural anthropology*. New York.

Hoebel, E. A. 1949. Review of Herskovits 1948. AA 51:471–74.

Homans, P. 1979. *Jung in context: Modernity and the making of a psychology*. Chicago.

Howard, J. 1984. *Margaret Mead: A life*. New York.

Hutchinson, E. P. 1981. *Legislative history of American immigration policy, 1798–1965*. Philadelphia.

Hymes, D., ed. 1972. *Reinventing anthropology*. New York.

————. 1999. Introduction to the Ann Arbor paperbacks edition. *Reinventing anthropology*, v–xlix. Ann Arbor, MI.

Joos, M. 1986. *Notes on the development of the Linguistic Society of America 1924 to 1950*. Ithaca, NY.

Joseph, J. E. 1996. The immediate sources of the 'Sapir-Whorf hypothesis'. HL 23: 365–404.

Jung, C. 1921. *Psychological types; or, The psychology of individuation*. Trans. H. G. Baynes. London (1923).

Koffka, K. 1921. *The growth of the mind; An introduction to child-psychology.* Trans. R. M. Ogden. London (1924).

Kroeber, A. L. 1917. The superorganic. In Kroeber 1952:22–51.

———. 1923. *Anthropology.* New York.

———. 1931. Historical reconstruction of culture growths and organic evolution. In Kroeber 1952:57–62.

———. 1935. History and science in anthropology. In Kroeber 1952:63–65.

———. 1952. *The nature of culture.* Chicago.

Lee, B. 1997. *Talking heads: Language, metalanguage, and the semiotics of subjectivity.* Durham, NC.

Lucy, J. 1992. *Language diversity and thought: A reformulation of the linguistic relativity hypothesis.* Cambridge, UK.

McDougall, W. 1908. *Introduction to social psychology.* Boston (1923).

———. 1920. *The group mind; A sketch of the principles of collective psychology, with some attempt to apply them to the interpretation of national life and character.* New York.

Mackert, M. 1993. The roots of Franz Boas' view of linguistic categories as a window to the human mind. *HL* 20:331–51.

———. 1994. Franz Boas' theory of phonetics. *HL* 21:351–84.

Malinowski, B. 1922. *Argonauts of the western Pacific: An account of native enterprise and adventure in the archipelagoes of Melanesian New Guinea.* London.

———. 1927. *Sex and repression in savage society.* London.

Manson, W. 1986. Abram Kardiner and the neo-Freudian alternative in culture and personality. *HOA* 4:72–94.

Mead, M. 1928a. *Coming of age in Samoa: A psychological study of primitive youth for Western civilization.* New York.

———. 1928b. *An inquiry into the question of cultural stability in Polynesia.* New York.

———. 1930. *Social organization of Manu'a.* Honolulu.

———. 1959. *An anthropologist at work: Writings of Ruth Benedict.* Boston.

———. 1972. *Blackberry winter: My earlier years.* New York.

Modell, J. 1983. *Ruth Benedict: Patterns of a life.* Philadelphia.

———. 1989. "It is besides a pleasant English word"—Ruth Benedict's concept of patterns. *AQ* 62:27–40.

Murdock, G. 1948. New light on the peoples of Micronesia. *Science* 108:423–25.

Perry, H. 1982. *Psychiatrist of America: The life of Harry Stack Sullivan.* Cambridge, MA.

Preston, R. 1986. Sapir's "Psychology of Culture" prospectus. In Cowan et al. 1986: 533–52.

Ross, D. 1972. *G. Stanley Hall: The psychologist as prophet.* Chicago.

Sapir, E. 1923. Two kinds of human beings [review of Jung 1921]. *The Freeman* 8:211–12.

———. 1928. Observations on the sex problem in America. *Am. J. Psychiatry* 8:519–34.

———. 1929a. The discipline of sex. *Am. Mercury* 16:413–20.

———. 1929b. Franz Boas [review of Boas 1928]. *The New Republic* 57:278–79.

———. 1930. What is the family still good for? *Am. Mercury* 19:145–51.

———. 1994. *The psychology of culture.* Ed. J. Irvine. Berlin.

Silverstein, M. 1979. Language structure and linguistic ideology. In *The elements: A parasession on linguistic units and levels, April 20–21, 1979,* ed. P. Clyne et al., 193–247. Chicago.

————. 1981. Reinventing the will: A philosophy of the elements of the human mind [review article on Tyler 1978]. *Revs. in Anth.* 8:311–34.

————. 1986. The diachrony of Sapir's linguistic description; or, Sapir's "cosmographical" linguistics. In Cowan et al. 1986:67–110.

————. 1992. Sapir's psychological and psychiatric perspectives on culture. *Cal. Linguistic Notes* 23(2):11–16.

————. 1996. Monoglot "standard" in America: Standardization and metaphors of linguistic hegemony. In *The matrix of language: Contemporary linguistic anthropology*, eds. D. Brenneis & R. Macaulay, 284–306. Boulder, CO.

————. 2000. Whorfianism and the linguistic imagination of nationality. In *Regimes of language*, ed. P. Kroskrity, 85–138. Santa Fe, NM.

————. n.d. Discerning 'cultural' concepts: Whorf on linguistically mediated (mis)recognition. Ms.

Stocking, G. 1968. *Race, culture, and evolution: Essays in the history of anthropology*. New York.

————. 1980. Sapir's last testament on culture and personality. *Hist. Anth. Newsl.* 7(2):8–10.

————. 1985. Philanthropoids and vanishing cultures: Rockefeller funding and the end of the museum era in Anglo-American anthropology. HOA 3:112–45.

————. 1989. The ethnographic sensibility of the 1920s and the dualism of the anthropological tradition. HOA 6:208–76.

————. 1995. *After Tylor: British social anthropology, 1888–1951*. Madison, WI.

Stocking, G., ed. 1974. *The shaping of American anthropology, 1883–1911: A Franz Boas reader*. New York.

————, ed. 1996. Volksgeist *as method and ethic: Essays on Boasian ethnography and the German anthropological tradition* [HOA 8]. Madison, WI.

Tyler, S. 1978. *The said and the unsaid: Mind, meaning, and culture*. New York.

Tyler, S., ed. 1969. *Cognitive anthropology: Readings*. New York.

Tylor, E. 1888. On a method of investigating the development of institutions, applied to laws of marriage and descent. *J. Anth. Inst.* 18:245–72.

Whorf, B. 1956. *Language, thought, and reality: Selected writings of Benjamin Lee Whorf*. Cambridge, MA.

Woolard, K. 1989. Sentences in the language prison: The rhetorical structuring of an American language policy debate. *Am. Ethnologist* 16:268–78.

Yans-McLaughlin, V. 1986. Science, democracy, and ethics: Mobilizing culture and personality for World War II. HOA 4:184–217.

JAIME DE ANGULO AND ALFRED KROEBER:

Bohemians and Bourgeois in Berkeley Anthropology

ROBERT BRIGHTMAN

After recounting an incident of "stench and scandal" involving anthropology faculty and graduate students at the University of California at Berkeley in 1926, Alfred Kroeber concluded that "every month passed makes me more un-relenting to Jaime" (KP:AK/B. Rudovic Pinner 5/9/26). Some twenty-five years later, Jaime de Angulo expressed succinctly to Ezra Pound his mature reflec-tions on Kroeber: "He is a Bastard" (GA 429).

Alfred Kroeber (1876–1960) established the Department of Anthropology at the University of California and was, after Franz Boas, the central figure in the theoretical agendas and institutional structures of American anthropology in his time. Jaime de Angulo (1887–1950) was a rancher, medical researcher, author, and scholar without formal portfolio who, peripheral position notwith-standing, made substantial contributions to the linguistics and ethnology of Native California and Mexico.

Angulo's involvement with anthropology appears in retrospect to have been dominated by patterns of paradox and irony. Possessing neither formal aca-demic credentials nor any inclination to acquire them, and exhibiting, more-over, personal dispositions at some variance with then-prevailing notions of re-spectability, Angulo aspired both to professional recognition, which he readily achieved, and to a permanent position within academic anthropology, which forever eluded him.

Though they were disinclined either to procure credentials for Angulo or to

---

Robert Brightman is Greenberg Professor of Native American Studies in the Depart-ment of Anthropology at Reed College. He is currently conducting research on hunter-gatherer castes in South Asia, and on a variety of topics in the urban anthropology of North America.

appoint him to academic positions, Kroeber, Boas, and Edward Sapir neverthe-less made extensive use of his professional abilities. Angulo's de jure exclusion from anthropology was thus complemented by a considerable measure of de facto inclusion. Working intermittently by means of small grants irregularly disbursed, he composed grammatical sketches of at least seventeen indigenous languages of California and Mexico (eleven published), published thirteen ethnological and eighteen linguistic articles, and left an unpublished legacy of thirty-four additional linguistic manuscripts (LH 521–29; GA 453–58). Kroe-ber and Boas also exploited his pedagogical skills and his contacts in the California Indian *rancherías*, periodically referring graduate students to him for informal instruction and placement. Angulo published in leading journals and corresponded with major figures in the discipline. With all of this, the only teaching position he held was a summer lectureship at Berkeley in 1920.

The article is composed of five parts. Following (1) a summary of Angulo's life and scholarly career, subsequent sections revisit certain career contexts in greater detail in order to evaluate two explanations for his marginalization: that (2) he lacked professional credentials and expertise, and that (3) his bohemi-anism adversely affected his career in the context of his personal relations with Kroeber. The following sections examine (4) Angulo's tactics in accommodat-ing himself to academia and pursuing a scholarly vocation outside of it, and (5) certain paradoxical characteristics of anthropology and anthropologists exem-plified in the Angulo-Kroeber relationship.

Angulo on the Margins of Academia

Born in Paris to aristocratic Spanish parents in 1887, Angulo received there (unappreciatively) a Jesuit education, and immigrated to America in 1905, in-tent on a career in ranching. In 1906, he began medical studies at Cooper Union in San Francisco, later transferring to Johns Hopkins University where he met and married his fellow student, Cary Fink. Angulo received his medical degree in 1911 and relocated with Fink to California in 1913, where they settled in Carmel. After a period of medical research, Angulo again looked into stock raising. His interests in the Indian people of California began when he met some Achumawis during a brief involvement in a ranch in Modoc County in 1914: "The sight of sagebrush forever is conducive to meditation but of a rather pas-sive inchoate kind. Humanity is not pleasing. It sounds an abysmal depth of vulgarity, from which I find relief sometimes in the company of Indians. Only their bodies are dirty" (GA 88).

Divested in Modoc County, Angulo next acquired a homestead in what was then the coastal wilderness south of Big Sur. Thereafter he moved between Big Sur, Carmel, San Francisco, and Berkeley. In 1915, increasingly estranged from

Jaime de Angulo and his Achumawi friend and consultant Old Blind Hall, near California, early 1920s. (Courtesy Gui Mayo.)

Fink, Angulo began a tentative involvement with Lucy "Nancy" Freeland, then visiting Carmel after completing her education at Vassar. His enlistment in the United States Medical Corps in May 1917 was followed by a reconciliation with Fink, and he was posted to Seattle while she returned, pregnant, to Carmel (GA 89–117).

Discharged in December 1918, Angulo returned to Carmel and was there reunited with Fink and their daughter Ximena. He was also reunited with Freeland, and the two resumed a more serious affair. He met the Berkeley anthropologists Kroeber and Paul Radin through Freeland; she had previously taken classes with them at the University. Angulo's friendship with Kroeber began an involvement with anthropology and linguistics that would continue for the rest of his life. In fall 1919, with Angulo's encouragement, Freeland entered the anthropology doctoral program at Berkeley under Kroeber's mentorship, with a specialization in linguistics. His earlier interests in exotic languages were rekindled and intensified by Freeland's studies; Angulo wrote Kroeber with questions on the subject in March 1920, initiating a period of informal tutelage in phonetics and morphology, and firsthand research on Eastern Pomo. There is no evidence that Angulo himself ever aspired to follow Freeland into the doctoral program or that Kroeber ever proposed such a course to him (GA 130–41).

In 1920 Kroeber invited Angulo to present a guest lecture and also offer two summer courses addressing the relations of psychology to anthropology, experiences that confirmed his desire for a permanent academic position (GA 134–42). After concluding his classes, Angulo resumed his residential alternations between Berkeley, Carmel, and Big Sur. Despite periodic co-residence, his marriage with Fink continued to unravel. Fink initiated divorce proceedings in 1920, and moved with their daughter to Zurich, where she became an acolyte of Carl Jung (GA 146–53).

Angulo's involvement with linguistics continued. In 1921 he began a decade-long correspondence with Sapir, and undertook his first fieldwork experience, spending approximately six weeks with the Achumawi. After separating from Freeland in 1922, he accepted a research position with Boas' student, Manuel Gamio, and commenced a productive period of research on Indian languages in Mexico (GA 150–94).

Angulo summarily abandoned the Mexican position in 1923 to return to the United States and marry Freeland (GA 194–201; LH 97–107). During a honeymoon visit to Zurich, he renewed contact with Fink, and established a personal friendship with Jung which possibly included analysis (GA 203–10). After their return to Berkeley, Angulo and Freeland became acquainted in 1924 with Mabel Dodge Luhan and her Taos Pueblo husband, Antonio Lujan. Angulo made multiple visits to Taos in 1924 and 1925, studying the Taos language and making the acquaintance of the visiting author, D. H. Lawrence. Angulo's and Freeland's son, Alvar, was born in spring 1924. On his last visit, he escorted the visiting Jung on a tour of the Pueblo (GA 203–48; cf. Angulo 1985).

In the mid-1920s, Angulo acquired professional visibility in American anthropology and linguistics, conducting fieldwork with many California Indian groups and publishing in professional journals. His research between 1927 and 1934 was supported by the ACLS-sponsored Committee on Research in Native American Languages (hereafter, "Committee"). Angulo and Freeland collaborated on much research and writing, although details are often obscure. Their daughter, Gui, was born in 1928. During 1930, Angulo attended the International Congress of Americanists in Hamburg and also worked with Carl Voegelin, the most distinguished of his de facto graduate students, providing both instruction and Pomo consultants. In 1932, Angulo and Freeland moved from Berkeley to the ranch at Big Sur and constructed a new house there (GA 249–314; LH 116–27, 198–298).

In 1933, Angulo was injured and his son, Alvar, was killed in an automobile accident at Big Sur. Angulo's extreme psychological trauma lasted at least until the end of the decade, and his scholarly activity was radically curtailed. He continued to correspond with Boas, but his financial support from the Committee ended in 1934. He conducted no further field research, and, excepting brief notes, published nothing in scholarly journals after 1935. A melancholy corollary of the accident was the suspension thereafter of nearly all of his professional friendships. He came briefly to national prominence in 1938 after shooting his neighbor's cattle and being charged with cattle rustling (Wall 1989:172; GA 341–43). Angulo's scholarly career, narrowly construed, ended quietly with transmission of a comparative Pomoan grammar to Boas in 1942. The manuscript was subsequently lost (GA 317–50; LH 130–35, 373–74).

Angulo and Freeland separated in 1939. Freeland and Gui returned to Berkeley and the couple divorced in 1943. During the 1940s, Angulo moved between Big Sur and San Francisco where he supported himself with odd jobs and by language instruction (GA 1995:344–79). His scholarly project during this period was an introductory linguistics textbook (*What Is Language?*) on which he labored between 1942 and 1948, but which was never published (LH 446–60).

Angulo's last years saw a return to his earlier literary activities and completion of the works of ethnographic fiction for which he is now best known. Diagnosed with prostate cancer in 1948, he returned to the Bay Area. Freeland, who had supported him intermittently in the intervening years, took him in again in 1949. Angulo remained in Freeland's home in the Berkeley Hills until his death in October of 1950 (GA 381–435). To the end, Angulo continued to hope for "recognition"(GA 416). He had initiated in 1948 an intensive correspondence with Ezra and Dorothy Pound. Through the Pounds and other literary connections Angulo's best-known writing saw posthumous publication: *Indians in Overalls* in 1950, and *Indian Tales* in 1953. In the 1970s and 1980s, both

Nancy Freeland de Angulo and Alvar de Angulo in Taos Pueblo, New Mexico, 1924. (Courtesy Gui Mayo.)

the Turtle Island Foundation, subsidized by Freeland, and City Lights undertook further publication and republication of Angulo's work (1974, 1976a,
1976b, 1979, 1985, 1990).

Though well-known to many writers, today Angulo lacks an academic reputation. A "History of Research" on Native California, for example, does not
mention him (Heizer 1978). Given the prevailing disciplinary amnesia, this is
unremarkable. More noteworthy was the total eclipse of his scholarly identity
in the fifteen years between his last field research and his death. Angulo's death
in 1950 went unnoticed in both *Language* and *American Anthropologist,* and by
the scholarly community more widely (Olmstead 1966:1).

Credentials and Professionalism

There are two distinguishable facets of Angulo's marginal disciplinary status.
First, he was never recommended for or offered an academic position. Second,
his privileged position as contract field linguist for the Committee ended in the
mid-1930s, never to resume. Leeds-Hurwitz has argued that Angulo enjoyed
professional status during the 1920s, but became professionally obsolescent following the advent of the first generation of university-trained anthropological
linguists around 1930. As contributory factors, she cites the psychological effects on Angulo of the 1933 accident, and the effects of the Depression on research funding (LH 24–29). These explanations are cogent and relevant, but
would benefit from some qualification and an understanding of context.

It is possible that Kroeber may have intended Angulo's 1920 summer lectureship as a probationary conduit to a more permanent position. Kroeber's interest in Angulo and Freeland was motivated in part by the desire to "collect a
group of good linguists at the university" (GA 140). In 1921, however, Kroeber
informed Angulo that a second appointment was impossible. Credentials were
clearly not an issue initially (LH 14); that they were desirable but not essential
at Berkeley during the period is suggested by Kroeber's hiring practices. As it was
constituted in 1901, the department consisted of Kroeber, the graduate student,
Pliny Earle Goddard, as linguist, and the "physician and radio specialist," P. M.
Jones, as archaeologist (Kroeber 1970:63). Many of Kroeber's appointments
(T. T. Waterman, Robert Lowie) express his preference for the Boasian impri-
matur, but he also hired Edward Winslow Gifford, an ornithologist sans credentials, as museum curator in 1912. Gifford advanced through the ranks and was
eventually promoted to Full Professor in 1945, "thus becoming one of the very
few men in the country to achieve such distinction without having gone to
college" (Foster 1960:328). In the teens and early 1920s at Berkeley, it seemed
credentials were requisite neither for appointment nor for advancement.

Further employment of Angulo at Berkeley would have made logistical sense in the department's division of labor. Around 1920, Kroeber shifted his research away from linguistics, opening a slot that Angulo might effectively have filled; recall Kroeber's use of him as informal preceptor for Voegelin and others. Different historians of the Berkeley department have converged on the same anomaly: that (after Goddard's departure) "no other linguist was hired" (Hymes 1964:701–2; cf. Steward 1973:10, 34). While it is not clear that Kroeber had means to add a position, he referred his decision, according to Angulo, not to fiscal limitations, absent credentials, or poor lecturing, but to a "bad reputation." Credentials influenced neither the initial offer nor the subsequent denial. Thereafter, the significance of credentials is unclear. While the value of the doctorate plausibly increased during the 1920s, Angulo's experience and increasing professional visibility might nevertheless have led to a position if he had enjoyed vigorous sponsorship. It appears, however, as though Angulo's later mentors had already ruled him out on other grounds.

Without an academic appointment, Angulo nonetheless enjoyed a privileged seven-year sinecure as field linguist with the Committee. In 1934, however, Committee support for his research was ended. As explanation, Leeds-Hurwitz emphasizes the increased salience of his "amateur" status during a transitional period of disciplinary "professionalism." During the 1920s, insufficient personnel existed to carry out Boas' salvage linguistics projects, and thus "amateurs" such as Angulo were employed. By 1930, the increased number of credentialed scholars gave Sapir and Boas an expanded and improved linguistic labor force; less accomplished amateurs could be excluded. "Due thus to a change of mental attitude as much to actual fact (after all, how many students actually obtained their degrees between 1927 and 1930?) . . . Angulo's career as part of the academic world was over within a few years" (LH 28–29).

The effects of emergent professionalism on Angulo must be examined in the context of earlier appraisals of his expertise during the 1920s. These include both negative and positive judgments, with the latter clearly predominant. In 1922, Kroeber judged his abilities as a phonetician to be "equaled by few anthropologists" (GA 176), and in the 1950s he recalled that he "had a good ear, a better one than his own" (Olmstead 1966:5). Kroeber's objections to Angulo's linguistics, expressed both to Angulo and to others, were that he produced incomplete grammars by neglecting problems that did not interest him, and that he did not collect sufficient texts (GA 175–94, 276). Initially skeptical of Angulo, Boas met him and Freeland during a 1927 visit to Berkeley, establishing a supportive friendship that endured until Boas' death (LH 48–52; GA 284–85).

Sapir's initial reaction to Angulo's work was ambivalent. In 1922, Kroeber debated with Sapir the merits of Angulo's Achumawi grammar relative to earlier work by Radin and Roland Dixon. Sapir expressed reservations about Angulo's Achumawi phonology, noting discrepancies with Radin's account and his own notes on the language. A revised version, written with Freeland, was later published in 1931 as "The Achumawi Language" (LH 95–96, 316–17; GA 188–90). Thereafter, however, Sapir praised Angulo's work and sponsored him in the Committee. Kroeber then wrote to Sapir and Boas, seeking to dissuade them from supporting Angulo's Californian research. Boas was sufficiently concerned to suggest making Angulo's payments conditional on receipt of manuscript, a tactic sometimes employed to extract publishable material from John Peabody Harrington. Sapir, however, vigorously defended Angulo's reliability and scholarship: "MS material of his that I have seen impresses me very favorably. . . . As a matter of fact, I have looked over his rather extensive MS on Achomawi Tone and Verb Forms and think it is one of the best American Indian studies now in MS" (GA 277). In a subsequent letter, Sapir again cited Angulo's "excellent work." Sapir's endorsement continued through 1928 when he wrote Angulo to tell him that his sketch of Eastern Pomo (1927a) was "exceedingly clear and highly instructive" (LH 27–28, 52–56, 83, 95–96, 235–37, 369).

By 1930, however, Sapir was evaluating Angulo by more rigorous standards of professionalism and finding him wanting. Comparing Radin and Angulo, Sapir wrote that "in many ways, Paul is obviously superior to such a man as Angulo in whom I have very little confidence at present" (KP:ES/AK 11/28/30). Sapir's larger point was that neither Radin nor Angulo were sufficiently expert to warrant further Committee support:

> The fact is that I think we are allowing too many poor or improperly qualified men to do linguistic work that should be entrusted to well-trained persons with a special flair for both phonetics and morphology. Boas has still very much the old pioneering attitude that the main thing is to rescue languages and put a lot of uncritical material on record. I do not subscribe to his view in the least. I think it is high time that all the work we sponsor be of a quality that is high enough to satisfy the requirements of a genuine linguist. (KP:ES/AK 11/28/30; cf. LH 28)

"One of the best" in 1927, Angulo was by 1930 "poor or improperly qualified." The Sapir-Angulo pedagogical correspondence continued through the following year when Sapir sent encouraging comments on Angulo's Karok grammatical sketch, together with a lengthy objection to the use in it of the term "neuter" (LH 55). Thereafter, however, it ceased abruptly, an interruption presumably linked to Sapir's diminished "confidence." By 1931 Boas also believed that the increase in "properly trained" students would improve the quality of linguistic research (LH 28), although he continued to view Angulo as "a genuine linguist," whereas Sapir, seemingly, did not. Angulo was "professionally qualified" to Boas but "professionally obsolescent" to Sapir, and thus he occupied for some time thereafter an ambiguous status that afforded continuing Committee support from Boas, but also portended eventual exclusion from academic linguistics as control of the latter shifted from Boas to Sapir, and thence, after Sapir's death in 1939, to his students and those of Bloomfield.

Sketch of Franz Boas by Jaime de Angulo, circa 1928. (Courtesy Gui Mayo.)

Replacing Sapir as Angulo's advocate, Boas provided Committee and other support for his research through 1934; thereafter support was attenuated and then ceased entirely (LH 48–52, 120–27, 132; GA 310–11, 320–29). After 1935, the Angulo-Boas correspondence lapsed until 1939 when Angulo twice wrote Boas asking for work. Boas replied, "there was no money for fieldwork, although there was plenty to do." The correspondence resumed briefly in 1942 when Angulo wrote announcing completion of his comparative Pomoan grammar. He added "a personal note": "I am living like a hermit on my mountain, not because I like it, but because I don't know how to get out. I am not actually starving but I am near it. . . . I will take any job, anywhere" (GA 348). Boas responded to acknowledge receipt of the manuscript but had no advice on employment. His death within the year ended Angulo's last professional relationship (GA 348–50; LH 130–35, 373–74).

Because Boas continued to regard Angulo as professionally capable, this second phase of his marginalization requires explanation. Boas's impression of Angulo's psychological condition and productivity, as mediated through their correspondence, may have persuaded him to suspend further support. Financial circumstances of the Committee during the period are less a matter of conjecture. Established in 1927 and budgeted initially for five years, the Committee was thereafter chronically underfinanced. By 1936 it was effectively out of funds and was discharged by the ACLS in 1937. A "Continuing Committee" with Boas at its head was then established, but disbursed only small grants to support preparation of manuscripts begun under Committee auspices (LH 269–79). While the shortfall may have weighed more heavily on Angulo than on others, without a chronological record of Committee disbursements, there is no means to determine if Angulo's research was terminated while that of credentialed scholars was maintained.

If Angulo's car accident and the Committee's fiscal situation are proximal explanations for interruption of Angulo's support in the mid-1930s, his already marginal position in linguistics can be traced back to the extreme shift in Sapir's attitude toward him around 1930. Tensions between Boas and Sapir over institutional control of linguistic anthropology were evident at least as early as 1927, and came to a head with Sapir's failed conspiracy to displace Boas from control of the Committee in 1934 (Darnell 1990:279–84; LH 269–73). By 1930, the issue for Sapir was not one of credentials per se, but of specifically Chicagoan versus Columbian imprimaturs. Committee contracts were split between the students of Boas and Sapir, with more going to the former (Darnell 1990:281). Sapir arrived at Chicago in 1925, and by the early 1930s included among his students Morris Swadesh, Stanley Newman, Fang-kuei Li, Mary Haas, Harry Hoijer, Walter Dyk, and Voegelin (Mithun 1996:49). These students embodied Sapir's criteria of professionalism: linguistic specialization and phonemic analysis, both contested by Boas and best guaranteed through training by Sapir himself.

Angulo's correspondence with Sapir comprised his most significant professional training (LH 52–56), but he was Sapir's student only in this informal sense, and it is unclear how assiduously he kept abreast of Sapir's changing theoretical priorities after the publication of *Language* (1921), or whether Sapir undertook to impart these in his correspondence. Sapir's concern with phonemic as against exclusively phonetic analysis of sound was evident as early as his Takelma grammar (1922a) of 1904, and his increasing interest can be traced through the 1920s and 1930s (Sapir 1920, 1925, 1933a, 1933b). Thus by the mid-1920s, phonological descriptions sometimes distinguished in Sapir's terms between the "organic" (phonemic) units and their "inorganic" (allophonic) positional variants. His students were influenced by these innovations, and the transition to a fully phonemic orientation was in place by the early 1930s (Hymes 1983:273–74; Silverstein 1986). Angulo's concern with pattern, however, was limited primarily to describing free variation. Whether Angulo's indifference to phonemics influenced Sapir against him is unclear, but in one instance there is the possibility that Sapir might have objected to his work on precisely these grounds.

Recall Sapir's early reservations concerning Angulo's treatment of Achumawi phonology. In 1931 Freeland wrote to Angulo, comparing their

Achumawi grammar with Radin's, registering surprise at the scope of the discrepancies, and suggesting that Radin was correct in at least one respect
(LH 57). Angulo and Freeland (1931:78–80) treat the plain, glottalized, and as-
pirated forms of Achumawi stop consonants as in free variation. Based on work
in the early 1970s, Nevin (1991:111; 1998) published an analysis of Achumawi
phonology, demonstrating both that the three series are phonemically contrastive and that they had been so described (by Radin, Sapir, and Harrington)
prior to Angulo's work. It is conceivable that Angulo's analysis of the stops was
both the source of Sapir's initial reservations and a factor in his later reappraisal.
Angulo's subsequent "Addenda and Corrigenda" in collaboration with phonetician Hans Jorgen Uldall only partially improved the analysis (Nevin 1991:11).

Given the development of linguistics in the 1930s, Angulo's only hope for
continuing his semi-professional status would have been closer alignment with
Sapir and the interacting Sapir and Bloomfield "schools" that later emerged at
Chicago and Yale. Voegelin might have provided the linkage. In any case, in
the 1930s Angulo maintained contact only with Boas, seemingly ignored theoretical developments in linguistics, and was, for personal reasons, professionally inactive during the latter half of the decade. His indifference to phonemics
and morphophonemics in the 1930s and thereafter would have guaranteed
his exclusion by linguists who regarded "the phoneme as defining a boundary
between the washed and the unwashed" (Hymes 1983:131; 1997:personal
communication).

Angulo's subsequent reflections on the discipline of linguistics in the 1940s
appear in later correspondence. In a letter to Pound, he recalled both an incapacity and an indisposition to reacquire a professional identity: "Then slowly I
got sane again but when I tried to go back to work I was rusty there was a new
generation of youngsters and they seemed to be on a wrong track linguistically
lost in a forest of technicalities. . . . I gave it up" (GA 426). This suggests that
he made some attempt to read the current literature in the journals in which he
used to publish, but could not get through the "forest of technicalities"—surely
the phonological debates of the 1940s. Through the 1940s, he labored on an
introductory textbook on language, which he submitted for publication in
1948. His pessimistic speculations as to whether "the pundits will set aside their
professional prejudices and accept the book" indicate both the alienation he
felt, as well as a personal superiority to the new generation of academic linguists
(LH 452). Not surprisingly, the book "infuriated the more academic experts"
who vetted it, and it was twice rejected in 1948 (LH 452, 459). Near the end of
his life, he wrote to Pound that "of course, they advised against it, too icono-
clastic, unproved theories, unacceptable to the trade!!! The experts, the pundits, who are they, now that Boas and Sapir are dead? Little squirts who first
started to study linguistics with me and now they are professors" (GA 392).

The question of whether Angulo's scholarship was or was not "professional" in the 1920s and 1930s is complicated by the facts that he was active in two subdisciplines, ethnology and linguistics. As concerns linguistics, Angulo's work during the 1920s was positively evaluated by Kroeber, Boas, and Sapir. Angulo published repeatedly in *Language* and in *International Journal of American Linguistics*. As concerns the Committee, "between 1927 and 1937 Angulo was given more money (approximately $6250 in all) and worked on more languages than any other researcher for the Committee" (LH 117; GA 275). Angulo's ethnography was conventionally Boasian, although notable for its reflexivity and precocious attention to acculturation. In contrast, his ethnology reflects such influences as Jung, Lewis Henry Morgan, and Lucien Lévy-Bruhl. These *grand récits* of the human condition led him to some ethnological conclusions genuinely anomalous in the Boasian milieu (see Angulo 1926:352–53). This notwithstanding, Lowie published Angulo repeatedly in *American Anthropologist*, and also gave him books to review (LH 62); he published also in *Journal of American Folklore* and *Anthropos*. Within the context, then, of 1920s "four-fields" anthropology, Angulo exhibited professional qualifications. But relative to changing theoretical agendas in the increasingly autonomous discipline of linguistics, he was, indeed, professionally obsolescent by 1930.

Such evaluations are, of course, dependent upon perspective, as Sapir's changing attitude to Angulo attests. While Olmstead (1966:5) wrote that Angulo's Achumawi grammar "holds up remarkably consistently under the closest scrutiny," later assessments of Angulo's linguistics are mixed or negative (LH 344, 397; Nevin 1991). The merits of Angulo's linguistics as viewed from a historicist rather than a retrospectivist or presentist perspective remain to be assessed. On Sapir's warrant, it is probable that Angulo was better than most of his contemporaries, prior to the first generation of Sapir's own students. And given Boas' continued sponsorship, his "obsolescent" status does not directly explain suspension of his Committee support, although it speaks to his failure to maintain a professional identity in linguistics in the 1930s. All this suggests that Angulo's inability to find an academic position cannot be reduced to the question of professional credentials.

"Stench and Scandal"

An alternative explanation for Angulo's failure to secure an academic position is that potential employers or sponsors considered him to be personally undesirable as a faculty member or colleague. Angulo was imaginably problematic both in his psychological profile and his decidedly bohemian orientations.

A possible analysis with Jung notwithstanding, Angulo never sought psychiatric treatment, but suffered throughout his life from insomnia and nightmares, and acknowledged needs to establish relations with substitute father figures and to dominate and disparage women close to him. Episodic psychological abuse is a harrowing theme in his relations with his children. Angulo expressed fears of nervous breakdown, attempted suicide in 1943, and was briefly committed to a mental ward in 1944. His problems were exacerbated by personal tragedies, notably his son's death and his separations from Fink and Freeland. Angulo was hardly unique among scholars of the period in experiencing psychological problems. He wrote of them variously with self-pity and with ironic detachment, but intermittent objectivity did not consistently permit him to overcome their adverse effects on his life and relationships (GA 9, 171–77, 352, 356).

In regard to bohemianism, Angulo himself was disposed to trace the genesis of his self-conscious "rebellion" to his disillusionment with Catholicism in early childhood (GA 6–7). In any case, he came to America temperamentally predisposed to embrace the stereotypic forms of Murger-derived bohemianism present there. As his first wife noted, "We wanted to be free" (GA 69): thus socialism, feminism, primitivism, free love, alcohol, and wilderness. Angulo's "rebellion" was variously expressed in genuine obliviousness to social conventions and in self-conscious transgression of them. Upon first beholding the Big Sur wilderness, he recognized in it the ideal "place for a freedom loving anarchist" (GA 92). He drank heavily from adolescence on and was seemingly an alcoholic for much of his life. While appreciating formal clothing in professional contexts, his habits of dress otherwise ranged from bohemian dandyism through the equestrian costume of the Big Sur vaqueros to intermittent transvestism— although there is no evidence that his academic colleagues knew of this latter habit (GA 307–10). In his later years at Big Sur, Angulo grew increasingly indifferent to hygiene and clothing altogether (Wall 1989:172). His overlapping relationships with Fink and Freeland and his marriages to each of them were, in contemporary idiom, "open" in the sense that Angulo engaged in open extramarital liaisons.

Any or all of these factors might have persuaded Angulo's mentors that, professional qualifications notwithstanding, he would not have functioned effectively in an academic position. Angulo himself explained his marginalization in terms of the significance that his conduct assumed in the context of his personal relationship with Kroeber. By Angulo's account, his bohemianism had adverse effects on his career exclusively because of Kroeber's outraged reactions to it.

The Berkeley anthropology department was established in 1901 through a bequest from Phoebe Apperson Hearst, with Kroeber in effective control of the program from the beginning. At the time he met Angulo and Freeland, Kroeber was emerging from an extended period of personal upheaval brought on by the death of his wife, Henriette, in 1913, the onset of his Meunier's disease, and the death in 1916 of Ishi, the Yahi Indian resident in the University Museum. Kroeber took a sabbatical year of European travel in 1915–16, and then in 1917–18 underwent Freudian analysis in New York. He was sufficiently impressed with analysis to undertake its practice, and continued to see patients between 1918 and 1922 (Kroeber 1970:79–80, 86–107; Steward 1973:10–12).

Kroeber's initial relations with Angulo were cordial, Kroeber functioning as Angulo's informal adviser and instructor. Their correspondence exhibited such formal and ebullient salutations as "My Dear Kroeber" and "My Dear Angulo," among other signs of collegial good fellowship (KP: JA/AK 11/3/19, AK/JA 3/31/20). The friendship initially focused on shared experiences with psychiatry. During his military service, Angulo received three weeks of training in psychiatry at Johns Hopkins and was then assigned to identify and treat signs of mental trauma in flying cadets and pilots (GA 1995:101, 119–26, 130, 134). In spring 1920, the two men finalized plans for Angulo's courses on "The Mental Functions in Primitive Culture" and "The Relation of Psychology to Anthropology," their correspondence attesting to Angulo's Radin-inspired understanding of the elastic relationship between courses and their descriptions: "And from what Paul tells me, it makes very little difference what you announce for your courses. Then you can give what you like. Isn't that so?" (KP:JA/AK 11/15/19). Angulo taught the two courses in the summer and seemingly acquitted himself well (LH 87).

Yet Angulo's first teaching appointment at Berkeley would also be his last. Still married to Fink, he resolved the question of summer-term lodging by living openly with Freeland in her home in the Berkeley hills. When Kroeber first learned of this arrangement—or of the ongoing Angulo-Freeland relationship—is unclear, but his reaction to it is distilled in a letter Angulo wrote to Fink over a year later. He apparently hoped his Achumawi linguistic and ethnographic material, once written up and published, would provide an entrée into a faculty position at Berkeley. Kroeber continued a collegial correspondence with him while he was in the field in fall 1921, encouraging him to take texts ("they are like a pile of ore dumped at the smelter entrance"[GA 157]) and providing maps and copies of Dixon's earlier linguistic work. Upon returning to Berkeley in November, Angulo met with Kroeber and raised the question of a position in the Department. "Kroeber told him that on account of his reputation—that is, his affair with Nancy—Jaime had no chance at all" (GA 158). Specifically, "Kroeber felt that this was scandalous and immoral, and gave the university, and his department a bad name" (GA 142). Here we encounter Kroeber at the limits of his appreciation of the "relativity of morals, customs, and comparative etiquette," a theme he had urged Angulo to address in his guest lecture at Berkeley in spring of 1920 (GA 138). Kroeber's decision to "keep clear of both of us" prompted Angulo and Freeland to discuss marriage and then to separate in April 1922 (GA 159; LH 87–88). Incongruously, he continued during this period to rely on Kroeber for odd services such as overseeing the welfare of his Achumawi consultant, Jack Folsom, then passing through Berkeley on his way north to Modoc County; Kroeber wearily agreed to "do what I can" (KP: AK/JA 3/13/22).

The scandal rendering Angulo unfit for employment might as easily have rendered Freeland unfit for doctoral training. In any event, her separation from

Angulo seems to have altered Kroeber's attitude. He wrote her a friendly letter in June, addressing her as "Dear Nance," thanking her for an invitation to a Miwok Kuksu ceremonial, and dunning her for $1.45 in department fees (KP:AK/NF 6/22/22). Thereafter (until April 1923), Freeland held the posts of research fellow in the Department and continued to study for the doctorate under Kroeber's supervision (LH 98).

Kroeber's misgivings about Angulo extended also to his prospective professional employment elsewhere. In fall 1921, Sapir wrote Kroeber, inquiring about Angulo's suitability for a position as his field assistant in Ottawa. Kroeber's testimonial to his "exceptionally keen intellect" was submerged overall by emphasis on "instability," "vehemence," transient "enthusiasms," and "infantilism," and by a lukewarm assessment of his prospects. Sapir responded, predictably, "I had better steer clear of Angulo" (LH 90; GA 157–58). Thus Kroeber obstructed Angulo's exposure to the finest linguistic training in the discipline and probable later access to academic employment. Julien Steward knew both Kroeber and Angulo, and it is interesting to consider in this light his assessment of Kroeber in the capacity of referee: "On occasion he pointed out the person's shortcomings in ways that were not altogether appropriate" (Steward 1973:21).

In the immediate wake of the Angulo-Freeland separation, Kroeber wrote quite a different reference letter in May 1922 to Manuel Gamio, recommending Angulo for the research position in Mexico in very positive terms (GA 176). Having received the offer, Angulo wrote happily to Kroeber whose support must have seemed enigmatic to him: "Dear Boss, You are a brick to have landed me that job—and such a job—*fait tout exprès pour moi*. . . . And I who was all set to take a job as janitor. But it's the work that I'm keen on. What an opportunity! Well, I am so happy I don't know what to do" (GA 179). This evoked both a cordial response and a prophetic reservation: "I was not sure how you would feel about going to Mexico" (KP:AK/JA 6/26/22). Gui de Angulo notes that Kroeber's letter to Gamio, in contrast to its predecessor to Sapir, seems "partly inspired by desire to get Jaime employed somewhere out of Kroeber's sphere of influence, where Jaime wouldn't be leading Kroeber's students astray and wouldn't be hanging around the University without a position" (GA 176).

With Angulo in Mexico in 1922, Kroeber resumed their pedagogical correspondence and vigorously promoted Angulo and his writing to Sapir and Boas (LH 95–97; GA 175–94). In April 1923, Angulo left Mexico and communicated to Gamio through an intermediary his intention to resign. Kroeber reacted with a degree of anger inexplicable even given his role as Angulo's reference. Kroeber wired that Angulo's behavior was "infantile," that "his resignation will close his anthropologist career," and that "his one chance lies in returning to Mexico." Long after Angulo made his peace with Gamio, Kroeber dwelt implacably on the incident as abiding evidence of his irresponsibility (GA 195–96; LH 103–06).

In January 1923, Freeland was formally advanced to doctoral candidacy (KP:AK/NF 1/17/23). Anticipating her completion, Kroeber had arranged for her to submit to the National Research Council a proposal dealing with the sex lives of the Pueblo Indians. Reunited with Freeland, Angulo persuaded her to submit a revised proposal including him as co–investigator. The rationale for their joint proposal was persuasive to its evaluators, but Clark Wissler's request to Kroeber for a recommendation for Angulo inspired "a letter so damning that it was marked 'personal' and later removed from the file" (GA 200). The Mexican affair, the Angulo-Freeland marriage, and Angulo's intervention in the NRC grant effectively ended the Kroeber-Angulo relationship, although Kroeber continued writing avidly and adversely about him to others for years to come (GA 194–201; LH 97–107).

To Kroeber's existing objections to them, the Angulos soon added the charge of maintaining a disreputable house. In the Prohibition-era 1920s, the Angulo-Freeland residence in the Berkeley hills took on the character of a well-lubricated salon-in-the-rough, one much-frequented, to Kroeber's dismay, by anthropology graduate students. As Steward recalled:

> During my graduate years at Berkeley a group of graduate students, together with certain other persons, had formed the habit of foregathering in the home of Jaime de Angulo. This group was known as the North Berkeley Gang. Whereas Lowie and Gifford attended the occasional festivities of this group, Kroeber, so far as I can recall, was never present. He gently warned us, however, to be careful of our behavior lest the university learn of it and we get into trouble. (Steward 1973:18; cf. Wolf 1981:62)

Kroeber's ongoing correspondence during the 1920s with Berna Rudovic [Pinner], his former student and Freeland's friend, exhibited marked disapproval of "life on the hill." For example, Kroeber wrote that he liked Freeland a great deal "even though her name is as water" (KP:AK/BRP 9/?/25), a closing simile that remains mysterious. Somewhat paradoxically, he brought his visiting mother to experience the Angulo-Freeland household in 1925, but elected "not to trouble her" with "the cruder aspects of the Freeland, Allison et al., ménages" (KP:AK/BRP 10/2/25; cf. GA 259). A spring 1926 visit to Berkeley by Bronislaw Malinowski resulted predictably in the latter's recruitment into the Angulo-Freeland circle and in further faculty-student intercourse, described by Kroeber in these terms:

> Our summer-school man Malinowski—Polish-English—has been annexed by the Jaimes. He was here on a preliminary visit for the Rockefeller people and gave a series of "seminars." [William Duncan] Strong brought an acquaintance, who brought Gladys [Franzen] and Mary Ellen [Washburn], who the next time brought Nancy [Freeland]. Mary Ellen encouraged Malinowski to make love to her (she will sleep with no one but her husband, it is said), which he was more than ready to. Nancy furnished the house, he was guest of honor at a couple of parties, Lowie let himself be dragged along not unwillingly, and there'll be stench if not scandal

all summer. Well, enough of that sort of thing—except to say that every month passed makes me more unrelenting to Jaime. (KP:AK/BRP 5/9/26; cf. GA 262–68)

Kroeber's departmental colleague Robert Lowie was often complicit in such proceedings. Robert Murphy (1972:34) recalled that he was "a devoted participant in the Prohibition-days parties held by the students" and that "his performance of the Crow war dances was considered the high point of an evening." In a 1925 letter to Sapir, Angulo wrote: "Robert was here last night, danced the Crow dance, and by God it is remarkable how well he does it" (GA 259–60).

Kroeber's marriage in 1926 to an anthropology graduate student, Theodora Krakaw Brown, a widow with two young children (Kroeber 1970:119–21, 132–33), seemingly worked no change in his animosity. His reflections on Angulo and Freeland's son Alvar appear in yet another letter to Rudovic: "Nancy and her kid [Alvar] bumped into Theodora the other day with the result that the brat was brought in for a quarter-hour to get acquainted with ours. He is very strange—not deficient, apparently docile without being scared, but lacking in the normal three-year-old's realization that speech is something to be used. Nor does he have the impulse to play with toys—they are things to wonder at and pick up and pick up again and hold. The drive to act isn't there but he seems both healthy and intelligent." Having thus pronounced clinically on the progeny, Kroeber proceeded to the parents: "Nancy is pathetic in her eagerness to reconcile Jaime and me. So much so that she loses all her tact of indirection and becomes transparent. What I can't tell her and she won't see is that anything I do for Jaime comes out of my hide" (KP:AK/ BRP 5/14/27).

In May 1927, Kroeber, having learned that the Committee proposed to support Angulo's linguistic work in California, was in extensive communication with Sapir and Boas.

Dear Dr. Boas:
In view of de Angulo's activity in language work and your Committee's prospective relations with him, I want to tell you my attitude to him. You are at liberty to use the following statements as you see fit, but on account of their personal nature I should not want them incorporated in any official record.

The fundamental bar to our maintaining any relations with de Angulo during the past couple of years is that his personal reputation in the University community and with the administration is such that his association or identification with our department would be prejudicial to its welfare. This may bring it about that it will be somewhat embarrassing if he works in the California field. I should therefore be personally relieved if his work takes place at Taos or elsewhere outside of our range. I should like however to be understood that if other conditions indicate California as the most desirable field for de Angulo, I will interpose no objection as long as it is clear that he has no . . . relations with the University of California.

> I do not wish to disguise from you that de Angulo and I had a definite misun-
> derstanding some years ago, as I felt that he did not manifest reliability in his sev-
> erance of relations with the Direction of Anthropology in Mexico. There is the
> further fact that his marriage to Miss Freeland completely interrupted her prom-
> ised and more than half-finished work with Miwok which she had done as part of
> her graduate training . . . at University expense; and that such linguistic work as
> she has done since then has been contributory to his. I realize that the responsi-
> bility in this latter point is hers as much as his; but inasmuch as he is the gainer
> by the outcome and the University's work the loser, it is perhaps natural that I am
> somewhat dissatisfied.

Kroeber went on to affirm Angulo's intelligence and also to criticize his inat-
tention to detail and to text collection. He concluded: "I think it is desirable
that your Committee try him out, largely because there is undoubtedly promise
in the man and it is unlikely that any institution could come to enter into permanent relations with him. At the same time, if your Committee acts without
understanding and cognizance of a quite unusual personality, I think that it is
likely to be disappointed" (GA 275–76). Here again, as in the earlier letter to
Sapir, the praise is more than faintly damned. Sapir, however, supported
Angulo ("I believe Kroeber may for personal reasons not be altogether fair to
Angulo" [GA 277]), and Kroeber was unsuccessful in excluding him from
Committee-sponsored California research.

Thereafter, there is little to add. Kroeber continued to write adverse letters
to the Committee, now emphasizing Angulo's linguistic shortcomings rather
than his character (LH 47). Angulo's attitude toward Kroeber during his period
with the Committee is distilled in a 1932 letter to Boas announcing plans to
study the Yurok language: "I kept out of it on account of Kroeber. But Kroeber
continues to boycott me, so why should I care?" (LH 380). In 1934, Kroeber dis-
suaded Boas from transferring to Angulo Radin's long-delayed Committee as-
signment on Patwin (GA 234). The same year, Boas alerted Angulo that he was
sending his student, Burt Aginsky, to him for briefing on Pomo. Angulo then
wrote Kroeber, describing his post-accident malaise, foisting Aginsky onto
him, and instructing him to "Give my love to Theodora" (GA 327–28). This is
the last known correspondence between them.

The strange tale of Freeland's dissertation also deserves notice. After her marriage to Angulo in 1923, Freeland's connection with the Berkeley department
appears to have ended, and her doctoral research on the Eastern Miwok languages was interrupted. When Sapir proposed in 1927 that the Committee support completion of her research, Kroeber took exception, writing that "the situation is so complicated that I recommend letting matters lie for the present" and
that "I would appreciate it if your Committee would leave to me the initiative of
any steps directed toward resumption of Mrs. De Angulo's work, if at any time
such seems desirable" (GA 278). As a result, the Committee did not fund her.

By 1930, Freeland apparently felt renewed interest both in Miwok and in the Berkeley doctoral program, and wrote to Kroeber (with the salutation "Dear Kroeber" and the signature "Nancy") to ask "Would you still like to have me do the Miwok?" (KP:NF/AK ?/?/30). Kroeber responded with a friendly letter encouraging her to complete her dissertation (KP:AK/NF 5/6/30). Freeland resumed her research (GA 304–7), and later reported on her progress: "I am so glad I never did complete it before, Kroeber, for what with the work I have done this winter (on all three of the dialects) and the help I have had from [phonetician] Hans Jorgen [Uldall], it does both you and me much more credit than it would have before" (KP:NF/AK ?/?/32).

Freeland wrote to Kroeber in 1935 announcing completion (KP:NF/AK 1/3/35). Kroeber answered cordially, acknowledging receipt of the manuscript and concluding incongruously with the charge to "give my best to Jaime and take it for yourself" (KP:AK/NF 1/22/35). Shortly after he commended her on the quality of her work: "[I] want to congratulate you on having done one of the best executed pieces of work in American linguistics and perhaps the very best expressed one" (KP: AK/NF 2/26/35). Thereafter their correspondence ceased.

Kroeber's commendations notwithstanding, he never took steps to confer the doctoral degree on Freeland. Freeland did not force the issue, but regretted the withheld degree (GA 2001:personal communication). Neither did Kroeber publish her grammar or attempt to place it elsewhere, a project that fell ultimately to Voegelin sixteen years later (Freeland 1951). It is of some interest that Freeland's analysis of Miwok sounds is fully phonemic.

This excursus on Kroeber's interventions in Angulo and Freeland's professional careers reveals, to say the least, a certain incommensurability between their conduct (cohabitation, interrupting a job, marriage, seeking coresearcher positions, entertaining students at drinking parties), and the intensity of Kroeber's reactions to it. It is plausible that Kroeber had genuine reservations concerning Angulo's professional suitability, but it is difficult to escape the conclusion that personal animosity for Angulo also entered, consciously or unconsciously, into his attempts to obstruct his career.

It was not that Kroeber genuinely doubted Angulo's professional abilities. However damning his assessments of Angulo's conduct, Kroeber seldom omitted reference to his brilliance. Angulo returned the favor in a letter to Pound: "What a goddamn son-of-a-bitch—But he was a good anthropologist . . . ["The Super-Organic"] was an idea of genius" (GA 430). Neither was it simply incompatibility between Germanic and Latin temperaments. United by a shared intellectual passion for Native California, Kroeber and Angulo were otherwise radically opposed in personality and in attitudes towards the scientific vocation, the politics of anthropology, and the uses of convention (Buckley 1997). Angulo and Kroeber afford, in fact, a privileged example of the kind of temperamental complementation famously prominent in literature and sociology—

if less frequently in lived experience—as a feature of enduring friendships. Kroeber was not adverse to eccentric colleagues at close quarters: consider his support of Waterman whose obituary he took as an occasion for remarking on the latter's "erratic" and "drastic" character (Kroeber 1937:529). But if Kroeber or Angulo ever felt, as writer John LeCarré has a character say, "Together we would have made one marvelous man," it was Kroeber's antipathy that dominated their relationship. As Thomas Buckley puts it: "In Kroeber's view, de Angulo—an activist for free love—was a bad influence on the embodied future of anthropology. In his perception of these (particularly, female) graduate students' welfare, the personal and professional met and coalesced in Kroeber's mind" (Buckley 1997).

Astute readers will already have noted the signature theme of *cherchez la femme*: Kroeber's interwoven personal and professional preoccupations with Angulo intersect in the person of Freeland. The jealousies underpinning Kroeber's animosity were obliquely revealed by Angulo in two opiated, but not dismissible deathbed epistles to Pound. In the first, Angulo recreated an imagined scenario in which his "reputation" is described to Boas: "[Boas] discovered that my stuff was being published in Europe, in Vienna, in Paris 'Who is this fellow Angulo? Living in California? Why isn't he publishing here?' 'Oh he had a fight with Kroeber—he married Kroeber's girl . . . he is a dissolute drunkard he is crazy'" (GA 424). In the second, Angulo enlarged on this aspect of Kroeber's enmity:

> That bastard he couldn't make up his mind between Nancy and another girl (a pretty fast one)—everybody on the campus thot she was his mistress—but she wasn't—I know—he supported her on condition she didnt fuck anyone—wanted to reform her—and he couldn't make up his mind about N—I was still married then—& i fucked both N. and the other girl—and that awful gossip of Paul Radin—with his long nose—of cors he found it out and gave it a trolley-ride around Carmel and Berkeley—you bet K loved me less than ever—
>
> The day I got my divorce I married N—and this is the letter Kroeber sent me: "I suppose you expect me to congratulate you—what you'll do with your marriage depends on you—you will probably continue to hide behind a woman's skirts and waste our time with your enthusiasm."
>
> In those days I was still trying to get into academic circles—whenever I was on the point of landing a good job, Kroeber wud spoil it for me—he would go out of his way to blacken my character—I did fuck around a good deal—but what has that got to do with anthropology? I was unknown and he had already an established position—time and time again I was on the point of landing a good position—until he sent his letter. (GA 429–30)

Angulo's account makes better sense of Kroeber's enmity than any competing explanations, although details remain obscure. Angulo's reference to Freeland as "Kroeber's girl" more probably refers to Kroeber's intentions rather than to an existing relationship: Gui de Angulo recalls being told that Kroeber was romantically interested in her mother but "stood no chance with her" (2001:personal communication). It is unclear when Kroeber became interested in Freeland, when he first learned of the Angulo-Freeland relationship, and whether his resentment was immediate or delayed. Angulo's first serious involvement with Freeland lasted from 1919 to 1922, and signs of Kroeber's animosity emerge relatively late, in November 1921. On the other hand, his friendly relations with both resumed shortly after their separation in 1922, and then went into dramatic eclipse one year later when the two married. Kroeber's desire for Freeland to study Puebloan sexuality under the auspices of the NRC's Committee for Research on Sex Problems still awaits elucidation. His ambivalence towards Freeland is foreshadowed in the mingled romantic and professional aspects of his relationship with the comparably emancipated Elsie Clews Parsons between 1918 and 1920 (Deacon 1997:201–13). The enigmatic "other woman" between whom and Freeland Kroeber "couldn't make up his mind" remains unidentified, but is possibly Berna Rudovic, his former student and a friend of Freeland, with whom he carried on an extensive correspondence in the 1920s (KP:Outbound AK/BRP:1925–1931). When or whether Angulo had relations with Rudovic, and whether and how Kroeber reacted, is unknown (GA 132, 134, 139, 181, 211).

If Freeland and possibly Rudovic composed for Kroeber a site of competition with Angulo, other disclosures to Pound suggest that sexual jealousy was the least of it:

> He [Kroeber] is a bastard. One day [early 1920s] we were sitting on the hillside back of the university talking. He was telling me about his having gone into "psychoanalysis," opened an office in SF etc suddenly he said "you see I am an anal erotic" "What the hell is that?" "I am stingy—you think I am your friend but I am not! I am jealous of you" I jumped 3 feet in the air—"Jealous of me???! Why?" "Because you are brilliant and i am not—I am a plugger—you are independent but I have to stick to my job." (GA 429)

With all due allowance for medication, wish fulfillment, and embellishment, it is possible that Angulo here related to Pound his memories of an actual conversation. Alternatively, the substance of the interchange may have been true even if the event never happened, Angulo fabricating a discourse that Kroeber himself never acknowledged or verbalized.

Kroeber inhabited the professional status to which Angulo aspired, a status, moreover, which Kroeber was empowered to bestow upon or to withhold from him, specifically on the Berkeley campus itself where Angulo could align his professional goals with his regional attachments. Angulo thus recreated for Pound his own plausibly incredulous reaction to Kroeber's jealousy in which "independence" and "brilliance" are contrasted with stolid intellect and onerous professional responsibilities. And while "independence" is here contrasted with "sticking to a job," Angulo possibly imagined Kroeber as envying a whole bohemian portfolio of drink, itinerancy, leisure, and—perhaps especially— free love. If Kroeber covertly envied Angulo's lifestyle, it is possible to discern elements of overdetermination in his preoccupation with the bibulous and li- bidinal conduct at 2851 Buena Vista Avenue in Berkeley.

In Angulo's letter, the reciprocal jealousy is figured as an ironic chiastic trope: the "positioned" Kroeber envies Angulo's "independence" and the "indepen- dent" Angulo envies Kroeber's "position." At the same time, one can surmise that each man appreciated his own situation, and regarded the other's with more than faint skepticism. Angulo's recollection is, indeed, about greener grass and roads not taken, but more fundamentally about a time and place in which "position" and "independence" assumed the character of irreconcilable alternatives. It is plausible that Kroeber and Angulo both valued and devalued the contrasting features of temperament and vocation distributed between them, and this is perhaps what the two of them most basically meant to each other. Behind these symmetries remains the fact that Kroeber could have cho- sen to become an independent bohemian scholar whereas, by refusing to hire Angulo and obstructing his access to other jobs, he withheld from him the op- portunity to elect the position of bourgeois academic.

Kroeber's adverse effects on Angulo's career were limited to refusing him a position at Berkeley and sabotaging Sapir's potential offer in Ottawa. But Kroe- ber was not the only or even the most important obstacle between Angulo and a position. Since Kroeber was unsuccessful in communicating his animosity to Sapir and Boas, other reasons must be sought for the fact that these later men- tors vigorously promoted Angulo's research and publishing in the 1920s, but never during this period sought to find him an academic position. Boas was both a tireless promoter of anthropology and a genuine friend to Angulo, but never included him among the lists of Columbia-educated scholars he recom- mended to employers. The probable explanation is that Boas and Sapir inde- pendently converged in defining Angulo as too "eccentric and difficult" to function effectively as a professional (Boas in LH 50–52). Angulo's prospects would probably have improved if he had been either eccentric but credentialed, or sans credentials but far more normal. The intersection of these disadvan- tages ultimately outweighed the value of his scholarship.

Since no one ever offered Angulo an academic position, the issue of his im- puted incapacity remains unsubstantiated. Angulo might have spent the 1920s yearning after a position that he was incapable of occupying, or that, if capable of occupying, he would have loathed. Alternatively, a position might have ex- erted stabilizing influences on Angulo, and he might have gone on to a distin- guished professional career in research and teaching.

There are grounds for speculation that the latter outcome was possible. An-

gulo's effectiveness as a teacher is corroborated in both academic and nonaca-
demic contexts. For a neighbor at Big Sur in the 1940s,

> Jaime was unquestionably one of the most brilliant men I ever met and the most
> eccentric. There was a feeling, especially when he talked of anthropology, lin-
> guistics, mathematics, physics, psychiatry, philosophy, fields he knew well, of ex-
> traordinary lucidity—rather like a pure gem in whose center existed a deep, still,
> quiet pool, rather like a crystal. The feeling one got at such moments was of pure
> beauty; and it was at times such as these that those who knew Jaime felt to the
> fullest the purity of his genius which, when so directly contacted, was akin to mu-
> sic, poetry, the stars, flame, the cosmos. (Wall 1989:173–74)

Less passionate, but also appreciative were the reminiscences of Edward Russo
who recalled Angulo as a presence in North Beach in the late 1940s:

> Jaime was a hell of a talker. He could talk about anything. Even when he was
> drunk. Hell, especially when he was drunk. Music, books, women, food, whatever.
> Chinese guy come in the place to clean up [the bar], he'd talk Chinese to him.
> Young guys in the bar, they'd start out making fun of him. Then they'd listen and
> then they'd just wind up listening to him talk. I brought my girl there to Ferone's
> on Kearney just so she could hear him talk. (Russo 1995:personal communication)

Similar sentiments were expressed by Carl Voegelin. After Angulo's death,
he told Freeland that Angulo "had great potentialities as a teacher, and could
inspire a young student as no one else in the field could do," and that "with a
feeling of security and a skilled stage manager, he could have had a marked success in the role of a member of a university faculty." Voegelin concluded, "it had
been a great loss to Anthropology, that Kroeber had been too timid to sponsor
Jaime" (LH 10). The two women who knew Angulo best, however, held different convictions. Freeland flatly disagreed with Voegelin's optimistic assessment
of her ex-husband's academic career prospects (LH 10), and in 2001, Gui de
Angulo expressed the same skepticism regarding her father's capacity for an academic position (GA 2001:personal communication).

Angulo's Tactics

The interpretation of Angulo's marginal status thus far is one of Kristevan ab-
jection and involuntary exclusion at the hands of academic powers-that-be.
But if he lacked the credentials or character conventionally requisite for an academic position, he was not uncreative in seeking to overcome these obstacles.
Angulo's "tactics" (see Certeau 1984:xix) comprised various adjustments, compromises, and decisions that addressed genuine or imagined incompatibilities
between his temperament, his scholarly vocation, and institutional academia.

He addressed these problems both by (intermittent) genuflections to convention, and by more mainstream strategies of professional networking and scholarly activity. Once banished from academe, he was not uncreative in seeking to pursue his anthropological vocation independently. Deprived of all affiliation and support, he continued his linguistic research in isolation. Intellectually predisposed both to scientific and artistic vocations, or perhaps to a vocation that fused the scientific and the artistic, Angulo ultimately sought their reconciliation in literature. Throughout the three decades in question, he additionally invented the rather different tactic of embracing and embellishing his "outsider" status.

Confronted with bourgeois opinion, Angulo intermittently attempted to conform to respectability—or at least to simulate such an alignment. While it is remotely possible that Angulo and Freeland believed their affair would go unremarked, Kroeber's reaction in 1921 provided them with an occasion to reflect anew on the wages of adultery. Taking Kroeber's discourse on morals at face value, Angulo and Freeland pragmatically discussed marriage: "He [Kroeber] for one has decided to keep absolutely clear of either of us. Well, it isn't worth the fight, we think, and we will take the risk of spoiling our friendship" (GA 159).

The occupational costs of the "fight" against puritanism were thus too high, and warranted the risks that marriage might entail for the Angulo-Freeland romance. Other damage-control tactics followed. Freeland took Angulo's temporary residence in her Berkeley house as an occasion to decamp to the Miwok "because she did not want further to scandalize Kroeber by being in her house while Jaime was there" (GA 164). Ultimately, they settled on separation: "Anyway, the long and the short of it is this: marriage is not possible for us. And keeping on as we have been doing is impossible—too much against the 'mores' of the community, it involves too much fighting (witness Kroeber's flat refusal to give me a job on account of it)" (LH 87–88).

In other letters to Fink in 1922, Angulo lamented that "I have thrown my usefulness away through lack of discipline in my own personal life" and asserted a determination "to rehabilitate myself in the eyes of the world." Imagining an omniscient Kroeberian super ego ("now we will see if he was merely philandering and playing or if he was honest"), he even swore to abandon Big Sur (GA 177–79). The research position in Mexico then afforded potential, though deferred, access to an academic position in the United States. In the event, Angulo resigned and returned to Freeland, Berkeley and Big Sur. His broadmindedness on the subject of convention, however, lingered on, nowhere better attested than in a 1923 letter outlining plans to end his four-month marriage with Freeland, remarry Fink, and then establish a residential ménage à trois with both of them and the children. Of this project, he wrote: "We will try to shock their [others'] conventions and opinions as little as possible" (GA 208).

A second group of tactics for reconciliation with academic anthropology comprised the more conventional practices of networking and professional activity. Angulo conducted privately financed research, established supportive personal relationships with the acknowledged leaders of the field, and began to publish in the leading anthropology and linguistics journals. Sapir and Boas promoted his publishing and also his privileged status as contract field linguist for the Committee. The Committee afforded a compromise resolution of the otherwise incompatible goals of "independence" and "position." While Angulo continued to hope that his relations with Boas would yield a "real position" (GA 286), his ambition for one may have attenuated, leavened by the prestige and monies of the Committee, and by the "free-lance" pleasures afforded by the Indian *rancherías*, Big Sur, the Berkeley *vie de Bohème*, and Freeland's independent income.

Angulo's idiosyncratic "independent position" ended in the mid-1930s. Estranged from an increasingly autonomous linguistic subdiscipline, he entered the 1940s as an independent scholar, but now without professional affiliation or mentors in high places. Academically banished, he pursued his linguistic vocation through work on his textbook, dedicated to Sapir and Boas, and envisioned as a meditation on Sapir's *Language* (1921). While Angulo was cautiously hopeful that the work might reestablish his academic identity, he took no great pains to align it with professional expectations. Written in an idiosyncratic phonetic notation, elliptical in structure, and addressed both to the lay public and students of linguistics, the book was rejected by two publishers, an outcome Angulo anticipated (LH 446–60). The book, nevertheless, afforded him both a retrospective synthesis and subjective closure of his linguistic career: "I found out, and that's enuf. *L'humanité je m'en fiche*" (LH 450).

Thereafter, Angulo abandoned scholarly writing and whatever hopes he might still have entertained for an academic position. He remained, nevertheless, intellectually engaged with the Californian cultures and languages that he had studied for over twenty-five years. His activities as a writer of poetry and prose had previously been subordinate to his scholarly work. In 1948, freed from the distractions of academic opportunities or aspirations, he returned to his earlier experiments with genres of ethnographic literature. Not surprisingly, he wrote about California Indian cultures and languages, and, in so doing, integrated his scholarship with a long peripheral, but now revitalized literary career.

Near the end of his life, Angulo recalled acquiring from his father a conception of the radical difference between science and art, and a disposition to value science at art's expense. He went on to describe his protracted emancipation from these early prejudices, and, climactically, the belated discovery of an artistic vocation (GA 401–8). While there is some evidence in 1915 for Angulo's disenchantment with medical science ("A pile of junk!! A true pile of junk; rusty pieces all disconnected. But Life is not there, the principle of life, of energy, energy itself, or whatever IT is" [GA 78]), there is none whatsoever for a protracted denial of his artistic vocation. Angulo's anthropological and literary interests coexisted and interacted from the 1920s to the end of his life. He wrote, for example, three novellas with Indian-related themes in the 1920s: *Don Bartolomeo* (published in 1925; reprinted in Angulo 1979), *The Lariat* (in Angulo 1979), and *The Witch* (in Angulo 1985). Angulo's literary activities bear comparison with the ancillary artistic avocations of others in the Boasian milieu. Less typical but not unparalleled was his interest in the aesthetics of American Indian oral literature and music (see Hymes 1999).

Leeds-Hurwitz (117–18) wrote that "de Angulo's nature was not really that of an academic, anthropologist or otherwise," and that he "saw the world with the eyes of an artist." The distinction expresses an extreme view of the divide between scientific and artistic practices and temperaments. This seems more the case since Leeds-Hurwitz proceeds astutely to locate Angulo's literary work within a larger Boasian context in which experimentation with ethnographic fiction prompted reflections both on contrasts and continuities between art and science. Inspired by Bandelier's *The Delight Makers* (1916), anthropologists in the 1920s were speculating that fiction might be superior to academic prose genres for purposes of representing intuited patterns and Indian subjectivities (LH 407–16; cf. Kroeber 1922, Sapir 1922b). Angulo predictably had little use for academic prose: he found Kroeber's style "flavorless" and complained to Sapir of the "perfectly flat monotonous drone" of academic writing (LH 409; GA 254–56). Angulo's enthusiasm for the deployment of artistic sensibilities and mediums to anthropological purposes had formed at least by 1928, when he announced that "every anthropologist would like of course to write like an artist, and see like an artist" (Angulo 1928:323). By the same time, the science-art oppositions notwithstanding, he had come to bracket ethnology with art ("we the artists and ethnologists") in distinction to all other vocations (Angulo 1927b; cf. GA 397).

In 1928, inspired by the mythological literature of the California Indians, Angulo composed "Indian Tales for a Little Boy and Girl" for his children (GA 294). By 1943, he had written an account of his fieldwork with the Achumawi (GA 351). His literary career and reputation derive primarily from what he made of these two works when he returned to them in 1948 and 1949. Both give expression to his ethnological vocation, but in different literary genres.

Angulo rewrote the Achumawi account as a series of letters to Blaise Cendrars, "saying just what I goddamn please, and to hell with the publishers" (LH 136). An account of three summers of Achumawi fieldwork, *Indians in Overalls* (1950) is literary rather than scientific in rhetorical form, and also didactically ethnographic, as it explores features of Achumawi language and culture through evocation of Angulo's interviews and other less formal interactions with his Achumawi friends and consultants. Anticipating most first-person fieldwork accounts by well over a decade, the book also prefigured disciplinary preoccupations with reflexivism that emerged in the 1980s, even as it fell predictably beyond the latter's notice. As its oxymoronic title would imply, the book was distinctive for its specific focus on a contemporary rather than pre-European horizon. Some Achumawi people have taken an interest in Angulo's portrait of their ancestors (Wilson 1990).

In spring 1949, friends in Berkeley learned of Angulo's "Indian Tales for a Little Boy and Girl" and arranged for him to read it in installments for broadcast on the listener-sponsored radio station KPFA. Aired that year as *Old Time Stories*, it was immensely popular and prompted an invitation to compose and rerecord for broadcast a longer version, upon which Angulo and his daughter collaborated (GA 391–95; LH 429–46). The genre affiliations of *Old Time Stories* are less readily identifiable. In its completed form, it is composed by a fictional connecting narrative in which Old Man Coyote and other animal personae travel across a primeval landscape of north-central California, visiting different animal (and other nonhuman) "tribes" that are modeled loosely on the societies with which Angulo conducted fieldwork. Within this frame, characters ask and answer questions, tell stories, and sing songs, all from Angulo's ethnographic sources and from his original translations and retellings of Indian literature.

A much edited version limited primarily to the linking narrative was published as *Indian Tales* (1953), and has been continuously in print ever since. Neither *Indian Tales* nor the excised sections later published (Angulo 1976a, 1976b) do justice to the complete text (1949) prepared for the radio recordings (LH 433–34). Angulo nevertheless would have appreciated Clyde Kluckhohn's review (1953), in which the book is characterized as correct but not dry, and as interesting but not romantic; and Gary Snyder's (1969) remarks on the brilliant textual evocation of the orality of Native Californian literature. The book exemplifies, in particular, Angulo (and Freeland's) long standing interest in speech registers, a subject which became topical in linguistic anthropology only long after Angulo's exclusion from it (Buckley 1997).

While Angulo nowhere explicitly confirms this, the claim seems plausible that he found in literature, as earlier in his participatory fieldwork, a superior means for a characteristically Boasian scientific intention: the apprehension and representation of Indian subjectivities (LH 17–18, 407–9; GA 395, 423). His guiding intentions can be read equally as the subordination of literature to ethnographic ends, or as the reverse.

Angulo came to his literary career circuitously by way of academic circumscription. If his exclusion followed primarily from others' adverse judgments of his character and comportment, the pains he took to elicit precisely such judgments deserve equal attention. Despite occasional genuflections to conformity, throughout most of his career Angulo adopted a renegade persona that acquired legendary dimensions in the years after his death. Through his literary

Jaime de Angulo broadcasting *Old Time Stories* on station KPFA in Berkeley, 1949. (Courtesy Gui Mayo.)

connections and posthumous publications, he became known to writers during the 1950s, notably, but not exclusively to the so-called Beats. Thus, Jack Kerouac wrote of "old Valencia, . . . the mad Spanish anthropologist sage who'd lived with the Pomo and Pit River Indians of California, famous old man, whom I'd read and revered only three years ago while working the railroad outa San Luis Obispo—'Bug, give me back my shadow!' he yelled on a recorded tape before he died" (1995:138). Of Bay Area writers, Gary Snyder played the major role in carrying Angulo's reputation forward into the 1960s and beyond (Snyder 1969; Tarn 1971). But Angulo's mystique is nowhere better expressed than in Henry Miller's portrait of him in the mid-1940s at Big Sur. Miller introduced Angulo to his Parisian visitor, Conrad Moricand, a very different variety of urban bohemian:

> Finally I hear them speaking soberly, earnestly as if it were a matter of great concern. It is about language. Moricand says but little now. He is all ears. With all his knowledge, I suspect that he never dreamed that on this North American continent there once were spoken so many varieties of tongues, languages, not dialects merely, languages great and small, obscure and rudimentary some of them, some extremely complicated, baroque, one might say, in form and structure. How could

he know—few Americans know—that side by side there existed tribes whose languages were as far apart as is Bantu from Sanskrit, or Finnish from Phoenician, or Basque from German. The idea had never entered his head, cosmopolite that he was, that in a remote corner of the globe known as Big Sur a man named Jaime de Angulo, a renegade and a reprobate, was spending his days and nights comparing, classifying, analyzing, dissecting roots, declensions, prefixes and suffixes, etymologies, homologies, affinities, and anomalies of tongues and dialects borrowed from all continents, all times, all races and conditions of man. Never had he thought it possible to combine in one person, as did this Angulo, the savage, the scholar, the man of the world, the recluse, the idealist, and the very son of Lucifer. Well might he say, as he did later: "C'est un être formidable. C'est un homme, celui-là!"(Miller 1957:347–48; cf. Brooks 1954:1920)

Miller here evokes multiple paradoxical attributes but the basic opposition contrasts Angulo's unworldly scholarship with his unscholarly worldliness. Drawing on Miller's language, this juxtaposition could be called the "renegade-scholar" identity. Both the charisma and the stigma of the identity derive from the compositional linkage of incongruous scholar and renegade attributes. To ask whether Angulo's renegade-scholar identity was ascribed or achieved invites the same problems of infelicitous dichotomy that characterize the identity itself. Angulo and his colleagues had very different conceptions and evaluations of this identity, and it is in their interaction that its biographical trajectory can best be appreciated.

Coexisting rebellious and scholarly dispositions reach back to Angulo's childhood, but the identity first coalesced in 1921 when Kroeber confronted him with the incongruity of scholarly respectability and renegade sexual conduct. While Angulo was not oblivious to the uses of conformity, his reactions to the disciplinary gaze sometimes took the form of yet further behavior that could only guarantee to make him intolerable to prospective employers. He was often confrontational on the subject, asserting, for example, to Fink in 1921 both his autonomous moral code and sovereign indifference to gossip (GA 148–49). He was also personally flamboyant, disposed to épater les bourgeois with profane language, exhibitionism, and other outrages in formal social contexts (GA 349). And while he expressed concern in the early 1920s with "living down" his bad reputation (GA 177–79), he appears by mid-decade to have been more concerned with perfecting it: the years of his major research activity were also the years of maximal "stench and scandal" in the Berkeley Hills. In 1930, Ruth Benedict recalled a New York meeting as follows: "Jaime has been here. We sat over whiskey and soda till after midnight one night, and I liked him just as I always have. With all the ostracism he courts—and gets— he hasn't a trace of a persecution complex, speaks the kindliest and keenest things of everybody, and—of all things—cares most about Nance's getting back to professional achievements, to linguistics that is" (1959:298).

Note that even Benedict, more appreciative of renegade-scholar juxtaposi-
tions than others in Angulo's professional circle, found his concern for Freeland's career incongruous. Many Boasians liked Angulo and respected his scholarship, but, from the perspective of a more genteel or housebroken academic
bohemianism, Angulo may have been, in a later idiom, "too real" to mesh
smoothly with received ideas of professional probity. As for Angulo himself, he
valued his bohemian comportment, his scholarly vocation, and, perhaps most
of all, their juxtaposition. Stereotypic bohemian dispositions are famously
Saussurean, deriving both content and charm from their oppositive value to
the practices of conventional others. So also with the renegade-scholar identity that at once differentiated Angulo from nonbohemian scholars and from
nonscholarly bohemians, notably those whose primary vocations were in the
arts. Everything appears as if adverse reactions to Angulo's bohemianism confirmed him in it, and as if external judgments of its incongruity with the scholarly vocation inscribed the identity more deeply in his persona.

Angulo's different evaluations of the identity appear in his late correspondence with the Pounds. In some contexts, he was disposed to critique the im-
puted incongruity between bohemianism and scholarship. Thus he appreciated
that Boas recognized his professional accomplishments without attending to
his personal comportment: "Boas didn't give a damn about my private morals as
long as my phonetics were right" (GA 424). In his writing, Angulo sometimes
simultaneously drew attention to the incongruity and expressed resentment of
others' reactions to it. Of his cylinder recording of Achumawi songs, he wrote:
"The university would not help me; took no interest; would not even give me
enough money to have the records transcribed and made permanent on modern disks. Decent anthropologists don't associate with drunkards who go rolling
in ditches with shamans" (Angulo 1990:53). But how would decent anthropologists have learned that he drank with Achumawi shamans if not, like the
reader, from Angulo himself?

In other contexts, Angulo emphasized the hybrid vigor rather than the mutual irrelevance of the juxtaposed attributes. Kroeber, for example, was "too
full of systematic archeology ever to grasp the mystical modality of [Indian]
thought" (GA 142)—but not, by implication, Angulo himself. Institutional
liminality, moreover, could be a virtue, affording autonomy from academic Babbitry. Angulo fondly recalled the mid-1920s in Berkeley where "I was accused
of every crime all those stories about me only one-third were true and how the
University hated me! I had no job, I was a free-lance anthropologist-linguist,
they cudnt fire me HOW THEY HATED ME . . . and of cors I took great delight in
circumventing the University arm-chair anthropologists . . . they would never
help me. . . . I spent all my own capital (I had inherited from my mother) on
those field-trips with Indians—that was all right" (GA 423–25).

If only a third of the stories were true, this was due not least to Angulo's own embellishments. So attached did he become to the renegade-scholar persona that he amplified it with invented self-aggrandizing exploits. Thus, by the 1940s, he was telling Big Sur neighbors that he was never rehired at Berkeley because of naked flagpole climbing and public transvestism, both of which renegade transgressions are almost certainly nonevents (Wall 1989:176–77). Henry Miller thought that Angulo was "his own worst enemy" and another Big Sur neighbor lamented the personal tragedy entailed by his "dramatic sense, his need to play a role, to be a buffoon, a star, a madman, a tragic figure, a rebel, a martyr" (Wall 1989:174). The professional costs to Angulo of inhabiting the renegade-scholar identity were not small ones. At the same time, the role afforded satisfactions absent from more conventional academic careers. A fragment of deathbed writing, probably intended for the Pounds, seems to be Angulo's meditation on his own obsession with the "renegade-scholar" legend and others' reactions to it:

> Jaime legendary—Full of violence and carrying his burning restless soul and body on a horse by sun and moonshine—fighting himself and the world, referring to himself as a living symbol—often, too often drunk and then dangerous—knife fights, gun-shooting among tough dancers, singing indian chants with them who did not know the meaning of it. His home perched on dizzying hilltop—hole in the roof for the ever-burning chimney smoke—a spot which smells of Andorra's smuggler—osteria. Jaime sitting in his raincoat under the leaking roof and full of bestemmia, gloria, and unconquered madness—they praise his bursting laughter with centuries of spanish grandeur behind it. Philo-semitic by protest against hitler, etc. As you'd say, endless in somma Refusing to be introduced to an English literatus, instead of which pulling his reddish beard—most of the time on horseback—once put in prison for a feud over a neighbor's cow which he had shot—getting freed by pleading and on the ground that he suffers from Claustrophobia—It takes Jaime to convince the Monterey Sheriff, etc. (P/AC:Folder 146)

Angulo genuinely wanted an academic position, but his pursuit of ostracism possibly answered to a coexisting and contrary desire to remain on the institutional frontiers. In certain times and places it was seemingly a hell of a lot of fun to be a renegade-scholar. Upon learning that his cancer was terminal, he wrote to Freeland, "I have had plenty of fun and plenty of sorrow, in my life, BUT IT HAS NOT BEEN A DULL LIFE, certainly" (GA 387).

Academic Anthropology and Its Discontents

Angulo's noncareer attests to incongruities between academic anthropology and bohemianism. If Angulo and his animus Kroeber appear to exemplify bohemian and bourgeois orientations, respectively, it is interesting to reflect that academe in general and anthropology in particular occupy parallel paradoxical positions. Anthropology and anthropologists commonly combine, in variable proportion, two sensibilities that might be labeled "Academic Babbitry" and "Bohemian Primitivism." Lévi-Strauss, for example, regarded anthropologists as the most extreme bearers of an "attitude of refusal toward the demands of the group" (1955:54) typical of scholars in the arts and sciences. But if a certain "attitude of refusal" (stereotypically a scholarly "otherworldliness") accrues to academics in general and anthropologists in particular, it coexists with an "attitude of acceptance" to institutional participations no less rigid and routinized than those of more worldly professions.

Nevertheless, anthropology and anthropologists exhibit a distinctive modality of this "attitude of refusal" in their particular choice of discipline and vocation. Until recently, anthropology was the study of exotic Otherness—the alterity of primitives and savages. And as a corollary, relativism and pluralism together instilled perspectives on Western conventions and institutions that were either detached or openly critical. The valuing of otherness together with a skeptical take on the customs at home continue to be a dominant motivation in anthropology. Moreover, they are commonly conjoined: the conviction that the fourth-world societies have exemplary lessons to teach us reaches from Rousseau through Boasianism and structuralism, and on to the theoretical orientations of the present day. It is plausible that many men and women come to the discipline, today as in the past, because it resonates with their own personal dispositions for detachment or refusal.

Here there is a partial resemblance between anthropologists and bohemians. Alike in their "attitudes of refusal," they also share an affinity for otherness, the former looking to non-Western societies and the latter more commonly to Europeans, the insane, and the underclasses. "Non-worldliness" is intrinsic in the labor of both groups. The occupational associations of bohemians are with *les beaux arts,* and those of anthropologists with scholarship, although it is instructive to recall that the original quartet of Murger bohemians included a philosopher. Nevertheless, the studied defiance of convention embodied in the personal behavior of bohemians contrasts semantically with the behavioral conformity commonly associated with academics, anthropologists included. The personal or professional "attitude of refusal" of anthropologists seems seldom to take the form of the adoption of bohemian conventions, but intersections have occurred during the 1920s (see Stocking 1992) and at other times. It is these incongruities (bohemians who are scholars rather than artists, scholars who are bohemians rather than bourgeois) that composed the "renegade scholar" identity ascribed to and inhabited by Angulo.

These considerations suggest that there is an abiding instability or ambivalence in anthropology and anthropologists. Anthropologists participate in bureaucratized and hierarchical institutions and identify with their values. But they do this precisely through participation in an academic discipline that is skeptical of these same institutions and values. Thus, the field is attractive to individuals predisposed to postures of detachment and critique.

Angulo and Kroeber appear to represent extreme and, as it were, concentrated expressions of "Bohemian Primitivism" and "Academic Babbitry" as paradoxical aspects of anthropological sensibility. Everything *seems* as if Kroeber's anthropological vocation was exclusively intellectual, divorced from personal affinities for what he called "the exotically primitive" (Deacon 1997:211) and its implicit or explicit critiques of civility. There is no trace of even qualified primitivism in his work. His theories and his texts are famously impersonal, lacking both reflexive turns and attention to human subjects. Kroeber's fieldwork practices exhibit a like detachment: he did not seek protracted residence with or participation in *ranchería* social life (Buckley 1997). Kroeber was institutionally an "insider" of high rank. He sought relief through psychoanalysis from what appear to have been symptoms of depression. He exhibited no evident dispositions for bohemianism or less routinized eccentricity.

Angulo, on the other hand, exhibits particularly well the "attitude of refusal" composing anthropology's "Bohemian Primitivism" tendency. His anthropology, in contrast to Kroeber's, was strongly reflexive and alive with human individuals. Angulo professed an extreme version of a more general skepticism regarding the methodological uses of objectivity in a profession where subjectivity, in variable measure, was "both the object and the instrument of their endeavor" (Stocking 1992:340; cf. LH 408). Dismayed by the "austere and impersonal" character of Boasian science (GA 256–57), he moved beyond the prevailing textual strategies, independently inventing fieldwork practices shortly to be expounded by Malinowski, but in a more assertively participatory mode. Thus, for Angulo, people who "forgot they were white and became Indians [were] in a way, the better ethnologists and artists" (1927b:352), and understanding of "the religious spirit" was possible only for a scholar with "that spirit of wonder in himself" (Angulo 1926:354). "Going native" became the means to a full-tilt immersion in Achumawi subjectivities (LH 19).

But if "going native" was for Angulo a means to scholarly ends, it also served other motives more attuned to his own subjectivity than that of the Achumawis. His primitivism took the form of challenging the sufficiency of science and rationalism, and arguing that "good hard logic and clear thinking" required leavening with the "spirit of wonder" embodied in Achumawi spirituality (GA 170, 223, 270). It also nourished a full-blown "Wannabee Indian" identity: Angulo sometimes claimed Indian ancestry among the Achumawi, and also assured Ruth Benedict that he was "half an Indian or more" (Benedict 1959:298). Such stereotypic bohemian behaviors were plausibly the primary explanation for his institutional exclusion.

While Kroeber and Angulo appear to typify the academic and bohemian polarities of anthropology, they cannot, of course, be divided easily between them. If the "spirit of wonder" is not salient in Kroeber's scholarship or biography, neither is it beyond investigation there, and Kroeber's relationship with "Ishi" is an obvious place to begin looking for it. Recall that Kroeber, on Angulo's warrant, fantasized about emancipation from his professional obligations, and also that in other contexts he expressed dissatisfaction with what he described as the "ascetic and passive" or "repressed" aspects of his personality (Deacon 1997:202–3). For his part, Angulo, for all his Jungian and primitivist excesses, wrote ethnographies and grammars that were, most of the time, perfectly objective by Boasian criteria. Further, Angulo's search for an academic position was plausibly motivated by precisely the obsessive desire for social validation of personal worth that bohemians are supposed to regard with contempt or indifference. Additional indices of "Bohemian Primitivism" in Kroeber and "Academic Babbitry" in Angulo could be cited. As with other anthropologists, their careers—including institutional locations, theoretical orientations, and geographic and topical interests—represent individual projects, conditioned by historical contexts and biography, in which these paradoxical tendencies are put into more (Kroeber) or less (Angulo) stable conditions of reconciliation and alignment.

> I a seal lie on the rocks warm in the sun.
>
> I remember the Esselen, the Mukne,
> the Saklan, all the tribes that lived
> From the Sur to San Francisco Bay
>
> I dive in the water, and my head looks like a man
> Swimming to the shore in the dusk.
>
> I like to wander along the bright streets
> at night in the crowd.
>
> *Jaime de Angulo*

Acknowledgments

First of all, my thanks to Gui de Angulo who generously invited me to her home, showed me manuscripts and photographs, discussed my ideas for the essay, graciously presented me with an offprint of her father's "Seven Indian Tales" (1952), and granted permission to reprint one of his poems, published originally in *Coyote's Bones* (1974). I am indebted to various archivists and custodians at the Bancroft Library at Berkeley, and also at the University Libraries of the Universities of California at Santa Cruz and Los Angeles. On the principle that two heads are better than one, Thomas Buckley and I originally planned to write this essay together. Contrary to all reason, Buckley elected instead to embark upon a self-navigated global odyssey in his sailboat, but left in his wake the gist of many conversations about Angulo over twenty-five years and also access to his unpublished writings. Among colleagues, Raymond Fogelson, Kathrine French, Dell Hymes, Paul Kroeber, Wendy Leeds-Hurwitz, Robert Moore, Bruce Nevin, James Shugrue, Shirley Silver, Michael Silverstein, and Chloe Blake Stevenson all provided varieties of assistance and inspiration. My thanks to Rupert Stasch, who gave the essay an especially close and constructive reading, and to Richard Handler, for his superb editing. Much of the material in the last section was prompted by dialogues with George Stocking. Maria Lepowsky has been an inspiring companion in research-related travels including descents into the archives and ascents to the Berkeley Hills and up the Jaime de Angulo trail (so-called) to Partington Ridge at Big Sur.

References Cited

While I have made use of a variety of published and archival sources, most material comes from the two basic sources, Wendy Leeds-Hurwitz's *Jaime de Angulo: An Intellectual Biography* (1983) and Gui de Angulo's *Old Coyote of Big Sur: The Life of Jaime de Angulo* (1995). Many themes in the present essay are already prefigured and discussed in these works.

AA   *American Anthropologist*
IJAL   *International Journal of American Linguistics*

Angulo, G. de. 1995. The old coyote of Big Sur: A life of Jaime de Angulo. Berkeley.
Angulo, J. de. 1926. The background of religious feeling in a primitive tribe. AA 28:352–60.
———. 1927a. Texte en langue pomo (Californie). *J. de la Société des Américanistes* 19:129–44.
———. 1927b. Review of *L'Art et la philosophie des indiens de l'Amérique du Nord*, by H. B. Alexander. AA 29:551–54.
———. 1928. Review of *Myth in primitive psychology*, by B. Malinowski. AA 30:322–26.
———. 1949. *Old time stories*. Angulo Collection, Special Collections, University Library, University of California, Los Angeles.
———. 1950. *Indians in overalls*. San Francisco (1990).
———. 1952. Seven Indian tales. *Hudson Rv.* 5(2):165–98.
———. 1953. *Indian tales*. New York.
———. 1974. *Coyote's bones*. Berkeley.
———. 1976a. *Shabegok* (*Old time stories*, vol. 1). Berkeley.
———. 1976b. *How the world was made* (*Old time stories*, vol. 2). Berkeley.
———. 1979. *The Jaime de Angulo reader*. B. Callahan, ed. Berkeley.
———. 1985. *Jaime in Taos: The Taos papers of Jaime de Angulo*. G. de Angulo, ed.
Angulo, J. de & N. Freeland. 1931. The Achumawi language. IJAL 6:77–120.
Bandelier, A. 1916. *The delight makers*. New York.
Benedict, R. 1959. *An anthropologist at work: Writings of Ruth Benedict*. M. Mead, ed. Boston.
Brooks, V. W. 1954. *Scenes and portraits*. New York.

Buckley, T. 1997. Love, rage and grief in salvage ethnography. Ms.

Certeau, M. de. 1984. *The practice of everyday life*. Berkeley.

Darnell, R. 1990. *Edward Sapir: Linguist, anthropologist, humanist*. Berkeley.

Deacon, D. 1997. *Elsie Clews Parsons: Inventing modern life*. Chicago.

Foster, G. 1960. Edward Winslow Gifford, 1887–1959. AA 62:327–29.

Freeland, L. S. 1951. Language of the Sierra Miwok. *IJAL* Supplement 17(1):1–199.

GA. See under Angulo, G. de.

Heizer, R. 1978. History of Research. In *Handbook of North American Indians, vol. 8: California*, 6–15. Washington, DC.

Hymes, D. 1964. Alfred Louis Kroeber. In *Language in culture and society*, 689–707. New York.

————. 1983. Essays in the history of linguistic anthropology. Amsterdam.

————. 1999. Boas on the threshold of ethnopoetics. In *Theorizing the Americanist tradition*, eds. L. Valentine & R. Darnell, 84–107. Toronto.

Kerouac, J. 1995. *Desolation Angels*. New York.

Kluckhohn, C. 1953. California Indians in word and picture. *Herald Tribune Book Review*, April 19:4.

Kroeber, A. 1922. Introduction. In *American Indian life*, ed. E. C. Parsons, 5–16. Lincoln, NE.

————. 1937. Thomas Talbot Waterman. AA 39:527–29.

Kroeber, T. 1970. *Alfred Kroeber: A personal configuration*. Berkeley.

Leeds-Hurwitz, W. 1983. Jaime De Angulo: An intellectual biography. Doctoral dissertation, U. Pennsylvania.

Lévi-Strauss, C. 1955. *Tristes tropiques*. New York (1973).

LH. See under Leeds-Hurwitz.

Miller, H. 1957. *Big Sur and the oranges of Hieronymus Bosch*. New York.

Mithun, M. 1996. The description of the native languages of North America: Boas and after. In *Handbook of North American Indians, vol. 17: Languages*, ed. I. Goddard, 43–63. Washington, DC.

Murphy, R. F. 1972. *Robert H. Lowie*. New York.

Nevin, B. 1991. Obsolescence in Achumai: Why Uldall too? *Papers from the American Indian Languages Conference held at the University of California, Santa Cruz, 1991*. Occasional papers in linguistics, Department of Linguistics, Southern Illinois U. Carbondale, IL.

————. 1998. Aspects of Pit River phonology. Doctoral dissertation, U. Pennysylvania.

Olmstead, D. L. 1966. *Achumawi dictionary*. University of California Publications in Linguistics. Berkeley and Los Angeles.

Sapir, E. 1920. Review of *The language of the Salinan Indians*, by J. A. Mason. *IJAL* 1:305–9.

————. 1922a. The Takelma language of southwestern Oregon. *Handbook of American Indian Languages: Part 2*, ed. F. Boas, 1–296. Washington, DC.

————. 1922b. A symposium of the exotic. *Dial* 73:568–71.

————. 1925. Sound patterns in language. In Sapir 1949:33–45.

————. 1933a. Language. In Sapir 1949:7–32.

————. 1933b. The psychological reality of phonemes. In Sapir 1949:46–60.

————. 1949. *Selected writings of Edward Sapir in language, culture, and personality*, ed. D. Mandelbaum. Berkeley.

Silverstein, M. 1986. The diachrony of Sapir's synchronic linguistic description; or Sapir's "cosmographical" linguistics. In *New perspectives in language, culture, and personality: Proceedings of the Edward Sapir Centenary Conference*, ed. W. Cowan et al., 67–110. Amsterdam.

Snyder, G. 1969. Review of *Indian tales*. In *Earth household*, 27–30. New York.

Steward, J. 1973. *Alfred Kroeber*. New York.

Stocking, G. 1992. *The ethnographer's magic and other essays in the history of anthropology*. Madison, WI.

Tarn, N. 1971. From anthropologist to informant: A field record of Gary Snyder. *Alcheringa* 4:7–13.

Wall, R. S. 1989. A wild coast and lonely: Big Sur pioneers. San Carlos, CA.

Wilson, D. B. 1990. Pit River country today: Destination unknown. *News from Native Cal.* 4(4):4–6.

Wolf, E. 1981. Kroeber. In *Totems and teachers: Perspectives on the history of anthropology*, ed. S. Silverman, 35–66. New York.

Manuscript Sources

KP   Kroeber Papers, Department and Museum of Anthropology Records, Bancroft Library, University of California–Berkeley, Berkeley, California.

P/AC   Pound-Angulo Collection, Special Collections, University Library, University of California–Santa Cruz, Santa Cruz, California.

A. I. HALLOWELL'S BOASIAN EVOLUTIONISM

Human Ir/rationality in Cross-Cultural, Evolutionary, and Personal Context

GEORGE W. STOCKING, JR.

[This essay was originally conceived as one part of a monograph, since abandoned, entitled "Anne Roe's Anthropologists"—itself part of a larger project on
"Anthropology Yesterday: From the Science of Man in the World Crisis to the
Crisis of Anthropology: 1945–72." Early in that postwar period, the social psychologist Anne Roe (wife of George Gaylord Simpson, the paleontologist) published a book called The Making of a Scientist (1953), based on research she
carried on in the late 1940s on sixty-four "elite" scientists in four disciplines (biology, physics, psychology and anthropology). The eight anthropologists selected
represented three of the "four fields" of anthropology: cultural anthropology
(Robert Redfield, Ralph Linton, Clyde Kluckhohn, A. I. Hallowell); archeology (Duncan Strong and Gordon Willey); and physical anthropology (Carleton
Coon and Harry Shapiro).[1] In pursuing the project, I began with the cultural

---

1. Of the eight, five (Shapiro and the four cultural anthropologists) were presidents of the
American Anthropological Association between 1944 and 1949. Although apparently one indicator of "elite" status, this office was neither a necessary nor a sufficient condition for inclusion in
Roe's sample: Neil Judd, president in 1945, was not chosen, nor was Ruth Benedict, who was president for six months before the reorganization of 1947. Judd was by no standards "elite"; Benedict,
who had died by the time Roe got to the anthropologists, would have been eliminated by Roe's prior

---

George W. Stocking, Jr. , the founding editor of *History of Anthropology*, is Stein-Freiler
Distinguished Service Professor Emeritus in the Department of Anthropology and
the Committee on Conceptual and Historical Studies of Science at the University of
Chicago, and is currently at work on a series of essays on anthropology in the United
States in the post–World War II period.

*anthropologists, taken in order of birth, beginning with Hallowell. As will be ev-
ident below, however, his selection was over-determined, and the essay took on
a life of its own. The present version is dedicated to the memory of Hallowell,
and to Murray Murphey, who were respectively my anthropological and historiographical mentors at Penn, and both members of my dissertation committee.]*

When Anne Roe wrote inviting him to participate in her study, Alfred Irving
Hallowell (then known to colleagues as "Pete") had six weeks before given his
presidential address to the American Anthropological Association.[2] Entitled
"Personality Structure and the Evolution of Man" (AH 1949c), it was the first
of a series of essays on the psychobiological and cultural evolution of the human species that Hallowell, who had studied with Franz Boas, contributed to
the neo-evolutionary movement in American anthropology during the 1950s.
Since Boas is characteristically (and not without reason) thought to have been
anti-evolutionary, and since the most vocal of the neo-evolutionists, Leslie
White, was staunchly, even obsessively, anti-Boasian (White 1966), it is worth
emphasizing this Boasian component of 1950s evolutionism. Manifest in the
work of Julian Steward, the leading proponent of "multilinear" cultural evolutionism (Hanc 1982), it is perhaps most strikingly evident in the later work of
Margaret Mead, whose early ethnography has been critiqued from a neo-
evolutionary point of view (Freeman 1993), but whose participation in the
Behavior and Evolution Symposium organized by Roe and Simpson in 1955

---

decision to exclude women and the foreign born, in order to reduce the number of variables that
might affect comparison (i. e. , "sexual" and "cultural" variation [Roe 1953a: 22–29; cf. GS2000a]).
Sampling considerations aside, the all male and overwhelmingly "waspish" nature of this group
seems worth noting, as perhaps reflecting more general cultural tendencies in a period when traditional gender roles and notions of American identity were being reasserted—the more so in a disciplinary tradition that has emphasized both its openness to women and its proximate origin among
persons of immigrant background.

2. Contemporary correspondence suggests that Hallowell began to be so addressed in the later
1930s. However, when I took two courses with him as a graduate student in American Civilization
at the University of Pennsylvania in the later 1950s, I did not call him "Pete." Born in the same
year as my own father, Hallowell was to become a kind of anthropological godfather to me. He was
an enthusiastic second reader of my doctoral dissertation on "American Social Scientists and Race
Theory, 1890–1915" (GS 1960) and the primary organizer of the Social Science Research Council's conference on the history of anthropology in 1962, at which I made my professional debut as
historian of anthropology. Although I do not specifically recall, it may have been from Hallowell
that I first heard of Roe's study—although it might have been from Murray Murphey, my primary
mentor in American Civilization, who was also much influenced by Hallowell (and did refer to him
as "Pete"). When Hallowell's Festschrift was being planned (Spiro, ed. 1965), I was among those
invited to contribute, but declined on the grounds that I had nothing then suitable for inclusion
that was not otherwise committed. In writing this essay, I have thought of it as a belated fulfillment
of a failed obligation. All of which I offer (and there could be more) as an indication of the personal motives that may condition my interest in Hallowell and more generally in United States anthropology in the post–World War II and Cold War period (see also GS n.d.).

provided for Mead "the necessary focus" and "a sufficient ground plan" for the work she subsequently published as *Continuities in Cultural Evolution* (1964:vii–viii; Roe & Simpson 1958). In contrast to White, Steward, and Mead, Hallowell was not concerned with defining long-term cross-cultural regularities in cultural evolution, or in the evolutionary implications of recent cultural change, but rather with the universal psychological concomitants of evolutionary change at a species level, in the context of his own ethnographic research among a particular Native American group.

In 1949, however, Roe was not yet aware of Hallowell's recently articulated evolutionary interest. She did know that he was then president of the Society for Projective Techniques and had used the Rorschach test in his fieldwork among the Lake Winnipeg Ojibwa in the later 1930s, but she felt that this would "not necessarily prevent its use" in their interview. Noting that he had already "heard something" from "various sources" about Roe's study, Hallowell recalled that during his recent term as Chair of the Division of Anthropology and Psychology of the National Research Council "we tried to set up a study along the same general lines but were not able to secure sufficient support for it." But because he was "tearing around so much that it's very difficult to get any sort of chance to talk with him," his meeting with Roe was delayed until early May 1950. In the meantime, Roe, as was her practice, familiarized herself with items on the bibliography she had requested (ARP:AR/AH 12/27/49; AH/AR 1/9/50; AR/AH 4/28/50; 1950 interview).

From Sunday School to Socialism, from
Social Work to Anthropology

The interview itself opened with "verbal discussion about some societal problems," which unfortunately (given the early motivations of Hallowell's anthropology), Roe felt offered "nothing that needs recording here."[3] The transcription proper begins simply "I was born in 1892 here in Philadelphia and have

---

3. Information not otherwise documented here is from the 1950 "interview" section of Hallowell's folder in the Roe papers (ARP:1950 interview) at the American Philosophical Society. Other materials in the folder are cited by the subject's initials and a section specifier (e. g. : ARP: AH Summary); in Hallowell's case, these include also the transcript of a taped follow-up interview in 1963 (ARP:1963 interview). In 1972, Hallowell published a brief autobiographical document, which provides additional information on his later career (AH 1972). In order to create a more coherent narrative than that in the somewhat rambling, imperfectly transcribed and perhaps edited 1950 "interview," I have drawn on all of these sources, as well as other materials in the Hallowell papers (AHP) at the American Philosophical Society, materials in the archives of the University of Pennsylvania, and the papers of other anthropologists. For a full bibliography of Hallowell's publications, see Boyer & Boyer 1991:xxxv–xlv.

lived here all my life." Hallowell's parents were also Philadelphia natives, and his father's parents, too, though his maternal grandmother had been born in England. When Hallowell's parents married, they moved in with his paternal grandparents, and although his grandfather soon died of tuberculosis, his grandmother continued to be part of the nuclear family unit—which was a small and focused one, since Hallowell was an only child, and had no cousins. The dominant figure was Hallowell's mother, who upon marriage had quit her job as a schoolteacher to take charge of the domestic sphere. His father, who had only a secondary school education and worked as a supervisor in a shipyard, was, in Hallowell's later estimate, "pretty much under my mother's thumb." There was "a lot of friction" between his mother and her mother-in-law, "possibly over me but over other things too." But although his grandmother took to "gallivanting around" (which Roe felt his mother might have resented), Hallowell was "very fond of her" and came to regard her as "kind of my confidante" (ARP:1950 interview).

Although the family "never were too well off," and baked their own bread, they always had an Irish servant girl, and "when one got married another one came." They were Baptists and "church people": his mother and grandmother both taught Sunday school, and Hallowell went to church "a couple of times" every Sunday, joining also in the church glee and mandolin clubs. His first formal schooling was in a private kindergarten run by "two Jewish ladies"; after that, the "regular public school"—where his father had gone and his mother had taught. Hallowell was "a pretty conforming fellow" whose mother "was interested in grades," and he did well, receiving "some kind of medal for something." But when it came to high school, he "began to rebel" against the "pattern of extended overprotection." His mother wanted him to go to the central high school, which had a "good classical curriculum," but he didn't "give a damn" about going there, because he had heard that "it was hard," and he didn't want to take Latin. Instead, he preferred to go to a manual training school near his home, because "they had a swell mandolin club." While he did not "hang around" his father and had not learned to do the "mechanical things" his father was adept at, his father supported his choice, and his mother consented, because the principal lived across the street and "they admired him." But Hallowell did not enjoy or do well in manual training courses, and took pleasure instead in working on the school newspaper. Although he was not athletic, and had a "very odd gait" that Roe thought suggested a disability, the only illness he had in childhood was typhoid in earliest infancy. In high school, he dated "quite regularly," and joined classmates in "raising hell" with the math teacher— never afterwards taking math again, and returning Roe's verbal-mathematical-spatial test with an apology for doing only the verbal portion (ARP:1950 interview; Summary; AH/AR 5/27/50)

Lacking direction upon his graduation in 1911, Hallowell entered the

Afred Irving Hallowell with his mandolin teacher. (Courtesy American Philosophical Society.)

Wharton School of Finance and Commerce at the University of Pennsylvania, where his mother thought he could prepare himself for a career in business— and where the admission standards were not so high, and there was a free choice of courses beyond the minimum required for a business degree. Although his poor performance in German barred him for a year from the glee club, which occasionally traveled for a week at a time giving concerts around Pennsylvania,

Hallowell sampled widely in history and the humanities. But what really engaged him was "social science." He took all the courses offered in sociology (where he read Herbert Spencer) and in economics (where he read John Stuart Mill). In his senior year, he took a seminar with Simon Patten, a maverick "in rebellion against classical economics," who dealt "with problems of social change and evolution and tried to open up a perspective emphasizing abundance rather than scarcity" (AH 1972:3). He was also influenced by Scott Nearing, a student of Patten who taught the introductory economics course, and whose public critique of child-labor and corporate greed placed him "at the epicenter of alarming opinions that were sending shock waves through the Wharton School and into the respectable society of Philadelphia"—resulting in Nearing's firing in a major academic freedom case within months after Hallowell graduated (Saltmarsh 1991:82, 91). Without reference to that controversy, Hallowell in 1950 simply noted that "the whole problem of social reform" began "to agitate his mind," and he decided he must "do something" about "bad social conditions." Twenty years later, in a less repressive post-McCarthy atmosphere, he recalled that he himself had had "socialistic inclinations"—which would not have surprised Nearing, who was the faculty advisor to the Penn branch of the Intercollegiate Socialist Society (ARP:1950 interview; AH 1972:4).

Given his socialist inclinations, it is not surprising that with the threat of U.S. involvement in the war in Europe, Hallowell had "a lot of discussion about going into the war" with "a couple of people," including a "Swedish fellow who told me a lot about the Germans." He later described himself as a having become a "convinced pacifist," although not a "consistent" one in the sense of refusing to register for the draft—hoping instead to work with the American Friends Service Committee. However, when he was called up, he was turned down for reasons he did not "to this day" understand, but which "had something to do" with his heart—though it never subsequently bothered him.

Concomitant with his early political development was Hallowell's "break away" from religion—without "crisis," but with "plenty of argument." His very first publication, in his church newspaper, dealt with "the functions of the church"—which at that point was embroiled in controversy over whether it was proper to use the Sunday school room during the week as a gymnasium for a boys' club. On this issue Hallowell and his parents were together on the winning "progressive" side. But as he took an increasingly sociological view of religion, and simply put "the theological question to one side," his failure to maintain "church affiliations" became a bone of contention with his mother, with whom he "always argued about missions and so on."

Throughout his college years, Hallowell clerked summers in a hotel, and was urged by the manager to "go into the hotel business"; but by the time of his graduation in 1914, he had given up the idea of a business career. Considering graduate work in sociology, he was encouraged by a professor first to try social

work "and then see how you feel about it." During his senior year he did volunteer work with the Society for Organizing Charity, and upon graduation was offered a job at $50 a month as a caseworker—which in a predominantly female
profession was at that time thought "a funny thing for a man to do." After a
"couple of years," he decided that he did indeed want to pursue sociology, and
began to take courses while continuing in social work, first as case worker for
the society, then raising money as its financial secretary, and finally as Executive Secretary of the Travelers' Aid Society.

During his eight years as social worker, Hallowell's interests shifted from sociology to anthropology, embodied locally in the person of Frank Speck, who
was to become for Hallowell the living exemplar of what it was to be a Boasian
anthropologist (see AH 1951a). From adolescence, Speck had been interested
in two of the research areas that were the thematic foci of his later anthropology: natural history, and Indian languages and cultures. Even before he began
training with Boas in 1904, Speck had coauthored with his undergraduate linguistics professor several articles based on his own research on the Mohegan-
Pequot languages, and under Boas he carried on fieldwork in the Indian Territory in Oklahoma. From 1907 on, Speck was associated with the University [of
Pennsylvania] Museum, but after 1910 his relationship with the new director,
the Harvard-trained archeologist George Byron Gordon, became increasingly
acrimonious. Arriving at work one morning in 1913 to find all his possessions
"piled in the Museum yard," Speck appealed his dismissal to the university administration, which appointed him acting chairman of a separately constituted
department of anthropology (Witthoft 1991:6–8; cf. Darnell 1998:161–66). A
man of empathic informality and "inimitable" humor (AH 1951a:74), Speck
was as at ease with students as with his Indian informants. Fortuitously, he was
also an active member of the same fraternity as Hallowell, who recalled him
as a wonderful raconteur whose stories about his "experiences with Indians"
sometimes included "delightfully funny arpeggios in dialect" (AH 1951a:75;
1972: 4). Although Hallowell had "never heard" of anthropology before meeting Speck in his senior year, he soon began to attend Speck's lectures when his
social work allowed. Attracted by anthropology's "skeptical" attitude toward
social evolution, by the idea of culture (which was not yet "in the sociologists'
kit"), and by the "very liberal" political attitude of anthropologists (which sustained his own opposition to World War I), Hallowell by 1919 had made the
shift from sociology to anthropology (AH 1972: 4; ARP:1950 interview).

Hallowell later spoke of Speck as a "mentor" whom he "imitated for a long
while," and the development of his own anthropology may be seen in terms of
its relationship to Speck's. Despite his motivating interest in "broad social
problems," Hallowell's work focused on "Frank Speck's pets"—the "primitive,
aboriginal people of North America," whose virtues Speck extolled as alternatives to "the general values of American culture" (AH 1972:5; cf. GS 1989).

From Speck, too, Hallowell absorbed a commitment to a remarkable "diversification" of anthropological interests, including ecology, animal behavior, ethnohistory, social organization, myths and tales, religious beliefs and rituals, all of which tended over time to converge toward an "inner core" or "common center" (AH 1951a:74–75). It was Speck—the "most persistent fieldworker of all Boas's students" (Fenton 1990:95)—who took Hallowell along on "odds and ends" of fieldwork among Northeastern Indians, including a "bully trip" to Labrador in the summer of 1923, and another in 1924, during which Hallowell complemented Speck's interests by collecting material culture and taking charge of the physical anthropological measurements (MHP:AH/M. Herskovits n.d. /23, 10/20/24; AH 1929). Looming behind Speck was, of course, Franz Boas, whose "austere intellectual influence and training" had given direction to Speck's "boyhood interest in Indians" (AH 1951a:68)—and whom Hallowell later remembered as "our god" (ARP:1950 interview; cf. 1938a).

What Hallowell did not get from Speck was his interest in psychology and psychoanalysis. As he recalled the situation to Roe, "there was no psychological aspect to anthropology at that time," and he himself had taken only one formal course in psychology. For him, it was in social work that "the psychological revolution began," and he felt especially the influence of three "pioneer" figures: Mary Ellen Richmond, who had been the head of the Philadelphia Society for Organizing Charity in the first decade of the century, and whose book, *Social Diagnosis*, Hallowell read when it came out in 1917; Jessie Taft, an innovator in psychiatric social casework with children, who settled in Philadelphia in 1918 (and who later wrote a biography of Otto Rank [1958]); and Virginia Robinson, Taft's "life long friend and companion" (Robinson 1962:7). It was in this context that Hallowell began to read Freud; performing an experimental test of the unconscious, he chose a number at random, and it made him "sit up and take notice" when it "turned out to be my draft number" (ARP:1950 interview). It was more than a decade, however, before this early psychoanalytic interest began to surface in Hallowell's anthropology.

A Boasian Relativist among the Lake Winnipeg Ojibwa/Saulteaux

Pursuing anthropology while holding a full-time job in social work, Hallowell did not get his master's degree until 1920, for a study of material culture—yet another of Speck's numerous ethnographic interests (AH 1920). By 1922, however, he had "determined to make anthropology his career," and with Speck's promise to get him hired as instructor, gave up his job in social work, relying for the time being on the income of his wife (a fellow social worker). During the 1922–23 academic year, when he held a university fellowship, Hallowell commuted weekly to New York to participate in Boas' seminar (which at that time included both Ruth Benedict and Melville Herskovits). His assigned reports were on Edward Westermarck's *History of Human Marriage* (1922) and John Dewey's *Human Nature and Conduct* (1922). Judging from Hallowell's later development, the former seems precursory to his biologically oriented evolutionary interests; the latter, although still resonant of evolutionary concerns, and cast in the rhetoric of "custom" rather than of "culture," would surely have been incorporated into a Boasian culturalist frame. Outside of the seminar, Hallowell and other students "met privately each week" with Alexander Goldenweiser, a maverick Boasian of broad-ranging comparative interests, who sometime in this period also gave a series of lectures on psychoanalytic theory at the Pennsylvania School of Social Work (AH 1972:4).

At about this time, Hallowell undertook dissertation research in a style for which he later apologized to Roe, but which was, in fact, not atypical of the postwar generation of Boasians. Rather than a field ethnography, which later came to be thought of as the prescribed initiation ritual, Hallowell (like Benedict, Herskovits, Mead, and Steward) wrote a library dissertation about the distribution of cultural traits over a geographical area. Conditioned in part by the availability of funding, such studies may also be viewed as transitional from earlier Boasian historical diffusionist ethnology to a more integrative synchronic culturalist approach (GS 1976b:137–39). In Hallowell's case, however, the preliminary survey and analysis of the existing literature foreshadowed the scholarly style of much of his later work, in which major research projects were prefaced by systematic investigations (fulsomely footnoted) of a wide range of relevant scholarship.

With Speck's encouragement, Hallowell chose as his dissertation topic the distribution of "Bear Ceremonialism in the Northern Hemisphere" from eastern North America westward across Siberia to Northern Europe (AH 1972:6; 1924; cf. Darnell 1977). At one level, the dissertation he produced was traditionally Boasian: starting with a critique of evolutionary assumptions, insisting on the need for specific geographical-historical study, eschewing ultimate origin for the tracing of historical relationships, and favoring the psychological over the utilitarian, it emphasized (at least in principle) the intensive study of particular *Weltanschauungen* from the "native point of view" as against broad ranging comparison of similarities and differences—all of which could have come from early Boas (AH 1924:1–21; cf. GS 1974). In light of Hallowell's subsequent development, however, what is striking is the dissertation's residual evolutionary assumption. Hallowell later recalled that he was "following a lead" from Sir James Frazer (specifically, the third edition of *The Golden Bough* [1911–15], which he frequently cited), and much of his monograph reads like a Frazerian anthology of the customs prevailing among different native groups.

Despite his insistence on the variability of "primitive cultures studied in recent times," Hallowell chose to "group them en bloc," and with a favorable reference to Lévy-Bruhl, contrasted the "folkloristic pattern" of thought with the "prevalent [i. e. , scientific] attitudes toward the animal kingdom found in Euro-American society" (1924:5, ll; 1972:6). In the end, Hallowell concluded that "a bear cult was one of the characteristic features of an ancient Boreal culture, Old World in origin and closely associated with the pursuit of the reindeer" (161)—a conclusion susceptible of both diffusionist and evolutionist interpretation, which may help to account for its subsequent citation in both continental European and Soviet Russian anthropological literature (ARP:1963 interview; AH 1972:7).

An atypically Boasian evolutionary interest is evident also in Hallowell's teaching during this period. In the summer of 1925, he traveled to Europe, to visit museums and "some of the anthropoliwogs"—including, apparently, George Grant MacCurdy, the director of the American School of Prehistoric Research in Europe. For the next several years, European archaeology was his special teaching interest—including "a whole year" on "the Paleolithic and Neolithic cultures alone" (MHP:AH/MJH 10/24/24, 8/13/26, 7/18/27). Given his background in social work and his familiarity with Westermarck, it is not surprising that during his early teaching Hallowell also gave a course on "Marriage and the Family." A draft manuscript on the topic suggests another major bout of reading, in which most of the titles are works of classical evolutionism and early-twentieth-century works in sociology and psychology, along with social anthropological writings of the later 1920s—including Malinowski on "sex and repression in savage society" and Radcliffe-Brown on Australian social organization. Although the influence of evolutionism is evident in topic headings ("the biological foundations of human mating"), in the appeal to comparison as a key to "the succession of modifications," and in references to "higher cultures," the emphasis was on a Boasian relativist approach to cultural conditioning, in the context of a functionalist insistence that "customs which at first sight may appear arbitrary, curious, bizarre, or 'savage'" in fact "fulfill important functions and meet human needs" (AHP: Series III, "Marriage and the Family," 1, 95–99; cf. Series V, "Marriage").[4]

In this context, Hallowell, in contrast to some more orthodox Boasians, became interested in "the relations between kinship pattern and social behavior,"

---

4. After a failed attempt to publish some of this material in 1941, and an aborted expansion into book form with Loren Eiseley as coauthor, Hallowell published an essay in 1942 (with a student assistant listed as coauthor) on "biological factors in family structure," which treated some of the same issues in the context of additional readings he did in the 1930s (AHP: Series 1, "Loren Eiseley"; AH & Reynolds 1942).

considered in historical terms on the basis of the evidence of kinship terminology. On one of his early trips to Canada with Speck, Hallowell had discovered "some old books" written in Algonquian by "one of the Jesuits about 200–
300 years ago" (MHP:AH/MJH 10/20/24; 1950 interview). Subsequently, on
one of several brief trips he made to the Abenaki reservation sixty miles east of
Montreal, seeking "the remnants of their aboriginal culture," he found an
eighteenth-century manuscript that enabled him to document changes in the
kinship system "unknown to the [present] Indians themselves." On a later visit
to Montreal he discovered more "old dictionaries" that seemed to suggest the
widespread early existence of cross-cousin marriage among Northern Algonquians. On this basis, he began to question the "prevailing point of view"
among Boasian anthropologists that kinship terms "were to be considered as
purely linguistic phenomena" and could not be used to reason backwards in
time to prior social behavior. Shortly after he advanced his aboriginal cross-
cousin marriage hypothesis at the meeting of the International Congress of
Americanists in 1928, Hallowell ran into William Duncan Strong, just back
from fieldwork in Labrador, who told him that it was still being practiced among
the Naskapi (AH 1928; MHP:AH/MH 11/24/28). After further library research, Hallowell was able to win a grant from the Social Science Research
Council for fieldwork in the Lake Winnipeg area to test his hypothesis among
Northern Algonquians living hundreds of miles westward. There, among the
Cree of the Ojibwa of the Berens River (locally called the Saulteaux), he discovered in 1930 "an aboriginal social organization" of this type still "essentially
intact" (1972:5–8; ARP:1963 interview).

   It was among the latter group that Hallowell was finally able to carry on intensive fieldwork during seven summers in the 1930s, aided by his "interpreter,
friend, and virtual collaborator" William Berens, the bilingual son of an Ojibwa
father and a mother of mixed Algonquian and Scottish descent, who was chief
of the band at the mouth of the Berens River (AH 1992:6, 13, 15; Brown 1987,
1989, 1992:xi). The most important of these field trips was the one Hallowell
took in 1932, when Chief Berens traveled with him by canoe 250 miles up the
river to the "still un-Christianized Indians" of the Pikangikum band. Starting
from what Chief Berens called "civilization," and moving along what Hallowell called a "cultural gradient," they entered into the "living past," where the Indians still lived in "birchbark-covered dwellings," and the conjurer in the "shaking tent" was able to summon the help of "other than human persons" when
some "serious problem" demanded it (AH 1992:8–10). It was in this context
that Hallowell's earlier interest in dynamic psychology came to the forefront of
his research, as he pursued the problems of world view and cultural personality
that were to be the main foci of his anthropological writing down to the time
of the first Roe interview.

Joe Keeper, Chief William Berens, Hallowell, and Antoine Bittern, on the Berens River Indian Preserve, Lake Winnipeg, circa 1935 (Courtesy Rose Berens Bittern and JoAn Boggs.)

Sometime after 1931 Hallowell became acquainted with Edward Sapir, the immediate intellectual progenitor of the emerging study of "culture and personality." Sapir had been a close friend of Speck from the time when, fresh out of Boas' seminar in 1908, the two were briefly colleagues and roommates at the University of Pennsylvania. In 1935, when Sapir chaired the National Research Council's Division of Psychology and Anthropology, he invited Hallowell to join the newly organized "Committee on Personality in Relation to Culture," on which he served as chair of a subcommittee charged with preparing a "handbook of psychological leads for ethnological fieldwork" (Darnell 1986: 174–75; cf. ARP:1963 interview). A venture in a tradition dating back at least to the 1874 edition of the British Association's "Notes and Queries on Anthropology" (GS 2001), the handbook was roughly contemporaneous with two other similar undertakings: the cross-culturally oriented "Outline of Cultural Materials" prepared by George Murdock and his colleagues at Yale—the preliminary draft of which was put together in 1937 (Murdock et al. 1950:xi)—and a never fully realized comparative project on the study of acculturation discussed by a committee of the Social Science Research Council in 1935 (Redfield et al. 1936; Madden 1999). Also conceived as a cooperative enterprise, Hallowell's handbook was intended as a similar orienting document for the emergent "culture and personality" movement, and was apparently circulated in mimeographed form in the late 1930s.[5]

As its extensive bibliography suggests, the introduction to the handbook, which Hallowell drafted early in 1936, was the product of another major immersion in scholarly literature. Organized into twelve major rubrics and a number of subheadings, the topics ranged from general psychology, the organic bases of behavior, animal and infrahuman primate behavior, and culture as a characteristic human trait, through social psychology and psychoanalysis, "unconscious" processes, communication and symbolism, to basic mental concepts and the cultural patterning of mental functions, to personality and culture, psychopathology and "the role of the individual in relation to culturally constituted values" (AHP:Series III, Handbook . . .). In the review process, Hallowell's earlier readings on psychoanalysis—"forgotten . . . in between times"—began "to take on a new aspect" (ARP: 1950 interview; cf. 1972:8–9).

Although a printed version was not published until after the war, Hallowell's introduction stands in retrospect as a conceptual and methodological agenda for much of the work of his later career. In contrast to the behavior of "infrahuman" animals, he emphasized the dominance of "acquired behavior patterns in human life" with specific reference to the work of Boas on perception (1937b:345, 349–50), and the consequent psychological implication "that the individuals of [different cultures] actually live in different [culturally determined] orders of reality" (355)—different "meaningful universes" with different "concepts of time and space," many of them inhabited by "beings of a purely conceptual nature" that could not be dismissed as "imaginary" or easily equated with the "delusional systems" recognized in "western civilization." So long as they acted "*as if* their beliefs were true, an understanding of their behavior must proceed from the premises implicit or explicit in their versions of reality" (363). Drawing on psychological and psychoanalytic literature, and on the work of Mead and Benedict, Hallowell went on to treat personality development from infancy in terms of variability around a culturally patterned norm, rejecting the "racial derivation" or stereotyping of cultural character, or individual maturational development in terms of the recapitulation of human evolutionary history, or notions of "group mind" or "pre-logical mentality." But if he was critical

5. As preserved in the Hallowell papers, the mimeographed handbook consisted of questions grouped into categories, each delegated to an anthropologist specialist, covering the various stages of the life cycle, followed by a single longer section covering a number of topics under the general heading "economics." The identity of some of the authors is revealed in a letter from Hortense Powdermaker to Hallowell (AHP:5/13/36), commenting on an early draft, in which she attributes a lack of unity "between the various contributions" to the "number of people working on the thing," mentioning herself, Benedict, Stanley Newman, and Father John Cooper. The opening page of the major section on "economics" bears the name of Ruth Bunzel—although it seems unlikely that she was the author of all of the headings in the 143 pages that followed.

of the ethnocentrism of Freudian theory, he had by no means abandoned it, nor did he embrace a complete relativism of "psychic disorders"; on the contrary, one of his goals was to facilitate the gathering of "comparative data from other societies which we can view with relatively more complete objectivity" (382).

It was to that end that Hallowell in 1938 became involved in Rorschach testing, which he later recalled hearing of for the first time when Benedict "uttered the strange word Rorschach" at one of the meetings of the Sapir committee.[6] His interest piqued, Hallowell went over "all the literature I could find," and then "worked up a procedure for myself"—later published as "The Rorschach Test as a Tool for Investigating Cultural Variables and Individual Differences in the Study of Personality in Primitive Societies" (AH 1941a & b). Although it was only after his first attempt to apply the test among the Ojibwa that he met Bruno Klopfer, the doyen of Rorschach testing in the United States (ARP:1963 interview; AH 1972:9), for the next fifteen years Hallowell played a central role in what might be called the "Rorschach movement" in American anthropology. Having adopted the test as a primary methodological tool in his own work (AH 1938c, 1940, 1942b), in 1942 he organized a Rorschach training seminar for leading anthropologists (CKP:AH/CK 10/21/41; 5/5/42; AHP:CK/AH 1/14/42), and subsequently took on the role of editing a cooperative volume on "cross-cultural Rorschach analyses" in conjunction with the project Laura Thompson was coordinating on "Indian Personality, Education and Administration" (AHP:LT/AH 12/6/43; cf. Thompson 1951:ix–xvii, 21).[7] After the war he served as president of the Society for Projective Techniques, and in the mid-1950s he offered a defense of the "inkblot" technique against critics who charged that it was "culture bound" (AH 1955b; cf. G. & L. Spindler 1991)

For the most part, Hallowell's work in a comparative psychological mode was a product of the postwar period. The culminating production of his earlier phase was a short monograph on "The Role of Conjuring in Saulteaux Society," written during the academic year 1940–41, when he held a Guggenheim fellowship. Offered as an attempt "to communicate the lineaments of a strange behavioral world," it sought to "make intelligible" the Berens River Ojibwa "system of magico-religious beliefs" by an analysis of the institution, which, "more than any other, reflects the kind of world in which they actually live"

---

6. Unlike the Thematic Apperception Test, in which the subject is shown, in a prescribed sequence, a standardized series of pictures "designed to tap different areas in human life and interpersonal relations," in order to elicit stories, the Rorschach subject is shown a series of ten bilaterally symmetrical inkblots with no evident representative character, thereby presumably minimizing the imposition of ethnocentric categories (Barnouw 1963:239–40, 26–61).

7. The cooperative volume seems never to have been realized. Although in 1952 it was apparently under consideration by the University of Chicago Press (AHP: LT/AH 2/14/52), and two years later was still spoken of hopefully as "forthcoming" (Kluckhohn 1954:688), it is not included in Hallowell's bibliography (Boyer & Boyer 1991:xxxv–xlv).

(1942a:5). It was a world in which powerful spiritual beings might interact with humans under certain circumstances, including conjuring performances by men whose special communicative abilities had been legitimized by a "dream blessing" during their puberty feast. Called upon to speak with the *pawáganak* about issues of pressing concern to members of the group (illness, sorcery, lost articles, departed relatives, the threat of cannibal creatures, the foretelling of events), the conjurer retired after dark to a small tent, from which the evidence of the spirit's presence was manifest to the surrounding (and usually very responsive) audience by the violent shaking of the tent and strange voices emanating from within. Hallowell attended three of these performances, which made a "deep impression" on him (44), and on one occasion hired a conjurer (for "a good fee" and "some tobacco") to find out how his seriously ill father fared back in Philadelphia (40, 46). Returning from his spirit journey, *mikinak* (the Great Turtle) reported that his father "was no worse"—which Hallowell discovered on his later return to Philadelphia "was not only judiciously phrased but quite true" (47).

Hallowell's own interpretations of the conjuring phenomena were also judiciously phrased. He noted (usually in one of his numerous lengthy footnotes) that some manifestations seemed to "violate the laws of physics," or depended on ventriloquism, or were similar to the "tricks" of western spiritualists, and that both conjurers and other Ojibwa would grant that some conjurers were charlatans (1942a:11, 22, 70). Granting that the viability of the conjuring system depended on a "threshold of credulity" kept low "so long as these powers are expressed in familiar native patterns" of belief (71–72), Hallowell made a point of keeping his personal threshold of credulity as low as his own patterns of belief would allow. In part, this was a matter of ethnographic tact: when a conjurer was trusting enough to violate "a rigid taboo" by expounding "a great deal of native theory" to him, he "did not have the impudence to insult him by inquiring how it *really* was done" (73). Nor was it ethnographically necessary to ask: to reject, "as we are inclined to do, all the a priori assumptions upon which their belief system is based" would be "actually indicting the foundations of their culture, which is irrelevant to the problem of how conjuring functions within that culture"(76). Among the Saulteaux/Ojibwa, conjuring served four social functions beyond its "ostensible and immediate purpose": providing "tangible validation of basic concepts" of the cosmos, already "familiar in belief and myth"; sustaining social structure "by exposing the dangers involved in a violation of the mores"; creating "a sense of security and confidence in the face of the hazards of life"; and offering "diversion and entertainment for those assembled to witness it" (85–87).[8]

----

8. Although there are marked similarities between Hallowell's interpretations and those of Evans-Pritchard in *Witchcraft, oracles and magic among the Azande* (1937), Hallowell's review of

In the spirit of Boasian cultural relativism, Hallowell had prefaced his book by suggesting that what was true of the "savage" was also true of "occidental man": both perceived the world "through the spectacles" their culture provided. And if ours were those provided by the results of "scientific investigation," as individuals we obtained them "in much the same way that any primitive has acquired his outlook." Nor could "we," by "intellectual" comprehension alone, "fully penetrate their behavioral world," or actually "*wear* their culturally tinted spectacles; the best we can do is to try them on" (1942a:1–3). Hallowell refused to speculate whether the world as viewed through the spectacles of science "more nearly approaches Truth in an absolute sense" (1). But as the residual evolutionism of his rhetoric ("savage," "primitive") implies, he seemed in little doubt as to which would in the longer run prevail. Anticipating in his peroration the ultimate "collapse" of the "behavioral world" and "belief system" of the Saulteaux under the impact of Christianity and "occidental culture," he foresaw a time when "institutions of occidental origin" would serve the social functions previously performed by conjuring (88). In the years after World War II, this implicitly evolutionary strain in Hallowell's anthropology was to come more to the forefront.

In contrast to other anthropologists who in various ways became actively involved in the war effort (GS 1974:159–68), Hallowell spent the early years of the war in Philadelphia, where he served as chair of the University of Pennsylvania Department of Anthropology. He was, however, seriously underpaid, and to meet family expenses (including the support of his parents, who lived with him, as well as alimony to his first wife, from whom he was divorced in 1942), he had to supplement his salary by teaching at Bryn Mawr and Columbia. When in 1944 his old friend Herskovits invited him to join the Northwestern department, in anticipation of its postwar expansion, Hallowell saw this as an opportunity to "combin[e] forces" at a moment when "many of the older men who built up A[nthropology]" were "now dead or in their 60s," in order to encourage the development of "new foci" (MHP: AH/MP 1/26/44). At the end of his second year at Northwestern, Hallowell embarked on what was to be his last fieldwork venture, leading a team of graduate students to Wisconsin, where they applied the Rorschach technique to the study of the "more highly acculturated" Lac du Flambeau Ojibwa (1955a:335). But in the spring of 1947, when Loren Eiseley, a student at Penn in the early 1930s, returned there as departmental chair to revive the program, his first move was to have Hallowell invited back, at a salary larger than his own. Accepting the offer, Hallowell remained at Penn until his retirement

---

Evans-Pritchard's later work does not suggest a direct influence (AH 1963d). There are, perhaps, similarities in ulterior intellectual motivation, insofar as Evans-Pritchard's interest in alternate rationalities may have reflected his brother's schizophrenia (Evans-Pritchard 1973:36).

in 1963 (LEP:Eiseley/G. Morrow 2/17/47; AHP:Morrow/AH 2/20/47; AH/ Morrow 2/25/47).

"An Anthropologist's Anthropologist":
Hallowell's Anthropological Trajectory
in Disciplinary and Cultural Context

Hallowell's anthropological career produced no "big book," theoretical or ethnographic.[9] But from the late 1930s on there was a steady flow of journal articles—a score of then collected in 1955—focused on and extending a central core of themes. He has been described as neither hedgehog nor fox, but something of a hybrid—a scholar whose work dealt "with a great many things, [but] is almost always concerned with one big thing": "the nature of man" (Spiro 1991:3, 6). Although he had decided early on to address particular topics rather than to "systematically collect material for standard ethnography," he felt that he had been "systematic in certain ways"; if he rejected the very idea of "theory" in the "strict sense" as inappropriate for anthropology, he had "increasingly been going in the direction of trying to see the meaningful character of some of these things" (ARP:1963 interview). Focusing centrally on the personality structure, world view and what he came to call "the behavioral environment" of the "most conservative" of the Berens River Ojibwa, he worked along a presumed acculturational gradient of Ojibwa contact with western civilization, forward into the present and backward into the recent historical past, and in that context was "inevitably led to a general consideration of the psychological dimensions of human evolution" (1972:11).

That phrase ("inevitably led"), from a short "semiautobiographical" essay Hallowell published two years before his death in 1974, would seem to imply the autonomous intellectual development of a personal ethnographic/anthropological career path. There are other passages in the same essay, however, that imply a more pluralistic contextual understanding. In its last paragraph, Hal-

---

9. Hallowell commented at several points in the Roe interviews on the discrepancy between the amount of ethnographic material he and other anthropologists were able to collect, and what they were able to publish. He apparently put aside in the late 1930s a comprehensive ethnography entitled "Pigeon River People" (Brown 1992:111). His only approximation of a systematic ethnography was a brief volume commissioned for the "case study" series edited by George and Louise Spindler. Begun in 1962, it was delayed in completion, then lost in transit to the Spindlers in 1967, only to be resurrected and edited by Jennifer Brown a quarter century later (Brown 1992:xi–xvii). But there were at least two other unrealized volumes (one of Ojibwa myths and texts, the other on the Rorschach), and the urging of his friend Herskovits that he put his "procrastinator to one side and get out his typewriter" suggests that there may have been more personal psychological or situational factors at work (MHP:MJH/AH 1/12/40)

lowell suggested that the essay was intended "to outline a personal record of my own experience in anthropology, of my changing values, and problems in field-work." True, it was only in the essay's opening passage that he referred specifically to his own values: noting Roe's finding that social scientists "often show a sense of rebellion against traditional family values," he remarked "I think this was true of me." But the reference—especially in the context of Roe's study—hints at an awareness of ulterior influences or contexts behind, beyond, or beneath the "inevitable" intellectual evolution he had recounted. And such a possibility was explicitly indicated in the essay's concluding sentence: "How this personal experience is related to the wider picture of the basic changes and emphases in the anthropological tradition and to changing values in the wider world, I leave to others" (AH 1972:12, 3). Taken together, these passages suggest three perspectives from which his intellectual biography might be further illuminated: developments within anthropology, changes in the wider world, and aspects of Hallowell's own more intimate personal history.

Although I have neither the competence nor the desire to interpret Hallowell systematically in "psycho-historical" terms, or to suggest specific relationships between intellectual production and "personality structure" as revealed in psychological testing (as Roe proposed to do), I firmly believe that the ideas of contributors in intellectual history do not develop in an intellectual historical vacuum; rather, that they are, in varying ways and degrees in different disciplines and different individuals, affected or conditioned by influences, external or internal, of which they may or may not be aware, including those of intimate personal history. I believe, furthermore, that a historical understanding of these actors (and their ideas) may be enriched by a cautiously contextual (rather than causal) and suggestive (rather than systematic) consideration of such influences. With these caveats in mind—and with Hallowell's partial authorization—we may venture beyond the "inevitable development" of his thought into other interpretive contexts, starting with the "wider picture of basic changes and emphases in the anthropological tradition."

While Hallowell's mature anthropological interests were all rooted in his own intellectual evolution, they were by no means disconnected from major developments within anthropology, psychology and the social sciences during the periods between and after the war in the United States. Theoretically eclectic, he read widely throughout his career, refiguring his own thinking in terms of current tendencies that seemed to articulate with the main line of his own work, including especially work in psychology and psychoanalysis, such as Rorschach testing, research on aggression, and ego-theory in psychoanalysis. Within anthropology, his work was clearly part of the culture and personality and "acculturation" movements within the Boasian tradition, both of which antedated Hallowell's own participation (GS 1976a). And although he suggested at one point that the "germs" of his later evolutionary writings could be found in the animal behavior interests of Frank Speck, he nevertheless regarded his thinking on "behavioral evolution" (most systematically elaborated at the Darwin Centennial in Chicago in 1959) as a contribution to the "renewed interest in cultural evolution on the part of anthropologists" in the 1950s (ARP:1963 interview; AH 1960a; cf. Wolf 1964:27–31).

Viewing mid-century American anthropology not as a congeries of separate "movements," but in terms of its unifying tendencies, Hallowell can be seen as a focal figure, in whose work a number of conceptually interrelated distinctive features of the anthropology of the period are manifest. In this context, it may be illuminating to examine a short essay on "Values, Acculturation and Mental Health" that Hallowell published in 1950, just as the study of "values" was coming to the forefront of anthropological research (see Kluckhohn 1952). Recognizing "the relativity of different value systems," Hallowell proposed, as a "hypothesis," that "from the standpoint of the psychodynamics of human adjustment," value systems might "vary" as "more or less efficient instruments in the molding of personalities that are fully capable of functioning at a level of mental health." With his own work among the Ojibwa as an example, Hallowell suggested that anthropologists might pursue this problem in two ways: by studying different value systems from "the standpoint of total personality integration and functioning viewed from the perspective of our knowledge of mental health"; and "by studying more closely the psychological aspects of acculturation" with reference to "personality structure and value systems." On the basis of Rorschach and Thematic Apperception Tests, he argued that a "psychological impasse" existed among the more acculturated Lac du Flambeau group he and his students had studied in 1946. With the "disintegration of the old belief system and the substitution of a superficially acquired Christianity as the basis of a new world view," the "functional support" provided for Ojibwa "personality structure" by the old "system of values" was "no longer available," and "contact with the version of Western culture available to these Indians has provided no substitute." And since "objective economic and other conditions" were not "conducive to any constructive resolution" of the impasse, the "inner core of their nonintegrative adjustment" might be characterized as "regression in the sense of a kind of primitivization" (1950)—an interpretation which, if not positively evolutionary, suggested, in Freudian terms, a corresponding devolutionary process.

From this point of view, Hallowell exemplifies a more general tendency for anthropological inquiries into culture and personality, worldview, values, and acculturation to be manifest as an overlapping and partially articulated set. Consistent with a postwar turn within the Boasian tradition from the culturally relative toward the universally human, they could all be treated in implicitly or explicitly evolutionary as well as in relativistic terms. And in a period when anthropology sought integration with and legitimacy among the newly rechristened "behavioral" sciences, these phenomena were often studied by methods and represented in rhetoric resonant of "science" (see Wolf 1964).

On the other hand, there are several respects in which Hallowell's mature anthropological interests were not simply carried along with the major currents of mid-century American anthropology, but eddied against them, or opened up new channels of inquiry. While the anthropological use of the Rorschach technique had other practitioners, and was subject to serious criticism even during its brief heyday, Hallowell's interest in personality theory and in individual variability in the relationship of personality and culture was a leavening influence on some of the more extreme manifestations of the "culture and personality" movement. His concept of "behavioral environment" and the five "basic orientations provided by culture" (self, object, spatiotemporal, motivational and normative) offered the possibility of a conceptual bridge between the mental world of the human individual self and the world of "culturally constituted symbolic forms" (1954:89–105; 1963b:297; cf. Spiro 1991). His interest in altered states of consciousness has been interpreted as the means by which "individual, internal" experience, "in the presence of systems of external shared symbolization, is turned into raw material for culture-building" (Bourguinon 1991:39). And while he later wrote apologetically of his early tendency to privilege the least acculturated Ojibwa, and to neglect the "total community" in which the Ojibwa lived (1972:58), several of his later essays have been read as contributions to a "decentering [of] acculturation studies by emphasizing the native side of the contact situation"—notably, in the idea of "transculturization" in reference to the process of "Indianization" (the "cultural assimilation of captured [European] individuals") that had fascinated American writers since the late seventeenth century (Fogelson 1991:14; AH 1963e: 499, 505; cf. 1957).

Hallowell's innovative role was even more evident in relation to his evolutionary interests. Emphasizing "the continuities as opposed to the discontinuities between man and the non-hominid primates," he sought to establish the psychological preconditions of "a human level of existence" (1967a:iii, viii). When he was asked to organize a symposium on "recent theory" at the meetings of the American Anthropological Association in 1952, he chose "human nature" as the topic—complaining to Robert Redfield that ever since he read Dewey's *Human Nature and Conduct* in Boas' seminar in 1922 he had "never been at any anthropological meeting of any sort where the subject has come up for formal discussion" (RRP:AH/RR 11/30/52; RR/AH 12/8/52). Appropriately, the resurgence of interest in "human design" in the "new anthropology" of the postwar period was subsequently traced to Hallowell's presidential address of 1949 (Wolf 1964:51).

Moving outward from developments within American anthropology, an understanding of Hallowell's anthropological work may perhaps also be enriched by viewing his writings from the perspective of the world beyond. Unlike Mead

or Benedict (and several of Roe's subjects), Hallowell was not involved in government work or applied anthropology, nor was he a spokesperson for anthropology to more general audiences. Among those who knew him in the postwar
period he is remembered as an "anthropologist's anthropologist"—a person of
wide-ranging anthropological interests, pursued both in the ethnographic field
and in the scholar's study, but not as a politically engaged intellectual. His published writings and his manuscripts offer only a few explicit references to events
or processes in the world in which he lived, and any attempt to explore such
matters in a textually or biographically grounded way must be suggested rather
tentatively, pending more systematic biographical research.

Starting from his youthful "socialist" inclinations (and the "progressive" milieu in which they were embedded), as well as his pacifist resistance to World
War I, one might patch together a short series of textual moments reflective of
the world outside of anthropology or of his own evolving political views. In the
1920s, these might include his reference to the "big crowd" Speck had in his
"Negro course—but not so many Negroes as we had hoped"; or his own missionary efforts to propagate the "newer ideas on race and culture" among social
workers and sociologists in a course on "Anthropology and Social Work"
(MHP:AH/MH n.d. 1923, 10/20/24); or his resistance to an appointment at
the University of Oklahoma, for fear of being "pocketed off there in the 'Bible
Belt'" (MHP: AH/MH 7/1827). A decade later, in discussing temporal orientation among the Ojibwa, he referred to the temporal disorientation the radical writer Ella Winter had experienced in Moscow, where "Russians had introduced the five-day week and abolished Sunday"—as recounted in her book, *Red
Virtue: Human Relationships in the New Russia* (AH 1937c:219). For the most
part, however, the occasional contrastive references to "western civilization" in
his Ojibwa ethnology, though they sustain a cultural relativist interpretation,
are subordinate to his explication of their "profound differences in psychological outlook" from that of "Western civilization" (234). If he emphasized
Ojibwa sharing of food and general "equalitarianism," and on one occasion
drew a contrast between their notions of property and those of "capitalistic society" (1943a:244), it was not to the end of cultural self-criticism in the aftermath of a decade of economic depression.

The period of the second World War offers more explicitly revelatory moments. In 1943, in a brief response to Ralph Linton's paper on "Nativistic
Movements," Hallowell suggested that there was not "such a far cry" between
"the situation in which primitive peoples have found themselves when their
fundamental cultural values have been threatened" and contemporary Americans "finding fresh virtues in Democracy" and "the values of our way of life" under the impact of "Nazi-Fascist ideology, implemented by armed force" (1943b).
Two years later, Linton invited Hallowell to contribute an essay on the "Sociopsychological Aspects of Acculturation" to a collective volume demonstrat-

ing the role "the science of man" might have in the "intelligent planning of the new world order which now appears inevitable" (Linton 1945:vii). Envisioning "acculturation" (as well as cultural anthropology itself) as an aspect of "the global expansion of European peoples" carried on by "military conquests or the threat of force," Hallowell suggested that it had resulted always "in the subordination of native groups to the power exercised by intruders" and that it had forced them "to make all kinds of cultural readaptations for which they were totally unprepared" (AH 1945:171, 192). Against the "culturalistic fallacy" that saw individuals simply as "passive vehicles or instruments," Hallowell insisted that "man derives his unique significance among all other living creatures as the creator of culture, not as a mere creature of it" (175). Specific cultures, however, might place limits on the range of adaptations: Hallowell recalled the recent destruction of "unsalable commodities" in Western society during the great depression as an instance of the human tendency "to solve problems in traditional ways instead of devising novel means" (178). In this context, Hallowell advocated the "study of the contact of specific peoples in a concrete historical setting" (as opposed to the traditional diffusionist study of "traits") in order to understand the variety of different modes of cultural "readaptation" (174). To this end, the analysis of "cultural changes" could draw on "contemporary learning theory" (Miller & Dollard 1941), moving beyond "our initial descriptive abstractions of stabilized cultural forms to readjustments on the part of individuals, and then back to the socially discernable effects of such readaptation which can once more be described as new or modified cultural forms" (177–78)—a study more Sapirian than Benedictian (or Kroeberian), foreshadowing more recent concerns with "culture and individual agency."

Hallowell's 1945 essay, with its references to Dutch colonial policy and "the global scale of the second World War" (187, 199), stands in striking contrast to his Rorschach studies of the same process—only one of which had so far appeared (AH 1942b)—insofar as the former argued the "pragmatic" adaptability of human beings in responding to the anxiety-arousing arrival of Christian traders and missionaries as a feature of the general process of European expansion, while the latter emphasized the disorienting and even regressive impact of Western culture within a single contact situation (see 1945:191 & 1950). Nor is there any piece in his later work in which the practical demands and historical processes of the modern Western world are so strikingly evident; once again, we are reduced to extrapolating from fragmentary textual moments—in this case, perhaps, to the critical attitude of some American anthropologists (including Herskovits) to British colonialism (Kennedy 1945; Herskovits 1944; Gershenhorn n.d.:528–30).

Other than Roe's tantalizing reference to a discussion of "some societal problems" at the opening of her interview in 1950, there is an apparent dearth of revelatory textual moments in the postwar decade and a half—a gap which, in the context of Hallowell's caution regarding his early socialism, might be interpreted as a reflection of the repressive atmosphere of McCarthyism. And there is in fact evidence that in the months before the Roe interview Hallowell was involved in one of the manifestations of that repression: the academic freedom case of Morris Swadesh, a leading linguistic anthropologist (and a sometimes outspoken radical). Shortly after Swadesh's appointment for one year as associate professor at the City College of New York in 1948, he had openly supported a student strike, and at the end of the year his appointment was not renewed. Hallowell had been a member of an American Anthropological Association Committee on Scientific Freedom appointed the previous year in connection with an earlier case, which had recommended that the Executive Board investigate "cases where the civil rights, academic freedom and professional status of anthropologists as such have been invaded," and "take action where it is apparent that injustice has resulted that affects their rights as citizens and scientists." However, in June 1949 when Swadesh addressed a letter to Hallowell as president requesting the intervention of the Association on his behalf, the matter was referred to the Executive Board. At its meeting that September, the Board found no cause to pursue the case, on the technicality that the bylaws of the Board of Education of New York City did not "require notification of intention to reappoint individuals on one-year appointments, and that, therefore, no violation of civil rights or legal forms is involved" (as quoted in Hymes 1983: 294). While there is no direct evidence of Hallowell's position on the question, his friend Loren Eiseley, writing from California prior to the September Executive Board meeting, worried that "left-wingers" might "precipitate the Association into no end of bickering and involvement if these things continue to get on the floor at the Annual meetings," and went on to note a colleague's confidence that Hallowell, with his "fine objectivity in general," would withstand the "pressure that some of the radical group have been trying to apply" (AHP:LE/AH 7/16, 7/24/49). When the matter was brought before the Council of Fellows at the November 1949 meeting of the Association, with Hallowell in the chair, the backtracking action of the Executive Board was sustained by a vote of 76 to 6, with 26 abstentions.

If the Swadesh case can be read as suggesting that Hallowell, like most of his anthropological colleagues, was reluctant to take a strong stand against McCarthyism, the major manifestation of the Cold War on the domestic front, other textual moments offer hints of his attitude on major international issues of the period. Writing to his wife from a 1959 conference on "The Social Life of Early Man" at the Wenner-Gren Foundation's newly renovated Burg-Wartenstein "castle" in the Austrian Alps, Hallowell commented on how the "Russian 'barbarians'" had "despoiled" the place, "pulling out *every spigot*" (AHP:AH/MFH 6/22/59; Dodds 1973:104–6). The following year he was among those who represented the United States—including Ralph Bunche,

W. E. B. Dubois, Langston Hughes, Martin Luther King Jr. , Joseph Alsop, and John Noon (once a student of Hallowell and Speck, but by then serving with the United States Information Agency)—at the installation of the Governor General of the newly independent Nigeria, B. N. Azikiwe, whom Hallowell had known in the 1920s when Azikiwe was a student at Lincoln University near Philadelphia. But there is nothing in his letter to suggest a concern with colonial issues or liberation movements, beyond his "feeling that things are on the move here" and his report that "Zik" wanted help in "building up the University of Nigeria (which he started)" (AHP:AH/Maude H. 11/17/60; cf. AH 1961b). In 1962, Hallowell traveled to Prague for a meeting to plan the 1964 Moscow sessions of the International Congress of Anthropological and Ethnological Sciences, where Herskovits anticipated that "the Russians were going to try to set up a line." Worried that "their attitude towards personality and culture"—that it was "something like racism"—would make it impossible to "talk to Russians," Hallowell was pleasantly surprised to find that they knew about both his Ojibwa work and the more recent "evolutionary business." Although he noted that "the intellectuals in Prague" were "very restive," on the whole he found it "a very rich experience" (ARP:1963 interview).

Insofar as one can discern a general movement in these moments, it is away from a mild early radicalism, attenuated in the 1930s and 1940s and repressed in the early Cold War McCarthy period, when he was recalled by colleagues as a Roosevelt and Stevenson democrat. Although there is evidence to suggest that he was a reader of the anti-Communist liberal journal *Encounter* (see AH 1961b), there seems also to have been a residue of sympathetic interest in the Soviet Union, which revived somewhat with the waning of McCarthyism. One colleague recalled that when the Soviet delegation arrived at the meeting of the International Anthropological Congress of Anthropological and Ethnological Sciences in Philadelphia in 1956 and another anthropologist made remarks critical of the Soviet Union, Hallowell bristled, but said nothing; in his 1963 follow-up interview (see note 3), he expressed a strong desire to attend the 1964 meeting in Moscow: "I really want to see it now."[10]

Widening the focus from the political to the cultural, one might construct a narrative of Hallowell's relation to "changing values in the wider world." Coming of age at the height of the Progressive Era, Hallowell experienced a mild rebellion against his lower-middle-class Anglo-American parents, refiguring their conventional religious values in socially functional terms. Troubled by the disturbing consequences of urban transformation in an era of unregulated economic competition, he was attracted to socialism and to sociology, and for a time actively pursued his social reform interests as a social worker. A pacifist during World War I, he shared the questioning of the values of contemporary

10. I have been unable to find evidence that Hallowell actually attended.

civilization by many left-leaning intellectuals, and was attracted by the cultural relativist and romantic primitivist tendencies of Boasian anthropology, which sustained a critical attitude toward the anti-relativist and racist social and political tendencies of the 1920s (GS 1986:5–7; 1989).[11] However, the processes of professional enculturation into the disciplinary world of anthropology and of immersion into the ethnographic other world of Native Americans encouraged a countertendency of withdrawal from or sublimation of active involvement in national political, social, and economic issues, especially during the depression years, when he carried on his major fieldwork among a Canadian Indian group he saw as documenting an aboriginal contrast to modern Western civilization. Although he continued to explore the alternative behavioral world of the Ojibwa, his conjuring monograph of 1943, which is a systematically relativist attempt to understand cultural behavior dramatically at odds with the norms of western rationalism in terms of the traditional (presumably precontact) beliefs and customs of a "primitive" group, may be taken as the culminating moment in the pre–World War II phase of Hallowell's anthropology.

In the years immediately before the war, however, other themes had begun to emerge in his work: fear, anxiety, and aggression in the traditional Ojibwa culture, and the psychological consequences of acculturation since first contact with Western culture. By 1950, the historical movement forward from the presumed precontact culture and personality of the Ojibwa was complemented by a backward movement deep into evolutionary time, to investigate the protocultural psychological preconditions for the emergence of fully human cultural behavior—the deep structure of "human nature" that was the universal substratum underlying the relativist diversity of subsequent human cultures. In suggesting that "we can learn something about the earliest stage of human adaptation from the cultures of the existing peoples who have survived as our contemporaries, despite the fact that, as observed, their cultures may not be completely aboriginal" (AH 1963c:315), Hallowell was in effect reaffirming one of the basic assumptions of "the comparative method" of nineteenth-century evolutionary anthropology (GS 1995:3–14; cf. AH 1963c). Hallowell's postwar evolutionary turn can thus be interpreted in terms of the underlying continuity of an evolutionary outlook that predated his encounter with Boasian anthropology. Alternatively, it can be seen as a reflection of the more general revitalization of universalist and evolutionary interests within American anthropology in the postwar period. But whereas in several other figures (including Redfield and Kluckhohn), there is evidence to suggest that this turn is associated with a

11. As an incidental reflection of the "Jazz Age," one might note Hallowell's suggestion, in offering to put Herskovits up in Philadelphia, that he stay over a day, "particularly if you like dancing," to join "a whole crowd of us" (including Speck and a number of students) who "always go to a dance on Friday nights . . . and have a jolly time" (MHP: AI/MH 3/22/24)

moral revaluation of the process of civilization in response to atomic and racial holocaust, in Hallowell's case, such interpretive enrichment may perhaps be found in a consideration of more intimate aspects of his personal life.[12]

The Boasian Relativist as Evolutionary Psychologist: Hallowell's Anthropological Trajectory in Personal Parental Context

By 1950, there had been dramatically disruptive changes in Hallowell's domestic situation—not all of them evident in the Roe interview. In 1919, he had married Dorothy Kern, a fellow social worker whom he had known since high school, and who, after receiving her doctorate in 1928, went on to a career as child psychologist specializing in the measurement of early child intelligence and the adjustment of adoptive children in foster homes. The marriage, however, was apparently not happy: Hallowell told Roe that the heavy work pace

---

12. Having myself referred elsewhere to the exclusion of women as one of several "exclusionary processes" at work in the anthropology of the early Cold War period (GS 2000b:253–54), it seems appropriate in considering the "external" cultural contexts of Hallowell's work to comment on the limited evidence that I have about his role regarding aspiring women anthropologists, a number of whom he taught at Bryn Mawr and Northwestern, as well as at the University of Pennsylvania. A classmate of mine at Penn once told me that she left anthropology after Hallowell discouraged her from going unmarried into the field (and in fact suggested another male graduate student as a possible husband). But when I mentioned this incident to two women anthropologists who knew Hallowell in the 1940s, they were both surprised, and found it inconsistent with their own experience (E. Bourguinon, 1/24/00; C. McClellan, 2/4/00)—and my friend had in fact been surprised at the time, since Hallowell had previously been supportive of her work. So was he also in the case of Ruth Landes, who wrote books titled *Ojibwa Sociology* and *The Ojibwa Woman* on the basis of fieldwork that he had in a minor way facilitated (Cole 1997:vii), and which he reviewed in the most favorable terms: "she is able to show, and rightly I believe, that women not only have an immense amount of freedom in this very individualistic society, but that they are often successful in flaunting customs and vetoing traditional standards" (Hallowell 1938d; cf. Landes correspondence, AHP: 1948–58). During a discussion of the job market in Anne Roe's follow-up interview of 1963, Hallowell commented on the difficulty of finding jobs for women (or, as he frequently called them, "girls"): "It's certainly not the same as getting a man a job. It's still that they prefer the men." However, he specifically rejected Roe's suggestion that they might have "problems in fieldwork." My friend thought Hallowell might have been concerned that she was "too small, young and feminine to live in a primitive culture on my own"—and it is possible that the fate of Henrietta Schmerler, whose rape/murder in the field in 1931 resonated for some years in the still small profession of anthropology, may have caused him to think of her as a risky case (Lavender n.d.). On the whole, it seems that, considered in the context of 1950s anthropology and the prevailing ideology of gender, Hallowell was among the more enlightened of male anthropologists—in contrast, perhaps, to his friend Herskovits, who in 1939 played a role in marginalizing Landes for allegedly violating traditional sexual standards during fieldwork in Brazil (Landes 1970:128–29; cf. Cole 1995; Yelvington n.d.).

he maintained "when living with my first wife" was in large part "compensa-tory," and that some time during the 1930s he "fell in love with someone else," and after "a long period" this "broke up his first marriage" (ARP:1950 inter-view). Shortly after the divorce, he was married in 1942 to Maude Frame, who had been employed "for a number of years" as an editor for a publishing firm, and who thenceforth worked closely with him (ARP:1963 interview). There was, however, one child from the earlier marriage, whom Hallowell and Kern had adopted as an infant in 1925—perhaps following the model of their social work mentor Jessie Taft, who tried to find "unusual homes" for "extraordinary children" (albeit at some "risk"), and who with her associate, Virginia Robin-son, adopted two such children in the early 1920s (Robinson 1962:72). Al-though William Kern Hallowell was gifted with an I.Q. of 124 and skipped half the second grade, by the eighth grade he was often truant, and by the time he was fourteen had been involved in a number of burglaries (*Philadelphia Inquirer* 4/24/47). Paroled to his parents on condition that he attend military school (*Philadelphia Bulletin* 12/1/47), he there became involved in a series of thefts from fellow students, and was sent to a private correctional school in Staats-burg, New York. However, when he left for summer vacation in 1939, he and a friend stole guns and ammunition from the military academy, and were subse-quently involved in a "running battle" with police in which thirty shots were exchanged. Charged with "assault with intent to kill" (*New York Times* 7/14, 8/23/39), young Hallowell was held in the Jamesburg Reformatory until Febru-ary 1941, when he went to live with his adoptive mother. In April 1947 (to her slowly dawning suspicion), he became involved in further robberies and auto thefts at gunpoint, culminating in a second automobile chase in which he shot and killed two policemen, and barely survived six bullet wounds in his chest. The event was given prominent coverage in all the Philadelphia newspapers at the time, and again later that year during separate trials for each homicide, each ending in a sentence to life imprisonment (*Philadelphia Inquirer* 4/23–29, 10/1–3/47; *Philadelphia Daily News*, 12/14/47; EBP:Maude H. /EB 10/7/47, 1/1/48). After seven unsuccessful attempts to win parole or commutation, William Kern Hallowell was finally freed in April 1972, and went to work at a company with a "program to give aid and assistance to people with problems." But when he lost that job in June of 1973, he and another man went to his adoptive mother's home with the intent to rob her, and in the process Hallowell—who was described by his accomplice as a "Jekyll and Hyde" when he drank—killed his mother with five blows from a claw hammer (*Philadelphia Bulletin* 7/6, 7/9, 7/11/73). Fifteen months later, his adoptive father died at the age of eighty-one.

Hallowell was present at the first of his son's two trials shortly after his return from Northwestern—and wrote to Herskovits that "'They' are out to get Bill by hook or crook" (MHP:AH/MP 10/18/47). But there is no mention of these events in the interview material in 1950, when Roe interpreted his Rorschach

Hallowell with his first wife, Dorothy Kern Hallowell, circa 1922. (Courtesy American Philisoph-ical Society.)

protocols as indicating a "very well organized personality," with "no evidence at all of anxieties" and "generally overall good adjustment."[13] He was also present in 1962, at an appeal for commutation of the life sentence, but when Roe asked in the follow-up interview of 1963, "what ever became" of his son, Hallowell sidestepped the issue, noting that he had "got into trouble" that was "too complicated to mention," and Roe moved quickly to "changes in the whole scientific field since you and I were young" (ARP:1963 interview).[14] That Hallowell might have preferred not to discuss his son's "trouble" is understandable, and newspaper accounts and surviving prison correspondence suggest that he distanced himself psychologically, as well as geographically and maritally, from

13. Roe felt that Hallowell's TAT's were "a fairly quiet sort of performance" with "very little concern with emotion" save for "one of general helplessness," and in one case "a pretty striking dependence" on parental figures. Several of Hallowell's picture narratives, however, involved parents and a son, and seem to an unsophisticated observer to bear some relationship to the events herein recounted. These include one about a mother and son and an absent father, which Roe interrupted at one point to ask "about the future"—to which Hallowell responded: "Who knows. Of course this is my story. I don't know. They are both very much concerned about the whole thing because neither one does know how it's going to turn out. That's why they are this way. She's wondering, she, and he's worried about it and it's a very uncertain situation and concerns the husband of one and the father of the other."

14. The actual passage in Roe's transcript of the 1963 interview reads: "Oh, this is too complicated to mention. Well, he got into trouble. . . ." Since the interview tapes were not preserved in the APS, there is no way of telling for sure whether those periods represent Roe's elision of disturbing material, a tape recording or transcribing problem, or simply aposiopesis ("a sudden breaking off of a discourse before it is ended, as if one is unable or unwilling to continue it"). However, I am inclined to assume the latter, on the basis of the Hallowell interviews as a whole, in comparison to other interviews in Roe's study. In general, Roe seems to have been guided by her subjects: if they responded to an issue she raised, it might be pursued at greater length, into areas that could be regarded as embarrassing. But she did not push. During the 1950 interview, she apparently said at one point (as indicated by a parenthesis in her transcript), "I'm not very clear about your interpersonal relations," to which Hallowell responded with the dates of his first marriage and divorce, the bare fact of an adopted son, and a comment about the breakup of his marriage, which in the transcript is followed by two parentheses: "(Here or elsewhere he said that he would tell me anything about it that I wanted to know if I would just ask questions)" and what was apparently her clarification: "(What I'm more interested in is the general psychosexual development)." Hallowell responded with general statements and vague specifics: "from high school days I went out with girls . . . I actually met my first wife in church . . . I never had any trouble"—this, in contrast to others in Roe's sample who spoke in rather more explicit detail. Roe then turned to a different topic—"Did you have any stormy times during adolescence?"—which although not unrelated, is not the same as "psychosexual development." While a mutual reticence on such matters is understandable, it is surprising in the case of an anthropologist who had just published (in obvious relationship to the Kinsey report) an article on "psychosexual adjustment" among the Ojibwa, based on detailed information (elicited by "systematic ethnographic inquiry, personal interviews, participant observation, and a Rorschach sample of the population") about positively, neutrally, and negatively evaluated sexual relationships and techniques, including masturbation, homosexuality, fellatio, etc. (AH 1949a:292ff).

Hallowell, followed by his ex-wife, Dorothy, leaving a courtroom in the Philadelphia City Hall, at the end of the opening session of the trial of their son, William Kern Hallowell (Courtesy *Philadelphia Inquirer.*)

him—in contrast to his first wife, who in 1947 vowed "to stick by my boy," and whose will left to him "everything of monetary value and anything else he wants" (*Philadelphia Bulletin* 12/1/47; *Philadelphia Inquirer* 1/18/62, 7/27/73).[15]

15. In 1978, William Kern Hallowell was granted a new trial after his accomplice, the chief prosecution witness against him, admitted he lied when he testified that he had not been offered leniency in exchange for his testimony. However, before the retrial began, Hallowell appealed instead to have all charges dropped. When this appeal came before the Supreme Court in 1981, the

What significance this horrific history of adoptive parenthood may have for an understanding of Hallowell's intellectual production is necessarily specula-tive. That Roe herself might have pursued the issue if Hallowell had followed her leading question seems unlikely, given the character of her published analy-ses, in which life history snippets were presented anonymously and her gener-alizing statements were of a collective character: thus, under "psychosocial development," she suggested that anthropologists ("over half" of eight), were more "rebellious" than psychologists, and both were more so than physicists and biologists (1953b:25; cf. 1952). The most venturesome specific thought preserved in her Hallowell materials is the parenthetic suggestion that his early interest in cross-cousin marriage might reflect the fact that he had no cousins (ARP:1950 interview)

In the present instance, a more individualized interpretation must begin by acknowledging that by the time of the murders in 1947, Hallowell's major an-thropological orientations were already well established, although his evolu-tionary interests had not yet come sharply to the fore. By the same token, it might be argued that the development of Hallowell's ethnographic interests in the 1930s reflected a dynamic internal to his own research: if he wrote about *Conjuring in Saulteaux Society,* it was because it was central to Ojibwa culture and had been mentioned in the literature for three centuries, because he was only the third professional ethnologist to have made "first-hand observations of such performances," and because he had a personal knowledge of the Ojibwa world view and "the role conjuring plays in their lives" (1942a:ix). In short, one might write a history of Hallowell's anthropology without reference to the trou-bling history of William Kern Hallowell.

On the other hand, there was a definite turn in Hallowell's later career that might be explained in other terms than "inevitable" intellectual evolution. Al-though there is no sharp chronological break, there are a number of indications of a shift away from a more traditional Boasian ethnographic orientation. Rather than the comprehensive ethnography he had at one point been plan-ning (Brown 1992:111), he produced only the short monograph on conjuring (1942a). And while Boasian cultural relativism was still there strongly mani-fest, he had by then begun elsewhere to explore topics in which a more univer-salistic and ultimately evolutionary interest in human nature was manifest—themes that can be interpreted as reflecting anxieties or sensitivities that might have been aroused in the parent of a psychologically disturbed adoptive child.

---

judges split evenly, and "the charges remained intact" (UPI regional news 7/8/81, as summarized on lexis-nexis.com). Allen Hornblum, a student of the Pennsylvania prison system (Hornblum 1998), with numerous contacts among current inmates, informed me (11/23/97) that William Kern Hal-lowell died in 1994 of natural causes, while still in prison, where he was known as a jailhouse lawyer and homosexual, who did legal work for sex with younger inmates, and was generally disliked.

Although Hallowell's first published paper on psychological topics (after a decade lapse of interest in the psychological literature) was obviously influenced by the recent work of Sapir, Benedict, and Charles Seligman, it is striking nonetheless that it dealt with "Culture and Mental Disorder" (AH 1934; cf. Sapir 1932; Seligman 1930; Benedict 1934). But to the present point it is perhaps more relevant to suggest a shift in his writings on mental illness from a predominant emphasis on the cultural relativity of mental disorder—its relationship to the "characteristic set of values" of a particular culture (1936:1297; 1937b)—to the more universalistic and evolutionary concerns of the postwar period, in which "mental health" was seen as "not altogether culture-bound" but as having "universal significance, both as a concept and as a value." Thus, in the discussions at the 1952 symposium on "Anthropology Today," Hallowell argued that while "persistent neurotic, psychotic, delinquent, or criminal behavior patterns may all be considered equally adjustive from the standpoint of a kind of psychological homeostasis, . . . they are not adjustive on the level of mental health." On the contrary, "our present knowledge makes it necessary to differentiate a positive higher or optimum level of psychological functioning from a lower or less positive one" (1953b:334).

There is evidence also to suggest the emergence of new themes in his ethnographic writing toward the end of the 1930s. Although his article on "Aggression in Saulteaux Society" was clearly influenced by the John Dollard volume on *Frustration and Aggression* and the Mead volume on *Cooperation and Competition Among Primitive Peoples,* it is worth noting that it was published a year after William Kern Hallowell's first gun battle with police, and that in it Hallowell spoke of having been "forced" after "more intimate acquaintance" to acknowledge the "aggressive impulses" and "undercurrents of hostility" that were among the "deeper psychological realities of Saulteaux life" (1940:278; Dollard et al. 1939; Mead 1937).

In the same period, Hallowell published an essay relating to the problem of juvenile delinquency: "Shabwán: A Dissocial Indian Girl," who was believed by the Indians "to be insane."[16] Because "mental derangement" was usually attributed by the Ojibwa to witchcraft, which might have caused her to "turn into a cannibal," her family were "terrified," and two boys were delegated to hold her down when she was "violent, moaned, yelled, laughed and talked in a silly fashion." Hallowell made a point of arguing that "the methods [they] used in restraining [her] and the diagnostic and remedial procedures undertaken were determined by culturally molded premises." Nevertheless, Shabwán's behavior,

16. In Hallowell bibliographies, the essay is cited as published in 1938, perhaps because volumes of the journal began in October, and is so cited here (as 1938b); internal evidence, however, suggests that, although the events took place in the summer of 1936, the essay was written during or after the winter of 1938–39 (1938b:329, 340).

which included asking the boys to release her arms momentarily so she could scratch her nose, led him to conclude that she was "malingering" to conceal her nighttime assignations with young men. Managing to win her confidence (indeed, her "positive transference"—she called him her "sweethard") Hallowell was able, by the promise of gifts for better behavior, to effect behavioral modifications that her parents and her grandfather regarded as a cure. In the present context, what is particularly striking is a single introductory sentence: "Despite the basic differences in the cultural patterns of Saulteaux society and our own, to which so much of the specific attitudes and behavior of the girl, her parents and the other Indians may be referred, there can be discerned, I believe, the operation of underlying psychological mechanisms and impulses that are familiar in comparable cases of revolt against parental authority in Western civilization" (1938b:330, 331, 336, 340). Here, by implication, is an appeal not only to universal human psychological mechanisms and to the diagnostic categories of Western scientific psychology, but to an experience of adolescent revolt that might be "familiar" to his readers, as it was to Hallowell.

Although his son's sociopathic tendencies were already at this time a matter of police record, and there might well have been inklings of more serious troubles yet to come, it is nevertheless quite a leap from Shabwán's "malingering," within the categories of Ojibwa belief, to the more radically transgressive behavior of William Kern Hallowell, which had not yet taken a homicidal turn. In placing Hallowell's history as an adoptive parent in an intellectually generative relationship to more general themes in his work, one must therefore hope for an interpretive tolerance similar to that he requested in 1936 in discussing several other case histories illustrating the relation of "Psychic Stresses and Culture Patterns" among the Ojibwa. Granting that "it would be difficult to comprehend them except in terms of the particular values and attitudes characteristic of Saulteaux culture," he acknowledged that "the psychological interpretation in each case is sheer guesswork on my part," for which "I crave as much indulgence as seems possible" (1936: 1298).

With a similar indulgence, it might be argued that from the moment of his adoption in 1925, William Kern Hallowell's behavioral future was a charged and problematic issue. His father-to-be was a social worker turned cultural anthropologist; his mother-to-be a social worker turning child psychologist; they acted at a cultural moment when issues of race and culture, of nature and nurture, of eugenics and environment were hot topics in both fields and in the broader culture, and when the family histories of the Jukes and the Kallikaks were still debated as exemplars of the heredity of feeblemindedness and criminality (Boas 1928:110; Zenderland 1998:143–85; Paul 1995:50). Both parents had felt the influence of a crusading psychiatric social worker, who had herself taken the same "risk" that they must have felt. While they were no doubt moved by more intimate marital motives, the adoption had from the beginning a cer-

tain experimental aspect, insofar as it could offer personal evidence for professional hypotheses on important issues of the day. And when there were first
inklings and then dramatic evidence that it was not working well, it does not
seem farfetched to suggest that personal questioning ("could we, as parents, have
made a difference?") may have been reflected, consciously or unconsciously, in
professional inquiry ("or was it something beyond our personal control, something that might be understood scientifically?").

Without venturing too far into the guesswork realm of psychological interpretation, it might be suggested that at the very least such a parental history
would have heightened Hallowell's sensitivity to particular ethnographic experiences (a previously unappreciated undercurrent of aggression, or the behavior of a "dissocial" adolescent). More generally, it might have inclined him to
the consideration of certain broader issues that were to become themes of his
work from the middle 1930s on: the definition and enforcement of behavioral
norms in different cultures; the socialization process which "limits the conditions under which personal adjustment can take place" (1955b:33); the cultural variability of personality structure; the cultural definition and boundaries
of the mentally and behaviorally "normal" and "abnormal"; the relation of the
"conscious" and "rational" to the "unconscious" and "irrational"; the way in
which generically human psychological processes manifest themselves in individuals in different cultures; and at a more general level, the relationship of the
culturally relative and the universally human in a broader evolutionary context. True, some of these questions, in various renditions and with varying answers, have long been central to the anthropological tradition, and by Hallowell's own historical account of the relationship of psychology and anthropology
were beginning to be addressed anew in the interwar years under the influence
of psychoanalytic theory (1954:205–29). However, they did not have the same
salience for every anthropologist, and it seems reasonable to assume (for those
who believe that intellectual production in the human studies can only for certain purposes be abstracted from personal experience) that one factor heightening their intellectual salience for Hallowell could have been his experience
as the parent of a "dissocial" child.

Insofar as his son's history heightened his awareness of such issues, it may also
have stimulated his hope that they might be amenable to scientific understanding. It is perhaps in this context that Hallowell returned to the literature
of psychology and psychoanalysis in the early 1930s, and that in collecting
"data" on the "personality and behavior of individuals in non-literate societies"
he turned from "impressionistic" methods to one that might facilitate "the use
of theoretical concepts of a scientific order," using the Rorschach method in
order to obtain "under controlled conditions [responses] that can be compared,
analyzed and interpreted according to well-recognized principles" (1941b:236).
And despite criticism that the Rorschach test was culture-bound, he continued

to insist that "the raw data necessary for interpretation" and cross-cultural com-parison could be elicited, if the tests were properly administered, "because a universal function of human perception is exploited" (1955b:45). Until the end of his active career, Hallowell remained convinced that human behavior was amenable to a type of inquiry he called "scientific," and which could pro-vide a form of knowledge that was both culturally specific and universally hu-man, insofar as it had to do with psychological processes that were common to all humankind.

The anthropological relevance of Hallowell's parental experience seems still manifest in two papers that in retrospect may be regarded as the culminating productions of the two major phases of his anthropology: the ethnographic in-terpretations based on his fieldwork of the 1930s, and the evolutionary inter-pretations of the postwar period (phases both mediated by his reemergent depth psychological interests of the later 1930s). Although building on his rel-ativist conjuring monograph of 1942, Hallowell's last major ethnographic in-terpretation, "The Ojibwa World View and Disease," was recast in the context of Redfield's "world view" studies and Kluckhohn's concern with cultural uni-versals. Starting from universal needs (including that of parents to know "Why is my child sick?"), Hallowell began and ended his discussion by contrasting Western "scientific" explanation with that "found in primitive societies," not simply as a culturally relative alternative world view, but as "of a different or-der," characterized "by a higher level of rationality, objectivity, and the avail-ability of tested knowledge." In between those affirmations, he argued by way of illustration that within the Ojibwa world view the "most ready explanation of events"—including the explanation of mental illness associated with ag-gression—was a "personalistic theory of causation. Who did it? Or Who is re-sponsible?"—an approach he suggested was based on an "unrecognized fallacy" of treating disease as a "dependent" rather than an "independent variable." Pushing the limits of interpretive indulgence, it may perhaps be suggested in this context that science for Hallowell may have had the implicit function of reassuring him that his son's crimes were not to be attributed to his son's or his own personal responsibility, but were the result of some determining processes which could be understood in scientific terms (1963a:392–93, 399, 403, 444), including perhaps those of human psychobiological evolution.

The culminating paper in Hallowell's evolutionary phase, entitled "Person-ality, Culture, and Society in Behavioral Evolution," built upon and extended arguments advanced in several papers of the preceding decade (1956, 1959, 1960a, 1961a). Hallowell here placed the major components of his evolution-ary argument within traditions of discourse ranging back to Darwin—in one in-stance beyond, to Theodore Waitz and J. F. Herbart—and thence forward in the British and the Boasian traditions, focusing particularly on the relationship be-tween anthropology and psychology (see AH 1954). During the early twentieth century, when these two disciplines were "developing their characteristic abstractions, concepts, and specializations," anthropologists, emphasizing the concept of culture, "reacted negatively to psychological concepts or theories which stressed innate behavioral determinants" (1963b:234). Although the culture and personality movement focused primarily on personality differences that "can be shown to be related to cultural differences," implicit in its data were "indications that universal dynamic processes are involved." These processes, which were "related to the psychobiological nature of modern man as a species," could no longer be simply taken for granted as part of an unexamined "psychic unity" of mankind. Psychoanalysis had shown that "the 'rationality' of the human mind is counterbalanced by an irrationality linked with biologically rooted forces which are intelligible in an evolutionary perspective" (237–38).

Proposing a new "*conjunctive* approach to human evolution" (1963b:241), Hallowell explored its psychological, social structural, and biological dimensions—in terms of both continuities and discontinuities, of preconditions and emergent distinctive features—from the primate and early hominid stages of "protocultural development," on up to a fully human cultural adaptation in which "cognitive processes were raised to a new level of functioning by means of culturally constituted symbolic forms" (1963b:291–97). Although we could "never check developmental stages in the enlargement of the brain by direct observation of behavior, we do know what the behavioral outcome was in the most highly evolved hominid": at this "more advanced stage, a normative orientation becomes an inherent aspect of the functioning of all sociocultural systems" (275–76). Furthermore, such an evolved system required human actors with certain psychological characteristics—including "a capacity for self-objectification, identification with one's own conduct over time, and appraisal of one's own conduct and that of others in a common framework of socially recognized and sanctioned standards of behavior"—which enabled them, by the use of "symbolic means" to play "sanctioned roles within a common framework of values" (276–77).

While the "evolutionary aspects" of self-awareness had been "scarcely touched" (1963b:279), they could be illuminated by recent psychoanalytic work on "ego theory," notably in the writings of Heinz Hartmann.[17] It is in the culminating portion of the essay, in which Hallowell speculated on the "phylogenetic roots of the ego" (282), that echoes of his personal parental experience may be heard. Defining culture as "an elaborated and socially transmitted system

---

17. My colleagues Ray Fogelson and Tanya Luhrmann have pointed out to me the significance of Hallowell's turn to Hartmann's ego psychology, which emphasized the impact of events in the "real world" (as opposed to internal fantasies), and the need to defend oneself, as Luhrmann suggested, "against the sorrows generated by historical crisis—and presumably, against the anguish of a child going crazy."

of meanings and values, which, in an animal capable of self awareness . . . makes the role of the human being intelligible to himself, both with reference to an articulated universe and to his fellow men," Hallowell went on to argue that "a human level of existence requires an evolutionary price." It was "not always easy, at the level of self-awareness, to reconcile idiosyncratic needs with the demands imposed by the normative orientation of the self," and "unconscious psychological mechanisms such as repression, rationalization, and other defense mechanisms" were "an adaptive means that permits some measure of compromise between conflicting forces," relieving "the individual of part of the burden" that was "forced upon him by the requirements of a morally responsible existence" (289). Quoting Franz Alexander, he suggested that "mental disease represents a failure of the ego to secure gratification for subjective needs in a harmonious and reality-adjusted manner and a breakdown of the defenses by which it tries to neutralize impulses which it cannot harmonize with its internal standards and external reality" (290). To the same point, it is worth noting that in a shorter paper published two years later on "Hominid Evolution, Cultural Adaptation, and Mental Dysfunctioning," Hallowell spoke in evolutionary terms of "the direction of ontogenetic development" as moving toward "the achievement of relative independence from erratic or unpredictable responses to impulsive demands"—responses, which in the case of William Kern Hallowell, had had fatal consequences (AH 1965a:47).

From an interpretive as well as a bibliographic point of view, it is striking that "mental disease," which was the topic of Hallowell's first statement of a relativist approach to culture and personality (AH 1934), should, thirty years later, figure so prominently in the culminating statement of his universalistic evolutionary interpretation of "the human nature of Homo sapiens"—just as it did in the culminating statement of his Ojibwa ethnography. Whether in each instance he had his son in mind remains speculative; but it seems possible that William Kern Hallowell's homicidal history may have been a factor in heightening and sustaining, if not motivating, his father's interest in the cultural and universal determinants of the borderline between human rationality and irrationality.

"What Would Pete Say?" A Reflexive Dialogical Interlude

Upon reading the preceding section, my dissertation mentor Murray Murphey, who first introduced me to Hallowell's work in 1956, sent me another long letter in a dialogue that had begun several months previously. From the first Murray had expressed reservations about interpreting Hallowell's anthropology in terms of his son's "homicidal history." Despite my protestations that my approach was "contextual," it seemed "still causal" to him, and in effect presented an "alternative hypothesis" to that of the purely autonomous development of

Hallowell's anthropology in "the normal course" of his research. Murray was willing to grant that there were cases where the decision between two such hypotheses was clear: William James' surviving letters convincingly documented a relationship between his "personal problems" and the "crisis" in his thought. But because there was no similar statement from Hallowell, or "others close to him," the two hypotheses "do not stand on equal ground." Moreover, "we both know that the second is the sexier, and that that is the one people will immediately adopt." Later, after reading a draft, and being struck by "just how little data you seem to have showing the influence of William's tragedy on Pete," Murray offered a counterhypothesis: "that he and his wife adopted the child, it being basically her idea though he agreed, that when it went sour he distanced himself from both her and William and went his way"—that is, proceeded on a research trajectory that had its own internal dynamic.[18]

As the terminology ("hypothesis," "cause," "data") suggests, there were epistemological as well as methodological and evidential issues involved in our exchange which had to do not only with how to understand Hallowell and how to represent his own understanding of his work, but also with what implications such an understanding might have for the pursuit of scientific "truth." It was not simply that over the last four decades I had moved away from the social science orientation of my doctoral dissertation toward a more interpretively permissive "contextual" approach, and that Murray had held to a more rigorously "causal" approach than I think appropriate for the interpretive purposes that interest me (see Murphey 1994). It was also that my interpretation seemed to call into question both the scientific status of Hallowell's work and his motives in pursuing

18. This section was added to the essay in response to the criticisms of a mentor and longtime friend who knew Hallowell over a longer period than I did. Reflecting on what I have written, I realize that while it is dialogical insofar as it is based upon correspondence with a critic, it is obviously a dialogue only in a limited sense, since its words were selected and arranged by me with a view to justifying the interpretation that elicited his criticism. Within the limits of this motivation, however, I have tried to represent Murray's position as fairly as I could—i. e. , in a manner that seemed to me consistent with his side of the discussion as I had experienced it, but which allowed me to continue in my own *contextual* interpretation (cf. Murphey 1994, where an argument for "*causal*" explanation" [my emphasis] is systematically advanced, and Hallowell is cited four times—twice on the basis of "personal communication.") By way of further dialogical contextualization, it is worth mentioning that Bob Richards, another colleague with whom I have long engaged in historiographic debate, who regards "contextualism" as a wimpish form of causal interpretation, has encouraged me to come out of the closet and admit that my interpretation is causal. I would like to think that my own position is somewhere between the two. Putting it as a matter of personal historiographical faith: while I cannot (nor do I seek to) establish what I would regard as a convincing "causal" connection between Hallowell's intellectual trajectory and his parental experience, my own life and intellectual experience makes it hard for me to imagine that the two are unconnected. On this basis, I have offered possible connections, which I hope readers may regard as relevant interpretive context (as I do)—or, if they prefer to think in causal terms, may reject or accept as they see fit.

it. Recalling the exact language in which Hallowell had once confronted a literary colleague about the latter's mode of textual interpretation (that it was
"not what we do in science"), Murray suggested that this phrase "made quite
clear the fact that Pete thought of himself as a scientist." More generally, what
was at issue was not simply the interpretation of Hallowell, but "the need to
protect the integrity of the intellectual process"—or, one might say, to protect
the human sciences from the science bashers.

That Hallowell, like many other anthropologists of his time (and some today), did indeed think of himself as a scientist (as did Roe), or at least as striv-
ing to be "scientific," seems evident to me, and indeed essential to my own
interpretation of the development and reception of his work. The question
remains, however, whether someone who strove to be "scientific" might *also*
(though not instead) be compelled by other unarticulated or unconscious motives—and whether (and how) a historian who in general privileges "the native point of view" (but who himself retains a qualified commitment to a universal scientific process) may responsibly attempt to understand and represent
such "ulterior" motives.

The answer will depend in part on one's prior assumptions about the possibility that such motives might have no effect on a thinker's thought, or none
worthy of serious interpretive consideration. My own presupposition—based
on life experience and self-analysis, flavored by a residue of Freudian assumption—is that, in the human sciences, where the subject matter is inherently
anxiety provoking, such cases of noninfluence are rarely if ever to be found (see
Devereux 1967). And while there may be good methodological reasons to attempt to recognize and control the influence of such ulterior motives in human
science practice, there is no reason to assume that they necessarily compromise
human science inquiry, or to exclude them from its historical interpretation.
Nor did Murray advocate doing so. But in response to his proposal that "zero influence" might stand as one pole in a typology of interpretive possibilities, I am
inclined to wonder whether in any particular exemplifying case of "zero influence" there was perhaps instead at work a process of denial—whether the apparently disciplined separation of the intellectual from the personal may not
have been at least in part a defense against the pain of traumatic personal experience, and to that extent (small, perhaps, but more than "zero") worthy of
interpretive consideration in a biographically-oriented study. And in the case
of an anthropologist whose later career focused on the limits of human rationality in cultural and evolutionary context, whose son's behavior radically transgressed those limits as defined in the culture they shared, I must confess that I
found it—and still find it—hard to believe that the anthropological project
would not in some way be influenced by the parental history. Not that the first
could be explained causally by the second, but that to write about the first as if

the second had not happened would be to offer an impoverished interpretation of a complex human individual.

None of this is intended to deny the legitimacy or utility of a more systematically elaborated investigation of the internal dynamic of Hallowell's research agenda than I have here attempted. It is rather to defend—and to delimit—a particular line of interpretation that I would like to regard as multi-contextual. On the other hand, there is one line of Murray's critique that I found compelling: the suggestion that because it came third, and was more extensively elaborated, and "sexier" than the others, the discussion of Hallowell's parental history would be taken by readers as "the heart of my explanation and interpretation of him and his work." While I would not deny a prior expectation that his son's story would engage my readers as it had engaged me, the placement can be defended in terms of the interpretive structure of the argument: a movement from intellectual development to external and then to interior context. And, as Murray implied, the elaboration of the latter did reflect an attempt to muster as much evidence as possible in entering what I acknowledged as a problematic interpretive realm. That said, however, I would insist again that my approach is in principle contextual, not causal; and that of the contexts of influence considered here, I would, as a matter of historiographic principle, privilege those contexts that were clearly evident in the development of the subject's thought itself as textually manifest, both as starting point and constant point of reference.

With all of this in mind, let Murray speak for a moment in his own voice, without elision, paraphrase, rearrangement, or interpretive intervention:

> My sense has always been that Pete's work is exceptionally coherent, compared with Mead or Geertz or etc. It has seemed to me that he followed a very logical progression, centering always on the Ojibwa and pushing to deeper and deeper levels, connecting up the different aspects of what he found there, and then drawing broad and often universal conclusions from his material. That he went from conjuring to aggression is it seems to me entirely logical in view of the relations of conjuring to aggression in the culture. Why is William necessary to account for this? [Hallowell's] interest in mental disease seems to me inevitable given his interest in personality variation between cultures; one would have to face the problem of when variation becomes abnormality. In short it seems to me that one interpretation of Pete's stuff is that it was generated out of the dynamic of his own research. This possibility you ignore, or very nearly so, in favor of the William interpretation. Now you are very careful to say that you are speculating in your interpretations. But you really don't make the alternative case in any detail, and your reader is left with the impression that this is the gospel.

Lest readers should be left with that impression, I might again reassert the privileged position, within a multi-contextual interpretation, of the author's textual representation of his thought. But given the structure of this essay, it is perhaps more to the point to agree that there is a logic to the development of Hallowell's anthropology, in both its genesis and in its final form—a logic which I found compelling as a graduate student, and which in some respects (or in some moments) I still do. And while I will not venture here to represent that logic in greater detail, Murray's brief statement may perhaps serve both as reaffirmation and as preface to a consideration of Hallowell's subsequent influence, where a central issue will be the influence of his research agenda as a unified program for anthropological research.

There is, however, one further dialogic issue raised by Murray that requires brief comment: that his own reaction to my interpretation "was probably in part from a feeling that Pete would not have liked having all this stuff brought up." He did not, after all, discuss it with Roe when she gave him the opportunity. But when he agreed to be interviewed by her, he knew that the materials of his life history, including the results of the same Rorschach and Thematic Apperception Tests he had used to get at the hidden motives of the Ojibwa, were to be preserved, and would be available for study ten years after his death—or so, at least, Roe's correspondence about the project would strongly suggest.[19] Twenty-five years later, and a half century since the events at issue, his life and thought have become part of the history of anthropology, of which he was himself a serious historian. He believed that this history should be studied "anthropologically" (1965b), and as an ethnographic anthropologist, he himself studied topics that in his own culture would have been thought "personal," "sensitive," or "ulterior" (from the point of view of intellectual history). Furthermore, his own autobiographical account acknowledged the possibility of other interpretations of his intellectual trajectory than its "inevitable" development. With that warrant, I am willing to assume (or at least to hope) that a part of him—the historian of anthropology part—might have found the interpretations suggested here worthy, in principle, of serious consideration as interpretive contexts, or "contexts of influence," useful in varying degrees for the historical understanding of his own anthropology.[20]

19. In writing to another of her subjects, Carleton Coon, Roe specified that "the record of each man is to be separately sealed and is not to be opened until ten years after his death and is then to be used only at the discretion of the Librarian of the Society" and went on to say: "I have asked each subject if he objected to this arrangement. None of them has. If any do, their files will be destroyed. As you realize, many of these data are unique and should be of immense biographical and psychological value. I have tried to arrange to make their use possible without in any way disturbing the subjects" (ARP:AR/CC 12/31/49). Although I did not find the same passage in the letters preserved in Hallowell's file, I assume that the issue was raised with him as well.

20. In the first draft of this essay, I quoted here a remark I have savored since Hallowell made it in 1960 upon reading my dissertation: "George, I really liked your dissertation. I read it almost word for word"—as if I imagined he might also approve the present interpretive effort. In later versions, I deleted that remark as childishly revelatory. But in the interest of greater reflexivity and full disclosure at a late point I decided after all to include it (see note 21).

The Janus Face of Influence: Hallowell
and the History of Anthropology

That Roe did not pursue the troubles of Hallowell's son may reflect not simply her sense of propriety, or an interviewer's tact, or a judgment about the kinds of influences relevant to her project. It may also say something about the place of "influence" in her study of "the making of a scientist." Although she recorded life histories and gave projective tests, her research was not really about the influences that might have formed the intellectual personae of her subjects and how such formative influences might be expressed in their intellectual productions. Despite the singularity of its title, the book she wrote was not about the "making" of any particular scientist, but about the making of scientists (or particular kinds of scientists) in general (Roe 1953a & b). In treating the thought and work of a particular anthropologist, however, the problem of "influence" presents itself in a more compelling way. And it does so with a Janus face: looking backward (influence/s on), there are all those influences out of whose confluence an anthropologist's thought and work are formed; and looking forward (influence/s of), the varied channels of effluence by which that thought and work may influence others. Having in the previous sections considered possible influences on the formation of Hallowell's anthropology, let me turn now to the problem of its influence, both in the present of its expression and publication during his lifetime, and in the time since his death.

Before turning to a specific consideration of Hallowell's influence, however, it may be helpful to consider briefly in general terms the problem of "influence" itself, beginning with schematic comments on the vicissitudes of its conceptual fashion in twentieth-century scholarship. Long the special province of literary historians, the traditional idea of "influence" as a relation "built on dyads of transmission from one unity (author, work, tradition) to another" suffered a general reversal of fortune (one might say an attenuation of "influence") in the years after 1950. The process was paralleled by the rising influence of notions of "intertextuality"—which has been seen either as a pragmatic "enlargement" of "influence" to encompass "unconscious, socially prompted types of text formation" and "other prior constraints and opportunities for the writer," or, in more systematic theoretical versions, as an alternative agenda advanced sometimes under the banner of "the death of the author." Reduced to two phrases, the shift was from "a literary history about agents" to a "literary history of meshing systems"—with a turn back toward agency at the end of the millennium (Clayton & Rothstein 1990:3–4; 17). The movement of literary studies is not unrelated, of course, to developments in other scholarly realms, including the history of science (paradigms and social constructions) and anthropology (from structure to agency)—although it might be argued that from the time of the "philosopher savage" to the time of the "colonial subject," anthropology has not in general been about the agency of named human individuals.

The situation, however, is different in the history of anthropology, which even when dealing with movements of thought has by and large focused on specific anthropologists, who only recently are being placed in supra-individual contexts of a more general systematic character. Perversely, the general movement of my own historiography has been in the opposite direction, from the consideration of categories of actors (American social scientists, 1890–1915) and structures of thought (the ideas of race and culture) toward biographical essays about individual anthropologists (from Boas via Tylor and Malinowski to Hallowell, among others)—or, in anthropological terms, from an "etic" toward an "emic" approach. Over the same period, there has also been a shift in my "historicism"—which is neither "new" nor "paleo" (in the sense that Marxism and other major meta-systems have been spoken of as "historicist"). Though I was once inclined to advocate "historicism" programmatically as a general historiographic approach to the history of the behavioral sciences, I am more inclined now to regard it as a personal historiographic credo in a field of inquiry in which "different strokes for different folks" may variously enrich historical understanding (GS 1965; cf. 1999). Loosely stated, this personal credo embraces the following notions: that insofar as possible, prior present interests should not be allowed to distort the interpretation of surviving evidences of the historical past; that the most important of these evidences are the words and actions of individual anthropologists; and that an understanding of these thoughts and actions may be enriched by considering them, in a conceptually eclectic manner, within the complexity of their various contexts: the inner psychological, the social interactional (institutional and disciplinary), and the cultural historical. Envisioned graphically, the credo might be represented as a series of concentric contextual circles, with vectors of influence focused on and emanating from the individual anthropologist subjects at the center. Or, to add a temporal dimension to the graphic representation, one might envision two cones of influence inverted on a single temporal axis, with their vertices each focused upon the subject/agent anthropologist.

To place oneself as historian within such a graphic representation would be daunting, both conceptually and graphically. The introduction of a temporal axis, however, suggests another shift in my historicism as it relates to the problem of influence. Although I still eschew the evaluation of past anthropologists in terms of prior normative notions of the presumed or advocated progress of the discipline toward the present and into the future, I am more inclined to consider past moments and figures in the history of anthropology in terms of their relation to later moments and figures, down to and including the present—in short, to consider the problem of "influence" from the perspective of each of its Janus faces. Having already dealt in preceding sections with influences that were (or may have been) formative of Hallowell's intellectual persona and production, the problem remains of exploring his forward influence on other anthropologists, both during his lifetime and in the years since his death. And furthermore, to do so not with the aim of resurrecting an unjustly neglected figure, or of offering his thinking as a model for the future direction of anthropology, or legitimating a present anthropological agenda, but in nonevaluative empirical terms, as a problem case in the historiography of anthropology—an inquiry Hallowell himself pursued in a methodologically self-conscious manner.[21]

Before considering Hallowell's case in specific detail, however, it may be appropriate to consider the problem of "forward" influence in general terms. Forward influence may be communicated by many means (oral, written, printed, and now electronic), in differing modes (consciously, unconsciously) or styles (self-serving, charismatic, self-effacing) to a variety of audiences (students, colleagues, individuals or groups beyond an immediate intellectual community), both contemporary and subsequent in time. Whether it is transmitted in partial or totalizing form (as idea or as system, as essay or as oeuvre, as image or as aura), an anthropologist's influence is subject to dilution, modification, fragmentation, transformation, and distillation, as it becomes successively or recurrently "available" (or simply "resonant") to different individuals or groups in changing historical contexts. At every stage, the forward impulse of influence must overcome resistances of reception, whether individuated or more broadly contextual. On the one hand, these resistances may be expressed in the selections and adaptations as well as in the repressions or denials of students and followers, and the qualifications or dismissals of critics. On the other hand, they may be expressed in the changing structure of debate within a disciplinary community (whether conceived as progress, fashion, pendulum swing, or paradigm

---

21. At this point, it may be appropriate to offer a few glimpses into the "black box" of my own motivation both in the study of influence in general, and specifically the influence of A. I. Hallowell. In regard to the study of influence in general, the most important "ulterior" influence is perhaps my disillusionment with Marxism in the course of my departure from the Communist Party in 1956, which on the one hand made me skeptical of all systematic historical meta-theories, and on the other made me sensitive to the complexity of motivation of individual historical actors hoping to change the world. In regard specifically to Hallowell, the most important ulterior influences are anxieties relating to my own disciplinary marginality and personal mortality, in ways I will not attempt to explicate here (cf. GS n.d.). In regard to both the general and the specific case, I suspect that my pervasive underlying pessimism about the future of the world, and of anthropology within it, may be a factor. On the principle that sauce for the subject goose may be sauce for the historian gander, I will note also the suggestion of my colleague Ray Fogelson, who was also a student of Hallowell in the 1950s, that my tendency "to minimize his influence" might reflect an unconscious oedipal need to slay my intellectual father. Accepting that this may not be totally irrelevant (cf. Bloom 1973), I would (in the spirit of Murray Murphey) insist that my interpretations can also be treated as conceptually independent and empirically grounded.

shift)—or more broadly in the fluctuating preferences of the surrounding political, ideological, or cultural milieu. At any point in these historicizing processes, influence may be manifest in different but not mutually exclusive ways—some positively generative (thinking with), others primarily referential (thinking of)—to different but not mutually exclusive ends. On the one hand, it may be manifest constructively, as a fund of substantive material, or a model of method, or a source of analytic concepts, or a framework of interpretation; on the other, toward the legitimation of intellectual authority, or the constitution of a school, a lineage, or a canon. Thus considered, the forward fate of influence is always problematic, both in its historical production and its historiographical reproduction. For most anthropologists, its half-life is probably less than their own life expectancy; and even that of the more influential anthropologists is subject to the dissipation of authorship, whether by diffusion into a faceless fund of disciplinary common sense, by incorporation into the evolving structure of discourse, by dispersion into the pastiche of intertextuality, or simply into the darkness of the library stacks. With their actual work then no longer read, the ideas of anthropologists are subject to paraphrase and reinterpretation, and their contributions to reinvention—perhaps later to be rediscovered as referential precursors, or in some cases to be reread regeneratively, although in contexts quite different from that in which they were formed and into which they were published.[22]

It is by the creation and recreation of such connections and channels by anthropologists and their historians forward and backward in time that "influence" may be established and traced in the history of anthropology. To investigate Hallowell's "influence" systematically in these terms would be a daunting task—the more so since direct interpersonal influence may leave no explicit textual trace, and more diffusely discursive or "atmospheric" influences are at once easy to exemplify and difficult to document empirically. One hopes, however, that such typological considerations may provide a conceptual context for briefly suggestive comments on the reception and influence of Hallowell's work at the time of its publication and in the years since.

The fact that Hallowell was not a self-promoter, that his preferred "pattern of transmission" was the "descriptive-theoretical paper" typical of scholars in

---

22. Ray Fogelson, with whom I had several helpful conversations about Hallowell's influence, reminded me of various ways in which it may leave no readily discoverable historical trace, suggesting (with examples) that some who may have been influenced by Hallowell might fail to recognize it, or minimize or even deny it, whether consciously or unconsciously. While I am sure that such processes operate—and that it is possible that Hallowell's notion of a "culturally constituted behavioral environment" may lurk in the intellectual background of those who speak today of "cultural construction" without reference to his work—I have for the most part limited the present discussion to aspects of influence that are easier to document. On the idea of "relexification," see Brightman 1995; on "resonance," see GS 2000b:254–56.

the biological sciences, that a number of his more important papers were published in venues not customarily read by anthropologists, and that there was no "general text" or "book-length theoretical synthesis" of his work may have militated against his influence in "the mainstream of anthropology" (Spindler, G. & L. 1975:143–44). As measured in the rough terms of the *Social Science Citation Index* over the years from 1965 to 2000, it has been substantially less than that of the other three cultural anthropologists Roe studied.[23] On the other hand, an anthropologist whose students and colleagues produced not only a Festschrift (Spiro 1965), but three posthumous collections (Fogelson et al. 1976; Nash, ed. 1975; Boyer & Boyer 1991) is clearly one whose influence, at least in the short run, must be taken seriously.

There is evidence to suggest, however, that by the time of the appearance of his major published work, the essays collected as *Culture and Experience* in 1955, Hallowell was already somewhat marginal to the changing anthropology of the postwar period. Rather than being assigned to one of his own interwar cohort, his book was reviewed in the *American Anthropologist* by David Aberle, a member of the rising postwar generation who had by this time become quite critical of Boasian anthropology. Aberle had been initiated into southwestern ethnography by Kluckhohn as an undergraduate at Harvard in the late 1930s, and then apprenticed to the culture and personality school by Benedict (and Linton) as a graduate student at Columbia. After three and a half years in the military—during which he administered Rorschach tests as chief clerk of an army psychiatric unit, Aberle returned to complete a dissertation on divergent anthropological views of Hopi culture (see Bennett 1946). In the later 1940s, however, as an instructor in the Harvard Department of Social Relations (Aberle et al. 1950), he was resocialized into the systems theory of Talcott Parsons and into British social anthropology—most notably, in his participation in the seminar on matrilineal kinship held at Harvard in the summer of 1954, out of which he prepared a comparative statistical analysis of "Matrilineal Descent in Cross-Cultural Perspective" (1961). By 1956, Aberle had settled into a tenured position at the University of Michigan, where he "became involved in the materialism and evolutionism" of Leslie White, and was a contributor to the critique of Boasian anthropology in its culture and personality reincarnation (Donald 1987:12; Aberle 1960).

That Aberle could begin by frankly "scanting" not only Hallowell's work on kinship (by then two decades and more in the past), but also his ethnology is itself suggestive of a changing disciplinary milieu (1956:920). Hallowell's early essays had in effect challenged a prevailing Boasian orthodoxy that rejected

---

23. Data compiled by my research assistant, Byron Hamann, indicated that of the total number of citations for the group of four over the whole thirty-five year period, Hallowell had 18.8%, Linton 21.5%, Kluckhohn 27.8% and Redfield 31.7%.

Hallowell, in Ann Arbor, Michigan, in 1953, as photographed by Leslie White (Courtesy American Philosophical Society.)

reasoning backward from present kinship terms to past practices, as the nineteenth-century American evolutionist Lewis Henry Morgan and the early–twentieth-century British diffusionist William Rivers had done. In contrast to the more recent functionalist approaches, however, Hallowell's approach to kinship was still "historical" in so far as it brought together the evidence of historical documents and present practices to confirm a hypothesized change in the kinship system (AH 1928, 1937a). While there were Americanists (such as Fred Eggan) who still pursued historical issues in the postwar period, this was not characteristic of those influenced by postwar British social anthropology and Parsonian sociology (see Eggan 1950 and Schneider & Gough 1961).

By 1956, moreover, the ethnographic focus of American anthropology was rapidly shifting from Native [North] Americans to populations overseas, and the term "ethnology" itself was being abandoned by those committed to—as well as some of those worried by—the newer theoretical approaches of "social anthropology" (see Kroeber 1953:366). Within this more restricted American-ist sphere, however, Hallowell's work remained influential. When the "Subarc-tic" volume of the *Handbook of North American Indians* was published a quarter century later, he was still among the most frequently listed authors in the gen-eral bibliography (Helm 1981:741–804). Save for several "short-term, special-ized studies," his work was all that was then "available for the development of an ethnography of the Lake Winnipeg Saulteaux" (Steinbring 1981:255). By that time, however, ethnographic issues foreshadowed in Aberle's critique—and reflecting the changing disciplinary context of Hallowell's ethnographic work—had also come to the fore among students of native North America.

One of these had to do with whether hunting territories in which families had proprietary rights were aboriginal among the Subarctic Algonquians. As part of the Boasian critique of "crude evolutionary theories of cultural development"—and in defense of traditional Algonquian land rights at a time when they were threatened—Hallowell's mentor, Speck, had argued that "family hunting ter-ritories" were in fact aboriginal forms of private property, and therefore should be protected from expropriation by Euroamerican whites (AH 1949b:35; cf. Feit 1991:123). But during the post–World War II neo-evolutionary revival, the priority of "communal ownership" advanced by Morgan (and embraced by Marxist or Marxish anthropologists) was reasserted, on the grounds that fam-ily hunting territories were a postcontact accommodation to the European fur trade (Leacock 1954). Prior to that, Hallowell himself had in fact cautioned that "our very devotion to cultural description and historical explanation" had perhaps "blinded us to the relevance" of "non-cultural" data to the explanation of the "actual dynamics of the hunting territory system," and had offered a methodologically-oriented case study in cautious support of what was in effect a third "ecological hypothesis." Nevertheless, his own position tended still to be linked to Speck's, for which he had previously provided ethnographic support (1949b:35; Rogers 1981:25–26). In a similar ideologically conditioned ethno-graphic context, there was debate in the same period as to whether the Ojibwa were socially and psychologically "atomistic"—as Hallowell was taken to have argued—or "cooperative" (Rogers 1981:28; G. & L. Spindler 1975). From a disciplinary point of view, it might be suggested that at a time when sociocul-tural evolution was being reasserted by critics of Boasian assumptions, Hallow-ell was, in effect, charged with being traditionally Boasian—in a field (Native American ethnography) which was, in any case, rapidly declining in interest to American cultural anthropologists.

Even so, at the turn of the millennium there were still a number of Algo-nquianists who may be considered in one way or another "Hallowellian," including Robert Brightman, Jennifer Brown, Mary Black-Rogers, Richard

Preston, Colin Scott, and Adrian Tanner, who "all still cite and use Hallowell, re-working his theoretical approaches to 'religion' and other topics" (Brightman 2/7/01). In the words of one, Hallowell's work has been "generative on a different plane than the theoretical or 'scientific'; it is *useable* [emphasis added] for those who come after across the Algonquian subarctic." Working among the Ojibwa and Cree people, "we find all the time how helpful he is, how well his work stands up"—not only the work "on culture, world view, persons, dreams, etc.," but "the particulars of his information" (Brown 2/19/01; cf. Fogelson 1/2/01). On the other hand, in the case of the "new ecological anthropologists," there seems rather to have been a "partial reinvention of a Hallowellian wheel" insofar as "new descriptions and interpretations of non-Western ecological and environmental ideas appear to be largely uninfluenced by Hallowell"—although "at least one practitioner claims partial inspiration from him" (Brightman 2/7/01; cf. Bird-David 1999).[24]

In contrast to his "scanting" of Hallowell's ethnology, in 1956 Aberle had quite a bit to say about his work "in the general field of culture and personality." Although lauding it as "refreshingly sane" and free of "the absurdities and extremes" of "so many psychoanalytic essays into anthropology," he nevertheless felt that it manifested the characteristic Boasian resistance to "conceptualizations of sociocultural systems" that "integrate the materials theoretically, from the observer's point of view"—specifically those manifest in the "renewed interest in [socio-cultural] evolutionary and structural-functional theory." Granting the insights provided by Hallowell's focus on "the orientations of the individual" toward the spirit world, Aberle insisted that the attempt to explain "cultural facts as psychological precipitates" neglected the total social framework of "regulatory mechanisms"—with the result that "internal social or cultural change seems to be merely a result of deviance." While the "sanity and clarity of the[ir] psychological analysis" would long make the essays "fruitful reading," it was nevertheless essential to see "their shortcomings" as "a warning for future efforts" in the field of culture and personality (Aberle 1956:921–23).

In retrospect, however, it is clear that by 1956, "culture and personality" was already on the wane in American anthropology. Shortly after the paperback edition of *Culture and Experience* appeared in 1974, George and Louise Spindler, who in the 1950s had conducted acculturation studies among the Wisconsin Menominee in a Hallowellian Rorschach mode (L. Spindler 1978), published a review essay entitled "A Man and A Book." Recalling Hallowell's first en-

24. A scan of three volumes of the *Papers of the [nth] Algonquian Conference* in the later 1990s suggests only a limited continuing influence: of the 27 articles in the 28th Conference Hallowell is cited in 2 (Pentland 1998); of 31 in each of the 25th (Cowan 1994) and 26th (Pentland 1995) he is cited in 4 and 3, respectively.

counter with Aberle after his 1956 review, at which they chanced to be present, the Spindlers suggested that in "laying upon" Hallowell all the problems facing "personality and culture" studies in the mid-1950s, Aberle had failed to appreciate "the major, creative, pioneering contributions of his work" (1975:150). If Hallowell had "superimposed an alien methodology and conceptual scheme" (the Rorschach), his emphasis on "the standpoint of the individual within his cultural setting"—what by 1975 was being called an "emic approach"—was the defining characteristic of his work, anticipating "the emergence of ethnoscience." Granting that it was unwise to "reify 'basic personality,'" but worried that anthropology as a discipline was becoming "politicized," the Spindlers defended the "psychological persistence" of Ojibwa culture against criticism that such a view was a "dangerously conservative" apology for the economic status quo. When they sent out a brief questionnaire to twenty anthropologists to measure Hallowell's influence, a major theme among the sixteen respondents was the "cultural constitution" of the "behavioral environment" and of the "self" as fundamental to a "phenomenological anthropology." Although the general feeling was that in a period dominated by neo-evolutionism, structuralism, and cultural ecology, Hallowell's contribution had not had "the recognition it deserves," the Spindlers predicted the emergence soon of a "psychological anthropology, different from the old 'culture and personality' field," which would be based in large measure on "formulations, concepts, and interpretations drawn from or heavily influenced by the work of A. Irving Hallowell" (1975:150–55).

Two years later, when George Spindler edited a volume on *The Making of Psychological Anthropology*, it was dedicated to Hallowell, "whose influence on the making of psychological anthropology is pervasive and profound," and to his wife, Maude, "without whom this influence would have been much diminished" (Spindler 1978:iv). In the volume itself, his generative influence was most evident in the work of those who had used the Rorschach method to study acculturation; but over the longer haul, it has been manifest primarily in relation to the concept of the "self," usually with specific reference to his two essays on "The [Ojibwa] Self and its Behavioral Environment" (1951b & c). In 1980 and 1981, when a "colloquy of cultural theorists" (several of them Hallowellians) discussed the "symbols-and-meanings conception of culture" that had emerged "over the past twenty years or so," Hallowell's concept of "the self"—posed against the more relativistic approach of Clifford Geertz—was described by Robert LeVine in generative terms as "a nice conceptualization of which aspects of the self are universal and which are culture-specific" (in Shweder 1984:13). A decade later, however, citations of Hallowell were often simply referential: on one occasion he was referred to as "an early pioneer" who had "produced a competent structural-functionalism" [!] (Whitaker 1992:203). More commonly, he was seen in terms more relativist than universal, on one occasion being characterized as "protophenomenological" (Csordas 1994:334).[25] Not, however, without corrective criticism from Melford Spiro, who reacted against "contemporary anthropologists [who] view the self . . . as *wholly* culturally constructed" by quoting Hallowell to the effect that concepts of the self were only "*in part* culturally derived" (1993:110). Among Hallowell's students, it is Spiro who has consistently insisted on the universalist impulse in his view of human nature—and in this way, highlights once more the tension in Hallowell's work between cultural relativism and evolutionary universalism; or, to put it another way, between his Boasian interest in a "culturally constituted behavioral environment" and his Darwinian interest in the "behavioral evolution" of the human species.

Insofar as Hallowell's influence has been sustained among Algonquianists, psychological anthropologists, or cultural anthropologists more generally, it has been manifest primarily through the "behavioral environment" half of his larger anthropological project, to the almost complete neglect of his writings on "behavioral evolution." This was foreshadowed in Aberle's review, which quoted Hallowell's preface on "the necessary and sufficient conditions" of a human existence—including "a unique biological structure and a sociocultural mode of life," as well as a "distinctive kind of psychological structuralization" —but which made no reference to the volume's opening essay, Hallowell's presidential address on "Personality Structure and the Evolution of Man" (Aberle 1956:920; Hallowell 1949c).

This neglect may perhaps be understood as a reflection of the fact that neo-evolutionism in the 1950s was not a unified movement. Aberle was then closely identified with the cultural evolutionism of Leslie White, which was rooted in the Morganian tradition and vigorously anti-Boasian, whereas Hallowell's emerged from within the Boasian tradition itself. Although insisting on the human capacity for "symboling" as a precondition of cultural evolution, White's "culturology" focused on the stages and processes of the subsequent evolution of "culture as a whole," and was in principle and in practice as independent from the "science of psychology" as it was from that of biology (White 1949:121–45; 1947:112–14). In contrast, Hallowell's evolutionism took seriously the problem of the emergence of a fully human "cultural level" of adaptation from an early hominid "protocultural" level, in both its psychological and biological aspect. And if for him the emergence of a capacity of symbolization was a critical moment in "behavioral evolution," it was not (as it was for White) the basis for a generalized cultural evolutionary sequence. Rather, it was a prerequisite for the "cultural [or symbolic] constitution" of a multiplicity of "behavioral environments"—of which the Ojibwa were the paradigmatic exemplar. However, if in textual practice he tended to pursue the two inquiries along separate lines,

25. I am indebted to Byron Hamann for a survey of the volumes of *Ethnos* in the 1990s.

"behavioral evolution" and "behavioral environment" were for Hallowell in principle part of a single anthropological project that focused on the manifestations of human symbolic processes through evolutionary time and in their ethnographic variety.

In this context, one might well ask what influence Hallowell may have had on the rise of "symbolic anthropology" in the 1960s, and more generally, what happened to "behavioral evolution" as part of an integrated anthropological project. As to the former question, whatever contribution he may have made seems to have received little recognition: he is not mentioned in a review of "theories of culture" published in the year of his death (Keesing 1974), and also a quarter century later in a recent historical treatment of the culture concept heavily weighted toward "symbolic anthropology" (Kuper 1999), as well as in recent biographical accounts of two of its leading figures, Clifford Geertz and David Schneider (Inglis 2000; Schneider 1995). While the testimony of one colleague suggests that this may be an instance of "unmarked influence,"[26] there may also be more general reasons for this neglect, reasons relating to the fate of "behavioral evolution."

Most of Hallowell's writings on "behavioral evolution" date from the later 1950s and early 1960s, toward the end of the neo-evolutionary movement's postwar efflorescence. When Sol Tax organized a series of Voice of America broadcasts by younger anthropologists in 1962, the cultural evolutionary viewpoint was still clearly in evidence (Tax 1964; cf. Wolf 1964). Thus the talk contributed by Geertz, based on his earlier essay on "The Growth of Culture and the Evolution of Mind," reflected a clear debt to Hallowell's ideas on "behavioral evolution" (Geertz 1962:61, 64, 65, 79). But when that essay, along with a later one on "The Impact of the Concept of Culture on the Concept of Man," was reprinted in 1973 in *The Interpretation of Cultures*, these two were clearly separated from the more commonly cited foundation documents of "interpretive" or "symbols and meanings" cultural anthropology (1962, 1964, 1966, 1973; cf. Shweder 1984). In retrospect, Geertz recalled that Kluckhohn, "who liked Hallowell, had surely put me on to him," while Geertz was at Harvard in the early 1950s, but that he himself "was not big on behavioral 'evolution,' but am on 'the behavioral environment'" (Geertz 1/3/01). Personal experience (as well as the overwhelming evidence of recent citations) would suggest that the same attitude is widespread among cultural anthropologists. "Behavioral evolution" has not been systematically pursued by Hallowell's students, and to the extent that it has been studied by others, there seems to be little if any referential evidence to suggest Hallowell's generative influence. Nor has there been a systematic attempt to follow further the programmatic trajectory of Hallowell's

26. Nancy Munn, after having heard the seminar presentation of portions of this paper, volunteered the influence of Hallowell on her own anthropology.

work: the integration of behavioral environment and behavioral evolution.[27] Theodore Schwartz, who had intended a career in physical anthropology before he was diverted to psychological anthropology by several courses he took with Hallowell in the early 1950s, has attributed this neglect primarily to Hallowell's own failure to pursue "the further behavioral evolution of human nature through the process of cultural evolution" (Schwartz 1991:183, 187). However, other more "external" contexts are suggested by Schwartz's further comment that Hallowell's failure (and that of "most other anthropologists") to pursue behavioral evolution into the cultural realm had to do "with a perception that culture evolutionism was associated with racism, ethnocentrism, unilinearity, superorganicism, recapitulationism, and that it was, moreover, empirically incorrect" (191). These associations, however, were problematic not simply as conceptual issues within anthropology (both for Boasian and Whitean evolutionists), they were also ideological and political issues within the discipline and in the surrounding world. One such "external" context for understanding the eclipse of Hallowell's behavioral evolution may well have been the anthropological status of "race" in the years following the "massive resistance" to integration and the civil rights movement in the South, in the course of which southern racists appealed to the work of the physical anthropologist Carleton Coon. After the publication in 1962 of Coon's controversial neo-polygenist study of *The Origin of Races*, the executive committee of the American Anthropological Association asked Sherwood Washburn—a leading figure in the neo-evolutionary movement in biological anthropology—to devote his presidential address in 1962 to "The Study of Race," and during the next few months Coon's book continued to be attacked as scientifically unsound and politically dangerous (Coon 1962; Washburn 1963; Shipman 1994:210–16). In this charged context, speculation about the cultural aspects of human biological evolution became a topic both politically and ideologically problematic, insofar as it may have suggested the possibility that living populations might have followed different paths of biopsychological development, or been left behind as "less advanced." This was to become even more the case with the onset of the debate over "sociobiology" in the 1970s (Segerstråle 2000), and it has remained so since. In this context, cultural anthropologists were unlikely to be receptive to interpretations linking cultural and biological evolution, even when advanced by one of their own. On the other hand, sociobiologists, who might have found Hallowell's work more relevant, seem to have been unaware of his

27. While Hallowell's thinking on "behavioral evolution" was reflected in several psychological anthropological writings of the 1960s and 1970s (Wallace 1961, LeVine 1973, Bourguinon 1979), a survey by Hamann of the *Biennial* and *Annual Review[s] of Anthropology*, the *Science Citation Index*, the journal *Evolutionary Anthropology*, as well as a number of relevant monographs suggests little if any referential influence in the last two decades.

writings on "behavioral evolution." Embraced by neither of two warring camps, Hallowell's evolutionary thought seems scarcely reflected in recent work on human biological and cultural origins.[28]

As Schwartz's listing of guilt by associational "isms" suggests, however, it was not simply racism (which remains to this day both an issue within anthropology and a force impinging upon it from "outside") that made such evolutionary speculation problematic. The disillusion with cultural evolution (and its congeners, "modernization"and "development") reflected as well events in the postcolonial world, including the Vietnam War, which made ideas of differing degrees of advancement toward European cultural forms—especially, perhaps, those measured in terms of technologically based "power"—seem politically and ideologically problematic. Accompanying this disillusion was a resurgence of relativism both within anthropology and, albeit unevenly, within Euroamerican culture generally (see Sahlins 2000). In this context, "behavioral evolutionism" has seemed to most cultural anthropologists not simply an unlikely project, but an ideologically questionable one—the more so insofar as it implied or assumed that there was a significant difference between "primitive" mental "traits" or "states" and others that were more "modern" or "advanced" (Schwartz 1991:197).

More generally, it would seem that once beyond the Algonquian lineage, the anthropology of the "self," and a few references in works on the status of psychological anthropology (Bock 1988, 1994; Schwartz et al. 1992; Ingham 1996), Hallowell has only a limited place in the disciplinary consciousness of anthropology at the turn of the millennium (see Darnell 2001:4–5, 241–46). Personal experience would suggest that few younger anthropologists or graduate students have read his work or even heard his name. Whether this nescience will continue in the new millennium remains to be seen.

Hallowell and the History of Anthropology

There is, however, one more area of the recent history of anthropology in which Hallowell's generative influence can be traced: the writing of the history of anthropology itself. By the time he had begun serious ethnographic fieldwork, Hallowell had already established an anthropological orientation that

28. Hallowell is not referred to in Durham 1990 or Klein 1989, or Durham 1991—although the latter lists Hallowell 1961a (incorrectly) in its bibliography. A similar neglect was revealed in Segerstråle 2000, as well as in a survey of recent sociobiological and biological anthropological literature by Hamann, and confirmed in conversation with my colleague Russell Tuttle. Cf. Schwartz, who suggested that "the study of the behavioral evolution of the human mind and personality as both contributor and consequence to cultural evolution" was "the concern of few current scholars" (1991:184).

was textually and historically grounded—on the one hand, in those character-istic immersions in the literature of whatever general topic he was investigat-ing (whether bear ceremonialism or contemporary psychology or hominid evo-lution), on the other, in the published and unpublished historical materials relevant to his specific ethnographic interests—including missionary records and other sources dating back several centuries. His more serious interest in the history of anthropology per se, however, developed in the postwar period, and was first systematically manifest in a cooperative volume edited by his friend, John Gillin. Conceived after the initial exclusion of the social sciences from the National Science Foundation—and with a "sense of greater urgency" after the "unlocking of the atom in 1945"—the volume was an attempt to show that convergences between "the three 'core' behavioral disciplines" (cultural an-thropology, psychology, and sociology) might provide the basis for a "common scientific understanding of social man" (Gillin 1954:7–11). To this end, Hal-lowell was delegated a review of the relations between psychology and anthro-pology. Characteristically, his essay was the longest in the book, covering de-velopments from 1800 to 1950—and was extensively footnoted, despite the volume's prefatory suggestion that documentation would be minimal.

A year later, Hallowell drew on this material for a graduate course on the "History of the Behavioral and Social Sciences" (Fogelson 1/10/01). In 1958, when his friend Frederica de Laguna at Bryn Mawr began work on a volume of *Selected Papers from the American Anthropologist, 1888–1920,* Hallowell was del-egated the background essay on "The Beginnings of Anthropology in Amer-ica" (1960b)—an extended, almost monographic treatment, useful to this day, covering the period from the voyages of Columbus until the opening of the twentieth century. At about the same time, he broadened and deepened his vi-sion in a year-long course on the "History of Social and Cultural Anthropol-ogy." Beginning with a comparison of the spatial and temporal orientations of Medieval Europe and those of the Ojibwa as two forms of "folk anthropology," he followed the gradual development within the European tradition of a "sci-entific anthropology," down to the functionalisms of Malinowski and Radcliffe-Brown (GS course notes, 1958–59). In 1961, he chaired the planning group for a conference on the history of anthropology sponsored by the Social Science Research Council, which was attended by anthropological elders with an in-terest in the history of the discipline, by historians and sociologists of science, and by several intellectual historians—one of whom had been trained in part by Hallowell (GS 1960). By that time, there was already interest in the history of anthropology stirring among other intellectual historians, independently of Hallowell (Stanton 1960, Resek 1960). It seems fair to say, however, that his ef-forts, both scholarly and organizational, marked the emergence of a history of anthropology that was at once historiographically professional and at the same time sought to treat "The History of Anthropology as an Anthropological

Hallowell, with Meyer Fortes, in London, England, at the CIBA Foundation Symposium on Transcultural Psychiatry, February 23–25, 1965. (Courtesy American Philosophical Society.)

Problem"—the title of a paper he published in 1965, drawing on material previously presented at the SSRC conference, and before that, in his courses (Hallowell 1965b; Darnell 1977; GS 1976a).

Rereading that essay today, however, it is evident that the "anthropology" Hallowell had in mind was in important respects different from that prevailing (although not without contestation) at the end of the millennium. For Hallowell, studying the history of anthropology as an anthropological problem meant treating it in terms of his version of the anthropology of the postwar period. It was an anthropology not yet shaken by the "crisis" of the later 1960s or responsive to the call for "reinvention" in the early 1970s; it was an anthropology whose scientific self-image had not yet been systematically called into question, in which the disciplinary ideal of a potentially integrated "four field" anthropology was still (in the United States) generally accepted, and in which neo-evolutionary assumptions were widely held. In juxtaposing the spatio-temporal categories of the Ojibwa and of Medieval Europe, Hallowell was suggesting a categorical similarity, not an evaluative or substantive equation. If "all cultures provide answers to anthropological questions," there was nevertheless a fundamental "intellectual shift from the level of folk anthropology" to "the development of modern science as a rational approach . . . which transcends folk knowledge on all fronts"—including the anthropological. It was only in "western culture that man has become most completely aware of his own unique being and the possibility of making himself the subject of rational objective inquiry" (1965a:21, 22, 33, 34). Those who were subsequently often called "Others" had "folk" anthropology; it was only within the Western tradition that anthropology developed in the disciplined, professional, scientific sense. Like many other boundaries, this one has by now been much blurred, and the history of anthropology greatly broadened—along lines, however, that Hallowell might nevertheless have appreciated, since the angle of his vision, although (like all such angles) bounded, was in its time a widening one.

What Hallowell's own place may be in the unfolding history of anthropology he helped to establish is an issue of influence that only its future will resolve. Considered in their past historical context, it seems retrospectively appropriate that he should have been chosen for Roe's study of elite anthropologists of the mid-twentieth century, insofar as he exemplified many of the tendencies of the later Boasian era and of the postwar neo-evolutionary moment. Viewed from the present, however, his interests, even in their more innovative aspects, seem grounded in an anthropology now a half century gone by—American Indian studies before Native Americans became activists; acculturation studies before postcolonial critique; culture and personality studies before they were redefined (and marginalized?) as psychological anthropology; evolutionary studies before they were tainted by sociobiology; "four field" anthropology before its fragmentation into a mélange of "adjectival anthropologies"; "scientific" anthropology before the Kuhnian critique of science. All of which may not augur well for his generative influence in an era when anthropology itself has been transformed, if not reinvented, in a world where the last of those Hallowell still called "primitive" are being incorporated into a transnational economic system, one media step away from political and cultural globalization. And even less so, since his students are passing and the students of his students have learned to speak a different discursive language, to which their students are now native, in a context of creeping disciplinary amnesia and of conceptual linkages that may be obscured by relexification or reinvention (see Brightman 1995).

On the other hand, to the extent that problems relating to those that motivated Hallowell's research continue to be investigated, it is possible that his works may be reengaged, and that, recontextualized, they may still provide a regeneratively influential fund of aperçus, concepts, and interpretations, as well as problems. And should the history of anthropology be more recursive than either Hallowellian or postmodern progressivism would imply, it is not impossible that his larger project of integrating behavioral environment and behavioral evolution—the relativist diversity of human cultures in the context of an evolving human nature—may again become a central anthropological concern. But whatever his place in the future of the discipline, his role in mid-twentieth-century anthropology, both as exemplar and innovator, should for some time to come guarantee his relevance to anyone with a serious interest in its modern history.

Acknowledgments

I would like to thank all of those mentioned under "Oral and Written Informant Sources," including Murray Murphey, to whom my debt is abundantly evident in the text itself, and Raymond Fogelson, who generously offered many leads from the mental store-house of his wide-ranging bibliographic knowledge of the history of anthropology—only a few of which I have been able to pursue and incorporate here. Among archivists, I would like to thank the staff of the American Philosophical Society Library, who facilitated my work in the Hallowell and Roe Papers during research visits over the course of several years, and especially Rob Cox, who responded to numerous inquiries along the way. Also very helpful were Dan Meyer and the staff of the Department of Special Collections of the Regenstein Library at the University of Chicago, Patrick Quinn and the staff of the Northwestern University Archives, and the staffs of the several other archives in which I did research relevant to this project (see under Manuscript Sources). Kevin Caffrey and Byron Hamann, who served as research assistants during the course of the project, were also of great assistance. Others who contributed in various ways were Ira Bashkow, Matti Bunzl, Richard Handler, and Raymond Smith, as well as students in my seminars on "Anthropology Yesterday." Helpful comments were offered also by members of the audiences in colloquium presentations to the anthropology departments of the University of Chicago and the University of California, Santa Cruz, the history of science program at Northwestern University, the Morris Fishbein Center Human Sciences Workshop at the University of Chicago, and a session of the Denver meetings of the History of Science Society. My research during the period of working on this essay was facilitated also by grants from the Wenner-Gren Foundation for Anthropological Research and the Lichtstern Fund of the Department of Anthropology of the University of Chicago.

References Cited

AA   American Anthropologist
HOA   History of Anthropology

Aberle, D. 1956. Review of Hallowell 1956. AA 58:920–23.
———. 1960. The influence of linguistics on early culture and personality theory. In *Essays in the science of culture in honor of Leslie A. White*, eds. G. Dole & R. Carneiro, 1–29. New York.
———. 1961. Matrilineal descent in cross-cultural perspective. In Schneider & Gough 1961:655–730.
Aberle, D. et al. 1950. The functional prerequisites of a society. *Ethics* 60:100–111.
AH. See under Hallowell.

Barnouw, V. 1963. *Culture and personality.* Homewood, IL.

Benedict, R. 1934. Anthropology and the abnormal. *J. Gen. Psych.* 10:59–82.

Bennett, J. 1946. The interpretation of Pueblo culture: A question of values. *Southwestern J. Anth.* 2:361–74.

Bird-David, N. 1999. "Animism" revisited: Personhood, environment, and relational epistemology. *Curr. Anth.* 40 [supplement]:s67–s91.

Bloom, H. 1973. *The anxiety of influence: A theory of poetry.* New York.

Boas, F. 1928. *Anthropology and modern life.* New York (1962).

Bock, P. 1988. *Rethinking psychological anthropology: Continuity and change in the study of human action.* New York.

———, ed. 1994. *Psychological anthropology.* Westport, CT.

Bourguinon, E. 1979. *Psychological anthropology: An introduction to human nature and cultural differences.* New York.

———. 1991. A. Irving Hallowell, the foundations of psychological anthropology and altered states of consciousness. In Boyer & Boyer 1991:17–43.

Boyer, L. B. & R. M. Boyer, eds. 1991. *Essays in honor of A. Irving Hallowell (The Psychoanalytic Study of Society,* vol. 16).

Brightman, R. 1995. Forget culture: Replacement, transcendence, relexification. *Cul. Anth.* 10:509–46.

Brown, J. 1987. A. I. Hallowell and William Berens revisited. In *Papers of the eighteenth Algonqian conference,* ed. W. Cowan, 17–27. Ottawa.

———. 1989. "A place in your mind for them all": Chief William Berens. In *Being and becoming Indian: Biographical studies of North American frontiers,* ed. J. A. Clifton, 204–25. Chicago.

———. 1992. Foreward, preface, & afterword. In Hallowell 1992: vii–x, xi–xviii, 111–15.

Clayton, J. & E. Rothstein. 1991. Figures in the corpus: Theories of influence and intertextuality. In *Influence and intertextuality in literary history,* 3–36. Madison, WI.

Cole, S. 1995. Ruth Landes and the early ethnography of race and gender. In *Women Writing Culture,* eds. R. Behar & D. Gordon, 166–85. Berkeley.

———. 1997. Introduction. In R. Landes, *The Ojibwa Woman,* vii–xviii. Lincoln, NE (reprint).

Coon, C. 1962. *The origin of races.* New York.

Cowan, W. , ed. 1994. *Papers of the 25th Algonquian Conference.* Ottawa.

Csordas, T. 1994. Self and person. In Bock 1994:331–50.

Darnell, R. 1977. Hallowell's bear ceremonialism and the emergence of Boasian anthropology. *Ethos* 5:13–30

———. 1986. Personality and culture: The fate of the Sapirian alternative. *HOA* 4: 156–83.

———. 1998. *And along came Boas: Continuity and revolution in Americanist anthropology.* Amsterdam.

———. 2001. *Invisible genealogies: A history of Americanist anthropology.* Lincoln, NE.

Devereux, G. 1967. *From anxiety to method in the behavioral sciences.* The Hague.

Dewey, J. 1922. *Human nature and conduct: An introduction to social psychology.* New York.

Dodds, J. 1973. *The several lives of Paul Fejos: A Hungarian-American odyssey.* New York.

Dollard, J. et al. 1939. *Frustration and aggression.* New Haven.

Donald, L. 1987. Introduction. In *Themes in ethnology and culture history: Essays in honor of David F. Aberle,* 9–33. Delhi.

Durham, W. 1990. Advances in evolutionary theory. *Ann. Rev. Anth.* 19:187–210.

———. 1991. *Coevolution: Genes, culture and human diversity.* Stanford, CA.

Eggan, F. 1950. *Social organization of the western Pueblos.* Chicago.

Evans-Pritchard, E. 1937. *Witchcraft, oracles and magic among the Azande.* Oxford.

———. 1973. Fragment of an autobiography. *New Blackfriars* (Jan.):35–38.

Feit, H. 1991. The construction of Algonquian hunting territories: Private property as moral lesson, policy advocacy, and ethnographic error. *HOA* 7:109–34.

Fenton, W. 1990. Frank Speck's anthropology (1881–1950). *Man in the Northeast* 40:95–101.

Fogelson, R. et al. , eds. 1976. *Contributions to anthropology: Selected papers of A. Irving Hallowell.* Chicago.

———. 1991. A. I. Hallowell and the study of cultural dynamics. In Boyer & Boyer 1991:9–16.

Frazer, J. 1911–15. *The golden bough; a study in magic and religion.* 3rd ed. , 12 vols. London.

Freeman, D. 1983. *Margaret Mead and Samoa: The making and unmaking of an anthropological myth.* Cambridge, MA.

Geertz, C. 1962. The growth of culture and the evolution of mind. In 1973:55–83.

———. 1964. The transition to humanity. In Tax 1964:37–48.

———. 1966. The impact of the concept of culture on the concept of man. In 1973: 33–54.

———. 1973. *The interpretation of cultures.* New York.

Gershenhorn, J. n.d. Melville Herskovits and the racial politics of knowledge. Ms.

Gillin, J. 1954. *For a science of social man; convergences in anthropology, psychology, and sociology.* New York.

GS. See under Stocking.

Hallowell, A. I. 1920. The problem of fish nets in North America. Master's thesis, U. Pennsylvania.

———. 1924. Bear ceremonialism in the northern hemisphere. Doctoral dissertation, U. Pennsylvania. *AA* 42 (1926):1–175.

———. 1928. Was cross-cousin marriage practiced by the North Central Algonquin? *Proceedings, 23rd International Congress of Americanists,* 519–44. New York.

———. 1929. The physical characteristics of the Indians of Labrador. *J. Société des Americanistes de Paris* N. S. 21:337–71.

———. 1934. Culture and mental disorder. *J. Ab. and Soc. Psych.* 29:1–9.

———. 1936. Psychic stresses and culture patterns. *Am. J. Psychiatry* 92:1291–1310.

———. 1937a. Cross-cousin marriage in the Lake Winnipeg area. In Fogelson et al. 1976:317–32.

———. 1937b. Psychological leads for ethnological field workers. As reprinted in *Personal character and cultural milieu,* 3rd ed. , ed. D. Haring, 341–88 (1956).

———. 1937c. Temporal orientation in Western civilization and in a preliterate society. In 1955a:216–35.

———. 1938a. Review of Boas, *The mind of primitive man. ASR* 3:580–81.

———. 1938b. Shabwán: A dissocial Indian girl. *Am. J. Orthopsychiatry* 8:329–40.

———. 1938c. Fear and anxiety as cultural and individual variables in a primitive society. In 1955a:250–65.

———. 1938d. Review of Ruth Landes, *Ojibwa sociology* and *The Ojibwa woman. ASR* 3:892–93.

———. 1940. Aggression in Salteaux society. In 1955a:277–90.

———. 1941a. The Rorschach test as a tool for investigating cultural variables and individual differences in the study of personality in primitive societies. *Rorschach Research Exchange* 5:31–34.

———. 1941b. The Rorschach method as a tool for investigating cultural variables and individual differences in the study of personality in primitive societies. *Character and Personality* 9:235–45.

———. 1942a. *The role of conjuring in Salteaux society.* Philadelphia (1971).

———. 1942b. Acculturation processes and personality changes as indicated by the Rorschach technique. *Rorschach Research Exchange* 6:42–50.

———. 1943a. The nature and function of property as a social institution. In 1955a:236–49.

———. 1943b. Discussion [of Linton's "Nativistic Movements"]. AA 45:240.

———. 1945. Sociopsychological aspects of acculturation. In Linton 1945:171–200.

———. 1949a. Psychosexual adjustment, personality, and the good life in a nonliterate culture. In Hallowell 1955a:291–305.

———. 1949b. The size of Algonquian hunting territories: A function of ecological adjustment. AA 51:35–45.

———. 1949c. Personality structure and the evolution of man. In Hallowell 1955a:2–13.

———. 1950. Values, acculturation, and mental health. In Hallowell 1955a:358–66.

———. 1951a. Frank Gouldsmith Speck, 1881–1950. AA 53:67–87.

———. 1951b. The self and its behavioral environment. In 1955a:75–110.

———. 1951c. The Ojibwa self and it behavioral environment. In 1955a:172–82.

———. 1953a. Culture, personality, and society. In *Anthropology today: An encyclopedic inventory*, ed. A. L. Kroeber, 597–620. Chicago.

———. 1953b. Contributions to discussion. In Tax et al. 1953:96, 129–30, 170–73, 332–35, 355.

———. 1954. Psychology and anthropology. In Fogelson et al. 1976:163–229.

———. 1955a. *Culture and experience.* New York (1971).

———. 1955b. The Rorschach test in culture and personality studies. In 1955a:32–74.

———. 1956. The structural and functional dimensions of a human existence. *Quarterly Rev. Biol.* 31:88–101.

———. 1957. The impact of the American Indian on American culture. AA 59:201–17.

———. 1959. Behavioral evolution and the emergence of the self. In *Evolution and anthropology: A centennial appraisal*, ed. B. Meggers, 36–60. Washington, DC.

———. 1960a. Self, society and culture in phylogenetic perspective. In *Evolution after Darwin*, vol. 2, *The evolution of man*, ed. S. Tax, 309–72. Chicago.

———. 1960b. The beginnings of anthropology in America. In Fogelson et al. 1976:36–125.

———. 1961a. The protocultural foundations of human evolution. In *The social life of early man*, ed. S. Washburn, 236–55. New York.

———. 1961b. To Nigeria! *Phila. Anth. Soci. Bul.* 14:7–11.

———. 1963a. Ojibwa world view and disease. In Fogelson et al. 1976:391–448.

———. 1963b. Personality, culture and society in behavioral evolution. In Fogelson et al. 1976:230–310.

————. 1963c. Review of E. R. Service, *Primitive social organization: An evolutionary perspective*. ASR 29:314–15.

————. 1963d. Review of E. Evans-Pritchard, *Essays in social anthropology*. ASR 29: 424–25.

————. 1963e. American Indians, White and Black: The phenomenon of transculturation. In Fogelson et al. 1976: 498–529.

————. 1965a. Hominid evolution, cultural adaptation and mental dysfunctioning. In *Transcultural psychiatry*, ed. A. de Reuck & R. Porter, 26–61. Boston.

————. 1965b. The history of anthropology as an anthropological problem. In Fogelson et al. 1976:21–35.

————. 1967a. Preface to paperback ed. of Hallowell 1955a, iii–xiv.

————. 1967b. Anthropology in Philadelphia. In Fogelson et al. 1976:126–58.

————. 1972. On being an anthropologist. In Fogelson et al. 1976: 3–14.

————. 1992. *The Ojibwa of Berens River, Manitoba: Ethnography into history*. Ed. J. Brown. Fort Worth, TX.

Hallowell, A. I. & E. Reynolds. 1942. Biological factors in family structure. In *Marriage and the family*, eds. H. Becker & R. Hill, 25–46. Boston.

Hanc, J. 1982. Influences, events, and innovations in the anthropology of Julian H. Steward: A revisionist view of multilinear evolution. Master's Thesis, U. Chicago.

Helm, J., ed. 1981. *Handbook of North American Indians*, Vol 6. *Subarctic*. Washington, DC.

Herskovits, M. 1944. Native self-government. *Foreign Affairs* 22:413–23.

Hornblum, A. 1998. *Acres of skin: Human experiments at Holmesburg Prison, a story of abuse and exploitation in the name of medical science*. New York.

Hymes, D. 1983. Morris Swadesh: From the first Yale school to world prehistory. In *Essays in the history of linguistic anthropology*, 273–330. Amsterdam.

Ingham, J. 1996. *Psychological anthropology reconsidered*. Cambridge, UK.

Inglis, F. 2000. *Clifford Geertz: Culture, custom, and ethics*. Cambridge, UK.

Keesing, R. 1974. Theories of culture. *Ann. Rev. Anth.* 3:73–98.

Kennedy, R. 1945. The colonial crisis and the future. In Linton 1945:306–46.

Klein, R. 1989. *The human career: Human biological and cultural origins*. Chicago.

Kluckhohn, C. 1952. Universal values and anthropological relativism. In *Modern education and human values*, 87–112. Pittsburgh.

————. 1954. Southwestern studies of culture and personality. AA 56:685–708.

Kroeber, A. 1953. Concluding review. In Tax et al. 1953:357–76.

Kuper, A. 1999. *Culture: The anthropologists' account*. Cambridge, MA.

Landes, R. 1970. A woman anthropologist in Brazil. In *Women in the field: Anthropological Experiences*, ed. P. Golde, 119–42. Chicago.

Lavender, C. n.d. The many deaths of Henrietta Schmerler: Murder, race, and power in the Depression Southwest. Ms.

Leacock, E. 1954. The Montagnais "hunting territory" and the fur trade. *Memoirs of the Am. Anth. Assn.* no. 78. Menasha, WI.

LeVine, R. 1973. *Culture, behavior, and personality*. Chicago.

Linton, R. , ed. 1945. *The science of man in the world crisis*. New York.

Madden, D. 1999. Culture, personality, and the philosophy of social science among the Chicago-area anthropologists in the 1930s: A history of the Social Science Research Council's Sub-Committee on Acculturation. Ms.

Mead, M. ed. 1937. *Cooperation and competition among primitive peoples*. New York.

———. 1962. *Continuities in cultural evolution*. New Haven.

Miller, N. & J. Dollard. 1941. *Social learning and imitation*. New Haven.

Murdock, G. et al. 1950. *Outline of cultural materials*. 3rd rev. ed. New Haven, CT.

Murphey, M. 1994. *Philosophical foundations of historical knowledge*. Albany, NY.

Nash, D. , ed. 1975. *An appreciation of A. Irving Hallowell*. Ethos 5:1–118.

———. 1975. Hallowell in American anthropology. Ethos 5:3–12.

Paul, D. 1995. *Controlling human heredity: 1865 to the present*. Atlantic Highlands, NJ.

Pentland, D. , ed. 1995. *Papers of the 26th Algonquian Conference*. Winnipeg.

———, ed. 1998. *Papers of the 28th Algonquian Conference*. Winnepeg.

Redfield, R. , R. Linton & M. Herskovits. 1936. Memorandum for the study of acculturation. AA 38:149–52.

Resek, C. 1960. *Lewis Henry Morgan, American scholar*. Chicago.

Richmond, M. 1917. *Social diagnosis*. New York.

Robinson, V. , ed. 1962. *Jessie Taft: Therapist and social work educator, a professional biography*. Philadelphia.

Roe, A. 1952. Analysis of group Rorschachs of psychologists and anthropologists. *J.
Projective Techniques* 16: 212–24.

———. 1953a. *The making of a scientist*. New York.

———. 1953b. A psychological study of eminent psychologists and anthropologists,
and a comparison with biological and physical scientists. *Psychological Monographs:
General and Applied* 67(2):1–55.

Roe, A. & G. G. Simpson, eds. 1958. *Behavior and evolution*. New Haven, CT.

Rogers, E. 1981. History of ethnological research in the subarctic shield and Mackenzie
borderlands. In Helm 1981:19–29.

Sahlins, M. 2000. *Culture in practice: Selected essays*. New York.

Saltmarsh, J. 1991. *Scott Nearing: An intellectual biography*. Philadelphia.

Sapir, E. 1932. Cultural anthropology and psychiatry. *J. Ab. and Soc. Psych.* 17:229–42.

Schneider, D. [& R. Handler]. 1995. *Schneider on Schneider: The conversion of the Jews and
other anthropological stories*. Durham, NC.

Schneider, D. & K. Gough, eds. 1961. *Matrilineal kinship*. Chicago.

Schwartz, T. 1991. Behavioral evolution beyond the advent of culture. In Boyer & Boyer
1991:183–213.

Schwartz, T. et al. , eds. 1992. *New directions in psychological anthropology*. Cambridge, UK.

Segerstråle, U. 2000. *Defenders of the truth: The battle for science in the sociobiology debate
and beyond*. Oxford.

Seligman, C. 1930. Temperament, conflict and psychosis in a Stone-age population. *Br.
J. Medical Psych.* 9:187–202.

Shipman, P. 1994. *The evolution of racism: Human difference and the use and abuse of science*. New York.

Shweder, R. 1984. A colloquy of cultural theorists. In *Culture theory: Essays on mind,
self, and emotion*, eds. R. Shweder & R. Levine, 1–26. Cambridge, UK.

Spindler, G. , ed. 1978. *The making of psychological anthropology*. Berkeley.

Spindler, G. & L. 1975. A man and a book. *Revs. in Anth.* 2:143–56.

————. 1991. Rorschaching in North America in the shadow of Hallowell. In Boyer & Boyer 1991:155–82.

Spindler, L. 1978. Researching the psychology of culture change and urbanization. In G. Spindler 1978:174–200.

Spiro, M. , ed. 1965. *Context and meaning in cultural anthropology.* New York.

————. 1991. Alfred Irving Hallowell: An appreciation. In Boyer & Boyer 1991:1–7.

————. 1993. Is the Western conception of the self "peculiar" within the context of world cultures? *Ethos* 21:107–53.

Stanton, W. 1960. *The Leopard's spots: Scientific attitudes toward race in America, 1815–59.* Chicago.

Steinbring, J. 1981. Saulteaux of Lake Winnipeg. In Helm 1981:244–55.

Stocking, G. 1960. American Social Scientists and Race Theory, 1890–1915. Doctoral dissertation, U. Pennsylvania (University Microfilms 60-3698).

————. 1965. On the limits of "presentism" and "historicism" in the history of the behavioral sciences. In *Race, culture and evolution: Essays in the history of anthropology,* 1–12. New York (1968).

————. 1974. The basic assumptions of Boasian anthropology. In *The shaping of American anthropology, 1883–1911: A Franz Boas reader,* 1–20. New York.

————. 1976a. Introduction to Part II, History of Anthropology. In Fogelson et al. 1976:17–19.

————. 1976b. Ideas and institutions in American anthropology: Thoughts toward a history of the interwar years. In 1992:114–77.

————. 1986. Essays on culture and personality. *HOA* 4:3–12.

————. 1989. The ethnographic sensibility of the 1920s and the dualism of the anthropological tradition. In 1992:276–341.

————. 1992. *The ethnographer's magic and other essays in the history of anthropology.* Madison, WI.

————. 1995. *After Tylor: British social anthropology, 1888–1951.* Madison, WI.

————. 1999. Presentism and historicism once again: The history of British anthropology as intellectual and personal history. *J. Victorian Culture* 4:328–35.

————. 2000a. Anne Roe's anthropologists, c. 1950. Ms.

————. 2000b. "Do good young man": Sol Tax and the world mission of liberal democratic anthropology. *HOA* 9:171–264.

————. 2001. Reading the palimpsest of inquiry: *Notes and Queries* and the history of British social anthropology. In *Delimiting anthropology: Occasional inquiries and reflections,* 164–206. Madison, WI.

————. n.d. Glimpses into my own black box: Apologia pro historia mea. Ms.

Taft, J. 1958. *Otto Rank; a biographical study based on notebooks, letters, collected writings, therapeutic achievements and personal associations.* New York.

Tax, S. ed. 1964. *Horizons of anthropology.* Chicago.

Tax, S. et al. , eds. 1953. *An appraisal of anthropology today.* Chicago.

Thompson, L. 1951. *Personality and government: Findings and recommendations of the Indian administration research.* Mexico, DF.

Wallace, A. 1961. *Culture and personality.* New York.

Washburn, S. 1963. The study of race. *AA* 65:521–32.

Westermarck, E. 1922. *The history of human marriage*. 5th ed. , 3 vols. New York.
White, L. 1947. Evolutionism and anti-evolutionism in American ethnological theory. In *Leslie A. White: Ethnological essays*, eds. B. Dillingham & R. Carneiro, 97–122. Albuquerque, NM (1987).
———. 1949. *The science of culture: A study of man and civilization*. New York.
———. 1966. *The social organization of ethnological theory*. Rice University Studies 52. Houston, TX.
Whittaker, E. 1992. The birth of the anthropological self and its career. *Ethos* 20:191–219.
Witthoft, J. 1991. Frank Speck: The formative years. In *The life and times of Frank G. Speck, 1881–1950*, ed. R. Blankenship, 1–8. Philadelphia.
Wolf, E. 1964. *Anthropology*. Englewood Cliffs, NJ.
Yelvington, K. n.d. Finding Africa in the Caribbean: Melville J. Herskovits, Fernando Ortiz, and Jean Price-Mars, 1928–1941. Ms.
Zenderland, L. 1998. *Measuring minds: Henry Herbert Goddard and the origins of American intelligence testing*. Cambridge, UK.

Manuscript Sources

AHP   Alfred Irving Hallowell papers in the American Philosophical Society Library, Philadelphia.
ARP   Anne Roe papers in the American Philosophical Society Library, Philadelphia.
CKP   Clyde Kluckhohn papers in the Harvard University Archives, Cambridge, MA.
EBP   Copies of letters provided to GS by Erika Bourguinon.
LEP   Loren Eiseley papers in the University of Pennsylvania Archives, Philadelphia.
MHP   Melville Herskovits papers in the Northwestern University Archives, Evanston, IL.
RRP   Robert Redfield papers in the Special Collections Department of the Regenstein Library, University of Chicago.

Oral and Written Informant Sources

In the course of my research on Hallowell, I have spoken to or corresponded with a number of anthropologists who were his students, his colleagues, or otherwise influenced by him, as well as others writing on related topics who provided helpful source or background material, or who commented on drafts or portions of the essay. These include Marsha Abrams, Erika Bourguinon, Jennifer Brown, Robert Brightman, Sally Cole, Raymond Fogelson, Clifford Geertz, Jerry Gershenhorn, Allen Hornblum, Igor Kopytoff, Catherine Lavender, Tanya Luhrmann, Catherine McClellan, Henry Michael, Murray Murphey, Marshall Sahlins, Richard Shweder, Melford Spiro, Russell Tuttle, Anthony Wallace, and Kevin Yelvington. In the case of those who are quoted without identification in the text, they are cited parenthetically by surname and date, in the form (Jones 1/2/02).

IT WAS NO "PINK TEA"

Gender and American Anthropology, 1885–1903

JOY ELIZABETH ROHDE

On June 8, 1885, ten women convened in the home of Washington ethnologist Matilda Coxe Stevenson to inaugurate the Women's Anthropological Society of America (WASA). They welcomed all women "clear in thought, logical in mental processes, exact in expression, and earnest in the search for truth" to contribute to anthropology and thereby enhance the status of women in science (Anon. n.d.:11). Envisioning their association as a child that would grow through careful maternal nurturing, the women waxed eloquent about the fecundity of their organization. One wrote, "to [Stevenson's] energy, ability and fostering care are due its birth and larger growth." With such care, the success of the Society and that of anthropology would only multiply. WASA would be "the minute seed from which a great forest will spring" (McGee 1889:240, 242). The organization, in the eyes of the women, would prove that they, as mothers and careful observers, were perfectly suited to cultivate scientific knowledge.

Thirteen years later, they appeared to have accomplished their aspirations. In November 1898, the forty-nine WASA women were invited to join the influential Anthropological Society of Washington (ASW). Scholars have asserted that this move demonstrated male acceptance of women in the budding discipline. Nancy Oestreich Lurie, for example, claims that "the disbanding of [WASA] . . . was in itself a recognition of the universality of work carried out by the very first women anthropologists" (1999:58). The circumstances of the merger, however, suggest a different interpretation of the absorption of WASA into ASW. Rather than representing a victory for women anthropologists, it signaled the deterioration of a visible community of women contributing to

Joy Elizabeth Rohde is a graduate student in the Department of the History and Sociology of Science at the University of Pennsylvania. She is currently studying anthropologists' roles as policy advisors and public intellectuals in postwar America.

the discipline. Notable individual women, such as Stevenson and Alice Cunningham Fletcher, continued to pursue anthropological research despite the demise of the women's association. Meanwhile, their WASA peers disappeared from the historical record. By 1900, only a quarter of the WASA women remained ASW members and WASA itself had faded from Washington's scientific landscape. This decline only intensified in the first decade of the twentieth century as male anthropologists struggled to redefine anthropology as a serious scientific career.

The burgeoning participation of women in anthropology in the last quarter of the nineteenth century occurred in tandem with the reorientation of American anthropology around stricter standards of scientific practice. To assert the legitimacy of their pursuits, practitioners proffered a model of science as rigorous, rational, and impersonal. Philadelphia anthropologist Daniel Garrison Brinton explained that scientific truth "deals with the actual world about us, its objective realities and present activities, and does not relegate the inquirer to dusty precedents or the mouldy maxims of commentators. The only conditions which it enjoins are that the imperfections of the senses shall be corrected . . . and that their observations shall be interpreted by the laws of logical induction" (1895:3). So defined, anthropology was incompatible with Victorian femininity. Women were delicate, subjective, irrational, and emotional, and the woman scientist was thus a contradiction in terms; she was unnatural, defeminized. At most, a woman could be a dilettante, for her mental constitution instilled her with characteristics that would only contaminate her attempts at objective observation and reduce her conclusions to unreliable musings (Cott 1987:216–27; Keller 1985:6–7; Parezo 1993a; Rossiter 1982:xv; Silverberg 1998).

For women anthropologists, however, the Victorian construction of femininity and the conventional definition of objective science were not necessarily contradictory. Faced with the discord between femininity and science, women fashioned a variety of novel identities and career patterns based upon Victorian gender characteristics to attain status in the anthropological community. Fletcher adopted the Victorian rhetoric of feminine morality, sympathy, and maternity to create a niche for herself in ethnological investigation. Stevenson rejected outright many of the sex-based restrictions upon scientific study, but retained Victorian gendered rhetoric when it proved a boon for her fieldwork. Others—most notably Zelia Nuttall and Phoebe Apperson Hearst—remained content on the fringes of the anthropological community, but mobilized their financial resources and social connections to create niches of institutional influence for themselves within the science.

Within anthropological institutions, however, the ideal of scientific rigor intersected with Victorian femininity to constrain women's participation. Although the rhetoric of feminine sympathy and maternity provided women anthropologists with justification for research, it simultaneously warranted their exclusion from the highest ranks of the anthropological community as gender became encoded in the new institutional structure of anthropology. The rhetorical tools women anthropologists mobilized to reconcile the conflict between femininity and science smacked of the amateurism Brinton and his cohorts sought to banish from the field. As WASA women struggled to gain admission to masculine institutional spaces, their male colleagues used the women to bolster their own claims to intellectual expertise and institutional supremacy in a divided anthropological community. While their numbers gave WASA women some institutional power, their femininity rendered them expendable. In the fits and starts of the movement from localism to a national scientific community, women anthropologists became pawns in the power plays of their male peers.

The Women's Anthropological Society of America

In the late nineteenth and early twentieth centuries, local scientific societies dominated the anthropological landscape. Most anthropologists formed their collegial affiliations through local scientific organizations such as the American Philosophical Society in Philadelphia, the Anthropological Society of Washington, the American Ethnological Society in New York, and the Peabody Museum in Cambridge. From these insular institutions, clusters of anthropologists vied for intellectual control of the discipline. At the same time, scholars such as Brinton and Boas worked to create a national organization that would challenge the local alliances and amateurism of the burgeoning science of man. University programs were scarce and anthropologists were not specialists trained within the discipline. According to an early history of the ASW, of the nearly five hundred members of the Society in 1906, the majority were physicians or employees of various government bureaus (Lamb 1906:578). Only the Bureau of American Ethnology (BAE) boasted multiple talented and nationally recognized scientists (Darnell 1969; Hinsley 1981).

Women were consistently excluded from these circles of anthropological research and publication. In 1885, after spending six years as an unpaid assistant at the BAE, Stevenson applied for membership to the all-male ASW. The ASW denied her application despite her unusually high scientific credentials (Parezo 1993b:55). Stevenson had studied geology, as had many of the prominent members of the BAE, and chemistry (Visweswaran 1998:115 fn. 14). In addition, she devoted far more of her time to fieldwork than most of the male members of the organization. Since 1879, Stevenson had accompanied her husband, Col. James Stevenson, on BAE expeditions in the Southwest where she collected ethnographic information and material culture from the Zuni Indians. Stevenson's fieldwork formed the basis for her 1881 publication, "Zuni and the Zunians." Many of the men in the ASW had never published an ethnographic work, and the majority were only marginally interested in the discipline and attended Society meetings sporadically (ASWM).

Renowned British ethnologist E. B. Tylor had observed Stevenson working beside her husband in the field in 1884. At a subsequent meeting of the ASW, he preached the advantages of women's involvement in anthropology. Addressing the men of the association, Tylor stated, "to get at the confidence of a tribe, the man of the house, though he can do a great deal, cannot do all. If his wife sympathizes with his work, and is able to do it, really half of the work of investigation seems to me to fall to her, so much is to be learned through the women of the tribe, which the men will not readily disclose" (1884:550). Encouraged by Tylor's support of women in the field, Stevenson responded to her rejected membership bid by creating WASA, one of the first American scientific associations founded and maintained exclusively by women (Croly 1898:341; McGee 1889:242).

Acutely aware of the tensions between traditional female identity and science, Stevenson and her cohorts designed their research programs to legitimize their participation in anthropology. Rather than rejecting Victorian notions of femininity, they argued that their feminine attributes—motherhood, sympathy, patience, piety and emotional intuition—endowed them with superior insight into particular realms of anthropological investigation. Late-nineteenth-century anthropologists drew a parallel between the phases of social evolution and those of child development. The Society women emphasized their gendered roles as mothers to argue that their daily lives furnished multiple opportunities for investigating human evolution. Motherhood, for example, provided ideal circumstances for anthropometric and developmental study: "In Anthropometry and in the earliest unfoldings of thought, language and belief, who can collect so valuable materials as can mothers?" (Anon. n.d.:9).

Other feminine social roles qualified women for investigational pursuits; the domestic sphere furnished multiple rich avenues for cultural research. Women interested in African Americans found that the middle-class home provided easy access to informants. According to WASA president Fletcher, "There are opportunities for the ladies to collect a good deal from their servants. Others are Southern born and can gather about their old homes" (in Mark 1988:208). Domestic spaces abroad supplied ample material as well. Mary Parke Foster, a diplomat's wife, presented an address on "The Ancient Ruins of Mexico" after spending seven years in Mexico. Even social calls within Washington afforded opportunities for anthropological investigation: Hannah L. Bartlett produced the "Habitations of Man" based upon her "researches concerning the dwellings of a large number of civilized people" (McGee 1889:242). Defining feminine spheres of activity as locations for anthropological research, WASA members stressed that they did not need to leave their cities, nor even their homes, to contribute to science: "the new fields that open before us are not those requiring new occupation, but, rather, new observation. Women are not exhorted to *leave* present life-conditions, but to *master* them in the interest of science" (Anon. n.d.:9).

Although WASA women stressed that they had no intention of trading child-rearing and home-making for fieldwork, they covertly pursued a public voice through their studies. As bastions of Victorian moral authority and pious virtue, women gained access to the public realm through reform (McCarthy 1990:1; Silverberg 1998). The members of Sorosis, an exclusive women's club for aspiring writers and journalists, for example, argued, "in woman resides a latent power for restraining evil" (Clymer 1890:26). In the 1880s and 1890s, many women increasingly combined reform with their growing scientific knowledge and thus actively mobilized gender roles to fashion their public scientific personas (see Kunzel 1993:11, 38–40).

The women of WASA deployed Victorian sentimentalism as a tool of scientific reform. The sympathy with which women were endowed allowed them to observe as well as aid fellow humanity (Anon. n.d.:12). Most of the women in the organization experienced firsthand the problems of urbanization—slums, indigence and immorality—that were perceived to threaten the moral order of American society, and they directed their benevolent interests toward Washington. In 1896, WASA participated in a house-to-house survey of impoverished regions of the city. Upon receiving the study's results, the women immediately helped form the Sanitary Improvement Company which planned to construct 808 new low-rent dwellings in the city. In 1897, the women became stockholders in the enterprise (Kober 1927:10, 19, 52).

Despite their ostensibly superior capabilities for scientific reform and social evolutionary research, WASA members faced the challenge of dispelling the skepticism of male scientists who predicted the women's society would never mature past its first years (McGee 1889:241). Women's clubs proliferated in the 1870s and 1880s, but many were literary societies—informal gatherings intended to foster sorority, social connections and personal development rather than scholarly work (McCarthy 1990:43; Blair 1980:57–58). To separate themselves from popular women's clubs, the Washington women emphasized the serious nature of their scientific endeavors. They wrote that "the object of the Society shall be to encourage the study of Anthropology, to arrange systematically and to preserve information relating to this science, and to hold meetings for the reading and discussion of papers" (Anon. n.d.:13).

Moreover, rather than accepting that science was implicitly masculine and therefore flawed, WASA members sought to prove that women and science were not necessarily contradictory. The Society's statement of organization included a detailed outline of the "departments of anthropology" modeled upon National Museum associate Otis T. Mason's program for anthropological inquiry, illustrating the women's commitment to the anthropological project pursued by prominent Washington anthropologists. The WASA Constitution also required that the Society focus solely upon serious anthropological inquiry. Merely literary work and speculative dabbling into human history, disparaged by anthropologists such as John Wesley Powell, Brinton and Boas, were strictly prohibited. A. N. McGee, the daughter of Simon Newcomb and wife of BAE anthropologist W. J. McGee, informed skeptics, "the majority of the papers [read at society meetings] represent the results of personal observation on the part of their authors. They are real contributions to knowledge, generally much condensed from abundant material collected. . . . It results from this custom that no discussion has ever been given to the origin, antiquity or primitive condition of man" (1889:241).

Painfully self-conscious of the marginalization they faced, WASA women were intent upon observing rigid standards. The women modeled their Society upon the ASW, but added a significant restriction to the structure of their meetings. Their Constitution declared, "No refreshments shall be served at the meetings of the Society" (Anon. n.d.:15). A. I. Hallowell patronizingly observed that "these women must have been terribly serious-minded and self-conscious. . . . An Anthropological Society meeting was not to be confused with a pink tea!" (1967:2). Indeed, the women set standards for membership far higher than those of the ASW. Applicants were required to gain three supporters in the association and two-thirds of the members had to endorse each neophyte. Furthermore, the women avoided publishing their own research under Society auspices. Instead, the only two anthropological publications the society produced were "designed to direct the members in their work" (McGee 1889:241). WASA women envisioned the society as a means by which they could gradually prove their aptitude for scientific work. McGee proclaimed that she and her peers were "satisfied to work out our own problems in anticipation of the time when science shall regard only the work, not the worker" (1889:240–41).

Gender and Exclusion in the American Scientific Community

WASA women internalized their Victorian identities as mothers, moral exemplars and empathetic observers to illustrate that feminine qualities were scientific assets. Male scientists, however, did not generally subscribe to such an interpretation of female involvement in the sciences, and few women interested in anthropological research found any success within the larger American scientific community. Late-nineteenth-century scientific societies, from the American Association for the Advancement of Science (AAAS) to local associations, consistently excluded women from membership. The AAAS was a forum for discussion, meetings and publication for all men interested in science whether dilettantes or professional investigators. Membership in the society was open; any interested man could join, and applicants were rarely denied

(Kohlstedt 1976:102). But women were elected on a case-by-case basis; only three women were admitted to the organization before 1860 (Rossiter 1982:76). In 1859, the president of the association wrote in the *New York Times* that although women were not banned from the organization, "it is probable that no others will consent to be named, lest it should be deemed a challenge to the public to admire their scientific achievements" (in Kohlstedt 1976:103).

As the social taboos surrounding women's presence in the public sphere loosened in the wake of the Civil War, more women began joining the organization. By 1872, over six percent of the Association's membership was female. This proliferation of feminine, and, therefore, necessarily lay interest posed a threat to serious scientific discussion, and the AAAS changed its policies to limit female participation. In the 1870s, the executive committee created the 'fellow' level of membership for individuals who were "professionally engaged in science, or have by their labors aided in advancing science." With the creation of ranks, the sex divisions in the society were fortified such that the highest orders—officers and fellows—were almost exclusively male (Rossiter 1982:76–77). The Association reinforced the traditional Victorian notion, already supported in smaller scientific societies and universities, that career scientists were men, and thus created a *de facto* exclusion of almost all women active in science.

Only two female anthropologists attained membership in the higher tiers of the Association. Erminnie Smith was elected as a fellow in 1880, as was Fletcher in 1883. Smith was both a cousin and informal student of Frederick Ward Putnam, the nation's premier anthropologist and the Permanent Secretary of the Association since 1873 (Rossiter 1982:77). In addition, she was an acquaintance of the renowned anthropologist Lewis Henry Morgan and a collaborator with the BAE as a specialist in Iroquois languages. Fletcher, a Special Agent in Indian Affairs for the government at the time as well as an experienced fieldworker, had studied informally under Putnam since 1879. Smith and Fletcher, however, were the exceptions. Between 1881 and 1884, they delivered eleven of the fourteen papers by women listed in the proceedings of the organization, and their connections with Putnam undoubtedly had a great impact upon their visibility in the AAAS. In 1885, after presenting a number of papers to the organization, Smith became the first woman to be elected to an AAAS office, as the secretary of Section H, the Anthropological Division of the Association. Eleven years later, Fletcher was elected the chairman of Section H, also the first woman to achieve such a position (Rossiter 1982:80).

The ASW avoided the issue of female members in their association for years after the AAAS allowed women to join their ranks. After Stevenson's rejected bid for membership in 1885, no other women applied to the Society. In 1891, the members of the ASW reversed their previous decision and welcomed Stevenson into the association. By this time, she had published a number of ethnographies and had taken up her late husband's research in the Southwestern

United States as a salaried employee of the BAE. Following Stevenson's admittance, the ASW accepted women into the association much as the AAAS had—they elected them individually. They invited Fletcher to join in the spring of 1892. By this time, she was already nationally known both for her ethnological work and her reform activities, and had received a fellowship through Harvard to support her future work. Neither Stevenson nor Fletcher was nominated for office in the ASW, and few other women were admitted to the organization until WASA was invited to join the ASW in 1898.

In the context of rigid sex-based exclusion in scientific associations, WASA was a novel project indeed. Providing both an environment for scientific study and a basis for women's claims to anthropological knowledge, the organization offered aspiring female anthropologists a community in which they could pursue studies virtually forbidden to them in the company of male scientists. But WASA alone did not supply would-be female anthropologists with adequate intellectual and political leverage in the broader scientific community. Fletcher's career demonstrates both the successes and setbacks women faced as they attempted to reconcile Victorian womanhood with the creed of science.

Sympathy and Science: Alice Cunningham Fletcher

Like her WASA peers, Fletcher conceived of her anthropological investigations in traditional Victorian terms. Fletcher's ethnological work was an outgrowth of her labors for social and moral reform. Already forty when she commenced ethnographic study, she had been involved in women's clubs and temperance movements for at least a decade. She was a member and secretary of Sorosis in the 1870s, and a founding figure in the Association for the Advancement of Women (see FI 1874–1883). Confident of her values and interested in applying scientific knowledge to reform, she turned to ethnology as a way "to do good" (in Mark 1980:62). When Fletcher set out for the Omaha Indian reservation in 1881, she wrote to an associate at the Peabody Museum in Cambridge that "there is something to be learned in the line of woman's life in the social state represented by the Indians that . . . will be of value not only ethnologically but help toward the historical solution of 'the woman question' in our midst" (in Mark 1988:62). Asking BAE director Powell for advice, Fletcher justified her novel field project as one open only to a woman: "I wish to get at Indian women's lives from the inside, and as the segregation of the sexes is marked among barbarious people, I think that being a woman I may be able to observe and record facts and conditions that are unknown or obscure owing to the separateness of the male and female life [sic]" (BAER: 10/8/81). Within a month of her arrival, Fletcher was investigating women's societies, marriage, and the daily life of Native American women (FD). By orienting her work toward the scientific study of women, she created an ethnological niche while simultaneously maintaining the feminine pursuit of reform.

Fletcher's foray into the impoverished world of the reservation proved an eye-opening experience, and she quickly reoriented her scientific interests toward ascertaining the most pragmatic solution to "the Indian question." She arrived in Omaha in the midst of a burgeoning social concern for the victimization of Native Americans at the hands of land-hungry settlers. As firsthand witnesses to the demoralization of Indians in the face of white westward migration, reformers and reservation officials began agitating for programs that would assimilate Indians into American civilization—their last chance for survival in the rapidly industrializing American republic. Fletcher embraced the assimilation agenda and began working with prominent Omaha men to further the cause of their people both on the reservation and in Washington. Profoundly disturbed by the conditions at government reservations, she asked, "how can Indians do better, hemmed in as they are at the agency, deprived of their native life, . . . and not fully introduced to our ways. They are stranded between two modes of life" (FD).

Fletcher fashioned a sympathetic and maternal role through which she could raise the status of Native Americans by socializing them as American citizens. Claiming her insight into their predicament stemmed from her firsthand experience and feminine sympathy, she wrote: "I have worked myself round to where the Indian stands and looked at his life and ways as he does" (in Mark 1988:63). Acutely aware of the responsibilities associated with her sex, Fletcher framed her work as a maternal rescue narrative; she was self-identified as mother and savior to all Indians—"those little ones whom I found in need of a friend" (FO: AF/Rhoads 4/7/87). Upon her arrival at the Omaha agency in 1881, she reported, the Indians waited for her to help them, "with all the confidence of children for their mother." According to a newspaper biography, this maternal feeling gave Fletcher, hitherto a childless woman, "the strength of a regiment of men" (FM: *Buffalo Courier* 8/31/96).

Fletcher experienced her reform work, particularly the Omaha Allotment and Dawes Acts, through the biological metaphor of the female capacity for giving life. She told the Board of Indian Commissioners that "it is like the birth, a dangerous time, but it is the only chance for life" (in Mark 1988:107). Posing as a bearer of civilization, Fletcher styled herself the mother of a new generation of Indians whom she would provide with a healthier future than the previously unsympathetic federal government had. Finding Morgan's rhetoric of savagery and barbarism pejorative, Fletcher reformulated her understanding of "life-stages" of society as a process of increasing individual maturation. The Indians were not barbarians or savages; rather, they were children who had to be reborn as assimilated and civilized members of American society (Mark 1988:108).

Fletcher's philanthropic sensibilities proved invaluable to her scientific work.

Her willingness to appeal to federal legislators on behalf of the Omaha generated opportunities for observation of Omaha culture unavailable to other ethnologists. She presented herself as a reformer and observer who was convinced that American mistreatment of Indians was founded upon white ignorance, and she gained the confidence of many Omahas. Her close Omaha friend Rosalie La Flesche Farley wrote to her, "I don't think there is anyone who understands the people as you do, and whatever you want to do for them is for their own good, and not for yours" (FI:2/23/86). Lucy La Flesche informed Fletcher that "I felt you loved and cared for us. . . . My dear friend I thank you *very very* much for your love, kindness and interest in us" (FI:2/21/87).

Such trust generated unprecedented anthropological access. Within a year of her arrival at the Omaha reservation, Fletcher witnessed and recorded the White Buffalo ceremony, never before observed by any white American, man or woman. She met Sitting Bull, and at his request helped raise money for the education of Omaha youth (FD; FI: Secretary of War/ACF 11/12/81). Her informants advised her that her access to their cultural life was due to the fact that she "had done so much for them in their trouble" (in Mark 1988:84). From 1881 to 1892, Fletcher focused her research on the contemporary predicaments facing Native Americans and continued her ethnological research on the side.

Fletcher was an immediate success among elite white reformers. Less than a year after Fletcher's first trip to the Omaha Reservation, Emily Talbot, corresponding secretary of the American Social Science Association, requested her attendance at an 1882 meeting of the Woman's National Indian Association to inform its members of "the means to be used, schools, land, homes, everything which will be tried to advance [Indian] civilization" (FI:5/13/82). At the same time, her public renown among members of Congress and influential Washington socialites grew. In November 1883, Alaskan missionary and education reformer Sheldon Jackson wrote that Fletcher was "a power in Washington" (FI: Fellowes/AF 11/19). She was welcomed into the homes of a number of wealthy Washington women to discuss the victimization of American aborigines (FI 1882–1883). With the support of Washington officials, she created a bill in 1883 that granted private property allotments and citizenship to Omaha Indians.

Fletcher's fame from successful reform work led Washington anthropologists to take an interest in her scientific endeavors. In 1881, prior to her first field trip, she wrote to Powell in search of advice and potential funding for her future research at the Omaha reservation, but Powell did not reply (FO: 8/10; 11/16). By 1882, J. O. Dorsey, Bureau ethnologist and missionary to the Omahas, wrote to Fletcher from the Kaw Agency, "I wish you could see these Indians! They have lost all energy, and seem doomed to gradual extinction. . . . I think, if here you might do some good and rouse them; but alas! it cannot be" (FI: 12/25).

Combining her novel scientific authority with traditional feminine sympathy, Fletcher entered the ranks of the scientific community. At an AAAS meeting in 1882, she delivered an address on "The Civilization of the American Indian." This paper spurred so much discussion that the Association scheduled her to speak again three days later and named her a Fellow. After Fletcher's Congressional accomplishment in 1883, Brinton took an interest in her work; beginning in 1884, he wrote her regularly for advice and information (FI: 1/20/84; 11/21/93). By 1898, Mason and BAE anthropologist Garrick Mallery expressed interest in cooperating with Fletcher's scientific pursuits (FI 1898), and Native American visitors to the capital extended their stays to meet her.

Throughout the 1880s, Fletcher devoted the majority of her energy to the contemporary problems of the Native American. She was hired by the Bureau of Indian Affairs, and as early as 1883, was paid five dollars a day, the same wage as any male Special Agent to the office (FI: Office of Indian Affairs/AF 4/21; 5/17). After Fletcher completed her allotments of Omaha land, she traveled to Alaska on behalf of Native American sympathizers to collect information on the problems facing natives in the territory. In 1887, after the Dawes Act was passed, Fletcher was enlisted once again as a Special Agent to carry out allotments for the Winnebagos, and in 1889 for the Nez Perces. She was an indispensable resource to the government program; her devotion to the contemporary problems of the Native American, her unswerving ambition to "do good," as well as her need for a steady job to finance her anthropological studies ensured she would complete the task at hand.[1]

As a woman scientist, Fletcher faced the constant threat of ostracism from the anthropological community. Her mentor, Harvard's Putnam, was essential to her anthropological success. Fletcher's ambitions as an anthropologist lay dormant until Putnam insisted that she could, despite her sex, carry out scientific investigations. One of the few late-nineteenth-century men who facilitated the careers of female investigators, Putnam encouraged Fletcher to study ethnology and archaeology informally at the Peabody Museum. By 1880, Fletcher was a regular visitor to the museum. With Putnam's encouragement, she joined the Archaeological Institute of America in 1879 and fostered the knowledge and connections that would allow her to present papers to the AAAS. Putnam was instrumental in securing Fletcher's Thaw Fellowship in the face of the sex bias of the Harvard administration. In 1891, Mary Copley Thaw, the philanthropic widow of a steel magnate, granted Fletcher a thirty-thousand-dollar lifelong fellowship to continue her reform work and her investigations at the Peabody. The fellowship was administered through Harvard, which barred women from affiliation as faculty members or students, and Fletcher faced the possibility of losing the grant due to her sex. The trustees of the University and the Museum stressed that they would have denied Fletcher a Harvard position, as well as a

---

1. The allotment program, although fervently supported as progressive in the 1880s, quickly proved devastating to the Omaha, Nez Perce, and Winnebago tribes.

large fellowship, if the decision had been theirs. The treasurer of the Museum wrote, "the appointment was made by Mrs. Thaw. No doubt we have the right to remove Miss Fletcher at pleasure, but until we do so she holds the fellowship, as it seems to me, by Mrs. Thaw's appointment, and not by ours" (in Mark 1988:205). The University and Museum authorities made it apparent that Fletcher's affiliation was by no means unconditional. Rather, Fletcher was the one exception, and according to the treasurer, perhaps a temporary one, to the rigid sex exclusion at Harvard.

The trustees' negative reaction diminished Fletcher's already meager confidence in her scholarly abilities. Fletcher expressed discomfort with her role as a woman scientist. Afraid she would be an embarrassment to Putnam, she wrote, "I hope no body blames you because I am a woman" (in Mark 1988:206). Even after Putnam secured her Thaw Fellowship, Fletcher remained insecure with her status and continued to send drafts of her unpublished papers to her mentor before submitting them for publication. During her WASA presidency (1889–1899), she wrote to Putnam for advice on how best to pursue the interests of the society. Although a well-established scientific figure, as vice president of Section H of the AAAS, Fletcher appealed to Putnam's counsel on every detail of her work from the titles of her addresses to the procedures of the Association (Mark 1988:255; FI: FP/AF 5/13/91; 9/8/91; 10/18/91).

Fletcher was uncomfortable with the disjunction between her sex and Putnam's encouragement of her scientific research. In the early years of her career, she was certain that as a woman she was incapable of contributing to the advancement of knowledge, and so presented herself as an assistant at the Museum. Fletcher did not enter anthropological inquiry intending to become a scientist; rather, in 1879, she envisioned herself as 'servant' to science, a potential popularizer and fund-raiser. In addition to writing popular ethnographic articles, Fletcher presented numerous public lectures as a means to attract attention and money to the science. In 1880, she told Putnam that through her public lectures she was "trying to do her small share to strengthen the hands of scholars by awakening a public response" (in Mark 1980:64).

Although she gained notoriety for her achievements, Fletcher continued to envision herself as Putnam's assistant for much of her career. In her obituary in the *American Anthropologist*, she was eulogized for "render[ing] valuable assistance to Putnam" in the form of fund-raising (Hough 1923:254). In the late 1880s, she contacted the affluent acquaintances she had made throughout the course of her reform efforts to help Putnam purchase and preserve the Serpent Mounds in Ohio. Putnam had been engaged in the project for a number of years, but Fletcher's social networks brought success to the plan. During the course of her conservation fund-raising, Fletcher wrote to Putnam that she had motivated a group of wealthy Rhode Island women to form an association for the preservation of American antiquities: "They are all rich. I told them of your work and that you were the person to lead them in this enterprise. . . . I will keep hold of them and help you all I can" (in Mark 1988:141).

Fletcher's form of science mingled with Native American reform made the Peabody Museum director anxious, and he attempted to steer her career away from such unscholarly efforts: "You want to give up this government work and devote yourself to writing and study. . . . There is so much in your head that must come out and be put in print that you must give your time to that work" (FI: 6/25/91). Sensing Putnam's uneasiness with her benevolent and feminine activities, Fletcher emphasized that the museum remained her foremost priority. In the midst of her allotment work for the government, Fletcher pled with Putnam: "I'll do good Ethnological work both Omaha and Winnebago [sic]. *Don't take me off the Museum.* I'll work hard for you" (in Mark 1988:158). Fletcher found it difficult to reconcile her benevolent interests with Putnam's single-minded commitment to science and often wrote to him that "I felt I was disappointing you" (in Mark 1980:71). Yet, she discovered validation in reform work and found her access to anthropological knowledge most rewarding when addressed through her feminine sensibilities.

Fletcher's self-styled maternalism and feminine sympathy allowed her to produce anthropological knowledge but served simultaneously to hamper her scientific status. Reviewers denigrated her *Indian Story and Song* (1900) as an unscientific work. Washington Matthews wrote in the *American Anthropologist,* "Her little collection . . . must prove entertaining and instructive to all readers." The scientific basis of the work, after all, rested not in Fletcher's analysis of the songs, but in John Comfort Fillmore's musical notation (1900:748). Many of Fletcher's male peers viewed her work as inadequate when it stood alone. A reviewer for the *Washington Times* recommended her publication on Indian music be read as a supplement to "a much larger book of Indian folklore which appeared a year ago, Jeremiah Curtin's work on the Indians of North America" (FM: *Washington Times* 3/18/00). Some members of the anthropological community argued that Fletcher's feminine sympathy caused her to misrepresent her subject. In *Nature*, one reviewer wrote, "Her monograph [*The Significance of Life to the Omaha*], the result of arduous and protracted toil, is the record by a field worker of wide sympathy and insight of investigations. . . . Some American ethnologists even go so far as to say that she reads into the native mind ideas that it does not contain" (FM: n.d.).

Although her maternal and sympathetic posture gained her access to new areas of anthropological research and won the confidence of many informants, Fletcher never achieved a comfortable reconciliation between her Victorian identity and that of the career scientist. Joan Mark has argued that a recurring theme throughout Fletcher's life was the constant "struggle" she faced against male authority and gender restrictions (Mark 1988:xv). This battle was as much internal as external. Despite Putnam's encouragement of her scientific work, Fletcher could not resolve the tension between her sex and science. As she wrote to her friend and mentor, "I am sometimes tempted when I think of the Museum and of what I could possibly do there, to wish that I never did wish, to be a man! I am aware that being a woman I am debarred from helping you as I otherwise could—but the bar is a fact" (in Mark 1988:243).

Transgression and Tactical Access: Matilda Coxe Stevenson

Like Fletcher, Matilda Coxe Stevenson struggled with Victorian gender conventions to create a place for herself in the anthropological community. Stevenson approached gender restrictions aggressively while internalizing the rigors of scientific practice. Eschewing feminine entrapments such as benevolent reform and unpaid assistantships, she sought recognition strictly on the basis of her research. She contested the popular notion that women were incapable of scientific expertise. Stevenson had dreamed of a career as a scientist and explorer before she met her geologist-turned-anthropologist husband, Col. James Stevenson. Tilly, as she was called by family and friends, used her marriage to gain access to the exclusive male realm of career anthropology.

Beginning in the 1870s, Stevenson spent six years with her husband engaged in geological investigations. As she worked next to James, Stevenson began to build the knowledge, skills, and social networks she would require to achieve a scientific career (Stevenson 1904:17, 19). When James, a close friend of BAE director Powell, joined the Bureau in 1879, Powell accepted Tilly as James's unpaid assistant or "volunteer coadjutor ethnologist." Both Powell and Spencer Baird welcomed her presence on ethnological and archaeological expeditions in the Southwest because she complemented her husband. For years, Tilly's involvement in anthropology would not be separated from her husband's scientific career (MCS).

During the ten years Stevenson worked with her husband, she remained hidden behind his reputation. James Stevenson preferred collecting and exploring to synthesizing his material for publication, and his wife penned many of the articles published in his name. In addition, she painstakingly sketched drawings of artifacts collected on Southwest expeditions, wrote object descriptions and prepared the items for exhibition. She initially felt it was her duty to aid her husband, but after three years as his assistant and ghost writer with no scientific career or identity of her own, her frustration mounted, particularly after her own publication, "Zuni and the Zunians," went unnoticed in the Washington anthropological community (Lurie 1999:34; Parezo 1993b:53–54). In the *Annual Reports* Powell prepared for the Smithsonian, which accounted for the work of each Bureau member during the fiscal year, he mentioned only her "important assistance" on the Southwest expedition in 1885, although she had spent months each year since 1879 rendering such aid (Powell 1884–1885:xxix). In the 1881–1882 *Reports*, James Stevenson included a letter thanking Frank Hamilton Cushing and Victor Mindeleff, both salaried members of the Bureau, for their aid on the expedition, but never mentioned his wife (Powell 1881–82:517). In fact, he acknowledged her assistance publicly only once, at a lecture given to the ASW in 1885, in which he remarked that he was "indebted" for her illustrations, which accompanied his paper (Parezo 1993b:54).

During this period, women were tolerated as data collectors at the BAE, and Powell was especially willing to send Stevenson into the field because she could gather information on women unavailable to male ethnographers. Stevenson, however, was more drawn to the religious life of the Zuni than the daily lives of Zuni women and their childbirth and childcare rituals. To gain a reputation as an indispensable fieldworker at the BAE, she strategically combined Powell's expectations with her interests and in 1884 produced "The Religious Life of the Zuni Child" (Stevenson 1884).

Stevenson had lofty ambitions for her scientific work despite marginalization by her husband and his associates. She desired "to have my work live and receive favorable criticism from great men" (MCS21: MS/Watkins 5/2/14). Realizing she was relegated to the sidelines of anthropology due to her sex, Stevenson set especially high standards for her scientific work. She crafted monographs that conformed to Brinton's exacting standards, keeping her feelings and sympathies buried under the guise of scholarly objectivity. At Zuni, she used multiple informants to verify every piece of information she uncovered: "Every word recorded by me is vouched for by at least three well informed men or women or both, neither one knowing that I have studied with another. When my information comes through three who agree that the matter is correct, I feel that the material may be recorded for publication with perfect safety. This is a very slow way of study but it is the only sure way" (MCS21: MS/Watkins 5/2/14). She continued, "I know that I am more tardy than other students in completing work for publication but I also know that when my work is published neither the Bureau nor myself can be called upon to correct errors of statement regarding the Pueblos." Stevenson even began signing her works "Matilda" rather than "Tilly" as the former sounded more professional and respectable.

Despite her diligent work, Stevenson was not officially hired at the BAE until her husband died suddenly in 1888. Powell appointed her to a temporary, but salaried, position to organize James Stevenson's field notes. In 1890, Stevenson apparently proved her worth to the Bureau, and Powell granted her an official position that included fieldwork funds. Stevenson thus became the first woman to hold a position as an official government anthropologist. From 1888 to 1906, she was paid only $1500 per year, although James Stevenson had earned twice that. In 1906, Stevenson received a three-hundred–dollar raise (BAE18). Despite financial discrimination, she was one of the only female anthropologists of the era with a steady source of income as well as the finances to pursue research.

Yet Stevenson's colleagues continued to assess her science on the basis of her sex. In his introduction to the *Reports*, Powell often gave a synopsis of the articles included in the publication. His brief prologues to most of the papers pointed to interesting material included therein. When it came to introducing women's papers, however, he felt compelled to justify their inclusion. He introduced Stevenson's first paper by focusing upon its gendered content: "Her researches were mainly among the women of the tribe and directed to an understanding of domestic life. . . . No male investigator, whose relations in respect to the religious orders and ceremonies must be exclusively with the men, can become acquainted with the peculiar beliefs and rituals among the women" (Powell 1883–84:l–li). Stevenson's sex was the source of her worth to the Bureau and her contributions to the scientific community. Other scientists pointed to the scientific value of her feminine sensibilities; Brinton told Stevenson, "What impresses me in ["The Sia"] differently from any other work of its class that I now call to mind, is the genuine sympathy revealed throughout its pages. . . . You have brought forward the human element of their lives, a feature so often overlooked in the description of scientists" (MCS: 6/18/95). The anthropological community acknowledged Stevenson not in spite of her sex, but because of it.

As irked as she often was at the gender-based limitations placed upon her, Stevenson herself maintained that her feminine sensibilities were an asset in her fieldwork and she embraced them unself-consciously when outside of Washington. Like most Americans of the period, she envisioned women as repositories of the virtues of civilization, and she approached ethnology, in part, as a moral calling. Because popular opinion dictated that Pueblo cultures would soon be irretrievably lost to encroaching civilization, Stevenson approached the collection of ethnographic data as a lifelong duty: "I am more than willing to make any sacrifice in order to record, ere it be too late, the records of these peoples" (MCS21:MC/Watkins 5/2/14). Male scientists, too, in the late nineteenth century, framed their work as a sacrifice for the benefit of humanity. But whereas the male anthropologist's sacrifice led to public esteem and the glory of the pursuit of pure knowledge, a female investigator such as Stevenson relinquished her femininity but gained little renown in return. In 1909, as Bureau funding for her research dwindled, Stevenson resigned from all scientific societies in order to save every penny for the continuation of her work (MCS).

Stevenson also desired to benefit the Zuni by providing them with the accouterments of civilization; she collected Pueblo material culture for display at the Smithsonian, and in exchange gave the Zuni soap, candles, lamps, window glass and milled lumber (Stevenson 1904:380). Stevenson took pride in her Zuni name, "Washington Mother," and referred to the Zuni as her childlike dependents: "these children of nature are like civilized beings of tender years and can be controlled through kindness or firmness, as occasion requires, by those for whom they entertain profound respect" (Stevenson 1904:204).

Stevenson's determined and often unladylike character, both in the field and at the BAE, quickly gained her a reputation as a stubborn shrew. Although she was hired in an official capacity, Stevenson faced constant animosity at the BAE. While her husband was alive, Powell and McGee viewed Stevenson as a benign presence, easily controlled by and complementary to her husband. However, as her stint at the BAE extended indefinitely, Powell and McGee attempted to expel her from the Bureau. Powell fired her routinely and McGee occasionally neglected to provide Stevenson with her paycheck (BAER). Like many female scientists of the era, Stevenson had friends in high places and reacted quickly and powerfully when she felt the Bureau, and Powell in particular, had mistreated her. One Bureau member recalled that each time Powell fired Stevenson, "she would threaten to invoke Congress on him and get herself restored to office" (in Lurie 1999:70).[2]

Powell and McGee tried to place Stevenson on sick leave in 1901, claiming her productivity was inadequate, although they actually anticipated offering her salary to a male ethnologist (BAE18; Parezo 1993b:44). Stevenson responded forcefully. In 1900, physical and mental exhaustion threatened her exacting diligence. On August 15, she wrote to Powell to inform him that her Zuni monograph was yet unfinished: "I thought I could return to my old way of working ten and twelve hours a day (I was soon compelled to cease the long hours as my brain positively refused to work after five or six hours) and I fully intended to do so" (BAE18). Despite her reduced productivity, Stevenson was determined to produce a master ethnography:

> My desire that the work should be thorough and classic must be my excuse and apology. I think you . . . must agree with me that preparing a number of separate or isolated papers is one thing and writing a comparatively complex and connected history of an aboriginal people whose thoughts are not our thoughts, weaving all the threads into an intelligent and satisfactory whole for the civilized student is quite another. . . . It is my wish to erect a foundation upon which students may build. I feel that I can do the most for science in this way.

Powell found Stevenson's mere six hours of work a day inadequate, and as he considered removing her from the BAE staff, Stevenson struggled to convince him of her productivity. She informed him that, despite her health, "I have nevertheless pushed on with the determination to accomplish that upon what I had set my mind and heart. And while I have labored under the oppression of

---

2. According to Bureau oral tradition, Stevenson was ultimately responsible for Powell's death. May S. Clark, Stevenson's assistant at the Bureau, apparently reported to another Bureau member that on one occasion, "Tilly stormed in the door, leaned over Powell's desk and shaking her finger in his face, shouted, 'Major Powell, you are a damned liar!' The Major, face flushed, rose in his chair and fell back with the first of the strokes which later resulted in his death" (in Lurie 1999:70).

wretched health, and at times found it very hard to work, I have worked, and, I shall succeed in spite of the oppressing forces. . . . Please permit me to say you are in error if you think I am unable to continue my work" (BAE18: 5/23/01).

Having decided Stevenson suffered from neurasthenia, Powell placed Stevenson on furlough from the BAE effective in August of 1901; if she completed her Zuni manuscript, she would be paid by the word rather than receive her Bureau salary. Powell, however, never mentioned his decision to Stevenson; rather, McGee broke the news. He informed her that Powell "gave me the data for the Plan of Operations for the next fiscal year. . . . In this plan the only references to your work are as follows: 'It is recommended that the method of obtaining ethnologic data by the purchase of manuscript be continued. . . . Our object in recommending the further increase is to provide for obtaining ethnologic data on this basis from Mrs. M. C. Stevenson, whose state of health does not permit regular duty'" (BAE18: 6/5/01). Unlike J. N. B. Hewitt, who was notorious for failing to complete his work, but was never fired from the BAE, Stevenson was pushed out because she failed to meet the exacting standards placed upon her by her male peers.

Her forced furlough was only temporary. Stevenson called upon her friends in Washington, presumably family acquaintances affiliated with her late father, a prominent Washington attorney, who included a number of generals, senators, the Speaker of the House, and Supreme Court Justice Oliver Wendell Holmes (MCS). After months of negotiations and the aid of Smithsonian Regent and Congressman Robert Adams, Stevenson was reinstated to the Bureau in May 1902 and BAE members abandoned their schemes to fire her. Yet the harassment she faced did not cease. She returned to the Bureau to find that sections of her Zuni manuscript had been "misplaced" in a safe and accompanying illustrations were damaged after being left in a furnace room (BAER). Additionally, Powell demanded as a condition of her reinstatement that Stevenson work at the office so he could "examine [her work] daily" (BAE18: 1/21/02). By July 1, she had finished the manuscript and was en route to the field.

Stevenson was not bluffing when she threatened to use her political connections against Powell, and after his death, against McGee. Congress kept a watchful eye on the Bureau, fearful they were squandering government funds on impractical investigations, and Stevenson exploited the tension between the money-providing arm of the government and Bureau directors. After a 1903 Congressional hearing on the Bureau, at which Stevenson gave a scathing account of McGee's mishandling of the organization, she was left alone to continue her fieldwork—which spanned another twelve years—without aggravation from the Bureau.

Many Bureau anthropologists remembered Stevenson for her personality rather than her work. According to Smithsonian associate Neil Judd, Powell "almost immediately began to regret [her] appointment" at the BAE, for she was "strong-willed and dominating," unacceptable characteristics for a late-Victorian woman (1967:56). Stevenson's personality became a newsworthy subject in 1886 when she and her husband were involved in an altercation with a group of Pueblo people who objected to their questions. In the article, "Cowed by a Woman," Stevenson was portrayed not as a heroine who saved her husband and herself from a group of "craven red devils," but as an unwomanly tyrant. Stevenson protected her husband by "shaking her fist in the face of a hunchbacked savage" (MCS: *Illustrated Police News* 3/6/86).

Other stories, too, abound in BAE legends of Stevenson. Her male contemporaries are remembered for laughing over the fact that, although the Zuni told Stevenson the Indian name they gave her meant "Little Mother," it actually meant "big broad buttocks like a mesa" (Lurie 1999:70). Perhaps one of the greatest injustices to her anthropological work came through her affiliation with John P. Harrington. Stevenson taught the aspiring ethnologist and ethnomusicologist fieldwork technique. But after she died, Harrington co-opted her notes and incorporated them into his own, including her original research, which she had accomplished with great difficulty, regarding a Taos pilgrimage. According to one scholar, "he presumably intended to publish the Stevenson material under his own authorship since the original . . . clearly shows that he scratched through Stevenson's name and put his own on the manuscript" (Bodine 1988:91).

Stevenson's behavior, which often transgressed traditional expectations of feminine activity and temperament, played a role in restricting her from attaining the scientific renown she sought. Unlike her contemporary, Fletcher, she consciously eschewed feminine entrapments such as passivity and study restricted solely to women in order to gain respect for her work based upon its scientific value. But like Fletcher, she was confined to a marginal space in the anthropological community. Neither the strategy of gender accommodation nor that of gender transgression provided women with unrestricted access to the masculine world of anthropology. Both Fletcher and Stevenson relied upon male mentors to carry out ethnological investigations. Stevenson, through her affiliation with her husband and powerful Washington political players, maintained her position at the BAE. Fletcher, as Putnam's protégé, gained prestige otherwise unknown to women in the anthropological community.

Anthropology and Philanthropy:
The Authority of the Pocketbook

Other women, such as Zelia Nuttall and Phoebe Apperson Hearst, were able to contribute to anthropology regardless of their sometimes-cool reception by scientists of national renown. Utilizing financial resources and social networks rather than appealing to feminine sensibilities or masculine forms of scientific self-presentation, these women entered the anthropological community in the late nineteenth and early twentieth centuries. They remained, however, on the margins of scientific production and achieved only limited recognition in the anthropological institutions they helped to found.

Born into a rich San Francisco family, Nuttall was independently wealthy and well traveled in affluent philanthropic social circles (Thoresen 1975:258). Having spent much of her youth in Europe, she received a diverse but thorough education. In 1880, she married the French linguist and folklorist, Alphonse Louis Pinart. Although their marriage lasted only a few years, Nuttall was able to glean anthropological knowledge and training from her husband during a field trip to the West Indies. After their separation in 1884, Nuttall visited Mexico on a family holiday and began investigating Mexican antiquity and ethnohistory (Tozzer 1933:475–76). Her affluence as well as her social connections granted her the investigative freedom both Fletcher and Stevenson lacked. In 1902, Nuttall purchased the mansion, Casa Alvarado, in Mexico, its backyard literally filled with Aztec pottery—an archaeologist's buried treasure. She divided her time between excavations in Mexico and visits to European museums and archives that housed antiquated, forgotten and even unknown documents concerning the pre-Columbian history of Mexico (Tozzer 1933:477–78). By the early 1890s, Nuttall earned a reputation for finding valuable manuscripts—or codices—in Europe, which she copied, translated from indigenous script, and made available to the public.

Although Nuttall's financial freedom allowed her to pursue independent anthropological investigations, it also reinforced her social distance from the anthropological community. By 1886, Nuttall had published a number of papers on the Mexican calendar system that sparked Putnam's interest. The same year, she attended a meeting of the AAAS, and met Putnam who appointed her an honorary assistant in Mexican Archaeology at the Peabody Museum. Through her felicitous association with Putnam, Nuttall became a member of the Archaeological Institute of America at the age of twenty-nine. In 1893, she befriended Fletcher, who became her mentor and advised her on the finer points of gaining Putnam's approval (Mark 1988:235, 243). She made few lasting scholarly connections, however, with American anthropologists.

Nor did her work garner her lasting renown. Nuttall was remembered for her discoveries of forgotten manuscripts rather than for her anthropological publications. According to her obituary, "Mrs. Nuttall's fame rests more firmly upon her ability to find lost or forgotten manuscripts and bring them to the attention of scholars." In addition, Nuttall was known for creating controversies due to her "independent will, and a remarkable belief in the truth of her theories." She was characterized not as a careful, objective scientist, but a capricious and stubborn meddler—"a remarkable example of nineteenth century versatility"—antiquated by the standards of twentieth-century professional anthropology

(Tozzer 1933:477–80). According to Putnam, Nuttall was an anthropologist and collaborator with his museum because of her "family associations and long residence in [Mexico]" (in Tozzer 1933:476).

Nuttall's importance to anthropology came not from her scholarly work, but from her financial resources. A socialite with connections to wealthy, philanthropically minded Americans, including Hearst, Nuttall's friendship was a valuable commodity in the anthropological community. Boas, in particular, nurtured and maintained his correspondence with Nuttall. The two maintained a steady friendship for decades (Parmenter 1966). Boas's cordiality was conditional, based primarily upon her ability to provide him with the financial resources he needed to develop the scientific institutions that would allow him to carry out his vision for American anthropology. Boas and Nuttall became associated at an AAAS meeting in 1886, presumably through their mutual acquaintance with Putnam. They met again in 1893 at the World's Columbian Exposition in Chicago, where both Boas and Nuttall curated exhibitions. By 1901, Boas had risen to the top of the field. A professor at Columbia and a key figure in a number of anthropological organizations, the "father of American anthropology" had clearly laid out his plans for the discipline. And the prospect of creating an anthropology department at Berkeley, a scheme in which Nuttall was deeply engaged, attracted Boas's attention.

In the late 1890s, Phoebe Apperson Hearst desired to create an anthropological museum in San Francisco. At Nuttall's urging in 1901, Hearst donated almost $203,000 to build the museum that would house many of the artifacts uncovered on global expeditions Hearst had sponsored (Bonfils 1928:112). As the primary patron of the proposed anthropology department at the University, Hearst wielded some institutional clout, and she appealed to Nuttall, as well as Fletcher and Putnam, for advice. Nuttall suggested that Boas head the California department (Parmenter 1966:94–95; Thoresen 1975:266).

Boas had plans for the proposed anthropology department, but he had little influence on its configuration from his location in New York City. In his efforts to assert a more systematic American anthropological discipline and to eclipse the eclectic pursuits of Washington ethnologists, Boas unflaggingly labored to spread his influence across the anthropological institutions of the nation (Darnell 1969; Hinsley 1981:267–70; Stocking 1960). Though unable to leave his position at Columbia to run the California department, he did not want to relinquish its control. He appealed to Nuttall to speak to Hearst on his behalf, and recommended his student, Alfred Kroeber, for the job. In a detailed letter, Boas explained to Nuttall his longterm plans for the young science, emphasizing the need for a more systematic training of ethnological students. He wrote, "I have tried to develop [my work] in such a way that it will ultimately result in the establishment of a well-organized school of anthropology. . . . For this reason I am trying to develop the collections of . . . [The American Museum of Natural History] in such a way that they will ultimately form the basis of

university instruction in all lines of anthropological research" (FBC 5/16/01).
Boas was, in effect, coaching Nuttall on the important features of a university
museum. He continued, "it is my strong endeavor to find as soon as possible
men upon whose shoulders the carrying out of certain parts of these plans may
be transferred." Thus, Boas recommended two of his students, Kroeber and
Roland Dixon, for the position in Berkeley, and suggested Hearst allocate funds
to continue the education of the two under himself at Columbia for ethnological study and under Putnam at Harvard for archaeological education.

Boas's letter to Nuttall was less a reflection of his deep respect for her anthropological work than an argument to gain Hearst's support for his plans in
the California department in the face of potential BAE intervention. Five years
earlier, Nuttall had convinced Hearst to grant money to Cushing of the BAE
for an expedition in Florida (Thoresen 1975:259). Hearst, too, was a supporter
of Cushing; when he was accused of fabricating an artifact, Hearst hired him
legal counsel (Mark 1980:117–18). Thus, it was possible that Nuttall and Hearst
might recruit a Washington anthropologist for the department.

In September, Hearst created the anthropology department in California.
Although Nuttall did not heed Boas's plea to wait five years before hiring a student, she convinced Hearst to hire Kroeber. Nuttall urged Hearst to act quickly:
"I hope, that if at all possible this chance of securing this promising young man
will not be missed and that he may be lost to us by being employed by another
institution [sic]" (in Thoresen 1975:264). Although Boas was initially angered
that the Department had been founded so quickly against his counsel, he continued to support Kroeber and maintain contact with Putnam, who was in fact
a Board Member and the main authority behind the museum.

Despite her involvement with Boas, Nuttall never gained an influential position in the California department and she remained on the periphery of the
American anthropological community. Hearst's authority in the California department was limited as well. Her pocketbook allowed her to claim some administrative clout; as a benefactor of an anthropological museum, Hearst played the
role of "the power behind the Director" (see Rossiter 1982:58). But her interest
in anthropological work was considered that of a dilettante at best—directed toward the collection of ancient Old World material culture for aesthetic rather
than scientific benefit. As a result, she was not accepted as a member of the scientific community, but her money provided her with limited access to the nation's
premier anthropologists in the late nineteenth and early twentieth centuries.[3]

3. Affluent Philadelphia socialite Sara Yorke Stevenson played a role similar to that of Hearst.
Through her acquaintance with a collector of antiquated artifacts, Stevenson became interested in
archaeology, particularly Egyptology. Following her marriage to a wealthy Philadelphia man, Stevenson met William Pepper, the gentleman archaeologist in charge of the collections housed in the
University of Pennsylvania library. During the 1890s, Stevenson convinced Pepper to establish a

Maintaining the Status Quo: WASA, ASW and AAA in the Formation of a National Association

Early women anthropologists used a variety of means to gain a foothold in anthropology, each of which reflected the degree of their personal acceptance of traditional gender characteristics and the new construction of objective and rational science. Each also relied upon contacts with established men in the anthropological community who themselves struggled with the role of women in anthropology. While Putnam encouraged Fletcher and Nuttall's research, other men, such as Powell, fought to keep women on the fringes of science. Boas's inclusion of women was conditional, based upon what individual women might offer in support of his aspirations for career science. But in the midst of the institutional upheaval that took place in the anthropological community at the turn of the twentieth century, most prestigious men withdrew support for women's scientific work as they sought to further their own visions for the future of the science of man. While such leading figures as Boas, Brinton, Powell, and Putnam worked to shape the discipline to their own agendas, the women mentored by such men were pushed aside, or when incorporated into negotiations, were used as pawns in the battle for institutional and intellectual domination. Indeed, in the late 1890s, WASA women would find themselves in the midst of a battle over disciplinary power that resulted in the incorporation of WASA into ASW in 1898. The amalgamation of the two societies, however, was justified by the women's financial and numerical strength rather than their scientific acuity.

As late as 1898, anthropology remained a discipline dominated by local scientific communities. Section H, the anthropological branch of the AAAS, was the sole site for national anthropological gatherings and the *American Anthropologist* remained the organ of the ASW. Non-Washington anthropologists had limited access to publication in the journal as ASW members controlled its

---

museum to house the growing collection. Sensing Stevenson's interest, Pepper quickly named her Honorary Curator of the Egyptian section of the University museum. The University had restricted women from entering its programs, but Stevenson was accepted due to her financial contributions to the new museum, which opened in 1894. The University awarded an honorary doctorate and granted her increased authority in business matters at the museum. Although she was never paid for her services, Stevenson remained a curator, board member and secretary of the institution until 1905. Stevenson did not achieve the scientific respect accorded to women such as Fletcher, but she wielded power that caused career anthropologists at the museum to chafe under her direction. Stewart Culin blamed Stevenson for the lack of professionalism in the institution. Stevenson's authority was evanescent, however, despite years of dedication to the museum. When her funds dwindled, Stevenson left the world of science unnoticed by the anthropological community (Darnell 1969:82; Meyerson and Winegrad 1978:119–28).

editorial board and far outnumbered recognized men from other locales. Boasting the BAE, the United States National Museum and the ASW, Washington men dominated the field with their privileged access to publication, wide institutional affiliations and great numbers.

Non-Washington anthropologists sought to challenge the supremacy of the Washington men. The American community of anthropologists had outgrown the small format of the *American Anthropologist* and began to agitate for a national journal. Washington anthropologists were unwilling to sacrifice their institutional domination of the field, but by late 1897, the ASW faced dire financial circumstances. Many members had failed to pay their dues and the treasury of the ASW was nearly empty. The Society was unable to pay its current publication bills; by early 1898, it was clear the ASW could no longer afford to produce the journal, let alone expand the size of the *Anthropologist* (McGee 1903:178–79). The ASW Board of Managers resolved to find a means by which they could publish the journal "outside the Society and at less expense" (ASWM). Meanwhile, Society finances continued to dwindle; by August of 1898, the ASW account held only $27 (PASW:Records of the Treasurer).

Seizing their opportunity to reduce the clout of Washington ethnology, the power players of anthropology began to negotiate the transformation of the *American Anthropologist* into a national journal. Despite its financial insolvency, the ASW sought to maintain its editorial control of the journal. Washington anthropologists remained certain they could simultaneously retain de facto control of the journal and rid themselves of its financial burden. The ASW men continued to hold their institutional ground, demanding that the majority of the editorial board, including the managing editor, be composed of Washington ethnologists, and insisting the name, *American Anthropologist,* be retained (ASWM:3/15/98). Brinton staunchly opposed the ASW's demands; he was determined that a national journal be distanced from the power of the Washington crowd. He charged that under such a plan, a "new journal would be nothing but a continuation of the *American Anthropologist,* in name, management and treatment." (FBC: DB/FB 6/13/98). After lengthy negotiation, Boas, Brinton and McGee compromised—the subscribers to the new journal would decide its name (BAE7:WM/DB 9/1/98).

It was no coincidence that the Board of Managers of the ASW began to consider inviting the participation of WASA at this time. The ASW Board realized the forty-nine WASA members were an untapped resource for Washington ethnology. Three years earlier, when the women had requested representation on the Joint Commission of Scientific Societies in Washington, the ASW Board of Managers blocked their application (ASWM: 11/18/95). But the women had been collecting dues for over a decade, spending almost none on publication or, of course, on refreshments at meetings. Not only would an increased membership guarantee the ASW the votes necessary to retain the journal's name; as a condition of the transfer of the journal to national hands, the

ASW was required to provide at least 250 subscriptions to the journal from their own ranks (BAE7: WM/W. Flint 11/22/98). New members would allow the ASW to meet this requirement with ease and increased the likelihood that the Society would retain its prominence in the *Anthropologist*.

The ASW's plan was successful. On the same day the Board of Managers of the ASW informed its members that the women were invited to join, President Powell and his cohorts adopted the following resolution: "we accept the proposition [to transfer the journal], on the condition that the name American Anthropologist be retained" (ASWM: 11/25/98). With the addition of new members, McGee threatened Boas and his camp, informing them that the ASW would continue publication of the journal if the Society's terms were not accepted (BAE7: WM/FB 11/28/98). Lacking the resources to call McGee's bluff, Boas acquiesced, writing he "must necessarily accept the demand of the . . . [ASW] with reference to the name of the new journal for the simple reason that the decision by the [ASW] Council . . . means 200 votes for the name" (FBC:FB/WM 11/29/98). The ASW had successfully used the WASA women to maintain control of the publication. And although the journal was ostensibly national, its contents following the transfer continued to perpetuate the overrepresentation of male Washington anthropologists.

The Washington men's tactical exploitation of the women of WASA heralded the decline of women's participation in Washington anthropology. Only fifteen WASA women joined the ASW and three resigned after less than a year of membership (ASWM: 1898–1900). The new ASW women were not incorporated into the higher tiers of the Society, nor did their membership provide them increased opportunities for scientific publication or speaking appointments at Society meetings. Rather, it appears the women of WASA were unable to compete with the authoritative male voices of the association and were quickly discounted as innocuous and unproductive members.

With the merger of WASA and the ASW, the majority of WASA members quickly faded from the scientific landscape.[4] Mary A. Owen, an author and instructor at Vassar, was ostensibly adopted as a tribal member of an unspecified Native American group in 1892 (Anon. 1943); yet her anthropological work is absent from the historical record. Other WASA women, such as Olive E. Hite, attempted to establish connections with male members of the anthropological community, but failed to gain recognition for their work. Hite's interest in folklore led her to compile her own study, which she presented to ASW member Frank Baker in 1898. Fully aware of the difficulty of publishing her work without male patronage, she wrote to Baker that publication was a "greater honor than I could ever possibly hope for" and asked him to suggest a "semi-scientific"

4. Interestingly, the Women's National Science Club, founded in 1891, also disappeared at the end of the century. Many of the members of this society were also active in WASA (Rossiter 1982:94–46; Croly 1898).

journal that would accept her work (PASW: 1/22/98). As the anthropological community became increasingly masculinized, most women interested in the discipline retreated to more feminine pursuits; they sought careers in teaching and memberships in feminine and dilettantish literary societies (see Anon. 1943; Croly 1898). Although women such as Fletcher and Stevenson continued their anthropological investigations, the increased ranks of women in the ASW had little effect upon women's participation in anthropology.

The upheaval in the national anthropological community and the exclusion of women from the higher ranks of anthropological societies only increased with the creation of an ostensibly national anthropological publication. Shortly after the *Anthropologist* changed hands, anthropologists again began agitating for a national society, and disagreements over the institutional nature of the discipline became heated. Between 1896 and 1902, men from Washington, Cambridge, Philadelphia, New York and Chicago debated admission criteria for the proposed national organization. Boas and his followers stressed the need for an exclusive organization composed solely of career members—educated men employed as anthropologists. He argued that should those lacking in formal training be invited to join, "the greater is the danger that meetings may assume the character of popular lectures" (1902:805; see Stocking 1960). The amateur element "endanger[ed] the permanent interests of science" (FBC: FB/WM 1/25/02). Boas's standards of membership would have excluded the most notable women anthropologists of the era. Women like Nuttall and Hearst, involved in so-called amateur aspects of science like popularization and patronage, certainly did not belong in an exclusive society devoted to the advancement of technical scientific knowledge. Even more successful women such as Stevenson and Fletcher had little access to formal scientific training and employment because they were women.

Boas's plan for strict exclusion failed. Nonetheless, the more inclusive organizational structure of the newly formed American Anthropological Association barred women from the higher tiers of anthropology. In 1902, forty hand-picked anthropologists convened for the founding meeting of the AAA. Fletcher was the only woman invited to the gathering, and as a result was the only woman eligible for any office in the organization during its first year (McGee 1903:185). She was nominated to the lowest rung of office as a councilor, while the other WASA women were virtually invisible in the organization. Only two—Sarah Scull and Marianna Seaman—joined the newly formed society, and as a result women were no better represented in the national organization than they were in local scientific societies. In all, less than two percent of the members of the AAA in its first years were women. Had the organization been established exclusively as a professional organization as Boas argued, it is doubtful that any women, perhaps with the exception of Fletcher, would have been permitted to join.

The Enduring Salience of Gender

Women anthropologists at the turn of the twentieth century sought to prove that objective, rational science and femininity were not necessarily contradictory, but in the context of institutional battles, they were pushed out of the discipline. Although the AAA constitution officially admitted "persons interested in anthropology" who lacked scientific credentials, the tiered membership structure of the organization relegated women to the margins of anthropological inquiry (McGee 1903:187). Fletcher was the only woman to hold an office in the AAA in its early years.

By the 1920s, the situation appeared to have changed radically. Boas was strongly supportive of the women who inundated his Columbia department during and after the war. In 1920, Boas informed a colleague: "I have had a curious experience in graduate work during the last few years. All my best students are women" (in Deacon 1997:255). Boas was so encouraging of women, in fact, that he lost two secretaries to the discipline, Ruth Bunzel and Esther Schiff Goldfrank. The institutional and intellectual commitment of women such as Bunzel, Ruth Benedict, and Margaret Mead became a valuable asset for Boas in the face of severe financial cutbacks and drastically reduced support of anthropology at Columbia (Deacon 1997:196; cf. Stocking 1992). Between 1920 and 1940, nearly half of the Ph.D.s awarded in anthropology at Columbia went to women (Babcock 1993:112). Yet, despite decades of dedicated service to Columbia, Benedict was not appointed full professor until the year of her death in 1947 (Babcock 1993:125; cf. Goldfrank 1978:110–11). Mead remained at the increasingly insular American Museum of Natural History for much of her career. Boas's academic support notwithstanding, notable women anthropologists in the interwar period failed to attain an institutional status equal to their male peers.

In spite of their unparalleled access to university training, women anthropologists continued to argue, like Fletcher and Stevenson, that their sex afforded them unique anthropological insights. In her study of Samoan adolescence, Mead declared: "because I was a woman and could hope for greater intimacy in working with girls rather than boys . . . I chose to concentrate upon the adolescent girl" (1928:9). In 1940 Benedict remarked that "women in the field of anthropology have contributed to its development not only as trained anthropologists, but as women" (in Babcock 1993:123).

In fact, the gendered rhetoric of women's participation in anthropology has proven remarkably resilient. Seeking a feminist anthropological canon, Ruth Behar has asked if women anthropologists necessarily "write culture" differently than men (Behar 1995). Other anthropologists have contended that women, by virtue of their openness and sympathy, make better fieldworkers than their male colleagues (see Parezo 1993a:4–5). According to Laura Nader, women are more "person-oriented," and as a result, "women anthropologists, if they want it, have access to a wider range within a culture than men" (1986:113–14). Further, women anthropologists continue to use their research to grapple with the origins of gender discrimination; feminist anthropologists have suggested women attack social constructions of gender by studying Western domestic spaces rather than exotic societies (see Aggarwal 2000; Visweswaran 1994). A century after Fletcher and Stevenson entered the field, many women anthropologists continue to perceive their scientific status and research through the lens of gender.

Acknowledgements

Portions of the research for this essay were conducted during an internship at the National Anthropological Archives and funded by the University of Chicago. I am deeply indebted to George Stocking for his patient encouragement and indispensable advice. I also thank Rob Kohler, Susan Lindee, Ruth Selig, and Jeremy Vetter for their comments and support.

References Cited

AA   American Anthropologist

Aggarwal, R. 2000. Transversing lines of control: Feminist anthropology today. In *Feminist views of the social sciences, Annals of the American Academy of Political and Social Science* vol. 571. Ed. C. Williams, 14–29. Thousand Oaks, CA.
Anonymous. n.d. The organization and the constitution of the Women's Anthropological Society. Washington, DC.
Anonymous. 1943. *Who was who in America*, vol. 1 (*1897–1942*). Chicago.
Babcock, B. 1993. "Not in the absolute singular": Rereading Ruth Benedict. In Parezo, ed. 1993:107–28.
Behar, R. 1995. Introduction: Out of exile. In *Women writing culture*. Ed. R. Behar & D. Gordon, 1–29. Berkeley.
Blair, K. 1980. *The clubwoman as feminist: True womanhood redefined, 1868–1914*. New York.
Boas, F. 1902. The foundation of a national anthropological society. *Science* 15:804–9.
Bodine, J. 1988. The Taos Blue Lake ceremony. *Amer. Ind. Quarterly* 12:91–126.
Bonfils, W. 1928. *The life and personality of Phoebe Apperson Hearst*. Privately printed.
Brinton, D. 1895. The character and aims of scientific investigation. *Science* 1:3–4.
Clymer, E. D. 1890. Presidential address. In *Report of the twenty-first anniversary of Sorosis*. New York.
Cott, N. 1987. *The grounding of modern feminism*. New Haven, CT.
Croly, J. 1898. *The history of the women's club movement in America*. New York.

Darnell, R. 1969. The development of American anthropology, 1879–1920: From the Bureau of Ethnology to Franz Boas. Doctoral Dissertation, U. Pennsylvania.

———. 1998. *And along came Boas: Continuity and revolution in Americanist anthropology.* Philadelphia.

Deacon, D. 1997. *Elsie Clews Parsons: Inventing modern life.* Chicago.

Fletcher, A. 1900. *Indian story and song.* Boston.

Goldfrank, E. 1978. *Notes on an undirected life: As one anthropologist tells it.* Flushing, NY.

Hallowell, A. 1967. Anthropology in Philadelphia. In *The Philadelphia Anthropological Society: Papers presented on its golden anniversary,* ed. J. W. Gruber, 1–31. New York.

Hinsley, C. 1981. *The Smithsonian and the American Indian: Making a moral anthropology in Victorian America.* Washington, DC.

Hough, W. 1923. Alice Cunningham Fletcher. *AA* 25:254–58.

Judd, N. 1967. *The Bureau of American Ethnology: A partial history.* Norman, OK.

Keller, E. 1985. *Reflections on gender and science.* New Haven, CT.

Kober, G. 1927. *The history and development of the housing movement in the city of Washington, D. C.* Washington, DC.

Kohlstedt, S. 1976. *The formation of the American scientific community: The American Association for the Advancement of Science, 1848–1860.* Urbana, IL.

Kunzel, R. 1993. *Fallen women, problem girls: Unmarried mothers and the professionalization of social work, 1890–1945.* New Haven, CT.

Lamb, D. 1906. The story of the Anthropological Society of Washington. *AA* 8:564–79.

Lurie, N. 1999. *Women and the invention of American anthropology.* Prospect Heights, IL.

McCarthy, K. 1990. Parallel power structures: Women and the voluntary sphere. In *Lady bountiful revisited: Women, philanthropy, and power,* 1–31. New Brunswick, NJ.

McGee, A. N. 1889. The Women's Anthropological Society of America. *Science* 13:240–42.

McGee, W. J. 1903. The American Anthropological Association: Antecedent conditions. *AA* 5:178–92.

Mark, J. 1980. *Four anthropologists: An American science in its early years.* New York.

———. 1988. *A stranger in her native land: Alice Fletcher and the American Indians.* Lincoln, NE.

Matthews, W. 1900. Indian song and story. *AA* 2:748–49.

Mead, M. 1928. *Coming of age in Samoa.* New York.

Meyerson, M. & D. Winegrad. 1978. *Gladly learn and gladly teach: Franklin and his heirs at the University of Pennsylvania, 1740–1976.* Philadelphia.

Nader, L. 1986. From anguish to exultation. In *Women in the field: Anthropological experiences,* ed. P. Golde, 95–116. Berkeley.

Parezo, N. 1993a. Anthropology: The welcoming science. In Parezo, ed. 1993:3–37.

———. 1993b. Matilda Coxe Stevenson: Pioneer ethnologist. In Parezo, ed. 1993:38–62.

Parezo, N. , ed. 1993. *Hidden scholars: Women anthropologists and the Native American Southwest.* Albuquerque, NM.

Parmenter, R. 1966. Glimpses of a friendship. In *Pioneers of American anthropology,* ed. J. Helm, 83–149. Seattle, WA.

Powell, J. W. , ed. 1881–82. *Bureau of American Ethnology annual report 3.* Washington, DC.

————, ed. 1883–84. *Bureau of American Ethnology annual report* 5. Washington, DC.

————, ed. 1884–85. *Bureau of American Ethnology annual report* 6. Washington, DC.

————, ed. 1904. *Bureau of American Ethnology annual report* 23. Washington, DC.

Rossiter, M. 1982. *Women scientists in America: Struggles and strategies to 1940.* Baltimore.

Silverberg, H. 1998. Introduction: Toward a gendered social science history. In *Gender and American social science: The formative years*, 3–32. Princeton, NJ.

Stevenson, M. C. 1881. Zuni and the Zunians. S. n.

————. 1884. Religious life of the Zuni child. In Powell 1884–85:533–55.

————. 1904. The Zuni Indians: Their mythology, esoteric fraternities, and ceremonies. In Powell 1904:1–608.

Stocking, G. W. 1960. Franz Boas and the founding of the American Anthropological Association. *AA* 62:1–17.

————. 1992. The ethnographic sensibility of the 1920s and the dualism of the anthropological tradition. *Hist. Anth.* 6:208–76.

Thoresen, T. 1975. Paying the piper and calling the tune: The beginnings of academic anthropology in California. *J. Hist. Behav. Scis.* 11:257–75.

Tozzer, A. M. 1933. Zelia Nuttall. *AA* 35:475–82.

Tylor, E. B. 1884. How the problems of American anthropology present themselves to the English mind. *Science* 4:545–51.

Visweswaran, K. 1994. *Fictions of feminist ethnography.* Minneapolis, MN.

————. 1998. "Wild West" anthropology and the disciplining of gender. In *Gender and American social science: The formative years*, ed. H. Silverberg, 86–123. Princeton, NJ.

Manuscript Sources

All of the following are located in the National Anthropological Archives, Smithsonian Institution.

ASWM   Minutes of ASW meetings, Records of the ASW.

BAE7   Series 7, outgoing letters of W. J. McGee, 1893–1903, Records of the BAE.

BAE18   Incoming letters from Matilda Coxe Stevenson, 1890–1918, Records of the BAE.

BAER   Series 15, incoming letters 1879–88; series 16, incoming letters, 1888–1906; series 31, records relating to the investigation of the administration of the BAE, 1903; Records of the BAE.

FBC   Franz Boas Professional Correspondence, microfilm.

FD   Omaha and Sioux diaries, boxes 7, 11, and 12, Fletcher papers.

FI   Incoming correspondence, Fletcher Papers.

FM   Biography and memorabilia, boxes 12 and 13, Fletcher papers.

FO   Outgoing correspondence, Fletcher Papers.

MCS   Series 5, 11, 18, 23, and 25, Stevenson Papers.

MCS21   Series 21, Stevenson papers.

PASW   Papers of the ASW.

Index

AAA. *See* American Anthropological Association

Aberle, David, 133n, 241–46

ACLS. *See* American Council of Learned Societies

Adams, Robert, 278

Adler, Herman, 137n

Afrikaner Nationalist Party, 106

Aginsky, Burt, 176

Alexander, Franz, 232

Allan, William, 103–5

Alsop, Joseph, 219

American Anthropological Association, 135n, 140n, 196n, 197, 215, 218, 286, 287

American Anthropologist, 283–85

American Association for the Advancement of Science, 144, 145, 266–68, 270–71, 284

American Council of Learned Societies, 134n, 162

American Ethnological Society, 144n, 263

American Friends Service Committee, 201

American Journal of Physical Anthropology, 135n

American Museum of Natural History, 144n, 281, 287

American Philosophical Society, 139, 144, 263

American School of Prehistoric Research in Europe, 205

American Social Science Association, 270

Angulo, Alvar de, 162, 175

Angulo, Gui de, 162, 181

Angulo, Jaime de: career, 159–64; and Lucy Freeland, 161, 171–79; and A. L. Kroeber, 161, 164–66, 171–82, 191–92; and Edward Sapir, 161, 165–70, 176, 180, 183; as linguistic anthropologist, 165–70, 183; and Franz Boas, 165–68, 180, 183, 188; bohemianism of, 171–92; literary endeavors, 183–87

Anthropological Society of Washington, 261, 263–64, 266–68, 283–86

Anthropology and Modern Life, 144n, 152n

Archaeological Institute of America, 280

Association for the Advancement of Women, 268

ASW. *See* Anthropological Society of Washington

Azikiwe, B. N., 219

BAE. *See* Bureau of American Ethnology

Baird, Spencer, 273

Baker, Frank, 285

Barnes, Frances, 111

Barnes, John, 103, 111, 115–16, 119–20

Barnett, Homer, 134n

Bartlett, Hannah, 264

Bate, John, 12–15

Behar, Ruth, 287

Behavior and Evolution Symposium (1955), 197

Beit Trust, 103, 108

Benedict, Ruth, 133, 134n, 145, 149–52, 187–88, 191, 196n, 204, 208, 209, 216, 227, 241, 287

Berens, Chief William, 206

Black-Rogers, Mary, 243

Bloomfieldian linguistics, 134n, 169

Board of Indian Commissioners, 269

Boas, Franz: anthropological philosophy, 131–33; critique of evolutionism, 132–33, 137–41; and psychology, 132–33, 148–50; political activism, 135–41, 144; and four-field anthropology, 135n; critique of racial formalism, 136–39; and psychoanalysis, 148–51; and Edward Sapir, 165–68; and Jaime de Angulo, 165–68, 180, 183, 188; and P. A. Hearst, 281–82; and Zelia Nuttall, 281–82; and organizational politics, 283–86; and women in anthropology, 286–87; mentioned, 7, 158–59, 197, 204, 263, 266

Bohannon, Laura, 26

Brightman, Robert, 243–44

Brinton, Daniel G., 262, 263, 266, 271, 276, 283. 284

291